LATINX SHAKESPEARES

Latinx Shakespeares

STAGING U.S. INTRACULTURAL THEATER

Carla Della Gatta

UNIVERSITY OF MICHIGAN PRESS

Ann Arbor

For questions or permissions, please contact um.press.perms@umich.edu

https://doi.org/10.3998/mpub.12253912

Published in the United States of America by the
University of Michigan Press
Manufactured in the United States of America
Printed on acid-free paper
First published January 2023

A CIP catalog record for this book is available from the British Library.

Library of Congress Cataloging-in-Publication data has been applied for.

ISBN 978-0-472-07577-5 (hardcover : alk. paper)
ISBN 978-0-472-05577-7 (paper : alk. paper)
ISBN 978-0-472-90374-0 (OA)

*For Janet Adelman, who encouraged me to write,
and advised me to rewrite*

Contents

Digital materials related to this title can be found on the Fulcrum platform via the following citable URL: https://doi.org/10.3998/mpub.12253912

Acknowledgments

This project began more than a decade ago, so to thank all of the people who supported and encouraged me is a nearly insurmountable challenge, but one that I have been looking forward to for years. Working across Shakespeare studies, Latinx studies, and theater studies, I have had the opportunity to engage with brilliant scholars from various disciplines, creative and critical thinkers whose genuine interest in art and theory helped to shape not just this project, but my way of thinking.

The best decision I made as a graduate student was to ask Will West to be my mentor and dissertation chair. He granted me the freedom to think freely and creatively, and his genuine openness and care as a mentor is a model that I can only hope to emulate. The additional support from Alexa Joubin, who stepped into the project most graciously, and Henry Godinez, who provided encouragement always, cannot be understated. Together this committee offered me flexibility and freedom in the pursuit of my topic and trusted me to explore and discover on my own terms. Along with my committee, I would like to thank Kim Hall and Ayanna Thompson for their enthusiasm and support of my work at such an early stage.

I would not have made it through graduate school without the friendship of Gina Di Salvo, Jessica Hinds-Bond, Laura Lodewyck, and Katie Zien. I am grateful for how our friendships have grown over the last decade, through so many life changes, and have only gotten stronger, despite physical distance. Our graduate program, the Interdisciplinary PhD in Theatre and Drama (IPTD), created an ethos and scholarly community at Northwestern that has extended well beyond our years there. I am thankful to my cohort, the faculty, and all of the other students before and after me who have cultivated our IPTD community.

Outside of IPTD, both Paul Edwards and Frances Aparicio allowed me the privilege of independent study under their direction, and I am indebted to Nelida Aubeneau, Jorge Coronado, Mary Dietz, Lane Fenrich, Susan Manning, Jeff Masten, Michael Rohd, and Mary Weismantel for all that I learned from them. My time at Northwestern was also shaped by my participation in the Gender & Sexuality Studies Certificate program and through my work on the Graduate Leadership Council. Thank you to Bill Baber, Amy Blakeley, Shane Clauser, Katherine Lee Halboth, Chanté Mouton Kinyon, Danny Scuderi, and Dan Taber for easing my transition to academia during my early years as a graduate student from my first career in the corporate sector. I learned so much about the Chicago theater community from friends who have extended beyond, including Tony Adams, Gina Buccola, Peter Kanelos, Gregory Qaiyum, and Tlaloc Rivas.

I am grateful to have met Phil Allen, Narinder Badhan, John DeMita, Phil Ethington, Aubrey Hicks, Hannah Langley, and to have re-met Viola Lasmana during the years immediately following my PhD. This book reflects that time, during which I transferred my attention more closely to my work with the Latinx Theatre Commons. Joining the Steering Committee of the LTC and eventually the Fornés Institute, I have been privileged to work with and learn from Anne García-Romero, Brian Herrera, Patricia Herrera, Marci McMahon, and Olga Sanchez Saltveit. Thanks to an invitation from Barbara Fuchs, I joined the UCLA *Comedia* in Translation and Performance Working Group during my last year in Los Angeles. I am genuinely blessed to be part of the community of scholars who share a life in and of the theater.

My learning evolved from exchanges at a variety of conferences, including the American Society for Theatre Research, Association for Theatre in Higher Education, International Federation for Theatre Research, Latina/o Studies Association, Newberry Seminar on Borderlands, Association for Hispanic Classical Theater, British Shakespeare Association, European Shakespeare Research Association, Shakespeare Association of America, International Shakespeare Conference, and the World Shakespeare Congress.

Especially formative was my first ASTR meeting in 2014, in the working group hosted by Jorge Huerta and Tiffany Ana López. There I met future colleagues Noe Montez and Chantal Rodriguez, and my future mentor, Patti Ybarra. I enrolled in ASTR's Mentorship Breakfast, where I met another wonderful mentor, Jon Rossini; no one else in academia is as enthusiastic, especially at 8:00 a.m. At subsequent meetings, I was welcomed by the amazing Siglo de Oro scholars to their working group, and I had the pleasure of co-leading a session on Latinx and Indigenous theater with Courtney Elkin Mohler. The Newberry Library Seminar on Borderlands and Latino Studies was the first Latinx studies working group in which I took part; there I got to be in conversation with Karl Swinehart, Lee Bebout, Chris Tirres, and so many others over the years. I am indebted to CJ Alvarez, Gerry Cadava, Ben Johnson, Jason Ruiz, and especially to Ramón

Gutiérrez for feedback at a key juncture in the development of the project. Likewise, my service work on awards committees for ASTR and on the Governing Council for ATHE brought me into dialogue with scholars and artists whom I otherwise would not have met.

I benefited greatly from the exchanges I had at meetings of the Shakespeare Association of America, and from the organization's support. In 2015, I took part in the first NextGenPlen, and in 2016, I received the J Leeds Barroll Dissertation Prize for my work on Shakespeare and Latinidad. The encouragement from this organization changed the possibilities for this research; I have devoted the years since then to its service as a panel chair, serving on two awards committees, and twice as a seminar co-leader. I have met and gotten to know some amazing colleagues during SAA meetings, including Jonathan Burton, Rob Conkie, Holly Dugan, Adam Hooks, Colleen Kennedy, Jim Knapp, Doug Lanier, Jennifer Low, Kevin Quarmby, Stephanie Shirilan, Lisa Starks, and Jamie Sutton, as well as the Siglo de Oro Shakespeareans: David Amelang, Joyce Boro, Juan Cerdá, José Pérez Díaz, and Alexander Samson.

I conducted extensive research for this project at the archives at the Oregon Shakespeare Festival and over many visits to the New York Public Library Performing Arts Archive. My fellowship year in Madrid was filled with hours inside the Bilbioteca Nacional de España. This work would not be possible without the support of a New York Public Library Short-Term Fellowship, a Career Enhancement Fellowship from the Woodrow Wilson Foundation (now Citizens and Scholars), the Targeted Area Research Grant from the American Society for Theatre Research, Florida State University's First Year Assistant Professor Grant, and a Folger Shakespeare Library Short-Term Fellowship. The generosity of the community at the Folger during my brief time there enriched the project and moved me in a profound way. During the two-week summer session on public humanities through the Mellon School of Theater and Performance Research at Harvard University, I had the good fortune to participate in Andrew Sofer's writing workshop. His feedback, and that of the group, pushed me to the next level at just the moment the work was ready to go there.

I have boundless gratitude for Patricia Akhimie, Tom Cartelli, Michael Dobson, Barbara Fuchs, Diana Henderson, Rebecca Lemon, Erika Lin, Octavio Solis, Will West, and Harvey Young. I thank Adele Lee and Aneta Mancewicz for hosting me in London during my visits, Trevor Boffone for being my interlocutor on all things theatrical, Jane Barnette, Ryan Claycomb, Ariane Helou, Danielle Rosvally, Jonathan Shandell, and Jessica Young for the sense of community I feel even just by typing their names,

Brett Gamboa and Sam Wilson for the specificity of our conversations, Pablo Maurette, Rob Stilling, and Aaron Thomas for our chats in Tallahassee, John Pascarella for reinvigorating my sense of play, and Gabriela Nuñez for talking me through the decision to go into academia after my decade-long corporate career. There is no better editor than Jessica Hinds-Bond.

I am a theater historian and performance theorist, and this study has provided me with a remapping of my own relationship to my cultural background. I am half Hungarian Jewish, and my methods of inquiry are largely shaped by Talmudic thinking. The other half of my heritage and upbringing is a palimpsest of Latin American/Latinx/Latin/Hispanic cultures. My biological father was Colombian, I was raised in Los Angeles surrounded by Chicanx culture, I have lived in Spain for over three years of my life, and my legal father was proudly Italian but accessed his Spanish heritage through language and all forms of art. He spoke five languages, but his career as a Spanish and Spanish for Native Speakers teacher and his love of performance resulted in my attendance at Spanish-language theater and music concerts from before I could speak or read. Because of my parents' desire for assimilation, my sister and I were not taught Spanish in our home, and I was instructed to rid myself of my accent in order to start first grade. With immigrant grandparents on both sides, I was never vexed by cross-cultural, cross-religious, or cross-linguistic encounters; they are more indicative of my lived experience than a belief or desire for monoculture or an easy binary that polarizes differences. Living in partial identification, speaking my second language, and negotiating the location of home between countries and cultures imbues my perspective and therefore my scholarship.

This book stems from a decade of research, conversations, and interactions with artists, and engagement as a scholar with various theaters; it has pushed me to expand my vocabulary linguistically, theoretically, and artistically. This work is only made possible by listening to the voices of artists and attending to their art. I interviewed over forty artists and had the privilege of reading unpublished scripts, but not all of those conversations and productions made it into this book. I wish to extend my thanks to Alex Alford, Alex Alpharaoh, Frankie J. Alvarez, Laura Baglereau, Ben Bartolone, Alberto Bonilla, John Briggs, Chloe Broznan, Freda Casillas, Oscar Ciccone, Durand Garcia, Lydia Garcia, Meme García, Arthur Giron, José Cruz González, David Richard Jones, Kate Jopson, John Keller, Mark Lamos, Larry Loebell, David Lozano, Tom Mallan, Bernardo Mazón, Kristian Méndez Aguirre, Manuel Morán, Carlos Morton, Tara Moses, Antonio Ocampo-Guzmán, Julianna Stephanie Ojeda, Eric Parness, Tony Plana,

Ulises Rangel, Jesus A. Reyes, Allen O'Reilly, Javier Rivera, Herbert Siguenza, Caridad Svich, Mary Tilden, Carlos-Zenen Trujillo, Cecilia Vega, Edit Villarreal, and Roberta Wells-Famula.

Thank you to Diana E. Henderson and James R. Siemon for publishing my NextGenPlen speech in *Shakespeare Studies*; my early career plenary was a "greatest hits" of my dissertation, and some of those ideas survive in the manuscript. I wish to thank *HowlRound* for publishing my essays that result from working with theaters, and the Folger Shakespeare Library for the opportunity to share my research through *Shakespeare Unlimited* and *Shakespeare & Beyond*. The invitations I received to visit colleagues' classrooms, campuses, festivals, and theaters have provided some of my greatest pleasures as a scholar. I could not be a theater scholar without being in dialogue with theaters. Thank you to Chicago Shakespeare Theater, Classic Stage Company, Halcyon Theater, Hedgepig Theatre Ensemble, Shakespeare Center of Los Angeles, Shakespeare St. Louis, Shakespeare Theatre Company, the Public Theater, and Victory Gardens Theater for the opportunities.

My profound thanks to the team at University of Michigan Press and especially LeAnn Fields, who ushered this manuscript through with the greatest support and keen understanding of the challenges within a burgeoning field. I am indebted to the two reviewers of the full manuscript who provided outstanding and detailed feedback. Jordan Kessler assisted with research early on in manuscript development, and working with Natalie Tombasco kept me on a schedule with due diligence checks to see this project through to the end. I moved to Florida State University just before the Covid-19 pandemic began, and finishing the manuscript during these first years of the pandemic enhanced the isolation but also shaped my experience of it. I have felt the support of mentors, Celia Caputi and Anne Coldiron, and all of my colleagues at Florida State University despite the limited interactions we have had in person over the last few years.

The final stretches of finishing this book would not have been possible without friends and colleagues who generously read drafts of some or all of the manuscript. *Latinx Shakespeares* began with an absence in the archive of Shakespearean performance more than ten years ago, and today other scholars are working in this field. My sister, Joanna Della Gatta, has patiently listened to more about book writing than I know she ever wanted to do. My mother observed that the long hours she always devoted to reading and the long hours I always devoted to writing should never cause us to set aside our love of dance and music. Mom has now passed, the book is now done, and I can already hear and feel the rhythm of what is next.

Introduction

There are no Latinx characters in Shakespeare. Not one.

There are Spanish, Italian, and Greek characters, Latin words and phrases, and Iberian and Mediterranean settings in the Shakespearean canon. But Latinx, no. And this makes sense: Latinx refers to people in the United States who are from, or a product of, Spanish colonization and conquest of the Americas and comprise more than 18 percent of the US population today. This book describes what we learn about Latinx cultures, Shakespeare, and art-making in the process of exploring how the intersections of the colonizing and culturally elite structures of Shakespearean drama can be reimagined as operating in the service of a contemporary ethnic category. The book also engages with the intersections and divergences embedded in contemporary constructions of Latinx and Latinidad. "Latinidad," a presentist term that signifies a holistic idea of Latinity or Latin-ness, has influenced the interpretation of Shakespeare in performance since the 1950s and continues to do so today.

Latinx Shakespeares are textual adaptations or performances in which Shakespearean plays, stories, or characters are *made Latinx* through dramaturgy (integrating context into performance), aesthetics (including concept settings), processes for art-making (including casting), and/or modes of storytelling. There is not one unifying purpose or experience of Latinx Shakespeares. The very existence of these productions raises the question whether Shakespeare—the paragon of British, white, English-language literature—can truly be made Latinx. This book attends to productions that embrace that question, from a myriad of theatrical approaches, racial and national backgrounds, political and practical motivations, and with various dramaturgical results. In order to even broach this question of the theater, we need to define and challenge the categories it rests on.

Latinx Shakespeares challenge perceived boundaries of what constitutes Latinx theater, and they move Shakespeare studies forward into a wider purview of performance traditions and aesthetics. This book decenters a macronarrative of US American (hereafter simply "American")

Shakespearean performance that has previously excluded Latinx peoples and cultures. Latinx Shakespeares allow us to think about the construction of these categories through something that seems totally separate from them: Shakespeare. Latinx Shakespeares force audiences to step away from the hierarchies imposed by centuries of colonization and reinforced by perceptions of immigration to consider Latinx through a different aspect. The categories of "Latinx" (to signal culture or people) and "Latinidad" (to signal culture or cultural practice) are in active contention now; this project acknowledges the contradictions and complexities within the negotiations of Latinidad.

Latinx Shakespeares is not a study of the merits of Shakespeare but a reading of the way his works are performed today that takes seriously the important inflections brought through the introduction of language, sonorities, visual practices, cultural forms, and understandings of history shaped by heterogeneous but connected modes of storytelling. Nearly all Latinx Shakespeares include at least some Spanish, and many include other languages as well. The political currency of the Latinx body onstage meets with Shakespeare's textual authority and the sound of a foreign language that has been subjugated in American culture due to linguistic racism. Through Latinx Shakespeares, I examine the intervention of a Latinidad that, at a minimum, brings constrained forms of American whiteness into sharper view and, in their most fully realized forms, gestures toward possibilities for cultural healing and transformative futures. The predominantly white directors, theaters, and casts that mounted the earliest attempts at Latinx-themed Shakespeares often created productions that are better described as performances of American whiteness; they employed conscriptive Latinx tropes to bolster and demarcate whiteness. As Latinx Shakespeares developed since the 1990s dramaturgically and thematically, and through a diverse group of practitioners, Latinx identities and themes emerged not only as a focal point, but as a space for reimagining both Latinidad and Shakespeare.

FIRST INTERSECTIONS OF SHAKESPEARE AND LATINIDAD

Latinx actors have been performing Shakespeare in English on prominent US stages since at least the 1940s. In 1943 on Broadway, Paul Robeson reprised his role of Othello, which he had played in the West End thirteen years prior, and in so doing became the first Black man to play the role with a white cast on Broadway. Descriptions of this landmark production often focus on Robeson, rightfully, but they tend to overlook the fact that a Puerto

Rican actor, José Ferrer, played Iago.[1] Ferrer's status as a US citizen (Puerto Ricans became citizens in 1917) and racial whiteness spoke more loudly than the burgeoning classification of "Hispanic." The descriptions of Ferrer's performance do not contain any of the ethnic stereotypes that dominate reviews of Latinx actors today. Samuel Sillen's 1943 review in *New Masses* describes Ferrer's performance as "subtle," "plastic," "lithe, arrogant, cynical," invoking none of the familiar stereotypical descriptors."[2] Nowhere does he use words like "fiery," "hot," or "sultry" to describe the Latino actor. In the years since that performance, the theatrical landscape has evolved. Today, Robeson's casting as Othello wouldn't draw much attention, but a Puerto Rican Iago certainly would.

There were Spanish-language productions of Shakespeare in what is now the United States as far back as the 1800s, and twentieth-century US "concept Shakespeare" kicked off in 1936 with Orson Welles's famous Caribbean-set *Macbeth*, known as the "Voodoo *Macbeth*," for the Federal Theatre Project.[3] Most foundational to the Latinx Shakespeares that I explore in this book was the work of Joe Papp at the New York Shakespeare Festival (NYSF), which began in the 1950s, as the construct of "Hispanic" (and subsequently, "Latino") became prominent. Papp's influential vision for US Shakespearean performance included and promoted Black, Latinx, and Asian actors, with a range of US accents as well.

Along with its touring Mobile Theater unit, the NYSF ran a Spanish Mobile Theater (1964–66) that brought Spanish-language theater to the boroughs of New York, via Latinx and Latin American actors.[4] In 1965, the Spanish Mobile Theater turned to Shakespeare, with a Spanish-language production of *Romeo and Juliet*, directed by the Argentine director Osvaldo Riofrancos.[5] In 1966, both the Mobile and the Spanish Mobile featured productions of *Macbeth*. The English-language production was directed by Gladys Vaughn, the first woman to direct a play for the NYSF, while the Spanish-language production—which featured Puerto Rican actor Raúl Juliá as Macduff—was once again directed by Riofrancos.[6] The Spanish-language production ran in tandem with the English version, and both were met with coded, racially imbued criticism: the English-language version with African American actors James Earl Jones and Ellen Holly "did little to convey the power of tragedy," while the Spanish-language version was hardly "more satisfactory, raising the question of standards."[7] The Spanish Mobile was short-lived due to funding cuts, a challenge that would imbue much of Papp's experiments; it was the duration and expansion of the long-running Festival Latino that would generate key intersections for Shakespeare and Latinidad.

Papp, with Argentine Oscar Ciccone and Salvadorean Cecilia Vega, produced the Festival Latino in New York, which ran ten times between 1976 and 1991. It drew over fifty thousand people each year in its last few years, and included performances by Spanish and Latin American companies as well as Puerto Rican and Hispanic companies from within the United States. The Festival Latino was so popular that New York governor Mario Cuomo declared August 1989 as "Joseph Papp's Festival Latino Month."[8] By 1990, the festival spanned over a month, with more than two hundred scheduled events, including plays, concerts, films, and over one hundred hours of television programming.

The Festival Latino's 1991 production of *Sonho de uma Noite de Verao* (*A Midsummer Night's Dream*) from Brazil and a Venezuelan production of *La Tempestad* (*The Tempest*) were performed at the Delacorte. It was the first time, and the last, that the Festival Latino would coproduce the Free Shakespeare in the Park series. The 1991 *Othello* starring Raúl Juliá in the Delacorte was also advertised as part of the summer Festival Latino; although there was no Latinx or Latin American theme, and the production was staged by an Irish-born director, Juliá's ethnicity was enough to promote the show as part of the Festival Latino.[9] The Brazilian production drew a great deal of attention because it featured nudity, but some of the critique of the nudity was code for the critique of staging a foreign-language production at the Delacorte (it was entirely performed in Portuguese, just as *La Tempestad* was performed in Spanish). This was the final, most explicit attempt to integrate the Festival Latino with the NYSF, tying together the venue reserved for Shakespeare, the languages of Latin American countries, and Latin American bodies in Shakespearean productions. The controversial nudity and the sounds of foreign languages taking the place of Shakespearean English came to a head with Papp's death in October that year, and within months, the NYSF abruptly cut funding for the festival.[10]

But the twenty-first century has told a different story, one in which the English language is not necessarily the hallmark of Shakespeare. And ethnicized and racialized bodies onstage perform, move, sound, and signify differently than they did sixty years ago. The world and the stakes have changed; even ethnic and racial categories have changed. In 2013, the Census Bureau announced that it was considering including Hispanic as a racial (rather than ethnic) category for the 2020 census,[11] and although this change was not implemented, it shifted the discourse about race and ethnicity. As this book demonstrates, the theatrical possibilities and those who are involved in making theater have changed. The discomfort of talking about ethnicity extends from Shakespeare studies to the American theater to cultural norms and political policy; therefore, a new perspective is needed through which to understand contemporary theater.

Latinidad has permeated Shakespearean performance for over seventy-five years, and theater-makers and historians must acknowledge this presence and influence in order to truly engage the complexity of American Shakespeares. This intersection also must lead to a recognition of the important work of some Shakespearean adaptations and performances as part of Latinx theater. In doing so, this study paves new ground by both expanding our understanding of the cultural work carried on in the United States through and with Shakespearean texts.

WHAT IS LATINX? WHAT IS SHAKESPEARE?

Latinx is an ethnicity and can be of any race: white, Black, Indigenous, or Asian. These are the ethnic and racial categories defined by the US government, and the terminology as well as the groupings cannot be applied within other countries. Conceptions of Latinidad have historically been anti-Black, while Latinx theater and performance have more often included Indigeneity, typically with a marginalized presence and through religious representation. "White" is often used, as it is employed here, to mean racially white and non-Latinx; although "Anglo" historically fits this definition, it is outmoded and can lead to unintended associations with "Anglo-Saxon." Whiteness also connotes a set of power relationships. I am aware of the problematics of this terminology and the way that, conversely, "Latinidad" conjures an image of a racially white peoples, when it in fact includes many who are racially Black and Indigenous. Language is in constant change: Latinx use terms including "Latin," "Latino," "Latino/a," "Latina/o," "Latin@," "Latinx," and now at times "Latine" or "Latiné" to describe themselves and their cultures. I use "Latinx" because it acknowledges that gender is not a binary, it is intended to be inclusive to all, and because it contrasts with the gendered language of Spanish; it is not a word in any language, and for me, it encompasses the spirit of language play. But others find it offensive or not relevant to their self-identity.[12] My use of the term "Latinx" reflects these historical biases, and this book pushes on the problematic relationship of ethnicity to race, even within the Latinx community. This book historicizes and attends to language malleability, and I employ the terminology of my time to push on its limitations.

More than four hundred years after William Shakespeare's death, an international debate is underway about what "Shakespeare" means.

"Shakespeare" is the last name of the playwright, a signifier of his oeuvre, and the totality of his reputation, which exceeds his works.[13] He is the most-performed playwright worldwide, and his canon is the most-translated literature in the world. Shakespeare's contribution to the English language has become almost a cultural meme. His reputation as the playwright of English both elides the linguistic and cultural diversity in his plays and belies a cultural universality on his part. This motif was carried throughout worldwide festivals in the anniversary years in 2014 and 2016 (the 450th anniversary of his birth and the 400th anniversary of his death, respectively) to reinforce Shakespeare's "greatness." Or was it British greatness? Or English-language greatness? Or the reach of British imperialism?

These questions arise as more people of color perform and rewrite Shakespeare for their own purposes. This follows in the legacy of Shakespeare himself, who rewrote others' tales and stories for his purposes and for a new style of theater-making and performance. In the early modern period, it was Shakespearean innovation that moved theatrical practice forward, all during a time with state-sponsored censorship and a growing backlash toward performance. And yet the deconstructive rewriting of Shakespeare's plays by people of color has historically met a bitter response when a foreign language and unfamiliar cadences are mixed into the text with Shakespeare's verse and prose.

This was evidenced in the 2012 Globe to Globe Festival preceding the London Olympics, in which foreign theater companies were invited to perform Shakespeare's plays in their national theatrical traditions and primary languages, with English reserved only for the British Globe actors.[14] These debates extended to the United States with the Oregon Shakespeare Festival's 2015–18 *Play on!* initiative to translate Shakespeare into modern-day English, and the American Shakespeare Center's "Shakespeare's New Contemporaries" competition, launched in 2017. The World Shakespeare Festival in the United Kingdom, held as part of the Cultural Olympiad for the 2012 London Olympic Games together with the Globe to Globe, involved the United States as the second most represented country after the United Kingdom.[15] While each American and American-authored production (all of which were adaptations) took up race and/or ethnicity explicitly, they all promised the visual of inter-ethnoracial romantic pairings, but the division was merely heard and not seen mimetically. This kept racism a central topic without the audience having to confront the visual of interracial intimacy.[16] The Oregon Shakespeare Festival's *Play on!* initiative set out to translate all of Shakespeare's plays into contemporary English, translated and dramaturged mostly by people of color. This led to excessive pushback from fidelity critics and textual purists. The American Shakespeare Center responded in turn with a competition called "Shakespeare's New Contemporaries," seeking sequels, prequels, or plays that otherwise engage with Shakespeare's plays and demanding that they be able to be performed on the ASC's traditional Blackfriars stage without lighting or large sets, thus setting dramaturgical limitations on new play development. The poles of the scholarly and theatrical debate compete at every level not just about who gets to perform Shakespeare but also about what gets developed in his name.

MAKING SHAKESPEARE LATINX

In *Latinx Shakespeares*, I probe the slippage between race and ethnicity not just onstage but also in the scholarship and terminology used to define and categorize a diverse group of peoples. In recent years, Shakespeare studies has largely embraced the global—investigating Shakespeare in non-English-speaking countries—but it retains a distance from the diversified local. One cannot understand Shakespearean performance in the modern and contemporary United States unless one comes to grips with Latinx Shakespeares because of their extensive presence in US theater. My work intervenes in the field of Shakespeare and race by analyzing productions that deliberately address histories of ethnicity through the intentionally crafted portrayal of Latinidad.

I anticipate an expansion of critical inquiry in the decades to come, for example into productions in Puerto Rico, Guam, American Samoa, and other US territories, each with its own political and linguistic contexts. But in this book, I focus specifically on theater within the mainland United States, about productions and adaptations that are Latinx-themed. The book does not frame a dichotomy between white and Latinx; a heterogeneous network of practitioners and influences has contributed to Latinx Shakespeares, and nuances of ethnicity and identity are addressed throughout.

Although various chapters in this book, particularly its last, engage with understandings of Hispanidad (Spanish culture) alongside Latinidad (Latinx culture),[17] this book largely focuses on the latter to the exclusion of the former. Representations of Hispanidad have followed a very different path than have Latinx Shakespeares, despite the fact that the genealogy of Shakespeare and Latinidad arose at the same time as did a renewed interest in Hispanidad. This renewed interest came through academic inquiry into Shakespeare's lost play *Cardenio*, which was thought to be recovered through paleographic inquiry in the 1990s, only to be disproven.[18] Although *Cardenio* is Spanish themed—Shakespeare took the play's name from a character in a subplot story of Miguel de Cervantes Saavedra's *Don Quijote*—the many twenty-first-century adaptations and productions that it inspired were driven more by the quest to discover a "lost" Shakespeare play than by a desire to perform Spanish culture or themes.[19] The scholarly interest in the play and the creative work inspired by a Spanish Golden Age text did not prompt a sustained theatrical interest in Spanish culture or result in even a marginal number of Hispanic or Latinx actors being cast for primary roles.[20]

During the same period of time, more Latinx actors and characters would dominate productions and adaptations of *Romeo and Juliet*, which account for over 25 percent of Latinx Shakespeares. This is greatly due to Pablo Neruda's 1961 translation of the play, which would become the most famous Spanish-language translation of the play in Latin America, in part because Neruda would be named Nobel laureate in 1971.[21] Notably, *Romeo and Juliet* is a culturally unremarkable play that was adapted by Shakespeare from Latinate origins. Due to the legacy of *West Side Story*, the most successful Shakespeare adaptation and one that adapted and ethnicized a nonethnic play through a problematic depiction of Latinx, the whitewashed *Romeo and Juliet* became re-ethnicized in the twentieth century. This process positioned *Romeo and Juliet*, just about the most-recognized play of Shakespeare's, in a seeming inverse to *Cardenio*, the lost play. *Romeo and Juliet* picked up immense cultural baggage over the years due to its lack of cultural specificity (there is nothing Veronese about the Capulets or the Montagues), while *Cardenio* couldn't sustain its Spanish roots or alleged story, its revival only useful as evidence of Shakespeare's importance. Seen against plays that have a contemporary legacy of racially marked casting practices—*Othello*'s title character as a Black man, *The Tempest*'s Caliban as a racial Other, and (more recently) *Antony and Cleopatra*'s heroine as a Black woman—the new "Spanish Shakespeare play" did much to bolster attribution studies and little to advance a politics of production that would center Spanish or Latinx culture.[22] The theater and politics of Shakespeare and Hispanidad vary greatly from those of Shakespeare and Latinidad.

As Shakespeare began to integrate more into Latinx theater, he had also most certainly become a "multicultural" writer by this stage of the twenty-first century. If he could not be entirely co-opted for Latinidad, in a twisted logic, he could be banned for his relationship to Mexican American studies because of an association with the Caribbean. The May 2010 passage of HB 2281 and the subsequent December 2011 court hearing in Arizona, or the Arizona Book Ban as it was termed in the public consciousness, suspended the Ethnic Studies / Mexican American Studies program in Tucson. Despite the fact that over 60 percent of the school district's students were from Mexican American families,[23] conservative legislative efforts were directed at eliminating the teaching of alternative histories and ethnic culture, out of a fear of a fast-growing and therefore powerful minority.[24] Seven books, all written by Latinx, were identified by the school district and specifically mentioned in the court order that followed HB 2281.

But those seven books were not the only ones removed: a total of eighty-eight books deemed to be inappropriate by the majority-Republican legislature were banned from classrooms. The dividing line was whether they were used to talk about oppression; if they were used for other pedagogies, they were allowed in classrooms. More precisely, "According to the administrative court's ruling, its [sic] perfectly acceptable to teach on oppression, as along [sic] as it's not in an emotionally charged manner."[25] Key texts to the teaching of Mexican American studies were included in the ban, along with titles such as *The Fire Next Time* (1962) by James Baldwin, *Feminism Is for Everybody* (2000) by bell hooks, *Critical Race Theory: An Introduction* (2001) by Richard Delgado and Jean Stefancic, *Civil Disobedience* (1849) by Henry David Thoreau, *A People's History of the United States* (1980) by Howard Zinn, and *The Tempest* (1611) by Shakespeare. The inclusion of *The Tempest* in the Arizona Book Ban provided an unexpected point of solidarity and surprise for those unfamiliar with or unsympathetic to the Mexican American studies program.

The association of *The Tempest* with Caribbean culture and by proxy Latinx and Latin American cultures, or *The Tempest* as the play of the Americas, took hold at the turn of the last century. Nicaraguan writer Rubén Darío, the pseudonym of Félix Rubén García Sarmiento, wrote "El Triunfo de Caliban" (1898) as a response to the US victory in the war in which Spain lost Puerto Rico, Guam, the Philippines, Cuba, and other islands in its overseas empire. Darío's idealization of Spanish hegemony was formulated in order to counter a new American hegemony. It also places Latinx in a history of Shakespearean storytelling. Uruguayan writer José Enrique Rodó's "Ariel" (1900) responded with a reconfiguration that pejoratively aligns Ariel with whiteness, interiority, elitism, and education.[26] Arielismo, or Arielism, was immediately popular, as it critiqued Western white culture and literature and promoted Latin American aesthetics. This idea was reworked through French writer Dominique-

Octave Mannoni's *Prospero and Caliban* (1950), which bears the psychoanalytic trope of "The Prospero Complex" that asserts the dichotomy of Prospero-Caliban as colonizer and colonized, and Cuban Roberto Fernández Retamar's *Calibán* (1968) shifted the focus specifically to the Caribbean due to the play's island setting. More recently, José David Saldívar defines the parameters of the "School of Caliban," Armando García invokes Caribbean theorist Sylvia Wynter to incorporate the absent-present Sycorax into this problematic configuration, and Irene Lara articulates a decolonial feminist praxis for attending to Sycorax.[27]

In the theater, Latinx Shakespearean adaptations have engaged with this association in creative and nuanced ways.[28] In both Larry Loebell's *La Tempestad* (2005), set in Puerto Rico in 2002 before the invasion of Iraq, and Khristián Méndez Aguirre and Laura Baglereau's *The Tempest: A Gentrification Story* (2018), which takes on the gentrified community of characters in East Austin, Texas, the Caliban character triumphs more so than in Shakespeare's play, but Prospero and Ariel do so as well, and none escapes from the postcolonial paradigm. Playwrights Y York, Fengar Gael, Don Nigro, and Susan Gayle Todd have written plays that center Sycorax in an effort to disidentify with Shakespeare.[29] The Arizona Book Ban brought together people with antithetical political beliefs in agreement that any version of a book ban (how could you ban Shakespeare?!) was unethical. It clearly proved that Shakespeare was not ubiquitous; Shakespeare could be the ally to the underdog at the same time that he could be cast out by dominant (and white) hegemonic structures.

BEYOND REPRESENTATION

There isn't just one relationship to Shakespeare's language and cultural capital. It varies due to a wealth of factors, including heritage, the language spoken at home, and the relationship to the theater and the text. Veteran Oregon Shakespeare Festival (OSF) actress Vilma Silva, who was raised in San Francisco by Nicaraguan parents, states, "I had no problem claiming Shakespeare as *my* playwright."[30] When others expressed surprise that a Latina was performing Shakespeare, she remarked, "It never, ever occurred to me that it was unexpected or unusual. And so, I would want kids to know, absolutely claim it, it's yours. . . . Okay, he was white, so what; he's a great playwright."[31] By contrast, essayist and scholar Marcos Gonsalez writes, "I learn from this moment the language of Shakespeare is the language of whiteness. . . . His ideas and language were crafted in response to the culture he lived in, the poetic and dramatic traditions he was working through, the impacts colonization and enslavement his homeland Britain was fully participating in had upon his psyche."[32] The range of responses to Shakespeare by Latinx practitioners and scholars is demonstrated by the range of Latinx Shakespeares addressed in this book.

Historically, the Latinx body, and the sound of the Spanish language or accent, signals a foreignness on the American, English-language Shakespearean stage. This experience of being marked as a linguistic, and perhaps foreign, Other has a lengthy history. In the late nineteenth century, Italian actor Tommaso Salvini performed the role of Othello in the United States, speaking his lines in Italian while everyone else onstage performed in English. Joseph Falocco notes in reviews of the time a "conflation of Italy with Latin America" and with Africa,[33] due to the large number of southern Italian immigrants around the turn of the century, which led reviewers to describe Salvini's Othello in animalistic and hot-tempered terms such as those all-too-frequently used for Latinx and Black actors today.[34]

The pejorative ethnic and racial constructions that were associated with Salvini are echoed in culturally appropriative attempts at essentializing an entire culture in Latinx Shakespeares today. Such productions assume a monolithic and stereotyped representation of Latinidad and layer it on top of a Shakespearean play, in a process that playwright and director Tlaloc Rivas aptly called "Latino window dressing."[35] Latinidad is an expression of culture that connects a heterogeneous group of people from multiple nations and generations with varied linguistic patterns, and cultural, regional, national, and religious beliefs. The belief in authentic representation has been entertained since the early twentieth century with the fashion for naturalistic styles, the advent of Method acting, and the Method's reformulations, or what Cary Mazer calls "Stanislavski 2.0."[36] In contrast, I do not critique Latinx Shakespeares for any seeming lack of cohesion of representation; anachronism is part of cultural translation. What interests me and what prompts the necessity for scholarly analysis is the interest in Latinixing: how, why, where, for and by whom, and to what effect.

In some ways, Shakespeare provides a welcoming and inclusive point of entry for Latinx and non-Latinx audiences alike to gain access to Latinidad. Latinx Shakespeares have the utopian possibility of teaching people about historical or contemporary Latinx history and themes as they may reach a wider audience than Latinx-authored plays. The familiar narratives appeal to general audiences, and due to the predominantly white curriculum in secondary and higher education, Shakespeare's stories are familiar to wide audiences and open a door to a perhaps unfamiliar culture (either

Latinx or early modern British) while combating pejorative notions about Latinx speaking Shakespearean verse. In an act of disassociation or because of the Latinx absence from Shakespeare's playscripts, Latinx Shakespeares pose an opportunity to have Latinx bodies onstage without showcasing stories of immigration, assimilation, or the destitute, although some Latinx Shakespeares take up these themes. While superficial attempts to depict Latinidad are regressive and racist, the act of telling one culture's story through another can also be productive because it removes other tropes that have been commonplace in Latinx theater. According to actor Daniel José Molina,

> If us being Latin is a diegetic element in the productions that we're in, . . . it's a real privilege. We can contribute in some small way to the story of our respective cultures. Which means that, conversely, if a play never brings up the fact that we are Latinx, both Alejandra [Escalante] and I cherish that opportunity. Sometimes the representation is enough.[37]

Latinx Shakespeares have the potential to weave Latinx cultures into Shakespearean plays, cast the production with actors who can draw on their heritage, and allow actors and audiences to experience the interplay of languages and cultures.

A consistent and problematic purity test for Latinx representation, as well as Latinx identity, is fluency or familiarity with the Spanish language. The equivalence of Latinx peoples to the Spanish language obscures the variety of languages Latinx peoples speak and hail from, and it also reinforces the linguistic racism that led to English-only legislation (see chapter 2), especially when it is staged for humor or topically.[38] Increasingly, more and more people who identify as Latinx do not speak Spanish.[39] Yet Spanish is a theatrical signifier of Latinx identity and a claim to cultural heritage, which for some is a distant and unseen locale. Although the Latinx plays of the 1980s and 1990s included a significant amount of Spanish,[40] much of the Latinx drama that boomed in the twenty-first century was more English-dominant focused. Indeed, as of 2020, all the Latinx plays to have been nominated for or receive the Pulitzer Prize for Drama include substantially more English than Spanish, offering an appeal to wider (English-dominant) audiences.[41] In many ways, Latinx Shakespeares do not follow that same trend: rather, they have tended to integrate more and more Spanish into Shakespeare's plays as their genealogy progresses.

In 2011, Ayanna Thompson noted the instability of Shakespeare and of the relationship between Shakespeare and race studies and racial activism.[42] Her book *Passing Strange*, as she explains, "might just be a manifesto advocating for the maintenance of that instability."[43] Latinx Shakespeares heighten this instability due to the work of translation. The text is not stable, not just because multiple versions exist across folios, quartos, and editors, but because all Latinx Shakespeares confront translation and put the translator's interpretation into the dialogue of the text. This is confrontation with Shakespeare at its most extreme, taking his language out and replacing it with another's. And the translator is typically Latinx.

Shakespearean translation has historically been viewed as detrimental to maintaining the canonicity of Shakespeare as purveyor of the English language: "The very act of translation subverts the authority of Shakespeare's text."[44] Shakespeare has allowed practitioners to be coauthors, or at least editors, of his scripts for centuries. Latinx Shakespeares permit them to be translators as well, bringing forward Latin American and Latinx translations onto US stages.[45] A linguistic dramaturgy that mixes Shakespearean English and modern-day Spanish, or what I have termed *cross-temporal code-switching*, centers language play across centuries; the sound of Latinx Shakespeares is outside of any particular time period. The case studies in this book demonstrate the range and nuance of local circumstances that inform backstage processes, actor training, translation and adaptation strategies, and audience diversity that affect language play.

When theater companies attempt to represent Latinidad in service of a concept without integrating it into their production and practice (through local/specific dramaturgy, casting, a Latinx soundscape, etc.), the results can be incredibly harmful. In November 2011, the Shakespeare Theatre Company (STC) in Washington, DC, launched a production of *Much Ado about Nothing* set on a sugar plantation in 1930s Cuba. With a predominantly white cast, peripheral Spanish phrases, and sensualized music and dancing, the production largely alluded to Cuban culture rather than performed it. The production romanticized a dark time in Cuba's history for the purpose of playing on the stereotype of the erotic and sultry Latino. Dogberry's troupe entered singing "Guantanamera," a sexy tango number was added for Margaret and Borachio, and slight updates were made to the dialogue to push the concept setting. Most notoriously, STC's production renamed two minor and originally lower-class characters as "Juan Arroz" and "Jose Frijoles," inadvertently transforming a class distinction (in Shakespeare) into an ethnic divide. A letter-writing campaign by Latinx theater practitioners denounced the problematic staging, the stereotypes that the production fostered and upheld, and the casting choices (only a few actors of color appeared in the cast, and they were mostly in minor or villainous roles).[46] After facing a severe backlash, STC hosted a roundtable discussion, and the names of the characters were returned to Hugh Oatcake and George Seacoal. The theater was also asked to work with the Hispanic Association of Latin Actors (HOLA) to cast more Latinx actors in its future productions.

This production prompted a national conversation among Latinx theater practitioners, resulting in the creation of the Latinx Theatre Commons (LTC) in 2012, a movement that fosters and supports new work by Latinx artists.[47] The purpose of the LTC is to create "new models of engagement and presentation of Latino/a theater that will not only illuminate the wide expanse of the field but will allow audiences to update the US narrative by experiencing multi-cultural worlds on stage that reflect an ever-diversifying national reality."[48] The four pillars of the Commons are advocacy, art-making, convening, and scholarship. Since first convening in 2013, the LTC has produced festivals and initiatives that generate and promote Latinx theater. Ultimately, a new surge in Latinx theater resulted in part from the imperative to respond to a faulty attempt to Latinxize a Shakespearean play.

After the start of the twenty-first century, the National Endowment for the Arts (NEA) created a campaign to associate Shakespeare with the United States, whose marketing included Shakespeare's image transposed in front of the American flag. "Shakespeare in American Communities" began in 2003 and was followed by "Shakespeare for a New Generation" the following year. Both initiatives offered funding for Shakespeare productions throughout the country. As Dana Gioia, chairman of the NEA, argued, "It's impossible to understand American culture or American theater without understanding Shakespeare."[49] Initiatives such as these— alongside the now commonplace practice of nontraditional casting in American theater,[50] a bevy of Hollywood Shakespeare films from the 1990s, the nearly uniform national experience of reading a Shakespeare play in high school, the United States' claim to more Shakespeare festivals and theaters than any other country in the world, and the US position in the world economy (until the Trump presidency)—have cohered to make Shakespeare an American writer, just as he was made a German national poet centuries ago. Shakespeare, now indigenous to the United States, is not as associated with Britain and colonialism in contemporary culture today; his hegemonic status is emblematic of an adjacent, entirely English-language American problem; his cultural hegemony is pitted against and marked for diversity initiatives.[51]

The perception that "diversity" is an optional, cost-prohibitive aspect of theater-making has stained the development of American theater despite theater's need for new and broader audiences in order to sustain itself. Problematic attempts at equity, diversity, and inclusion have a lengthy history of little regard for what diversity actually means. Even when actors of color have been made central, often the productions of classical works are themselves in many ways traditional. Progressive casting choices do not necessarily make progressive Shakespearean productions.

For this reason, a move to decenter white canonical playwrights and their stories from American stages was underway in the realm of theater more broadly. The year 2020 had been slated by a coalition of theater folx across the country to be the year of the Jubilee, "in which every theater in the United States of America produces works by women, people of color, artists of varied physical and cognitive ability, and/or LGBTQIA artists."[52] This plan was canceled due to Covid-19 restrictions, and instead, audiences saw the rise of international and multicultural Shakespeares online.[53] The plays' availability in the public domain made them especially useful here, amid the severe financial losses incurred during closures due to the dual pandemics of Covid-19 and race-based violence in the country. While the public health pandemic closed the theaters and shifted much live art to online, the pandemic of racial violence has led to outpourings of support for Black Lives Matter and racial justice initiatives, igniting theater practitioners not just to reimagine the American theater, but also to formulate clear demands for change. In June 2020, thirty artists of color created a petition and statement addressing White American Theater (WAT). The petition for "WeSeeYouWAT" had fifty thousand signatories in the first twenty-four hours, and over one hundred thousand signatories by August. Along with a robust social media presence, the petition was succeeded by a thirty-page handbook of demands for theaters. The call for recognition and structural changes made by Black, Indigenous, and People of Color (BIPOC) hopefully will be a blueprint for rebuilding American theater.

ENCOUNTERING SHAKESPEARE

I came to this project through the realization of the inchoate relationship of aurality to ethnicity. During my freshman year in high school, I was assigned *Romeo and Juliet* in Honors English. The teacher showed the Franco Zeffirelli film, and after several days, I asked whether this movie came out before or after *West Side Story* because this Juliet was also Hispanic (in the 1980s parlance). The teacher responded that this film had come out later

(*West Side Story* was first performed onstage in 1957 and filmed in 1961; Zeffirelli's stage production was in 1960, and the film came out in 1968), and she corrected my statement: Olivia Hussey, the actress playing Juliet, was British. A student blurted out that it was obvious by her accent. Another student said she didn't look Hispanic, ostensibly due to her blue eyes and pale skin. It would take me several decades to learn that Olivia Hussey is half Argentine and the daughter of the famed Argentine opera singer Osvaldo Ribó (né Andrés Osuna).[54] As someone living between languages, what Walter Mignolo refers to as bilanguaging, I heard her Spanish inflection at moments through her British accent; what is regarded as the most British and traditional *Romeo and Juliet* film has a Latin American Juliet. Latinx and Latin Americans are so integrated into modern versions of this play that many audience members do not even know when they see and hear them.

At the same time, in high school, I was enrolled in Honors Drama, and I was in rehearsal for my first Shakespeare festival competition, where high school students perform scenes or abridgments from Shakespeare plays. The festival selects one comedy and tragedy each year, and that year's tragedy was *Romeo and Juliet*.[55] In this moment of curricular serendipity, my first real introduction to Shakespeare was unified through the timing and selection of the same Shakespeare play in two classes; I was assigned Shakespeare for the first time simultaneously in the English department and the theater department, a duality that informed my later interdisciplinary research and foreshadowed my career.

Latinx Shakespeares is also informed by my work as a scholar for the theater for various theater companies. As a theater historian and performance theorist, I prioritize my firsthand phenomenological accounts of these productions. I have had to reread reviews and texts for ethnic and cultural bias, and translate dialogue, from theoretical and historical texts and from practitioner interviews from Spanish to English. I have conversed with numerous practitioners about their art, including more than forty that I interviewed for this book.[56] The archive of theater resides in the libraries where I conducted research for this project—at the Folger Shakespeare Library, the New York Public Library, the Shakespeare Institute Library, and more—but the archive also comprises interviews with practitioners, for the means by which they are making work with these plays is itself an act of criticism, an interpretive engagement with the plays. Thus, I do not merely use quotations from artists to substantiate my claims; I put the analysis by theater practitioners on equal level with academic theorists. This is my training across and from within the arts, the "both/and" aspect of the scholar-practitioner. I utilize theory to form a critical interpretation of art, and I center the art and the artist, which invariably leads to a discussion of politics: economic, identarian, and social.

This project did not expose a through line from early modern Spanish-English relations to today's Latinx-white US relationships, or from Latin American Shakespearean theatrical practice to Latinx; these relationships include some similarities and analogies, but any lengthy comparisons would be methodologically unsound. Also, there is no strict linear genealogy of Latinx Shakespeares from theater by white practitioners performed in predominantly white theaters to Latinx practitioners and theaters of color, though as more theaters and artists of color helm these projects, the instances of blatant cultural appropriation decrease. An attempt to draw such a segregated trajectory of theater-making avoids the nuances and relationships that are crucial to this history as both linear time and ethnic categories are being challenged throughout this book. Instead, the through line is a consciousness of cultural difference: in Shakespeare's plays, he reveals such a consciousness, albeit flawed, and both this consciousness and many of its flaws repeat in contemporary American productions. *Latinx Shakespeares* moves toward healing by reclaiming Shakespeare as a borrower, adapter, and creator of language whose oeuvre has too often been mobilized in the service of a culturally specific English-language whiteness that cannot fully extricate itself from its origins within the establishment of European/British colonialism/imperialism. These origins are nonetheless often fixated on a moment of intracultural encounter that lends itself precisely to the kind of necessary engagements that manifest in Latinx Shakespeares.

In his book *Shakespeare in a Divided America*, James Shapiro posits division as a premise on which American identity is founded. I concur, but Latinx Shakespeares, which are notably absent from his narrative of Shakespeare in the United States, show us how division can move toward a desire for building community. When I first began researching Latinx Shakespeares, a simplified binary arose as a means to explain the American predilection toward division. In this book, I parse out the perceived oppositionality of Latinx and Shakespeare to implode the binary and relieve Latinx of the burden of being perceived as an (unequal) Other, on the Shakespearean stage and elsewhere. This process of building community, both onstage and offstage, is an antiracist practice. Latinx Shakespeares are one possible strategy for progress.

METHODOLOGY AND SCOPE

This book draws its methodology for attending to theater from Ric Knowles's *Reading the Material Theatre*, which triangulates the factors for reading theater: performance, the conditions of production (working conditions, funding structures, actor training, directing), and the conditions of reception (stage and place, positionality, public discourse). Meaning is made through the relationship of the three poles, and "the local specificities of production and reception."[57] The array of case studies complicates monolithic assumptions about either Shakespeare or Latinx theater-making. As a theater history and study of stage performance, this book reveals the complexity of racial and ethnic categories and the simplicity by which they have often been staged.

Contemporary theater history refutes the idea that only big-name, Broadway, and large regional theaters define or are representative of theater in the United States. In his study *Performance in America*, David Román promotes "the 'romance of the indigenous,'" by which [he means] the endorsement of community-based and often obscure cultural productions, venues, and genres that seem more rooted in the 'authentic,' and artists and icons who are linked to progressive social movements."[58] Some of the most revolutionary theater happens in smaller, independent performance spaces, and what is considered "fringe" or "low-budget" may signal what audiences see at large, established theaters in the years that follow.

I detail productions at a range of theaters and cultural institutions. The situations and art of the case studies vary, but they are all equal partners in theatrical constructions of Latinidad, ranging from using Latinx culture to define hegemonic American culture to offering thoughtful Latinx aesthetics and identity performance. The Latinx relationship to Indigeneity runs throughout many of the case studies; Afro-Latinidad is less present, reflecting cultural and theatrical biases that extend beyond Latinx Shakespeares. In Latinx theater, of which Latinx Shakespeares are a part, the world becomes different through Latinx eyes and interfaces with spirituality and ritual often decentered or devalued in a kind of American secular Shakespeare; likewise, language switching and play is liberated from the pedantic insistence on maintaining authenticity. This cultural work attends to the local, nuanced specificities of those ways of being and storytelling while maintaining in productive tension with a meaningful relationship with other American Shakespearean practices. Built into how theater gets produced is a series of arguments that perform a new type of criticism of Shakespeare that isn't valued widely in Shakespeare studies. I center this form of criticism because it does interpretive work; the archive of the theater—interviews, ephemera, dramaturgy packets, rehearsal processes, theater designs, production strategies—reveals how people working with these plays, how people produce art, *is* an act of criticism.

These productions are reshaping America. In her book *The Problem of the Color[blind]*, Brandi Wilkins Catanese writes, "On both institutional and cultural levels, performance has become the medium through which American anxieties about race (and in particular, blackness) are pondered, articulated, managed, and challenged."[59] Likewise, modern Latinx theater grew directly out of activism when Luis Valdez founded El Teatro Campesino on the picket lines of the United Farm Workers (helmed by Cesar Chavez and Dolores Huerta) during the Delano Grape Strike in 1965.[60] From its origin, Latinx theater was overtly political and united oppressed people; in the words of Jorge Huerta, it was "necessary theater."[61] It was founded on building community partnerships, efforts that today extend to the movement that is the LTC.[62] Latinx Shakespeares utilize the conformity that Shakespeare represents as a standard-bearer of monoculture and apply the radical alterity of Latinx bodies, non-English languages, and stories of Latinidad to open up affective communities. This goes beyond the oftentimes transactional exchange of "nontraditional" casting strategies and representation to the transformational change of fostering community and worldmaking.

Studies of contemporary Shakespeares often look to popular culture, film, new media, new technologies, and experimental (and immersive) theater. I refer to filmic versions of Shakespeare that address Latinx culture (see chapter 1) only as they relate to the cultural knowledge that informs practitioners and viewers of theatrical Latinx Shakespeares. In today's world of modern technologies, it is both an antiquated and revolutionary act to devote a book entirely to contemporary Shakespearean theatrical performance. My subjects of study are these performances, the material conditions shaping their making, and their contributions to a sense of belonging for Latinx people. In live theater, actors can feel the audience; even nonimmersive theater is inflected by the give-and-take between actor and performer. The presence of an audience changes the performance, and it is this component that is essential to the efficacy of Latinx theater as a tool of activism. Is it possible that Latinx Shakespeares, then, can function in this way?

The productions in this book demonstrate that possibility. For example, the most popular Shakespearean adaptation worldwide is an ethnicized one that centers Latinx characters (chapter 1). The largest repertory and regional theater in the United States mounted two back-to-back Latinx Shakespeares, pushing forward a diversity initiative that would inform not only its future seasons but become a model for other theaters (chapter 2). A Latinx Shakespearean play served as a space in which to make audible an extinct Indigenous language not broadly spoken for more than one hundred years (chapter 3). Theaters of color integrated Indigenous ritual and ceremony into Shakespearean plotlines as well as the theatrical experience (chapter 4) and created world-class puppetry from a US territory that is displayed in museums and festivals to tell the history of New York (chapter 5). And a Latinx Shakespearean history play became the first piece of theater to be performed in an urban space of renewal, thereby changing the landscape and ideas about where theater is made (chapter 6). But art cannot empower unless we are clear on how communities have been disempowered. These productions push against prevailing presumptions about Latinx theater, that it comprises only stories of immigration and assimilation; about Latinx actors, that they are not qualified to perform in Shakespeare; about Latinx cultures, that they can be subsumed under homogenous tropes; about Shakespearean performance, that there is an authentic or appropriate style; about Shakespeare's plays, that they contain ideas about humanity that apply worldwide.

I have been asked whether Latinx Shakespeares are good for Latinx people. Like all artistic efforts, they have their good and their bad, but Latinx Shakespeares offer a depiction of Latinidad through a poetic language that is familiar, to some extent, to all Americans. Problematically, even when adaptations and productions attempt to stage a specific culture—Cuban, Chicanx, Nuyorican—oftentimes an amalgamation of Latinx cultures comes across onstage. But at their best, Latinx Shakespeares can challenge faulty historical notions of Latinx people, present new aesthetic ones, and provide a physical and linguistic space to combat marginalization and racism. The Latinx Shakespeares I introduce here engage a range of macroidentities and introduce new artistic modes and aesthetics. Ultimately, due to the ubiquity of Shakespeare, these plays allow people to see Latinx culture and Latinx bodies performing in their local venues that they may not have otherwise seen.

LATINX SHAKESPEARES AS INTRACULTURAL AMERICAN THEATER

In Latinx theater, the plays do not need to revolve around a specifically Latinx-themed plot. Far from it: Jorge Huerta identifies Latinx theater as including any play with a theme that "explores the nature" of being Latinx,[63] while Brian Eugenio Herrera argues that Latinx theater is a tradition, not a genre,[64] and playwright Georgina Escobar focuses on aesthetics as the connective tissue across Latinx theater.[65] Shakespeare's plays, as they are written, are obviously not part of Latinx theater, but Shakespeare—when adapted and performed—can become part of Latinx theater.

Much has been written on intercultural theater and cultural exchange. Ric Knowles explores the purposes of intercultural theater, claiming that it could "decolonise the stage" or, in Richard Schechner's terms, "*produce the experience* of difference."[66] Knowles considers not just verbal language, but also "language of the body, issues of translation, and the negotiation of meaning in performance."[67] Yong Li Lan astutely argues that the "fiction of the intercultural" is that it is informed through audience reception. She argues that intercultural theater is a performative, a repeated gesture that invokes a cultural trope, rather than a mode of representation.[68] Further, Rustom Bharucha differentiates between the intercultural and the intracultural, arguing that "intracultural" denotes differences between cultures on regional levels and challenges ideas of homogeneity of caste and economic equality.[69]

Here I invert the narrative of Latinx (or any other nonwhite cultural group) Shakespearean performance as intercultural, postcolonial, postrace, and so on, and present these productions as American theater. I term these productions *intra*cultural, as a development in the American theatrical landscape. This is a study of the present state of the American Shakespearean stage, and Latinidad is part of American culture. Division and friction between Latinx and white hegemonic American culture exist for obvious reasons, including centuries of discrimination, linguistic racism, colonization, and marginalization. By terming Latinx Shakespeares intracultural, I do not subsume differences and division, but rather address both how this conflict has served as an essential construct of American theater and how community can take shape through a broader idea of what American culture means. Intraculturalism includes an unsteady interplay of ethnically and racially different bodies and various accents and languages. Latinx Shakespeares were initially premised on division, but they have extended to dramaturgies that include Latinx history, Latinx and Indigenous rituals and ceremonies, issues of colorism and anti-Blackness within Latinx communities, and Latinx theatrical traditions. Latinx, by definition, are American. This is American theater.

Latinx theater has a long tradition of taking up the classics for today, extending back to early Chicanx theater that adapted myth for the stage.[70]

Adaptations range from the Greeks to more recent classics such as Milton, Molière, Chekhov, Strindberg, and Brecht, to name a few. Numerous adaptations and translations exist of the Spanish Golden Age dramatists and early twentieth-century Spanish playwright Federico García Lorca. Yet Latinx Shakespearean adaptations, appropriations, and concept productions are the most common, due to the familiarity of the stories.[71] Latinx theater-makers have been reshaping American theater for years; this book unpacks and remaps the strategies by which they have been doing so through various forms of adaptation, appropriation, and concept productions.[72] In Leo Cabranes-Grant's study of Mexican theater and performance, he argues that the methodology for intercultural scenarios must include not just the unpacking of relationships, but also the remapping of the relational ties that made them viable. I reconfigure the history of American Shakespeares by revealing and realigning the triangulated power relationships (linguistic, theatrical/aesthetic, cultural-political) of Latinx and the dominant culture in the United States. As Yong argues that the intercultural is a fiction created through repetition onstage, I argue that the two key components of intracultural American theater are the historical premise of divisiveness and the remapping of what is needed for creating community through the process of making theater.

In Latinx Shakespeares, the triangulation of power relationships results in an elevation of the aural. Although casting choices and elements of the mise-en-scène contribute to cultural construction, the soundscape (language, accent, music, silences, noise, and sounds) is the key dramaturgical signifier used to convey Latinx culture. Spanish is often used to overcome the challenge of recognizing an "authentic" Latinx body onstage. The liminal figure of the Latinx presents a way of imagining a visually diverse group of people whose heritage ranges from California to Texas, Puerto Rico to Cuba, Chile to Argentina, and so forth. Because Spanish dialects, accents, and slang vary just as widely, oftentimes the musical soundscape is used to specify a Latinx culture where other auditory markers do not. When Latinidad is performed on the Shakespearean stage, the intersection of Latinx and Shakespearean language play—the division between languages that is remapped to Latinx Shakespeares' cross-temporal code-switching—coalesces to become the language of the intracultural.

The liminality of language play is germane to Latinidad. Bilingualism, "Spanglish," and code-switching all form part of Latinx identity and the generational changes that can be marked in part by language shifts. Similarly, for many, the pleasure of Shakespeare's works has much to do with the pleasure of language. The early modern playhouse was also a theater of oratory; words and phrases were coined, puns and bawdy jokes abounded, and stage directions as well as shifts in setting were conveyed all through the words spoken onstage. This book focuses on how aurality can both shape and challenge culture and the theatrical representations of it.

The emphasis on the aural is an original practice of Shakespearean performance, and it is something that adaptation through the musical genre or through translation can draw on. The position of Shakespeare in English-language teaching and colonization drives the importance of recognizing language as both a structure and an event; this is the very definition of discourse analysis, key to the methodology for performance analysis in this book. Just as "Spanglish" extends outside of English and Spanish, Latinx Shakespeares speak in two modes simultaneously to create something bigger than both Shakespeare and Latinx theater.

Language is often what brings people to Shakespeare, but it can also be used to subvert patriarchal and colonialist histories. My engagement with language functions on both levels at all times. Latinx are faced with the heterogeneity of Latinidad today, including those that do not speak the language(s) of their heritage. Latinx educated in the United States are guaranteed to learn some Shakespeare, though they may not learn Spanish. Bilingualism, semi-bilingualism, and language play vary across localities and individual experiences; this instability across all aspects of Latinx language leads to apprehension on the part of many for taking on Shakespeare, who is often cast as a fixed linguistic genius. The irony is that Shakespeare's texts are just as malleable, perhaps more so, than Latinx linguistic code-switching. Latinx Shakespeares work both for and against this idea, reinforcing the association of Latinidad with Spanish but also, through the inclusion of additional languages, breaking down that binary. The genealogy I trace of Latinx Shakespeares since the mid-twentieth century shows changes along the way, from using language to bolster division to *theatrical bilanguaging*, or the theatricalizing of life between two languages. Latinx Shakespeares force an examination of the relationship of Latinx identity and culture to the Spanish language, and to the English language, for that matter.

SHAKESPEARE FOR LATINIDAD / LATINIDAD FOR SHAKESPEARE

In this book, I explore how division leads to community and redefines what can be considered "universal," or in fact, ubiquitous, about Shakespeare. The disjunction between cultures, as theatricalized by linguistic division, is a step in the process of healing and worldmaking. I define the *West Side Story* effect, or the layering of cultural-linguistic division onto

Shakespearean plays that have no such division, as a now-dominant mode of Shakespearean storytelling.

My research on Latinx Shakespeares has taught me that audiences and critics have a harder time accepting theater by artists of color if they don't make an explicit statement about identity. If productions are not explicitly political, the motivations for them are, whether they address contemporary ethnic and racial dynamics, problematize language politics, or serve as memory-history recovery sites. All theater is inherently political, enmeshed in power relationships of the cultural moment. Early Latinx Shakespeares included the integration of fictionalized versions of political figures, including Fidel Castro and Oliver North, and others used international conflicts to establish the setting for concept productions.[73] Some artists took up local demographics and others staged the past, but only one took up a Shakespearean history play in order to look to the future (chapter 6).

Latinx Shakespeares have brought me to the theatrics of cultural appropriation, histories of brownface, the distinct geographic origins of music and dances such as tango, cumbia, and flamenco (although they are often elided onstage), and the white-centered logics in acting and vocal methods. They have also brought me into dialogue with scholars such as Gloria Anzaldúa, Jon Rossini, and Catherine S. Ramírez, as well as artists all over the country. I shift the East-West axis of traditional Shakespearean performance criticism to a North-South axis by using the work of Latin American and Latinx theorists such as José Esteban Muñoz, Walter Mignolo, and Leo Cabranes-Grant and theater-makers such as Georgina Escobar and Luis Valdez to analyze this new development in American theater. My employment of Latinx and Latin American theorists to examine these productions moves away from modes of multicultural Shakespearean analysis that foreground European and white ontologies.

The central concern of this book is the question of how and why artists make theater, not just an analysis of the theater created. The book comprises thematic chapters, each with case studies of Latinx Shakespearean dramaturgies. Together, they form one large case study of intracultural theater, of which some are ethnic theater, that may have applications to other groups in different locales. I refer to ethnic theater as "for us, by us," the theater by and for an ethnic or cultural group that includes peoples from either a shared national or linguistic background that do not necessarily organize along racial lines: examples include Yiddish theater, Latinx theater, and Armenian theater. What Shakespeare offers for Latinidad is a data set of over 150 Latinx Shakespearean productions that demonstrates the breadth of dramaturgies, identities, and geographically specific politics that can be incorporated into Shakespearean plays. What Latinidad offers to Shakespeare is the opportunity to expand the making of theater for those who are absent from the text or conception in the period that the dramatic literature was written. In exploring the desire to adapt, appropriate, and stage Shakespeare for Latinidad, *Latinx Shakespeares* reveals the possibility of remaking Shakespeare as contemporary ethnic theater.

Since the early 2000s, scholars of both Shakespeare and Latinidad have argued for a rhizomatic approach to their fields, a shifting away from hierarchical mappings to a more nuanced theorization of the interconnections between people, geographies, and events. Douglas Lanier urges a rhizomatic outlook for Shakespeare studies, stating that "within the Shakespearean rhizome, the Shakespearean text is an important element but not a determining one."[74] Likewise, Latinx studies scholar Cristina Beltrán argues that viewing Latinidad as rhizomatic "imagines transformational multiplicities, off-shoots, and unexpected alliances."[75] Both Lanier and Beltrán speak to a decentered formation. In fact, Lanier credits the Shakespearean films of the 1990s with popularizing new narrative settings and bringing "Shakespeare in line with late twentieth-century visual culture and in the process loosen[ing] the equivalence between Shakespeare and text,"[76] and these relationships are also taken up in the network theory that Thomas Cartelli, Valerie M. Fazel, and Louise Geddes apply to Shakespeare.[77] I understand these arguments in unison; to study Shakespeare and Latinidad conjuntos requires an approach that is branched rather than hierarchical, in motion rather than fixed.

The dramaturgies of Latinx Shakespeares that I detail in this book, illustrated through case studies, form "a 'complex structure': a structure in which things are related, as much through their differences as through their similarities."[78] My various thematic investigations are connected to my two overarching themes: division/intraculturalism and aurality. These themes intersect as intraculturalism constantly presses toward a division often most clearly manifest through a broad and excessive aural soundscape. While each chapter focuses on a particular critical concept, the case studies intersect across thematic concerns and practices. There is no one version of Latinx Shakespeares.

CHAPTER BREAKDOWN

In chapter 1, "Division: The *West Side Story* Effect," I describe a significant factor in the field of Latinx Shakespeares—the creation of division—which

I attribute to the influence of the musical and film *West Side Story*. I detail key changes in this watershed adaptation and explore how they inform theatrical representations of Latinx more largely. What I term the *West Side Story* effect is the staging of difference of any kind in Shakespeare—familial, cultural, class—as cultural-linguistic division. I argue that the musical's racializing of the Paris figure and softening of the Romeo character codified notions of whiteness and masculinity for the stage and in the 1961 film. I explore the breadth of factors for the predominance of *Romeo and Juliet* in Latinx Shakespearean productions. I draw on a genealogy of Latinx Shakespearean films to make this case, including Baz Luhrmann's 1996 *William Shakespeare's Romeo + Juliet*, which reclaimed Latinidad for stagings and film adaptations of the play. Ultimately, I argue that *West Side Story* engrained division as the trope for representing Latinx in subsequent productions and adaptations not just of *Romeo and Juliet* but of the entire Shakespearean canon.

In chapter 2, "Aurality: Hearing Ethnicity," I argue that the intermixing of Shakespearean English, modern-day Spanish, and Indigenous languages in Latinx Shakespeares renegotiates perceptions of Latinx. This cross-temporal code-switching, the movement between languages from different time periods, reflects an inchoate idea of the relationship between ethnicity and language. It facilitates understanding for audiences who may not speak any of the languages fluently and demonstrates how polyphony remakes the world both more richly and accurately. I begin with a bilingual production of *Romeo and Juliet* at Florida State University in 2005 to demonstrate the need for heightened attention to the aural. I argue that the Latinx soundscape is inclusive of language, accent, music, sound effects, silences, and noise, all of which contribute to a Latinx Shakespearean acoustemology that is a performance of aural excess, which I term *auralidad*. I use two productions from the Oregon Shakespeare Festival (OSF) as case studies: a 2011 production of *Measure for Measure* that was set in a border town with Latinx and bilingual actors and characters, and a 2012 production of *Romeo and Juliet* that was set in 1840s Alta California, with both houses as part of the landed Spanish gentry. While the former production unites Latinx culture and the Spanish language in opposition to a diverse but monolingual culture, the latter depicts interlingual households with accent and linguistic differentiation between generations and geographic spaces. Utilizing theory from sound studies, I argue for a Latinx acoustemology that permits varied audiences to attune to Latinidad.

The dramaturgies in chapter 3, "Identity: Remapping Latinidades," highlight Latinx Shakespeares that expand the parameters of Latinidad.

Case studies include Coeurage Theatre Company's 2016 *Twelfth Night*, which featured Filipinx twins, a Brazilian Malvolio, and a Jamaican Antonio, as well as a multiracial and multiethnic cast with a total of seven languages; José Cruz González's 2009 *Invierno* (*The Winter's Tale*), which includes the Indigenous language of Samala spoken by the Chumash of Central California and is set among the 1800s Californio ranches; and Alex Alpharaoh's 2019 *O-Dogg: An Angeleno Take on "Othello"*, a homage to street life that is set during the 1992 LA uprisings and addresses colorism and anti-Blackness within Latinx communities with an Afro-Latinx Othello and an Indigenous-Latinx Iago. I argue for remapping the very definition of Latinidad as a network or community of a shared feeling rather than an identity that can be mimetically represented onstage. Embracing theoretical approaches that emphasize process, aesthetics, and affect, the productions challenge the productivity and means of expression of identity as a category. All three productions are set and were first staged in California and take up an expanded idea of Brownness. I argue that "a sense of brown" extends to various ethnicities who experience immigration, migration, and linguistic isolation and that Shakespeare provides a porous site for absorbing these commonalities.

Chapter 4, "Decoloniality: Theatrical Bilanguaging," addresses the dramaturgical construction of Latinx subjectivity from both inside and outside decolonialist theater practices that seek to engage audiences through thoughtfully crafted portrayals of Latinidad. What I term theatrical bilanguaging offers a liberation from discrete styles of theatrical storytelling. I extend this concept of theatrical bilanguaging to the experience of Latinx actors in the rehearsal room of predominantly white theaters versus Latinx theaters. Drawing a distinction between anticolonial, postcolonial, and decolonial strategies in three *Hamlet* adaptations, I argue that the crisis of self is linguistic, onstage and off. I begin with Joseph Papp's 1968 *Naked Hamlet*, which cast the half-Spanish Martin Sheen in both the lead role and that of Hamlet's alter ego Ramon, a Puerto Rican, heavily accented and sometimes Spanish-speaking janitor who delivered the monologues. I contrast this formation of the self to two recent productions: Asolo Repertory's 2012 *Hamlet, Prince of Cuba*, which had the cast perform entirely in English for one month and then entirely in Spanish for several shows, and Tara Moses's 2018 *Hamlet: El Príncipe de Denmark* at Telétulsa in Oklahoma, which included ceremonial practice and was staged during the Day of the Dead festivities. These adaptations address coloniality and the resulting crisis of the self through multiple border crossings: linguistic and cultural, religious and ritualistic, within the play and without.

Chapter 5, "El Público: Healing and Spectatorship," begins with two theater projects that crossed the literal national border and performed Shakespeare jointly with Mexican actors in Mexico to reposition Latinx representation: the Old Globe in San Diego's 2005 Bi-National Project and Symmetry Theatre's 2019 Bridge Across the Wall Bilingual Theatre Festival. From there, I turn to theater-makers that cross borders within their own communities. I look to OSF's fully bilingual 2018 *La Comedia of Errors*, which included contemporary English and Spanish and was designed to move to various performance spaces in the local region, as an example of community-building within the frame of a Shakespeare theater. I then attend to Teatro SEA's 2015 *Sueño*, an adaptation of *A Midsummer Night's Dream* that was performed either entirely in Spanish or entirely in English in an outdoor urban space. It included Afro-Caribbean puppets ranging from handheld to gigantes, thereby shifting the focus away from the physical body to assert Latinx belonging in public spaces. I argue that creating an audience for bilingual and ethnic theater is an act of worldmaking, and it is possible at both white theaters and theaters of color. Both OSF and Teatro SEA integrated movements toward bilingual and ethnic theater into their organizations through long-term strategies for creating new audiences.

The subject of chapter 6, "Futures: Shakespearean Critical History," involves the negotiation of Shakespearean history plays and the histories that his plays invoke. The chapter centers on Herbert Siguenza's *El Henry*, a postapocalyptic version of *Henry IV, Part I* that resets the action in the year 2045. Although Siguenza has adapted other Western classics for Latinx culture to tell contemporary history, here he adapts a history play to Latinx aesthetics to speculate forward. I argue that Siguenza's *El Henry* models a form of critical analysis for a Shakespearean history play by overlapping British history with speculative Chicanx futures, thereby forcing new questions about historicity, temporality, and identity. I demonstrate that through the creative work of playwriting, Siguenza generates a mode of historical criticism that is not dependent on Western dualisms, ethnic and racial binaries, cultural division, or even linear time. Siguenza's play models how the creative work of Latinx Shakespeares can function simultaneously as a form of critical history and as speculative fiction.

ONE | Division

The West Side Story *Effect*

Arguably the single most important cultural work to shape the trajectory of Latinx Shakespeares is *West Side Story*, a musical adaptation of *Romeo and Juliet* that offers a backstory for the grudge between the households by transposing them to youth gangs, the Puerto Rican Sharks and the culturally diverse but racially white Jets. With its ethnically based divide, it became the template for cultural division as a primary trope for staging contemporary American Shakespearean productions, shaping not just subsequent iterations of *Romeo and Juliet* but also many other plays in the Shakespearean canon. The lasting influence of this musical has led to what I term the *West Side Story* effect: the staging of difference of any kind in Shakespeare (familial, cultural, class) as cultural-linguistic division.

Division has both textual and thematic roots within *Romeo and Juliet*, but as this chapter will show, *West Side Story* is what caused it to fully take hold in Shakespearean performance. The *West Side Story* effect became a mode of Shakespearean storytelling for the second half of the twentieth century, and although applied to other ethnic, racial, and cultural groups, the *West Side Story* effect was ultimately reclaimed for Latinidad, as evidenced in the boom of Latinx Shakespeares following the 1996 Baz Luhrmann film *Romeo + Juliet*. This film built off tropes that trace back to *West Side Story* in order to reclaim *Romeo and Juliet* as *the* Latinx Shakespearean play and division as an American mode of Shakespearean storytelling.

In order to illustrate how division became a hallmark of American Shakespeares, and how *West Side Story* has contributed to that trope, I first expand on the scholarship of key changes from *Romeo and Juliet* to *West Side Story* in order to argue that notions of masculinity and whiteness (as seen through the racializing of the Paris figure and softening of the Romeo character) codified the representation of Latinx on the Shakespearean stage. From there, I briefly examine how these notions played out in the Broadway premiere, the 1961 film, and subsequent revivals of *West Side Story*, for which the creators turned to changing tactics—ranging from brownface to Spanish-language insertions and a plethora of Latinx accents to casting choices—to mark the ethnic divide. I then briefly address how the 2021 film offers new strategies for the years to come. Finally, I draw on a genealogy of Latinx Shakespearean films to illustrate how the Sharks and Jets forever changed the Capulets and Montagues, as well as the broader canon of American Shakespeares.[1] Ultimately, I argue that *West Side Story*'s trajectory is a road map both for staging race and ethnicity throughout theater history and for Latinx Shakespeares' emphasis on aurality.

WEST SIDE STORY AS SHAKESPEAREAN ADAPTATION

Romeo and Juliet begins with a pronouncement of division, but a division tempered by sameness: "Two households, both alike in dignity / In fair Verona, where we lay our scene."[2] No reason is given for the animosity between the two families; they are from the same place and of the same stature. Thematically, the ancient grudge is revealed through the Prince's disdain toward both patriarchs for their disregard of Verona's laws, the way the gentlemen of each household cause chaos in the streets, and the young lovers' secret wedding and consequent actions.

Textually, *Romeo and Juliet* lends itself to the theme of division with its heavy use of contrasting images and its parallel structure. In Robert N. Watson's analysis of "doubled words and phrases," he concludes, "*Romeo and Juliet* is the only Shakespeare play where such pairs constitute more than 1 percent of the word count."[3] With opposition in the words and syntax throughout, division becomes more ingrained as the households are cleanly divided in their allegiances. Further, the exaggerated metaphors ("This precious book of love, this unbound lover"), use of paradox ("My only love sprung from my only hate"), and instances of antithesis ("More light and light, more dark and dark our woes!") all reinforce the theme of opposition. In Colleen Ruth Rosenfeld's analysis of early modern poetic figures of speech, she argues that "the formal insistence of *antithesis* on perfectly matched contraries renders narrative's imperative for resolution impossible."[4] The early attention to opposition found in the verse shows how cultural-linguistic division comes to enact a similar division in adaptations. Romeo and Juliet, Capulets and Montagues, Sharks and Jets: these oppositions together form a blank canvas on which race and ethnicity can be—and, after *West Side Story*, often are—layered. The work of division as a metaphorical concept produces wholeheartedly different results when it is based on the combination of ethnicity and language.

Notably, *West Side Story* in its original conception did not engage Latinx culture. The now famous premise of the white and Puerto Rican gangs dancing on the streets of New York was a belated addition to the musical. Jerome Robbins's original idea that he pitched to Arthur Laurents in 1949 was to depict the divide between (New York–based) Catholics and Jews at Easter/Passover. Unfortunately, preparations for the adaptation would stall for several years amid concerns that the theme was repetitive of a popular 1920s comedy called *Abie's Irish Rose*, that the Holocaust was too recent to risk staging the death of Jews, and that the stakes for representing Jews had changed. After six years of having other projects take priority, they gave the working project the title *East Side Story*.[5] Circa 1955, Arthur Laurents saw an article in the *Los Angeles Times* about a gang fight between two Mexican men.[6] He was inspired by the sense of friction between the Southern California Mexican gangs, but he wished to retain the New York setting and the premise of more substantive division. What had originally been proposed as a religious divide between Jews and Catholics thus became an ethnic turf war on the streets of New York.[7]

The original 1957 Broadway debut of *West Side Story* garnered the Tony Award for Best Musical and ran for over seven hundred performances before touring. The Broadway run was followed by a national and international tour of major cities, and a return to Broadway in 1960. The 1961 film starring Natalie Wood and Richard Beymer won ten Oscars from its eleven nominations, including Best Picture and a special Academy Award for Jerome Robbins for his choreographic achievement. The film also won a Grammy, a few Golden Globes, and numerous other awards. The musical had Broadway revivals in 1980, 2009, and 2020, a new film version in 2021, along with productions in theaters and schools all over the world. The musical would change the face not just of American and Latinx Shakespeares but of the broader musical theater canon, by mandating that performers be able to sing, dance, and act equally well.

West Side Story proved to be *the* representation of Latinx on Broadway for fifty years, a position that it would hold until the 2008 Broadway premiere of the musical *In the Heights*.[8] It would retain this position despite the near-total lack of Latinx actors in the original Broadway run and film. The first producer of *West Side Story*, Cheryl Crawford, wanted the musical to offer a "realistic" representation of Puerto Ricans, despite its genre and fictional storyline.[9] Unfortunately, this goal was not to be readily achieved, hindered not just by the lack of Latinx actors on Broadway but also by the original, non-Latinx source inspiration as well as the Jewish and queer underpinnings of the creative team.[10] The musical drew criticism even before it opened on Broadway due to pejorative stereotypes of Puerto Rico, such as "You ugly island . . . / Island of tropic diseases,"[11] with the editors at New York's Spanish-language paper *La Prensa* "threaten[ing] to picket the show's New York opening if the production arrived without cuts or alterations to the song 'America.'"[12] Not only were the lyrics insulting, but they also inaccurately represented Puerto Rico, as there was "no significant disease problem related to its tropical climate."[13] Ultimately, however, no changes were made for the stage (though they were for the 1961 film), and no protest occurred.

The show garnered immediate success, but not for any sort of nuanced ethnic representation, "realistic" or otherwise. Rather, the accolades were for the musical's depiction of the contemporary problem of gang violence, reflecting perhaps the greater efforts that the creative team put into bringing this aspect of the musical to life: during rehearsals, Robbins segregated the actors and "encouraged [them] to cut out newspaper accounts of gang rivalries and paste these to the rear walls of the stage," so that they could draw on this real-world subject matter while learning their songs and choreography.[14] Bernstein, Robbins, and Laurents received the Key to the City of Washington, DC, for *West Side Story*'s efforts to depict youth/gang culture. And in a 1958 CBS five-part series *Contemporary Theatre and Religion*, the host, Reverend Sidney Lanier, claimed that *West Side Story* "shows an especially American problem in an especially American way." His questions for members of the creative team, including Robbins, Larry Kert (Tony), Carol Lawrence (Maria), and Mickey Calin (Riff), focused on the issue of youth gangs, not on ethnic division.[15] And yet, even though the rehearsals and initial reception of the musical focused on the gang story almost to the exclusion of the ethnicity of the characters, *West Side Story* has long been understood as a sociological study of Latinx people and culture. This understanding is rooted in the musical's widespread success, as well as the dearth of Puerto Rican or Latinx characters and culture in other Broadway shows.[16]

Gangs became prominent in the 1950s, and urban youth culture and violence made headlines. Walter S. DeKeserdy and Martin D. Schwartz write that gangs for young men of color result from "status frustration,"[17] but the formation and visibility of the Jets as a white gang includes the advantages they are given based on their skin color, heritage, length of time in New York, and language. The Jets benefit from these qualities that inform their greater income possibility and paths to assimilation, even if these privileges are muted. Although the Sharks and Jets battle each other and the adult status quo (vis-à-vis Lieutenant Shrank and Officer Krupke) rather than the threat of communism, it is the bond of fighting, physically and ideologically, that unites them. The Jets and Sharks fight against a society and structure they see as unjust.

There are many readings of *West Side Story*, but here I focus on the consequences for Shakespearean storytelling of making the Sharks Latinx and in opposition to the Jets, who are border whites, a hodgepodge and precarious group who are a mixture of white European immigrants, slightly more accepted in society than the Sharks. This division and its lasting legacy are made possible due to the aural excess that is definitive of musical theater intermixing with auralidad, the aural excess that is key to theatrical depictions of Latinx. Each gang has its attractive qualities: for the Jets, it is their individual characters and for the Sharks the developed relationships between Bernardo, Anita, and Maria. But each has its problems: The Jets' animal-pack mentality and the Sharks' homogeneity. Both theatrical gangs are shaped by stereotypes, but the ideation of the Boricua Sharks, preceded and followed by few and problematic depictions of Latinx for decades, leaves a far more damaging and lasting legacy. Along with its implications for Shakespearean storytelling and Latinx representation, *West Side Story* both problematically stereotyped and substantially embedded Latinidad in the history of American musical theater.

In general, *West Side Story* follows the plot of Shakespeare's play: Tony (Romeo) and Maria (Juliet) fall in love, despite the societal/familial divide that separates them, and their love story comes to a tragic end after they cannot overcome the division. Some key differences separate the two stories, though, as Misha Berson names in her study of the musical: (1) the feud is motivated by cultural difference; (2) the musical omits any backstory about parents or former loves; (3) the assault on Anita is responsible for the failure of the important message; and (4) Maria survives at the end, unlike Juliet, who dies alongside Romeo.[18] To Berson's four differences, I will add three additional, interrelated changes that are essential to both *West Side Story* and the Latinx Shakespeares that followed it: (5) the Jets are the primary holders of public spaces, whereas the Montagues are not; (6) Tony makes no move to kill Chino, unlike Romeo, who kills Paris; and (7) Chino becomes the agent of death in the musical, unlike Paris, who kills no one. These changes are due to and result in an equation of whiteness with goodness: Tony is white, and Chino is not; Tony dies by Chino's hand.

These three key changes shape the Jets as more (not entirely) innocent and the Sharks as culpable. The Jets are given the initial physical space, displaying their rightful ownership and casting the Sharks as interlopers. Shakespeare's play begins with the Chorus's prologue, followed by a conversation between Sampson and Gregory, two Capulet men. When the Montagues approach, the two groups of men exchange harsh words and begin to fight. In contrast, *West Side Story* transposes the prologue and initial verbal exchange to physical movement—with each gang chasing the other down the streets, dribbling a ball on the basketball court, and cornering members of the opposite gang to play tricks such as pouring paint and stealing food—and the Jets are the first onstage, thereby making the Sharks (Capulets) intruders on their turf. *West Side Story* furthers this lopsided arrangement of ownership/displacement by removing scenes from Capulet-dominated spaces. For example, Romeo and Juliet meet after Shakespeare's Montague boys crash a party at the Capulet house, but in *West Side Story*, the meeting occurs at a neighborhood dance attended by members of both gangs. What's more, this space is not truly neutral, as the Jets are already at the dance when the Sharks arrive, causing the Puerto Ricans to again intrude on the Jets' space. And when the Sharks and Jets meet to decide the terms of the war council, they do so at Doc's store, where Tony works. The Sharks are therefore infringing on white-owned space, the site of revenue and upward mobility for the Jets' former leader, Tony. These small but integral shifts in who has claim to physical space demonize the Sharks, thereby whitening the Jets.

The pivotal scene in both Shakespeare's play and the musical occurs toward the end, after Romeo (Tony) has been mistakenly (deceptively) led to believe that his beloved is dead. In Shakespeare's play, Romeo encounters Paris on the steps of the Capulet tomb. Romeo has come to mourn Juliet, whom he has been told has died through causes unknown. Paris, rightfully thinking that a Montague would only enter the Capulet tomb with bad intentions, threatens Romeo, and Romeo kills him. This action validates Romeo's masculinity because he does not back down at the threat, although having not recognized Paris in the darkness, he laments the death after he realizes whom he has slain. In contrast, when Tony comes across Chino at the end of the musical, he has been told that Maria is dead and that Chino killed her out of anger. Chino stands in for an old-fashioned, distant cultural code in which he would conceivably kill a woman. Tony taunts Chino, and Chino shoots and kills Tony just as the latter sees that Maria is still alive. Chino kills Tony by shooting him in the back, offering no apology or even words afterward. Making Romeo's death the cause of a Capulet's hand (rather than by suicide), and making the killer both ethnic and unassimilated, reasserts pejorative tropes of Latinx.

This final scene unites how public spaces and the criminalization of Latinx function together in *West Side Story*. The only public spaces that the Sharks inhabit freely are in and around the home and the bridal shop where Anita and Maria work. Maria stands firmly in the space of both her fire escape and her bedroom before Tony arrives; in the Sharks' big musical number, "America" (co-ed in the film, girls only in the stage musical), they sing and dance freely on the rooftop of the apartment building, and Maria and her friends control the space of the bridal shop, all of which make visible the outdoors versus private spaces that Latinx inhabit without threat. By contrast, when Anita enters Doc's shop, she is assaulted by the Jets and subsequently disappears for the remainder of the musical. After these instances of either danger or death when Latinx enter white public spaces, Tony runs into the street shouting for Chino to appear; Chino does, only to kill Tony. This is the death of the (white) Jets' domination of public space, and it literally is the death of Tony.

Further, the specificity of Othering Chino through regressive gender norms that lead to a violent machismo helps to conflate a relative lack of cultural and linguistic fluency with a particular resort to violence. Maria has already made clear to Anita that she does not find him sexually exciting. Then Chino enters the bridal shop with Bernardo to greet Maria and Anita, and Maria has to coax him in: "Come in, Chino. Do not be afraid," to which he replies, "But this is a shop for ladies."[19] The second time he speaks is to threaten Tony at the dance; after Tony and Maria have met, Chino says to Tony, "Get away."[20] Even though he tells Bernardo not to yell at Maria and later reluctantly breaks the news of Bernardo's death, he quickly adopts a killing mentality: "*Coldly, Chino unwraps a gun, which he puts in his pocket.*"[21] Shakespeare's original distinction evinces particular forms of acceptable masculinity and functions to affirm Romeo within society through the development of the complexity of his speech and his later decision to fight when challenged. Chino's ability to kill with immediacy perpetuates the stereotype of the dangerous, uncivilized Latino.

MASCULINITY, WHITENESS, AND THE RACIALIZING OF CHINO

Romeo, by avoiding Tybalt's challenge, went against a masculine code of honor in dueling. Though Romeo blames his love and marriage to Juliet for his hesitancy to act, "O sweet Juliet, / Thy beauty hath made me effeminate,"[22] in fact, the audience does not know if Romeo would have participated in the opening brawl since he was not present for it. The troubled depictions of masculinity that *West Side Story* includes are the former gang member turned good (aspirational middle-class Tony); the white, fraternal, misogynistic, and potential rapist Jets; and the outmoded stereotype of Latino machismo encapsulated by Bernardo, Chino, and the unnamed Sharks. The musical shows the failings of all of these tropes. In so doing, it ties together a Cold War masculinity in crisis and an unstable whiteness that would characterize not just the Sharks and the Jets but also the Capulets and the Montagues for decades.

West Side Story gave Broadway audiences what they were missing from the era's configurations of the new common man: it gave them the visceral male body.[23] *West Side Story* uses dance to shift masculinity away from the gainfully employed Tony, giving the not actually employed Jets and the recently-arrived Sharks bigger group dance scenes than the leading white man. Tony does not participate in the opening Prologue with the other Jets and Sharks, or in the Jets' ensemble numbers, "When You're a Jet" and "Cool," all of which establish the Jets' masculinity and aggressiveness.[24] While it is commonplace in the American musical to have the lead roles absent from big group numbers, especially the opening number (*Brigadoon*, *Cabaret*, and *Chicago*, to name a few), the effect this tradition has on theater with ethnic division is that it makes the leading roles more docile and "whitens" their characters, as they are absent from the labor of physical movement and singing about tough, urban life.

In fact, Tony is not only disembodied but a seeming template for the new man. Tony never wears the standard Jets outfit of a form-fitting T-shirt and blue jeans; instead of street clothes, he is dressed in working-class / aspiring middle-class clothes: a button-down dress shirt to lift boxes at Doc's store. Even Tony's name is blandly male. When Maria asks what it is short for, he replies, "Anton"; Tony's name is Eastern European but culturally ambiguous, and also distinct from the juvenile names of the Jets such as Riff, A-rab, Action, and Diesel. This blandness and his generally absent personality (Shakespeare's Romeo enters lamenting unrequited love, yet Tony only sings about the vague feeling that "Something's Coming") both contribute to a softer, whiter masculinity.

David Morgan concludes that there are two versions of masculinity: "The one is collective, physical and embodied, and oppositional. The other is individualistic, rational, and relatively disembodied. These can be broadly described as working class and middle class masculinities, respectively."[25] We see this dichotomy mapped in the musical, with the former describing the Sharks' masculinity, and the latter the Jets', with Tony as a more extreme form of the Jets' masculinity, so distinct he is no longer in the gang. The Jets are constantly fighting to retain a traditional masculinity, but they are threatened from within: if the effeminate Baby John, the masculine Riff, the jokester A-Rab, the aggressive Action, and the tomboyish Anybodys can all be in the same gang, then there is no cohesion within white masculinity. The Jets sing their identity with songs such as "When You're a Jet" and "Cool," self-identifying and creating their persona through description. "When You're a Jet" advertises the advantages of the fraternity of gang life, while "Cool" is the necessary performance of masculinity that results from fear of the Sharks. By contrast, the Sharks do not second-guess their intent or allegiance and do not have to define their image: their gang consists only of the hypermasculine and a unified cultural background.

Along with a changing masculinity, *West Side Story* reflects the changing definition of whiteness in the United States, a definition that is itself politically and socially inflected. Although Puerto Ricans were declared American citizens in 1917, they were not made to feel welcome in the mainland United States during the heavy immigration period after World War II, with both language divides and shifts in racial classification serving as barriers to acceptance. Whiteness in the United States has historically been in a constant state of redefinition, much of which involves a fluctuation of the categories that are defined as nonwhite. Italian Americans, for example, were racialized in the nineteenth and early twentieth century but viewed as "white" by the mid-twentieth with the Immigration and Nationality Act of 1965.[26] Hispanic and Latinx Americans, on the other hand, were generally grouped as white *until* the mid-twentieth century, when they were increasingly ethnicized, in part by changes to the US census.[27] The rules for distinguishing "white" from "Hispanic" or "Latinx" have shifted again and again, each time creating a more limited definition of whiteness to place at the center.

Ethnicity in *West Side Story* functions like lineage in *Romeo and Juliet*: Tony and Maria are both racially white, and so they cannot see their own difference when they first meet because their mutual whiteness functions as a mask.[28] As of 2019, within the Hispanic/Latinx population in the United States, 65% of Hispanic/Latinx people identified their race as solely white.[29] Within the range of racial whiteness is a great disparity of complexion; the visual of race is not uniform or necessarily legible. Because whiteness entails more than just skin color, it is both precarious as well as elastic. The Jets are only slightly more accepted in society than the newly emigrated, bilingual Puerto Rican Sharks. Described by Laurents as "an anthology of what is called 'American,'"[30] the Jets are held together by a professed shared identity but not a shared cultural heritage. Instead, they are united by their social position, white skin, language, and, presumably, their masculinity.

Of course, "Hispanic" and "Latinx" are also inherently unstable categories. But whereas their instability reflects the complex intersection of racial, ethnic, cultural, linguistic, and national identities, the instability of whiteness as a category elevates it as a set of power relations, "a social construction with real effects."[31] Richard Dyer, in his influential book *White*, argues that "white as skin colour is just as unstable, unbounded a category as white as hue, and therein lies its strength. It enables whiteness to be presented as an apparently attainable, flexible, varied category, while setting up an always movable criterion of inclusion, the ascribed whiteness of your skin."[32] Jewish, Irish, and Italian immigrants became "white" in part because the color of their skin enabled them to do so. They also became white by assimilating linguistically and adopting the English language more quickly than other immigrant groups. They rose to prominence because their populations were quite large and because they self-aligned with established white populations against Black people and other minorities, including Latinx who are from the southern hemisphere, or immigrants who are viewed differently than European immigrants. The Sharks cannot assimilate because of the bonds of whiteness, from which the Jets benefit, even if the Jets do not feel a connection across class and generational lines; Lt. Schrank refers to himself as a "friend" to the Jets, and they laugh at him. After the opening fight choreography, Lt. Schrank calls both gangs "hoodlums"[33] and tells both gangs they can "kill each other! . . . But not on my beat."[34] But he then tells Bernardo to get his gang to leave, revealing the bias that the Sharks face to assimilation.

Whiteness involves an interplay of the power structures that inform hierarchies of class, gender, sexuality, ability, and nationality. As these dynamics intersect, the hue and color of white skin become less relevant, but they remain the unstated and unseen baseline. Whiteness theorist George Lipsitz argues: "As the unmarked category against which difference is constructed, whiteness never has to speak its name, never has to acknowledge its role as an organizing principle in social and cultural relations."[35] Whiteness in *West Side Story* is defined through its relationship to something else, an inexact binary that ultimately reveals a new, unattainable whiteness. Lee Bebout identifies a "whiteness on the border" that extends throughout the United States as "a discursive and ideological constellation in which representations of Mexico, Mexicans, and Mexican Americans are deployed to construct white identity; or more accurately white identity as American identity."[36] Tony and the Jets are not easily defined in terms of whiteness, as they reside on a metaphorical border as both a heterogeneous group of European immigrants and white men. In contrast to its Latinx characters, *West Side Story* presents not a group of ideal white people but rather a version of whiteness that deviates from the model citizen. Dyer writes: "Going against type is a feature of white representation . . . it is the foundation of both psychological realism—when we don't get superheroes or obvious stereotypes, we feel we're getting the real—and of novelty and transgression, where the bounds of the typical are exceeded."[37] In this way, the nonidealization of the Jets reinforces an absent, unattainable, and aspirational whiteness offstage while signaling faux "realism" of the characters onstage. The Jets are on a path to assimilation, and Tony's death, the death of an aspirational whiteness, is a part of that assimilation.

The musical aligns whiteness with a sense of goodness and inclusivity. For example, Tony's new love for (and pretend marriage to) Maria is the tool that they both naively believe will make her accepted into his society. Tony is normative (read: more white) in contrast with Maria, but he is *less white* than the non-Jet white figures (Shrank, Krupke, and Doc). Maria makes it clear that her Puerto Rican family will never accept Tony. Tony says, "I like [Maria's father]. He will like me," and Maria replies, "No. He is like Bernardo: afraid."[38] By contrast, Tony is excited for Maria to meet his family. He says his mother will "come running from the kitchen to welcome you," and only then does Maria get more hopeful and conclude that "Papá *might* like you."[39] She can conceivably cross into his border whiteness, but he cannot be accepted into the fixed, monolithic Boricua culture as depicted, and he can only fully be part of the dominant white culture by turning against the Puerto Rican Sharks.[40] With the arrival of the Sharks, Tony and the Jets have the ability to move upward in the societal hierarchy. The warring relationship the Jets have with the Sharks has somewhat to do with a desire to maintain their turf, and much to do with an effort to establish a more secure (and securely white) station in society.

In the end, Chino kills the potential new go-to American man, Tony. "Chino" is a derogatory term in Spanish, one with multiple meanings and origins. The *Dictionary of Latin American Racial and Ethnic Terminology* offers twenty-one definitions for "chino," including Chinese, Indian, various combinations of mixed-race heritage, slave, dark skinned, or low class.[41] It also indicates one with curly/kinky hair.[42] This ethnicized, racialized, and derogatory association matters greatly to Chino's limited but integral role. Similar to Paris, who speaks only twenty-three times in Shakespeare's play, with a total of seventy lines, Chino speaks only twenty-six times in the musical, for a total of ninety-five words. His last line of the play is in the

Figure 1: José de Vega as Chino. Film still from *West Side Story* (dirs. Jerome Robbins and Robert Wise, 1961).

first scene of act 2, when he tells Maria that Tony has killed her brother, Bernardo.[43] If he is rendered largely voiceless, however, his presence is yet reinforced by the repetition of his name, which occurs twenty-eight times in the second act, more than that of any other character. To reinforce his Otherness, Chino, like Anita, has always been ethnicized or racialized through casting; in the original Broadway musical, Chino was played by Puerto Rican actor Jaime Sánchez and in the film by Filipino/Colombian actor José de Vega.[44]

Shakespeare's Romeo dies by his own hand, out of a commitment to his vow as lover/husband. He cannot live without Juliet, so he enters her crypt and drinks poison by her side. In contrast, Tony wills himself to the violent Chino, or the violence of the streets from which Chino appears, to fulfill his wish of death. In an adaptation that pits one culture against the other, Tony (Romeo) becomes an inactive victim, the Puerto Rican Sharks (Capulets) become aggressive killers and hot-blooded Latinos, and the Jets (Montagues) become aligned with the new generation of whiteness, albeit flawed. In Shakespeare's play, both Romeo and Juliet commit agential violence through their suicides, and this unites them across any familial division even in their last moments and deaths. But the violence in *West Side Story* kills off Tony's genuine aspiration to the intracultural and distinguishes a criminalization of Latinx from white juvenile gang life with Chino's imminent arrest. Even though the Jets pose a danger to middle-class whiteness, they retain more power than the Sharks; when two different cultures are pitted against one another, one must be made Other through culture, language, and violence.

The musical ends with Maria pointing the gun that has killed her lover; the sexualized Latina (she is no longer a virgin) is now poised to commit violence as well. Taking on the words of Shakespeare's Prince about the role of society in the fatalities, Maria delivers the condemnation while pointing a gun at everyone onstage (and often the audience). Along with Anita's escape from sexual violence, Maria survives the violent streets, placing Latina subjectivity as a critique of machismo and a possibility for Latinx survival and futures. It is now the Latina who speaks to the repercussions for society. Much as with ethnic and race relations today, the lovers do not "bury their parents' strife,"[45] and the audience does not have resolution. The gangs unite to carry Tony's body offstage, but Chino's fate is a societal death, Maria has lost her brother and lover in one evening, Anita has disappeared, the Jets have lost both of their leaders, and none of the cracks in societal structures that led to this fatal divisiveness have been healed.

TWO HOUSEHOLDS BOTH (UN)LIKE IN DIGNITY

West Side Story's influence has proven transformative for its source material, Romeo and Juliet, reshaping the text as the Latinx Shakespearean play, with stagings and adaptations of Romeo and Juliet accounting for approximately 25 percent of Latinx Shakespeares. Of course, Romeo and Juliet is one of Shakespeare's most performed plays in general, so in some ways this high percentage is not unexpected.[46] But the quantity also reflects both the original play's adaptability (because there is nothing Veronese about Romeo or Juliet, the play is an easy textual palimpsest) and the musical's entrance at a time when there were so few Latinx plays on Broadway and in other big theaters.[47] West Side Story swept onto the stage and screen, claiming the Romeo and Juliet story for a representation (however problematic) of Latinx and ethnically rooted difference.

Other reasons exist as well for the wealth of Latinx-themed adaptations, translations, and appropriations of Romeo and Juliet. Shakespeare's play is inarguably one of the most popular stories of all time, and it expands outside the genre of theater through films, musicals, and reverberations throughout popular culture. It is also one of the most widely taught plays (Shakespearean or otherwise) in American schools: Romeo and Juliet is part of the reading curriculum for over 90 percent of American high school freshmen.[48] And it is a play about young people. By engaging young actors and working with student performers, theaters can attract new audiences. Finally, *Romeo and Juliet* is predominantly an ensemble piece rather than a star vehicle like *Othello* or *Hamlet*. Because it does not necessitate a virtuosic performance, it can more easily incorporate actors who have been historically and systematically left out of the pipeline of formal actor training.[49]

Beyond all these reasons, though, the storyline holds a thematic connection to perceptions of Latinx characters: Romeo as a lover appeals to an emotional strain that romanticizes a deep pain, or dying for love. This idea of fatalism, or *fatalismo*, resonates in a particular style of Mexican and Chicanx music and storytelling and allows the Romeo character to fulfill a certain fantasy of Latinx culture writ large. This notion of *fatalismo* is developed most fully in the work of the Mexican Nobel laureate Octavio Paz. Paz's 1950 book-length essay *El Laberinto de la Soledad* (in English in 1969, *The Labyrinth of Solitude*) posited Mexican culture as one of solitude, and one that celebrates death.[50] Fatalismo can also include the possibility of transcending one's lot in life or transcendence in the afterlife.[51] This trope of the glorification of death has translated to the remembrance and praise for the dead in Día de Muertos celebrations, which are reflected in *Romeo and Juliet* adaptations and stagings by Latinx playwrights and theaters such as Edit Villarreal's *The Language of Flowers* (1995) and Milagro Theater's *¡O Romeo!* (2014), both of which make the celebration of the dead central to the plot. The romanticization of an intense love that leads to death is often the teenage appeal to *Romeo and Juliet* and is key to directors' and adaptors' strategies for Latinx *Romeo and Juliet*s. The play, even in its Shakespearean form, draws on multiple tropes of masculinity—the lovesick protagonist, the Petrarchan lover now ethnicized through *fatalismo*, the hypermasculine urge to pick a fight—that appeal both to a choleric hotness in Shakespeare's play and a trope of Latinidad.

The legacy of *West Side Story* stretches beyond its impact on American musical theater, beyond its role as the first Broadway show prominently representing Latinidad, and beyond its status as a brand franchise that sparks immediate recognition almost to the same extent as Shakespeare. *West Side Story*'s popularity has made it central to the depiction of American division. It has become a *template* for staging cultural division in American Shakespearean performance, not just for subsequent Latinx productions of *Romeo and Juliet*, but also for other Latinx Shakespearean productions and non-Latinx productions and adaptations, including films. The trajectory of *West Side Story* entails a shift between visual and aural signifiers, from brownface to various strategies for auralidad—the aural excess that is a hallmark of theatricalizing Latinidad. *West Side Story*'s formation within the genre of musical theater, the use of Spanish even in its original production, and its progression to bilingual and semi-bilingual theater invoke an emphasis on aurality as a strategy for division and as a necessity for Latinx Shakespeares. Because of *West Side Story*'s influence, what is "Other" in early Latinx Shakespearean productions is, in fact, not Latinx culture or any other nonwhite group, but the type of storytelling that does not include cultural or linguistic division.

ETHNICIZING THE OTHER IN *WEST SIDE STORY*: SHIFTING VISUAL AND AURAL PRACTICES

West Side Story's theatrical and filmic history is a roadmap for strategies of ethnic adaptations in American theater history. Invoking the *West Side Story* effect challenges ideas about the visible legibility of casting practices and about representation in general. In production—both for various twentieth-century stagings and for the 1961 film—the process of making the Sharks look Puerto Rican has historically been thought to be possible by changing the color of their skin through the use of brownface. This practice was used to make evident the unified cultural heritage of the Sharks, but it also had the more significant (if unstated) purpose of making them indistinguishable and homogeneous. For example, in the film, dark brown makeup was put on Greek American actor George Chakiris (Bernardo) to make him appear Puerto Rican,[52] as it was on all of the Sharks, including Puerto Rican actress Rita Moreno, who played Anita.[53] Not only was dark makeup employed, but the same color of brown makeup was used for every actor.[54] In fact, Chakiris had played the Jet Riff in the West End production prior to filming. Midway through the twentieth century, the *only* thing necessary to make a Jet into a Shark, then, was brown makeup.

This desire for homogeneity among the Sharks results in part from a discomfort and lack of familiarity that white directors and audiences had for the complexity of Latinidad. Steve Garner writes: "One of the ways in which racism works is to treat people as the opposite of individuals, to deny this and instead produce them as merely representations of a form of person; any Asian can stand in for Japanese car-manufacturers, any black man can be a murder suspect."[55] While the *West Side Story* effect may generate particular understandings of ethnic division, the insidious problematics of brownface and the ways in which the performance of stereotype gets

reified speak to the power of the reductive and homogeneous visual signifier of nonwhiteness that becomes central.

The only exception to the use of brownface for Puerto Rican characters
in the film was Russian American actress Natalie Wood, who in addition to
needing to be initially visually undetectable as Puerto Rican to Tony at the
dance, was excused based on her celebrity status and starring role. She
attempted to perform the character's ethnicity through her voice, although
her Spanish-inflected English was heavily criticized, and her voice was not
strong enough to sing most of the songs. Brownface was used once again in
the 1980 Broadway revival, this time even for Maria, played by actress
Jossie de Guzman, who is of Puerto Rican descent.[56] The role of Anita, the
most dynamic, sexualized character, who is described as "too dark to
pass,"[57] has always been distinctly ethnicized and racialized in casting, like
that of Chino. The role of Anita went to a Latina (half-Puerto Rican and half
Scottish/Italian Chita Rivera) even in the original Broadway production, to
Rita Moreno (Puerto Rican) in the 1961 film, to African American Debbie
Allen in 1980, to Karen Olivo, who is of mixed heritage (Puerto Rican,
Native American, Dominican, and Chinese ancestry) in 2009, to Colombian-
American Yesenia Ayala in 2020, and to Ariana DeBose, who is of mixed
heritage (Puerto Rican, white, African American, and Italian) in the 2021
film.[58] Writing about popular culture, media, and music, scholar Frances R.
Aparicio states, "A Latina actress is discursively defined in the public
sphere because of her generalizability as a Latina rather than because of her
uniqueness as a Boricua or Mexican American or Cuban American."[59]
Thus, *West Side Story* has historically made a sweeping gesture to establish
the Sharks' identity, either through the use of brown makeup or through
the casting of anyone from a Latinx or Spanish-speaking background,
including Debbie Allen (who spent time in Mexico as a youth), suggesting
that there is not anything specifically Puerto Rican about the Sharks aside
from the fact that they reference the island a few times in dialogue and
music.[60]

More largely, the visual legibility of any specific regional or national
Latinx community is complicated by Latinx identities stemming from over
twenty countries, the vast regions of the Americas, and multiple racial configurations. Latinx is a US ethnic construct, and Latinx can be of any of the
four US governmental racial categories: white, Black, Indigenous, or Asian.
Moving away from the use of brownface, the 2009 Broadway revival of
West Side Story attempted to reverse the cultural stereotype of the Puerto
Rican gang member, as well as overcome the whitewashed casting of prior
stagings and the 1961 film, by having the Sharks sing and speak in Spanish.

Laurents decided to make the show bilingual to "at last elevate the Puerto Rican Sharks to their rightful place as equals to their deadly white rivals."[61] In many ways, this bilingual revival, created and directed by Laurents, responded to decades of criticism leveled at the musical for its representation of the Sharks.[62] Laurents wanted to adapt his own story to include the heightened premise of linguistic division, and it is this elevation of the aural that was intended to affirm the difference between the racially white Jets and racially white and ethnically Latinx Sharks.

Feeling that linguistic division grew naturally from the established cultural division, Laurents claimed that this premise was more realistic, as the Sharks would be speaking to one another in Spanish. Puerto Rico's linguistic history is complex, but the Puerto Rican characters in *West Side Story* would have been taught English throughout their secondary education.[63] If musical theater characters can be conceived of and perceived mimetically, the characters would likely prefer and be more fluent in Spanish, but the strict linguistic division that Laurents conceived does not apply to 1950s Puerto Rican and New York white characters. The homogenization of linguistic difference that comes from larger US society and here, from Laurents as director, oversimplifies the complexities of Puerto Rican culture and how it is distinguished linguistically from other Latinx cultures.

Along with calling for more "realistic" dialogue, Laurents made casting a priority, seeking a Latinx or Latin American cast because he was "not about to go slap some dark makeup on [Maria]"[64] as had been done nearly thirty years earlier. Before the move to Broadway, the show opened at the National Theatre in Washington, DC, in 2009. It featured costuming changes that attempted to modernize the 1950s setting, a newly determined sexual overtone, and the replacement of some of Robbins's iconic movement by choreographer Joey McKneely. And yet, even with all these changes, the most notable and advertised alteration was the translation of the Sharks' dialogue into Spanish. Lin-Manuel Miranda, who is of Puerto Rican descent, penned the translation following his successful Broadway show *In the Heights*.[65] But a challenge remained: a coherence in accent amongst the Spanish-speaking Sharks.

Washington critics were positive in their reviews of Laurents's revival, and during the long period of previews, New York critics anticipated the show with excitement. At the beginning of the previews in Washington, Laurents included supertitles for the audience to offer a translation of the Spanish. But he felt that the supertitles inhibited the experience, and once he removed them, the show earned standing ovations.[66] While there are some Spanish phrases in the original *West Side Story* stage musical and film, Laurents wanted to adapt his own story to include the heightened premise of linguistic division; in so doing, the taunts and slang were translated, and modernized. For example, in the opening scene, the Jets danced and their only verbal utterances were "Ha! . . . Beat It! . . . Come on! . . . [and] JETS!" This benign dialogue resulted in the Sharks responding with offensive remarks in modern Spanish, such as Pepe's snarky "¡Oye Mamao!," Inca's derogatory "¡Mira! [sic] Maricones!," and Tio's offensive "¡Polaco sangano!"[67] The script then instructed both gangs to ad-lib, and the Sharks continued to do so in contemporary Spanish slang while the Jets maintained the slang that Laurents penned for them in the 1950s. Even non-Spanish-speaking audience members could recognize contemporary profanity as just that; both the Jets and the Sharks executed gestures that were visually profane, but the audience *heard* twenty-first century profanity from the Sharks.

When the show moved to Broadway, however, it soon made headlines because much of the Spanish was removed. Laurents was cautious in his explanation for the changes, stating, "From the outset, the Spanish in *West Side Story* was an experiment. It's been an ongoing process of finding what worked and what didn't, and it still continues."[68] Some viewed the change for Broadway as catering to monolingual English-speaking audiences who were thrown off by the use of Spanish.[69] Regardless of the motivations for the change, a savvier use of Spanish took shape. For example, Bernardo would speak only Spanish. In contrast, Anita spoke both Spanish and English—at least until Bernardo's death. "After Bernardo is killed, Anita won't speak English," Laurents said. "She goes back to Spanish."[70] In this way, Spanish was no longer used to achieve a clean fifty/fifty divide, but to show intimacy, different emotions, and tone. Through this linguistic diversity, Laurents at last broke down the monolithic view of the Sharks.

After its Broadway run, the revival underwent yet another linguistic transformation, completing a trajectory from bilingual production (in DC) to musical with some Spanish (on Broadway) to more nuanced exploration of linguistic code-switching on a US tour in 2011–12. With casting changes and Laurents's death in 2011, the entire show was in a perpetual state of change. As it traveled, more Spanish was removed, so by April 2012, the production had been linguistically whitened and was only 12 percent in Spanish.[71] At that time, the most sophisticated use of the inclusion of Spanish involved the character of Chino. Undesired by Maria as a suitor and representative of the Old World, he only spoke Spanish until shooting Tony at the end, when Maria spoke one line to him in English and he clearly understood her. It fostered a greater sense of gravity in the final scene, for the characters (and the audience) to realize that Chino had understood everything the others were saying the entire time. It also made clear that linguistic assimilation is not necessarily the goal for a Latinx character.

The acoustic heterogeneity spoke to the essentializing of ethnic categories that strategies such as brownface attempt to present homogeneously. Casting a nationally and racially diverse group of Latinx and Latin American actors as the Sharks and allowing them to speak Spanish in their range of accents did not necessarily make for a cohesive-sounding gang; Josefina Scaglione, the Argentine actress who played Maria, attempted to alter her Spanish to fit among the Sharks. She said: "I speak Spanish . . . but I had to learn to speak it the way a Puerto Rican would speak it."[72] Despite Laurents's sophisticated linguistic differentiation, the changes in strategy for bilingual theater and the varied accents fostered a non-setting-specific, pan-Latinx-sounding Spanish for the Sharks;[73] this is a common phenomenon in Latinx theater and Latinx-themed productions.[74]

The reality of a Latinx group of actors having varied cultural and linguistic backgrounds reflects the heterogeneity within the ethnic category, but it also reveals the expectations that white directors and audiences have for white characters: accents and language must conform to the play's locale and characters' heritage. The same attention to detail proves more challenging for Latinx characters as many professional actors did not go through actor training in Spanish, and directors typically have little experience directing in a language other than English.[75] But the use of Spanish and Spanish accents (in Spanish or English) become markers for authenticity, even within the realm of musical theater.[76]

The 2021 film (dir. Steven Spielberg) was met with the same polarizing comments about authenticity, representation, and the priority of which stories get told in Hollywood that are inseparable from, and in fact shape, *West Side Story*'s history.[77] Spielberg and Tony Kushner, who served as the screenwriter, aimed for authenticity through dramaturgy, casting, and language.[78] A range of Latinx and Latin American actors portrayed the Sharks. Maria (Rachel Zegler) was racially white, and Anita (Ariana DeBose) was racially Black. If the short-lived 2020 Broadway version (dir. Ivo van Hove) was multicultural and "tougher," the 2021 film version filled in the gaps with dialogue that explicitly addressed the stakes of the ethnic division.[79]

The 2021 film adopted several new tactics for storytelling yet retained the same implications for ethnicizing through Shakespeare.[80] The sociology of gang life and urban renewal cycles was made explicit. For example, the

Jets removed a restaurant sign that reads, "Cocina Criolla," to reveal that it previously had been an Irish pub. Then the Latino owner yelled at them in Spanish as they passed by African American couples and families on the street. As these demographic changes are laid bare, Lt. Shrank (Corey Stoll) describes the Jets as "The last of the 'can't-make-it-Caucasians.'"[81] Although they meet in the bathrooms at the gym to decide on the rumble (rather than Doc's store), it is still Riff's (Mike Faist) naming of place and the Jets who are first to appear on camera and at the dance. Ultimately, the Jets' real threat is the loss of dominion of public space; with rubble and construction all around, and it is their defacement of a mural of the Puerto Rican flag which incites the opening fight between gangs. In contrast, the Puerto Rican neighborhood is shown in full vibrancy, and Puerto Ricans have autonomy in public spaces: Anita and the Shark girls stride confidently throughout various locations for "America," the Shark men have a safe space and source of possible income by training in the boxing club, and the Sharks dance joyfully in the streets, albeit as white tourists photograph them from their cars as they ride past.

The film gave Tony (Ansel Elgort) a violent past and Bernardo (David Alvarez) a less-violent present in order to displace stereotypes of masculinity based on race and ethnicity. This Tony is hardened, has been in jail, and dances a gangster pas de deux with Riff in "Cool."[82] Although Bernardo is a boxer and visibly muscular, he does not physically hurt anyone until the rumble, and he apologizes to Maria for behaving like a "gangster" at the dance.[83] In earlier stagings and in the 1961 film, it is Bernardo who attacks Baby John in the opening rumble, and he punches other men. In 2021, a group of secondary Sharks attack Baby John, and Bernardo appears only at the end and does not physically hurt anyone. If masculinist tropes are reversed, both whiteness and anti-Blackness are addressed within the dialogue and by casting across the heterogeneity of Latinx peoples. When Tony and Maria meet, Maria says, "You're not Puerto Rican?" and Tony replies, "You're just figuring that out?"[84] Along with a joke about his height, it is a savvy callout of the visual instability of whiteness and the demarcation of ethnic facial features. Tony then asks, "Is it okay, that I'm not?"[85] Here, whiteness holds its power as unnamed, yet it is discursively framed as *his* lack of ethnicity. If distinguishing ethnic from non-ethnic whites is worthy of conversation, Anita reminds Bernardo that he harbors anti-Black sentiments; she firmly states that he hasn't married her because she is "prieta" (mestizo or dark-skinned),[86] a fact he does not attempt to deny.

Throughout, the roadmap of tactics for staging ethnicity that *West Side*

Story reveals—from an initial topical engagement with ethnicity in 1957 to brownface in 1961 and later, followed by casting as a marker of authenticity, a linguistic dramaturgy in 2009, to a multicultural approach in 2020—the aural strategies became more nuanced, resulting in a near-mimetic script and soundtrack in 2021. In 2021, there were untranslated portions of Spanish when the Sharks spoke to each other, including the period-appropriate version of the Puerto Rican national anthem, "La Borinqueña," as the first song with lyrics in the film.[87] While the Jets and the white authority figures express anti-Spanish-language sentiment, it is Anita who can command the band at the dance because she speaks Spanish, and Valentina (Rita Moreno) who can help Tony learn Spanish so he can woo Maria.

Queerness is made explicit, and empowered. Anybodys (Iris Menas) shifted in characterization from a tomboy to trans and is the only character to single-handedly fight off five men and escape the police. The assault on the effeminate Baby John is all the more invasive, with Shrank asking, "Which one of them nailed you?"[88] But it was the queering of the narrative position that advances storytelling modes. Kushner and Spielberg pushed against the problems of a musical created over sixty years earlier by making explicit the female perspective or "female gaze" of Valentina. Likewise, when the Jets sing "Office Krupke," a female "streetwalker" (Nadia Quinn)—whose resemblance to Gwen Verdon invites yet another commentary—locks herself in a cage as protection from the juvenile men. When they sing "We are sick, we are sick," her mouth is agape, providing the audience with the feminine perspective.[89] The camera largely follows Anita throughout "America," giving a leading positionality in an ensemble number to an Afro-Latina. The songs were reordered in the film so that after the rumble all those remaining were sung by women, and the last dialogue in the soundtrack is spoken by women. Further, Kushner inverts some of Shakespeare's tropes. In Shakespeare's play, both Tybalt and Juliet separately recognize Romeo by his voice, but in the 2021 film, it is Maria who recognizes Chino (Josh Andrés Rivera) by the sounds of his movement. Maria has forgotten to punch her timecard, and she hears only the sound of metal rattling, causing her to ask, "¿Hola? ¿Quién está allí?" Chino merely replies, "Soy yo," from behind some boxes, and Maria responds, "¿Chino?"[90] She cannot immediately be sure that Tony isn't Puerto Rican while looking at him, but she can recognize the racially white Latino Chino without sight.

To "Other" Chino in 2021, Spielberg and Kushner queered their approach. Unlike prior casting and dramaturgical choices, Chino was the whitest of the Shark men, both in skin color and power dynamics. This Chino is absent from Shark group numbers such as the opening prologue and "America." Rather than being unassimilated and Spanish-dominant as he was previously, here he is unassimilated to gang life. Chino's moment of tragedy is not his decision to enact revenge; it is the moment when he helps Tony lift the gate so they may both enter the rumble. But Chino does not fight; he cradles Bernardo's dead body and crying, laments, "Que idiota, bendiga."[91] He later calls Bernardo a fool, and when he chooses to kill Tony, he shoots him twice (rather than the previously scripted and staged singular shot) to guarantee his fate. In the 2021 film, "Chino believed in the possibility and virtue of assimilation, [and] it is his subsequent loss of all hope for a better life that distinguishes his tragedy."[92] Although Puerto Rican, Chino was able to access the promise of white immigrants; his tragedy is the loss of belief in a white-standard idealized American Dream.[93]

Chino's masculinity and sexuality were inverted from the "hot-blooded Latino" trope of the past. Chino is an infantilized square; Bernardo buttons Chino's shirt and holds a glass for him to drink while Chino describes himself as a "lambe ojo" (brownnoser) who Maria cannot like, "who just works day and night" to study accounting and adding machine repair.[94] Maria refers to Chino as "that zángano" (asexual), and Chino does not appear to be romantically interested in her as she intently paints on Anita's red lipstick, or in anyone.[95] Chino is dressed in neutral beiges and browns, not aligned with any other characters. Although he says he does not dance, he subsequently removes his glasses, throws his jacket on the ground, and dances joyfully without touching or willfully partnering with anyone, even though Maria laughs and joins him on the dance floor.

The trajectory of *West Side Story*, from mostly monolingual in its inception, Broadway premiere, the 1961 film, and its initial revivals, to bilingual in the 2009 Broadway production where the Jets sang and spoke in English and the Sharks in Spanish, to semi-bilingual from 2009 to 2012 as it toured nationally, to mimetic and historically accurate code-switching in the 2021 film, illustrates the nuances of how language and music can connote or complicate the staging of ethnicity in the twenty-first century. In fact, the 2021 film—which is truly an adaptation, not a revival or reimaging, of the stage musical—includes some of *Romeo and Juliet*'s dialogue, uniting Shakespeare's words, Sondheim's lyrics, and the Spanish language at last.[96] This template for cultural-linguistic division shows how it can work for and against understandings of whiteness and Latinidad; in fact, the instability of racial and ethnic categories creates fissures in the template as dramaturgical and societal factors continue to change.

HOW THE SHARKS AND THE JETS CHANGED THE CAPULETS
AND MONTAGUES

What *West Side Story* helped reveal is that Shakespeare is not the playwright of universality; he is the playwright of cultural difference. Shakespeare's place in American culture both reflects and shapes the dramatization of divisions between cultural and linguistic groups. But it is the premise of *West Side Story*, rather than the Shakespearean play itself, that informs the dramaturgy of so many subsequent Shakespearean performances and films. *West Side Story* does not have this same resonance in Latinx theater, and it is not Latinx theater; Latinx theater engages Latinx experiences and identity, while *West Side Story* offers representation. Linda Saborío argues that "a performance of difference, then, provides a site from which subjects can effectively challenge essentialist, hegemonic, and patriarchal orders through a defiance of the body as signifier of fixed identities and a rescripting of the oppressive language used to define it."[97] A performance of difference can break down stereotypes and the systems of categorization that uphold them. Doing so through Shakespeare, rather than through works by Latinx, can result in culturally appropriative performances that invoke stereotypes, but they can also serve as a step in the process toward healing (see chapter 5). Integrating cultural-linguistic division into Shakespearean storytelling, the *West Side Story* effect illuminates the desire for a subtext that Shakespeare does not offer, closing off possibilities for a perceived universality of human experience and instead establishing division based on inequality as the norm.[98] It is precisely the fundamental lack of necessary difference in *Romeo and Juliet*, a feud of equals, that points toward this massive shift in which the story can no longer be told without the importation of difference. Plays such as *Othello*, *The Merchant of Venice*, and others do not transform over time in the same way, as they have cultural division within their storylines. *West Side Story* removed the "and" from *Romeo and Juliet*, its titular antithesis, yet ultimately created a story of greater divide.[99]

  West Side Story is so prevalent in the cultural consciousness that it has been an inspiration for both staged and filmic versions of its source material, *Romeo and Juliet*. In a circularity dissimilar to most adaptations, *West Side Story* has prompted the Romeo-killing-Paris scene to remain absent even in productions in which race and ethnicity are not at stake. The two English-language films of *Romeo and Juliet* that predate the musical (George Cukor's 1936 film and Renato Castellani's 1954 version) both include Paris's murder. But once *West Side Story* appears on the scene, Romeo's masculinity is softened; the innocent Romeo is a product of the cultural work of

West Side Story to ensure a whiteness freed from the culpability of violence, which gets framed repeatedly through Brown and Black bodies. The murder of Paris was left out of Franco Zeffirelli's 1968 film starring the half-Argentine Olivia Hussey and the British Leonard Whiting in the lead roles. Likewise, Neither Baz Luhrmann's 1996 film *William Shakespeare's Romeo + Juliet* (which includes Latinx culture) nor John Madden's 1998 film *Shakespeare in Love* (which adapts various Shakespearean plots) shows Romeo (or the Romeo character) killing Paris.[100] In fact, even in the all-white *Shakespeare in Love*, the Paris figure (Lord Wessex) is the villain, an echo of *West Side Story*'s influence on Shakespearean appropriations.

The *West Side Story* trope of cultural-linguistic divide had become so ingrained by the 1980s as a storytelling device that it was applied to non-Latinx, nonethnic divisions in filmic adaptations of *Romeo and Juliet*. In *Valley Girl* (1982), a punk/urban white male teenager (played by Nicholas Cage) introduces the pop/suburban white female teenager to the city and punk music, widening her purview as she learns his "language" of city life and a new genre of music. In *Fire with Fire* (1986), a white Catholic schoolgirl (played by Virginia Madsen) is introduced to sexuality through a white male teen in a parole camp. In *Thrashin'* (1986), director David Winters (who played Baby John in the original Broadway run of *West Side Story* and A-Rab in the film) creates a division between LA skateboard gangs, where Corey (played by Josh Brolin) falls for the visiting-from-Indiana preppy younger sister of the rival punk gang leader. Corey teaches her about skateboard culture as their romance develops and everything gets resolved at the downhill skateboarding competition, the "L.A. Massacre." All three of these films involve white actors and actresses in the lead roles as white characters, but they characterize the young men as educators to the untutored Juliet characters. The films invert normative cultural values, with punk standing for the music and culture that will liberate white teenagers in *Valley Girl*, incarceration standing in for the darker, sensualized, and rebellious side of teen life in *Fire with Fire*, and skateboarding culture as key to understanding masculinity, both familial and romantic, in *Thrashin'*.

Once the *West Side Story* effect had been explored through variations of whiteness, it became a trope for racial divide in subsequent filmic adaptations of Shakespeare's play. For example, *China Girl* (1987) involves an Italian man and a Chinese woman, and it recenters the *West Side Story* effect explicitly by setting the story in New York between opposing gangs fighting over space as neighborhood demographics change. In *Zebrahead* (1992), the Veronese lovers were transformed into a white Jewish boy named Zack (played by Michael Rapaport) from Detroit and an African American girl named Nikki who just moved from Brooklyn. The Juliet character was marked as Other not just by her race, but also through her class and geographic origin. The film includes multiple shots of Zack driving and listening to hip hop music to establish his character. Although Zack and Nikki speak English, the movie asserts that he can only access her Black urban culture through the music and language of hip hop. *Mississippi Masala* (1991) created division between African American Demetrius (played by Denzel Washington) and Indian American Mina, who is the daughter of immigrants. *Love Is All There Is* (1996) transformed the warring households into two Italian families but retained the issue of cultural-linguistic divide. The northern Italian family, which is wealthier and of a higher class, objects to their daughter Gina (played by Angelina Jolie) becoming involved with Rosario when the teenagers star in a production of *Romeo and Juliet* together. Here Gina is less assimilated than Rosario and is set to leave the United States to return to Italy, and she speaks with a heavy accent. All of these films use music, accent, and/or language to enhance the cultural divide.

Baz Luhrmann's *William Shakespeare's Romeo + Juliet* (1996) is the most famous and successful of the filmic adaptations in the past forty years, perhaps because it offers a nuanced version of cultural divide mitigated by two white celebrities in the lead roles, Leonardo DiCaprio and Claire Danes.[101] DiCaprio is part Italian but mostly of German descent, while Danes has described her ethnic background as being "as Waspy as you can get."[102] Even so, Danes's Juliet has a somewhat ethnic Capulet family. The Italian actor Paul Sorvino played Lord Capulet,[103] Puerto Rican / Colombian actor John Leguizamo played Tybalt,[104] and the British Australian actress Miriam Margoyles was cast as the comedic, Spanish-speaking, and Spanish-inflected-when-speaking-English Nurse. Panamanian Italian actor Vincent Laresca played Abra Capulet, and Mexican actor Carlos Martín Manzo Otálora played Petruchio Capulet.

Despite casting a white Juliet and a white Lady Capulet, Luhrmann Latinxized the Capulets through casting and characterization of the other family members and the Nurse. The Capulets were given Spanish/Italian names (Fulgencio and Gloria), compared to the Montagues (Ted and Caroline). At the Capulet ball, characters dress to type (Juliet as an angel, Romeo as a knight in shining armor, Tybalt as a devilish cat), but Fulgencio dresses up as Caesar, and Gloria becomes a bejeweled Cleopatra, invoking Shakespeare's Othered characters who are Latinate and North African, while Abra and Petruchio invoke Indigeneity through their Day of the Dead calaca (skeleton) costumes. Luhrmann also employed heavy Catholic imagery in both Juliet's home altar and at the Capulet tomb.

Figure 2: Carlos Martín Manzo Otálora as Petruchio,
John Leguizamo as Tybalt, and Vincent Laresca as
Abra. Film still from *William Shakespeare's Romeo +
Juliet* (dir. Baz Luhrmann, 1996).

The domestic and international popularity of the heavily musicalized,
somewhat-Latinx film was due to a celebrity cast in a modern-day take on
one of the most recognizable stories worldwide, but it was also due in part
to the liminal ethnicity of the Capulets. Luhrmann called on tropes from
West Side Story, for example by starting the film in a scene of turf war at a
gas station, where Tybalt's waving, flamenco braceo (flamenco-style arm
work) arms and latigo (whipping) footwork designate him as "Latin."[105] In
that moment, Luhrmann showcases a diversity of Latinx identities, from
the theatrical turf war depiction of Nuyorican culture in *West Side Story*, to
Spanish flamenco choreography, Leguizamo's Colombian / Puerto Rican
heritage, and the young Mexican actor playing a child with a toy gun,
whose blue eyes hold Tybalt's gaze.[106] With a toy gun pointed at Tybalt,
violence has already clearly influenced the young boy, and with his pale
skin, blue eyes, and status (he is wearing a suit and tie), he aspires to the
gang life that is entrenched in the culture. The boy points his toy gun at
Tybalt and yells at him, only for Tybalt to point his real gun and say "Bang"
in return. The Latinx / Latin American actors/characters do not hurt each
other; instead, Tybalt saves his violence for the Montagues. Luhrmann's
deliberate heterogeneous mixing of Latinx cultures indeed led him to a
diverse Latinx and Latin American cast, in part by employing locals (the
film was shot in Mexico City) as extras. While others critiqued him for cultural appropriation and a lack of specificity in the setting, Luhrmann
flipped Laurents's individuated "anthology" of (white) Americans and
applied the concept to Latinx as well. Luhrmann describes the Montague
boys as "quintessentially Anglo, Californian, but gang. . . . The world was
created. It looked a little bit like Miami, but it wasn't. We wanted also to
mix the metaphors."[107] The vague setting of "Verona Beach" and the cast-

ing of two white leads both contribute to a dislocation in setting, which prompts the twin responses of foreignness and a "universality" that led to the film's international success.[108] After earlier films that applied the *West Side Story* trope to other cultures, Luhrmann's film reclaimed the *West Side Story* paradigm for Latinidad. The celebrated success of *Romeo + Juliet* argues for the familiarity of investment in the Latinx component of the *West Side Story* effect.

What followed were Latinx-themed Shakespearean films, even when the source material was not *Romeo and Juliet*. *Tortilla Soup* (2001) centered on a Chicanx family with a patriarch (played by Héctor Elizondo) and three daughters and had mild *King Lear* elements except that the only character to die was the Clown, Gomez. Patrick Stewart starred in *King of Texas* (2002), also a version of *King Lear* set in the 1800s Old West, in which Lear and his family are wealthy white landowners, and cultural divide is enforced through a Mexican landowner who hosts the exiled youngest daughter of Lear and falls in love with her. That same year, a film version of *Richard III* entitled *King Rikki* (2002) and set in East Los Angeles created division between the northern (norteño) and southern (eme) gangs of California. Division was established not between ethnicities, but between the gangs, the class levels of main characters, and two news reporters—Latinx who came from the same area but had lost their Spanish accents and achieved a higher socioeconomic status. *Hamlet: Son of a Kingpin* (2015) turns back to ethnicity to create division, with Polonius and his family as white, while Hamlet is from a sensualized/Mafioso Latinx family.

Romeo and Juliet also made a comeback during this time, with adaptations that continued the *West Side Story* gang theme that had been revived through Luhrmann's film. These films propagate the fantasy of a dangerous divide that wants to refuse the historical family feud and instead blame existing material, social, and political tensions to keep people apart. Four films, *Barrio Wars* (2002), *Rivals* (2003), *In Your Eyes* (2004), and *A Gangland Love Story* (2010), connect hip hop music and gang life and use Spanish to varying extents, largely to show the generational differences between the parental figures and the lovers; like *West Side Story*, they depict a shared language of gang life but also contain a cultural-linguistic divide. All but one of them, *Rivals*, is also told in flashback.[109] *Barrio Wars*, which was advertised as starring Chino XL, the "Under Ground Latino Rapper," features Latinx Romeo and Juliet characters. Plato (Romeo) is a rapper who is looking for a female voice to complement his; Angelina (Juliet) sings R&B, and they unite to record a duet together. *Rivals* offers cultural, linguistic, and musical differentiation, with the doomed lovers, the Mexican Julio

(Romeo) and El Salvadorian Romina (Juliet). Romina's family is cast as more traditional, with an aversion to the English language and the hip hop music that mark Julio. *In Your Eyes* presented a Mexican Juliet (Cece) and an African American Romeo (Yusef), who choose to run away together at the end but (like the lovers in *Rivals*) are killed in a car accident. The film posits that the lovers cannot escape their destiny, playing into the theme of *fatalismo*. *A Gangland Love Story* reversed the construct with an African American Juliet (Julia) and a Mexican Romeo (Romano). Uniquely, the movie fractured what is most commonly a single divide, adding in Russian drug impresarios and the Asian Mikki, a friend of Julia's who kills nearly everyone at the end with a mixture of guns, blades, and karate. Julia and Romano survive, however, and in the credits their "wedding album" montage looks forward to their life as a couple with a child. In all these films, cultural-linguistic divide accompanied urban warfare.

Even when Latinx do not factor into the story, *Romeo and Juliet* films of this time tended to foreground gang violence and ethnic or racial divides, implicitly or explicitly continuing tropes begun with *West Side Story*. The film *Romeo Must Die* (2000) stars Jet Li and Aaliyah and sets the action in Oakland, California, between Chinese and African American mobster gangs. The hip hop musical film *Rome and Jewel* (2008) depicted an African American male teenager and a white female teenager, with the Juliet character adopting the "language" of hip hop to communicate with the Romeo character. The original theatrical trailer made explicit reference to the influence of *West Side Story*, with an image labeled "1635 [sic] *Romeo and Juliet*" followed by one from "1961 *West Side Story*" and then simply the label "2008" before fading into the film. In contrast to *Valley Girl* over twenty-five years earlier, the two sides are divided by class as much as by race (with Jewel being the daughter of the Los Angeles mayor, and Rome being the son of a preacher in Compton), but they are united through a musical genre. Jewel is differentiated slightly in that she sometimes sings R&B, though with her soprano voice, both hip hop and R&B sound forced. She attempts to co-opt musical styles that are associated with the Black characters and traditionally associated with Black musicians. Unlike Shakespeare's play, where Romeo advances his language through his relationship with Juliet, Latinx Shakespearean films often transpose masculinity, or machismo, to linguistic authority through musicality. These later films borrow the *West Side Story* formula and echo earlier efforts to center Latinx so that there is a Latinx essence even within a film with no Latinx characters.

This wealth of Latinx Shakespearean films makes clear that there is no division between Shakespeare and Latinx in film, just as there is none in the theater. Ruben Espinosa argues that "the near invisibility and misrepresentation of Latinxs in filmic productions of Shakespeare broadens what I term the Shakespeare-Latinx divide because such narrow perceptions suggest that either Shakespeare doesn't belong to Latinxs or Latinxs don't belong to Shakespeare."[110] But as demonstrated here, there are a wealth of Latinx Shakespearean films, and any problematic representation of Latinx is not specific to Shakespeare; it is an issue in Hollywood and mainstream theater more largely.

ON CULTURAL ADAPTATIONS: OR, IS THIS HOW THEY TALK IN AMERICA?

Onstage and in film, the whiteness perceived from skin color has proven to be questionable, requiring that ethnicity be marked in other ways. The genealogy of Latinx Shakespearean films illustrates how a resistance to visual homogenization, especially through brownface, has led to a presumption that aurality (language, accent, musical styles, noises, silences, etc.) trumps the visual, even if problematically, as a clearer marker of difference for and within the intersectionality of Latinx identities. The *West Side Story* effect shows us that a threat to the status of whiteness exceeds the theatrical ability to convey race or ethnicity only through the visual, making the acoustic prominent in twenty-first-century performances of ethnicity. What I am positing here is that the strategy propagated by *West Side Story* for more than six decades necessitates aurality to function as a strategy for division. This sense of division continues to escalate, with language looked to as a stand-in for difference in light of the difficulties of staging ethnicity visually and mimetically. Brownface only served to highlight the false premise of an inherent whiteness of the Jets; all of this changed in the twenty-first century when Spanish was more heavily incorporated to distinguish the Sharks as linguistically separate from the Jets.

West Side Story's legacy, clearly evidenced in Latinx Shakespeares, is that white skin color is neither a reliable marker of whiteness nor the theatrical counterpoint to Latinidad: monolingualism is. The original *West Side Story* does contain some Spanish phrases; even Maria and Tony first express their affection in Spanish, "Te adoro."[111] What Latinx Shakespearean productions share in common is the notion that incorporating the Spanish language is a necessary component to performing Latinidad. While the inclusion of Spanish is also a hallmark of early Latinx theater, and often spoken at least in some part in much Latinx theater today, it becomes a necessary through line for Latinx Shakespeares because of the distance (not divide) between Shakespeare and Latinx culture and characters. Applying a Latinx concept setting or integrating Latinidad into a Shakespearean character requires aural embellishment in ways that make identity legible that cannot be achieved through skin color without resorting to brownface.

Cultural-linguistic division has become so much the thing that one without the other no longer resonates with audiences. The 2013 Broadway revival of *Romeo and Juliet*, the first in thirty-six years, starred white Australian film actor Orlando Bloom and African American theater actress Condola Rashad. Despite the production's invoking racial division through lead casting choices, the two households had no cultural division, leading *New York Times* reviewer Ben Brantley to comment, "That one of them is white and the other black may underscore the division between their families, yet it registers as irrelevant when they're together."[112] The costumes were modern dress, but with a nearly absent set that made indoors and outdoors unclear, the setting was nondescript, dislocating racial division from context that would also resonate as cultural division. Compounded with Bloom's Australian accent, a British/South African Benvolio, and the partly Latinx Mercutio, many of the actors utilized a formal speaking voice, but ultimately the production was sonically dislocated as well. Visual racial division without cultural division or clear linguistic division is incoherent in the face of the *West Side Story* effect.

This division marked early Latinx Shakespeares, and, as the genealogy progresses, practitioners deviate from, and respond to, this trope. *West Side Story* is the subtext, intertext, and übertext with which Latinx Shakespeares continue to be in fraught dialogue today. The poetry and rhythms of Shakespeare, when adapted and ethnicized through music and musical theater, amplify the importance of aurality in staging difference and invite an exploration of division that informs American Shakespeares. The subsequent chapters explore how this relationship plays out—how it maintains, fractures, alters—well into the twenty-first century.

TWO | Aurality

Hearing Ethnicity

In 2005, Antonio Ocampo-Guzmán directed an adaptation of *Romeo and Juliet* at Florida State University (FSU) that interwove Spanish-language verse and cast Latinx actors. The Montagues spoke Spanish, the Capulets English, and Romeo and Benvolio shifted between languages.[1] Juliet was biethnic though not bilingual, and though the actors playing Romeo, Juliet, and Lord Montesco were Latinx, their national backgrounds and varied appearances did not signal a cohesive heritage. Language, rather than ethnicity, was the marker of divide.[2] The Montescos spoke Spanish, and the Montague boys switched between Spanish and English, with Romeo speaking some Spanish to Juliet.[3] The production would prove formative for Frankie J. Alvarez, the talented and bilingual undergraduate actor who played Romeo. Entirely new to Shakespeare at the time, Alvarez would go on to become a prominent figure in Latinx Shakespeares.[4] Asked about the experience of working across languages, Alvarez stated that when it comes to bilingual Shakespearean performance, "English might be a tactic, [but] Spanish is a guttural impulse. I keep that with me today."[5] Per his training, Alvarez learned about stasis and intrusion, given circumstances and tactics, in English, and he was not taught acting or vocal methods in Spanish. In the production, Spanish was used for moments of intimacy and heightened emotion[6] and complemented Alvarez's familial rather than academic experience with Spanish. In this case, and often with native Spanish speakers who perform in Latinx Shakespeares, the use of Spanish sounds more instinctual than Shakespearean dialogue in English, offering two different affective registers based on language. Whether the Spanish comes from the mid-twentieth century from Chilean poet Pablo Neruda, from the 1990s from Spanish scholar Angel-Luis Pujante, from a recent translation by Colombian poet William Ospina, or from translators prior to the twentieth century, the Spanish may be in heightened poetry like Shakespeare or not, but it is always in a more recent language than Shakespeare's English, offering a mixture of different temporal languages.[7] Although he did not want to "make a political statement, just an artistic one," after the show Ocampo-Guzmán concluded that there needs to be "a significant political context" to explain why one of the houses would be speaking a different language than the other.[8] Ocampo-Guzmán experimented with language *as* the dramaturgy;[9] Latinidad was invoked through language, alluded to through casting, but not integrated into the concept of the play.

AMPLIFYING AURALITY

This chapter takes up the question of how Latinx Shakespeares use aurality, or sonic phenomenology, to invoke ethnicity. Aurality serves as both marker and purity test for ethnicity; it is interpreted in our daily life and represented in art through literary, sonic, and visual signifiers. A focus on aurality extends Shakespeare studies' historical emphasis on rhetoric and poetry to other elements of the aural soundscape and complicates the long-standing heavy theorization of visual signifiers in the theater.[10] I attend to the complexity and consequences of aural strategies used in Latinx Shakespeares to create an affective soundscape that is a performance of aural excess, or what I term *auralidad*. Auralidad is not a word in Spanish, and my use of a direct translation that does not exist is purposeful. While the adjective "aural" may be translated to *auditivo* or possibly *auricular*, there is not a noun to ascribe to the idea of aurality. Here I draw on Diana Taylor's discussion of her use of *performático* for performative, a Spanish word to describe a concept in English, to signal that it "is a product of that same logocentrism rather than a confirmation that there's no there there."[11] Auralidad is not a direct translation of aurality; auralidad connotes the rich aural elements germane to the performance of Latinx cultures. I use the term "auralidad" to signal the constant tension of understanding and misunderstanding, of the act of translation that is always imperfect and often beautiful because it demands an alteration of terms and form, and as a constant reminder that in the theater that is Latinx Shakespeares and this book of the same name, we read and hear between languages to create new meaning.

In their work on sound in theater, Lynne Kendrick and David Roesner expand the elements of aurality, stating aural elements "all agitate received ideas of ocularcentric theatre semiosis."[12] The desire to focus on the aural extends outside of theater studies to sociohistorical research into the shaping of racial categories.[13] In his study of the role of music in American racial formation, Josh Kun uses the phrase "the American audio-racial imagina-tion,"[14] and what Jennifer Lynn Stoever calls "the sonic color line" func-tions "as an externally imposed difference."[15] While sound theorists make evident that sound has helped to define racial categories, these formula-tions typically address race, but not ethnicity.[16] But aural differences of eth-nicity can be profound; sound recordings of New York in the late 1940s reveal "white Americans most easily marked Puerto Ricans' difference audibly not visually."[17] Any study of Latinx, the theater and beyond, requires an attunement to auditory signifiers of culture, especially Latinx who are either racially white or racially Black, as the aural distinction may be more prominent than the visual, or it may be the only outward differ-ence at all.

In the theater, the soundscape includes all possible sonic elements: language, accent, inflection, music, affect, noise, sounds, and silences.[18] The richness of auralidad includes a heightened language play, which may take one or more forms within the world of the play.[19] Different types of language play are evidenced, for example, in *Romeo and Juliet* pairings that speak English to each other and Spanish to their parents, and in the immigrant characters in *Twelfth Night* and *The Comedy of Errors* who speak their home language when reunited with their lost relatives. This language play becomes a crucial step toward creating an identity of these characters, and of giving them a history through the legacies of col-onization, assimilation, and immigration. The assumptions in artistic practice about what theatrically constitutes Latinidad vary widely; theater-makers unfamiliar with Latinidad and who do not include Latinx artists in the development and performance of the work may default to established tropes or stereotypes. But the work of theater encompasses more power and analytic awareness than that: even as more Latinx peo-ple do not speak Spanish, auralidad is a savvy, and oftentimes necessary, means for theatrically engaging with Latinidad. With inclusion and a commitment to exploration, auralidad connotes a variety of expressive and specific aural components that integrate Latinx culture with Shake-speare's language and the command of vocality required for both con-temporary linguistic code-switching and Shakespearean acting.

Crucially, however, Latinx Shakespeares are a site of a particular type of language play that employs languages from different time periods. This *cross-temporal code-switching*, such as mixing Shakespearean English with modern-day Spanish, shifts the dialogue outside of any particular time period. Drawing on Ngũgĩ wa Thiongo's concept of orature, which includes "gesture, song, dance, processions, storytelling, proverbs, gossip," and more, Joseph Roach argues that "orature goes beyond a schematized opposition of literacy and orality . . . [and] that these modes of communication have produced one another interactively over time."[20] Although this is specific to performance (ritual, customs, etc.), not theater, the act of making meaning through hearing (rather than speaking) allows sound to cross between Spanish, English, Spanglish, and from New York to Texas to Los Angeles. Sound tells us certain things about culture; cross-temporal code-switching modernizes while it ethnicizes and reflects an inchoate idea of the relationship between ethnicity and language. As Latinx Shakespeares shape ethnically specific characters from Shakespearean plays that lack them, they give all of the characters in the production a disjunctive linguistic and aural history that opens up opportunities for audiences to attune to Latinidad.

ATTUNING TO LATINIDAD

The cultural/political work enabled by introducing audiences to Latinx characters mediated through the "legitimacy" of Shakespeare permits the discernment of Latinidad and Shakespearean meaning together onstage. Attuning to Latinidad provides recognition of representation, but it also moves an audience into the spaces of liminality, an experience provided by Latinx theaters but rarely by Shakespeare. In the interstices of the two, or borderlands, an audience that might not otherwise encounter this linguistic experience of bilingualism is invited to be immersed in it for over two hours.

Beyond the strategies to make the soundscape a signifier for Latinidad, I argue that in using the aural to theatrically depict Latinx, this theatrical work engages the audience in a differently sensorial world. Engagement in this sensorium supersedes merely registering the problematic visual difference created by brownface, as the defamiliarizing effect of Latinidad permits a meaningful attunement to a different perspective. This perspective shares sociocultural sensibilities with liminal and border experiences of between, both/and, and minoritized or marginalized points of view that might not otherwise be visible to the still mostly white upper-middle-class audiences of prominent regional and repertory theaters. Latinx Shakespeares emerge in the service of particular models of theater such as Shakespeare and social justice; they also emerge precisely out of the problematic intersection of these competing needs.

Examined together, the two case studies that follow reveal a Latinx "acoustemology," a portmanteau for acoustic epistemology, and a term that Steven Feld coined "to express the particular ways cultures experience their knowledge of the world through sound."[21] The centrality of acoustemology as a practice of identity begins to offer an alternative model of difference-making to the strong arm of visuality. A Latinx acoustemology for Shakespeare includes auralidad, the aural excess that counters and enriches an unreliable recognition of the visual of Latinx bodies onstage.[22] Shakespeare invites this process through the openness of his language, and in the unremarkable settings of some of his plays; Verona does not factor into the characterization, plot, or physical spaces of *Romeo and Juliet*, and *Measure for Measure*'s setting in Vienna is likewise irrelevant, as are the Italian names of its characters. Acoustemology is about meaning; in Marcus Cheng Chye Tan's impressive research on "an acoustic interculturalism," he writes, "Acoustemology establishes sound as culturally determined and symbiotic to cultural spaces."[23] In Latinx Shakespeares, the complexity of linguistic difference becomes a powerful interpretive tool for both performers and audiences to open up the nuances of identity and to reformulate the identity category of Latinx.

COMBATING LINGUISTIC HEGEMONY

Indeed, the heteroglossic language play, or the expression of two or more viewpoints through the intermixing of two or more languages, of Latinx is inherently liminal. This liminality is germane to Latinidad and, indeed, can counter stereotypes about linguistic deficiency or the valorization of language purity. In *Borderlands / La Frontera*, Gloria Anzaldúa lists eight different forms of Chicanx language[24] and argues that "ethnic identity is twin skin to linguistic identity—I am my language."[25] Juan Bruce-Nova advocates for interlingualism and against "language loyalty," and Frances Aparicio's notion of tropicalization—the process of essentializing Latinx identities through hegemonic discourses—argues the tropicalized (Latinx) can subvert such essentialism by writing in English and invoking Spanish and Latinx cultures, with "strategic self-tropicalization."[26] Ilan Stavans situates this type of linguistic diversity as a space that will "initiate a utopic future where equality means assimilation into a new hybrid culture."[27] These acts of reshaping and reclaiming identity through language play are part of everyday life for Latinx. Movement between languages is part of the Latinx experience, often even for those who consider themselves monolingual English speakers. The inclusion of slang, verbal expressions, and the application of syntax from one language to the words of another are all forms of language play. Likewise, Shakespeare's dialogue brings together words from a breadth of etymological sources, and it shaped and solidified the English language. Shakespeare's heteroglossia confounds a perceived purity of English, and Latinx language play amplifies this faulty perception. Latinx Shakespeares combine these histories and strategies for the theater, placing greater emphasis on the aural to discern Latinidad and Shakespearean meaning together onstage.

But linguistic bias against Latinx takes the form of the policing of Spanish in public spaces, and the pejorative dismissal of code-switching, often on both sides of a national linguistic divide. These biases conform with presumptions about class and education of Latinx based on accent, syntax, and vocabulary. Both Spanish monolinguals and English monolinguals have at times argued against the mixing of languages, with most often English monolingual Americans concerned with the preservation of "American" culture and a fear that the country is changing due to immigration from the southern border. Ana Celia Zentella notes that "bilingual dexterity" allows speakers to "poke fun at their own semantic and grammatical constraints,"[28] whereas John M. Lipski claims that it will ultimately result "in the deterioration of the Spanish language."[29] There is a narrative that code-switching is chaotic, transgressive, and it is sometimes called "alingulism" (having no control of any language). But code-switching does not break grammatical rules in any language.

A large portion of the divide today emerges out of the English-only legislation of the 1980s and 1990s. English-only legislation desired only one language used in schools, the government, and the workplace. English Plus, by contrast, advocated for bilingualism. The movements implied that access to English guaranteed economic benefits, which still remains untrue. The language issues of the 1980s gave way to the immigration issues of the 1990s that are today expressed through concerns of the undocumented Latino. The rhetoric about language contamination was a deflection from the human rights and foreign policy concerns that were conveniently masked by putting language front and center.

Latinx-themed Shakespeare productions challenge ideas about temporality by creating a Latinx world in disjunction with Shakespeare. I ground my discussion of auralidad in two Latinx Shakespearean productions at the Oregon Shakespeare Festival (OSF): Bill Rauch's 2011 *Measure for Measure* and Laird Williamson's 2012 *Romeo and Juliet*. OSF is the largest repertory company in the United States and a significant regional theater for the West Coast, and these were the first two Latinx-themed Shakespeare productions in the company's history. While the first was set in a 1970s diverse bordertown, with Angelo, Isabella, Claudio, and Juliet as Latinx, the latter was set in 1840s Alta California, with both households as members of the landed Spanish gentry and Paris and the Prince as members of the white militia. These two productions offer examples of how auralidad shapes and informs the theatrical depiction of ethnicity.

OSF was on a mission to diversify its processes, people, and productions, but was challenged to do within the frame of a Shakespeare festival. While both productions adhere to the *West Side Story* effect, using Latinidad and the Spanish language to mark differences between groups of characters, they each employ auralidad to connote ethnicity in distinct ways. *Measure for Measure* depicted Latinx culture by creating a division between the monolingual and the bilingual within a single society and *Romeo and Juliet* depicted language shifts across generations. OSF's first forays into Latinx Shakespeares provide an example of how a theater with immense resources—financial, dramaturgical, personnel—makes deliberate choices. The political economy of Shakespeare festivals inflects both the capacity and limits of this work.[30]

Utilizing sound studies as the theoretical lens of analysis, I argue that these productions model a Latinx acoustemology for Shakespearean performances and audiences. Both productions are examples of semi-bilingual theater, which I define as theater with less than 25 percent of its dialogue in a secondary language. Cross-temporal code-switching facilitates understanding for audiences who do not understand early modern English or modern-day Spanish fully, and with a small portion of the dialogue in Spanish, these productions convey Latinidad through other mechanisms of the soundscape. Further, they engage a soundscape outside the limits of linear time, one that emphasizes auralidad as a form of agency that combats dual forces of linguistic racism (both forces inherent in Shakespeare-as-gatekeeper and those prevalent in the United States today). Because the soundscape is not temporally situated, the elitism of Shakespearean linguistic hegemony fractures, easing understanding for those who may find it daunting and creating new meaning and creative practices as well.

OSF'S 2011 *MEASURE FOR MEASURE*

Three women, dressed as maids, clean an office space. As they clean, they sing acapella mariachi music in Spanish. They break out their instruments from their cleaning carts, and the deep-bodied sounds of strumming on a guitarrón, a large guitar, and the higher pitched vihuela, a five-string-style guitar, fill the theater. They begin singing "Ay Ay Ay Ay / Canta y no llores,"[31] the beginning of "Cielito Lindo," a folk nursery rhyme with a waltz rhythm that is *son huasteco*, a traditional Mexican style of song. One woman speaks directly to the audience: "Buenas Noches, Welcome to the Oregon Shakespeare Festival. Our casa es su casa. We have rules. Turn off your cell phone. Nada de texting." The last line she speaks is entirely in Spanish: "Bueno. Muchisimas Gracias."[32] This moment, the opening scene of OSF's 2011 *Measure for Measure*, set the tone for the whole production. This work of semi-bilingual theater foregrounded cultural and linguistic division and utilized music to create a soundscape that was both thematic and affective as well as accessible to the predominantly non-Spanish-speaking audience at OSF.

Set in a fictional 1970s inner city, resembling perhaps Los Angeles, this *Measure for Measure* interweaves class-based politics and Latinx as a prominent culture within an urban setting to stage the interplay between Latinx peoples and a diverse, yet monolingual, society. Staged indoors in the proscenium Angus Bowmer Theatre, the set featured white walls and a long rectangular table, and it transformed from office to bordello to court to convent through stark changes in lighting design, which maintained a bright, crisp aesthetic while accentuating similarities among the locations. The effect of the set was that it offered a visual consistency across the varied public and private spaces of the play, thereby suggesting the possibilities for justice and inequities that extend to each space. Siblings Isabela and Claudio, as well as Claudio's betrothed Julieta and the deputy Angelo,[33] were portrayed as Latinx and played by bilingual Latinx actors. Portraying Angelo as Latino (alongside the other Latinx characters) provided a backstory that Angelo (René Millán) had come up from the barrio but had increased his status.[34] The Duke, played by a white actor, leaves town and the responsibilities of governance to "an upwardly mobile Latino in Angelo who makes a clear example of a young Latino offender of the law in Claudio in order to show the greater community that he means to rule by the letter of the law regardless of any race-based sympathies."[35] The other prisoner, Barnadine (Jim L. "Jimmy" Garcia) was too played by a Latino actor, making Latinos the only incarcerated people the audience sees and hears.

The rest of the casting and characterization crossed ethnic, racial, and gender lines, situating Latinidad in opposition to a multicultural, though monolingual, urban US city. Mistress Overdone, at the bordello, was played as a drag queen by an Asian actor; the Duke's adviser Escalus was played by an African American woman with a Caribbean accent; and the fop Lucio was played by an African American man in a disco suit and an Afro.[36] These choices in costuming and characterization improvised on the bawdiness and humor of the play (after all, this is a comedy), and the diverse casting involved white actors and actors of color in both high and low character roles. Casting specific roles with Latinx actors to play them as Latinx characters was deliberate and essential to the storytelling to create an ethnic group that is both integrated with and restrained by the larger society. Spanish was also interwoven into the dialogue of non-Latinx characters, with a Spanish word sprinkled into a sentence spoken by a monolingual character, in the same fashion that popular Spanish expressions are appropriated into the English lexicon. For example, Mistress Overdone, who spoke only English, used the word *dolares*.[37] But outside of the Latinx roles, there was no unifying racial/ethnic concept, signaling a shift in the role language serves in being the Other to both white and nonwhite monolingual English speakers.

Although this production of *Measure for Measure* was not staged as a musical, the music—as embodied in Las Colibrí, the three-woman mariachi band—was a key component, representing a common thread between locations, complementing the dialogue, and advancing the unique affective soundscape of the play. Reminiscent of a Greek chorus, the women wove in and out of the scenes, becoming the music for the fiesta at Mistress Overdone's and the brooding component to Angelo's inner turmoil. The first time that the audience sees Mariana (Angelo's one-time fiancée), Las Colibrí appeared upstage in long, sexy, red dresses, singing "Aleja, ¡oh!, aleja esos labios" (Take, O, take those lips away). Sounds of thunder opened the scene, and Mariana appeared kneeling, praying, and suffering. Then Mariana abruptly turned the radio off, and the mariachi exit: in this moment, they were the song playing on the radio. Though they did not narrate the events of the story, their presence and music worked as a through line and accentuated the tone of the scenes. More than that, though, their singing cultivated the production's soundscape. The strategic but limited use of Spanish-translated Shakespearean dialogue may cause some audience members to feel distanced from the action if they cannot comprehend the words; Las Colibrí's music harks on an expansion beyond dialogue to the wider soundscape, offering affective qualities rather than conveying information, antithetical to how Shakespeare's music functions.[38] Las Colibrí facilitated the process of connecting the Spanish and the Shakespearean dialogue through their ongoing presence and Spanish-language, Mexican music.

The music generated an aural pathway to understanding, connection, and storytelling. While the traditional "Cielito Lindo" welcomed the audience through a popular lullaby, Las Colibrí then varied the styles of maria-chi music to both invoke the affect of different scenes and to introduce OSF's audiences to the diversity within mariachi. The song "Consoling Julieta" was a mariachi version of a ranchera, conveying the fatalismo of lost love when Julieta realizes that Claudio will likely be executed for impregnating her. The interlude into act 2 was a stylized huapango, "El Preso Número 9," originally performed by Ana María González and con-tinually covered by the likes of Joan Baez and Chavela Vargas. It tells the story of an imprisoned man confessing to a priest that he does not regret his actions, analogous to Claudio's prior scene with the friar. Las Colibrí also translated music directly from Shakespeare's play, performing "Take, Oh Take, Those Lips Away," in Spanish as a mariachi pop song. The last song of the play occurred when the Duke returned, and this joyous event was marked with the classic mariachi "En Tu Día," famously performed by both Pedro Infante and Javier Solís. Through the musical soundscape, Las Colibrí showcased a range of affective, aesthetic, and adaptation styles but also offered an unprecedented history of mariachi music for an American Shakespearean audience.

This aural pathway also served to nuance ideas about monolingualism and bilingualism in an integrated society, as well as how language can be a mode of intimacy as well as exclusion. OSF staged *Measure for Measure* as a linguistically integrated production: the Latinx characters spoke both in Shakespearean English and in modern-day Spanish, while those around them spoke in generally Shakespearean English, although OSF modern-ized some of the English as well. This shortened the temporal distance between the English and Spanish and depicted a society with language flu-idity. Spanish words were occasionally sprinkled into a sentence spoken by monolingual English characters, and taken together, the elements of lan-guage play worked with the music to depict a range of linguistic assimila-tion practices, from Julieta to Isabela to Angelo. OSF translated some of the English-speaking characters' lines to contemporary English, as Elbow's line "Marry, madam" was changed to "Ya Know, madam," and the use of "fourscore pound a year" by both Pompey and Escalus was changed to "much ready money."[39] This reduced the distance between temporalities— Latinx and Shakespeare—and prompted the audience to discern meaning from an integrated and varied aural soundscape.

For the character of Julieta (Alejandra Escalante), who becomes preg-nant by Claudio, language play isolated her, reinforcing her sense of social displacement and disempowerment. Julieta only spoke Spanish, needing a translator to communicate with the authorities to visit Claudio in the jail.[40] In the scene where she attempts to make her case of penitence to the friar (the Duke in disguise), the authorities provided a translator for her, and without the translator, her petition for Claudio's innocence was denied— her inability to speak English seemingly a factor. One of the members of Las Colibrí, who in this scene was a mother with a stroller also waiting for her time in front of the judge, began to play her violin. As she began to sing in Spanish, the scene transitioned, the other members of the mariachi band joined her song, and the scene segued to the next. In this way, the Spanish language left Julieta without access to the legal society and contributed to and reinforced her displacement; the soundscape more largely carried this presence forward.

The physical design of the stage remained, with lighting and furniture pieces to connote different locations within the setting, but it was the shifts between languages that enhanced the relationships and politics of each location. As much as Spanish isolated the Latinx characters from their non-Latinx peers, it also fostered unity among the Latinx characters themselves, signaling not just their shared culture but also their familial affection. This was never more important than in the exchanges between Claudio (Frankie J. Alvarez, who starred as Romeo at FSU six years earlier) and Isabela (Stephanie Beatriz). Visiting Claudio at the jail, Isabela tells him in English that Angelo is attempting to coerce her into bed in exchange for Claudio's freedom. During this heightened exchange, Claudio speaks in Spanish after she says she will have to sacrifice her virginity. They pray in Spanish together, whereby Claudio interrupts with English to ask her, "Have you affections for [the Duke]?"[41] Isabela responds with disgust in Spanish. This shifting between languages demonstrated not only the intimacy between Claudio and Isabela as siblings, but also a shared linguistic pattern of switching between Spanish and English in similar moments.[42] At the same time, the production retained enough English to allow the OSF audience to follow the dialogue.

Here I highlight an integral scene where the Duke speaks with Claudio in prison and the soundscape is accentuated through the visual language of Christianity—through costuming, props, and gestures. Lucio goes to the convent to inform Isabela of Claudio's fate and bring her to the jail to see him. Claudio is in jail, a barren room, and handcuffed. The Duke as friar enters, and Alvarez writes, "He slides a Bible towards me [Claudio], and I push it right back towards him. As his monologue begins, I dialogue with him physically."[43] Once Isabela enters and the Duke exits, Isabela says that

Figure 3: Stephanie Beatriz as Isabela, Anthony Heald as the Duke, and Frankie J. Alvarez as Claudio in *Measure for Measure* (dir. Bill Rauch, 2011). Photo by Jenny Graham. Courtesy of Oregon Shakespeare Festival.

there is only one way she can save Claudio, by sleeping with Angelo. Claudio shifts to Spanish with several phrases after Isabela refers to Angelo as "el diablo." When Isabela says, "Be ready, Claudio, for your death tomorrow," Alvarez notes, "We hold hands, place them atop the Bible and begin to recite the Apostles' Creed in Spanish."[44] Claudio, handcuffed and in a beige jail uniform, interrupts this moment of religious and linguistic intimacy to question if she should perhaps take the offer. On his knees on the floor he asks, "Oye, / What sin you do to save a brother's life,"[45] and he pushes the Bible away from the center of the table, away from Isabela. The dialogue moves between English and Spanish, between Shakespeare and a twenty-first-century language, but the physical dialogue speaks of the historical and complicated relationship of Latinx to Christianity, typically Catholicism. In this way, Latinidad is made central to the characters' choices, and religiosity as a key component of the play harks to the history of Spanish Catholicism as a colonizing practice.[46] In Rauch's *Measure for Measure*, the religious ethos that governs decision-making and is recalled in the title of the play is also an arm of coloniality.

OREGON SHAKESPEARE'S 2012 *ROMEO AND JULIET*

The following year, in 2012, the Oregon Shakespeare Festival produced its second Latinx Shakespearean production, again in the Angus Bowmer Theatre. Just as with *Measure for Measure*, this production incorporated notes of Spanish into the first moments of the play. After the house lights dimmed, blue lighting colored the background of the stage and two women entered from the audience. A recorded female voice, aged, English-speaking and Spanish-inflected, was heard: "En la Hermosa Verona, Dos familias, In fair Verona, two households"; the voice-over was that of the Nurse (Isabell Monk O'Connor), an Afro-Latina character with a heavy Spanish-inflected accent who was older and walked with a cane. She repeated the words of the prologue, speaking in Spanish, her voice aged and wistful. This Nurse is elderly, now blind, and recalls events long since passed. The rest of the cast entered from the wings and surrounded her, repeating the words of the prologue in English. If the Nurse was looking back on the past, the others filling onto the stage were characters from that past, and they all spoke the prologue to the audience. As the program explained, the play was reset as "a memory dream of the fabled world of the Spanish Californios."[47] The premise was that "Juliet's nurse . . . [comes] back to revisit this place which held tragedy in her life. . . . It's not so much that she tells the story but she conjures it up and the people will start coming out of the woodwork so to speak, as if they have been revived from the past."[48] And that past was seen not through the eyes of the now-blind Nurse, but told through the voices of the characters who lived it, young and old, with a range of languages, accents, and inflections.

This *Romeo and Juliet* was set in 1840s Alta California (the region that today encompasses California, Arizona, Utah, Nevada, and parts of Wyoming, New Mexico, and Colorado), a setting that director Laird Williamson chose in large part because the historical US military occupation added "another pressure on the play."[49] As Williamson describes, "Not only is there this conflict between the two families, but there's a whole new cultural influence, culture clash so to speak. . . . It adds to uncertainty."[50] In this play, then, the *West Side Story* effect involves a clash not between the two families (who are both part of the landed Spanish gentry) but between these families and the American (white) militia, to which both General Prince and Captain Paris belong. The set design conveyed the time period and location through a large facade of adobe housing that "gestured at a California pueblo town without recreating the romantic flowering balconies and plazas so often associated with imagined 'Old Spanish Days.'"[51] A warm color palette for costuming established the atmosphere and mood for scenes: costumes included serapes and bolero jackets, traditional Spanish music and dancing, and Aztec masks worn during the fiesta scene. For the bedroom scene, no set pieces were used and the lovers emerged from backstage wrapped in one sheet, later revealing Romeo bare-chested and Juliet in a white nightgown, and the floor of the stage was used as a bed. The austere set and minimal use of props allowed for a greater emphasis on the selected elements that alluded to Californio culture, without resorting to stereotypes.

Just as with *Measure for Measure*, music played a crucial role in fostering the play's soundscape and in reinforcing ethnicity. For example, in the opening scene, the sounds of intermittent guitar strums were heard from offstage to accentuate the challenges that each household spewed at each other, and there was music in the background of the fighting scenes, played for the audience as a sort of soundtrack that blended with sound effects connoting street noise and mayhem as the fight progressed. This music registered as "Spanish" because of stylized guitar strumming and periodic vocal accompaniment in Spanish. The music of Spanish boleros also played in the distance during the party scene. Choreographer Alonzo Moore pulled "movement and dances from the regions in Mexico and Nyarit and Tomaulipa [sic],"[52] including a waltz and a polka that were popular at the time. And the music brought together characters from distinct racial groups who were united ethnically, as when the white Latinx Mercutio sang the first words of a popular corrido "La Pastora," and the Afro-Latinx Nurse joined in.[53] *Romeo and Juliet* was inspired by events in which Spanish and Indigenous cultures were subjugated by (white) military force; having a white Latinx Mercutio and a Black Latinx Nurse, who evoked a shared culture through music and language, invoked migration patterns rarely represented on large repertory stages. Whereas the staging of *Measure for Measure* included few (yet integral) Spanish-speaking characters and live musicians onstage who sang Spanish-language mariachi music, here *Romeo and Juliet* offered a mostly Spanish-descended society, and the Spanish language and Spanish accents dominated the aural soundscape so much that it was less dependent on music for this function.

The dual device of Spanish language and flashback for the play's opening moments, however, established the Spanish language as a "linguistic veil,"[54] a conduit for entering the world of the play that simultaneously shields that world from those (characters and audience) who do not speak Spanish. In this, the framing device of memory is voiced by an Afro-Latinx character, played by an African American actress, evoking authority as the narrator and empathy as well.[55] While the Nurse spoke the prologue in Spanish, the large majority (roughly 80 percent) of the lines in the play were spoken in English, albeit with a variety of accents and inflections.[56] This linguistic, ethnic, and racial diversity comments on the complexity of US/Californio history; the intersectional interplay of tensions within Latinx identity today are historicized within the first moments of the production.

The setting of *Measure for Measure* was a few decades in the past, but here as in *Romeo and Juliet*, the linguistic veil served the play's concept of a flashback, as the audience could imagine that the Spanish takes us back to a historical period in which most all of the play is assumed to be in Spanish as well. This is both a common device in Latinx theater and a sign of an unresolvable problem. It signals the complexity of staging another linguistic culture through English, and here Shakespearean English, and how this can reinforce a colonial legacy. But it is also a potentially effective way to mark differences within the existing constraints of a primarily monolingual audience. Shakespeare has always used language as a marker of difference in precise ways (see chapter 1), and the ways that language difference is employed in Latinx Shakespeares reflects both this long-standing view of Shakespeare and a new one. Spanish was largely relegated to the background and the periphery, with "Possible Crowd Ad-Libs" in Spanish for key scenes offered in the dramaturgical work and director's prompt book.[57] It was only in the scene in which Romeo and his friends make various sexual innuendos through dialogue entirely in Spanish that the audience was left to follow along through gesture and possible familiarity with the text. The macaronic elements of Shakespeare's script remained, including Mercutio's French greeting, "Romeo, *bonjour*: there's a French salutation to your French slop,"[58] serving as a reminder that Shakespeare's audience and today's audience can enter into a world of a play that contains multiple languages. This chips away at both the idea that Shakespeare should only be spoken in the English that he wrote in and that his plays are only in English. Further, it allows Spanish into the soundscape and offers more than one strategy for its integration into the play.

Spanish and Spanish accents were used among the older, less-assimilated characters, both Capulets and Montagues, to show generational changes in the acquisition of English, but not without challenges. Alejandra Escalante (Juliet) and Daniel José Molina (Romeo), both bilingual actors, spoke unaccented English in their roles and interactions with each other.[59] The refusal to use stereotypical Spanish-accented English is a sign of an awareness of the reality of accents that are not so distinctly marked as an early generation of Latinx Shakespeares seemed to need in order to reinforce their problematically limited notions of authenticity. Escalante recollects, "For *Romeo and Juliet*, Dan [Molina] and I were asked on the first day, for the first read-through, to read with accents. . . . That whole idea kept getting tossed out, mainly really, because of Dan and me. Me crying, and asking, 'Please don't let us do this. It's going to be really bad. Please don't make us do this.' For lots of reasons, but mainly it was that we didn't want to seem like a weird, stereotypical story, and because there wasn't the research into what this accent would be."[60] Although Escalante and Molina were successful at pushing back on performing with an accent, to signal an older and less-assimilated generation, some characters were asked to employ a Spanish accent. One critic compared the ethnicizing of *Romeo and Juliet* to the prior year's *Measure for Measure* and noted, "In last year's production, though, no one spoke with fake quasi-Mexican accents."[61] What this critic alludes to is that not all of the accents were equally fleshed out or sounded as if they were from one place, making Lady Capulet sound as if she spoke English with a geographically appropriate accent, while Benvolio sounded vaguely European.

The already two temporally distinct languages spoken onstage became normalized against one another, making modern-day Spanish and Elizabethan English both more familiar by allowing a much less familiar third language to reside in the soundscape. Among the majority Spanish and English linguistic soundscape, the sounds of a third language became the marker for denoting class, racial, and religious difference. As Romeo approached the Apothecary, dulcet, nonlinguistic sounds were heard along with the shaking of beads. The Apothecary in *Romeo and Juliet* was portrayed as an Ohlone medicine woman by Cherokee actress DeLanna Studi, and Williamson changed the "needy shop" to a "hut."[62] Traditionally, Indigenous representations in predominantly white theaters, in Shakespeare theaters, and in much Latinx theater, conform to monolithic and stereotyped portrayals. Yet this racist practice was overthrown here in the careful assertion of precise Native histories attached to the specificity of location and through casting. The presence of the Ohlone Apothecary accentuates the ways in which Hispanidad (Spanishness) and Latinidad can become sites of contestation about the relationship of Indigeneity to Latinidad. Here, Blackness is integrated into the Spanish-descended Californio culture through the Nurse with the Capulets and Balthazar (Mikkei Fritz) with the Montagues, but the Indigenous character is unaffiliated with either household. Courtney Elkin Mohler describes "the scene in Mantua begins as Studi sings vocables dressed in carefully rendered traditional Ohlone clothing, including a large deer hide, a shell and feather

Figure 4: DeLanna Studi as the Apothecary / Ohlone Medicine Woman in *Romeo and Juliet* (dir. Laird Williamson, 2012). Photo by Jenny Graham. Courtesy of Oregon Shakespeare Festival.

prayer necklace, and a brown cloak containing various medicines."[63] While Shakespeare's Apothecary references his own poverty, differentiating his class status from that of the two families, and his medicine is deadly in contrast to Friar Laurence's faux-deadly potion, there is no linguistic difference between the Apothecary and others in the text. The linguistic difference was conveyed through the addition of the Ohlone woman's "vocables," or nonlexical syllables that do not have meaning, without altering the dialogue.

Just as Indigeneity was conveyed through the sounds of the Ohlone apothecary's vocables, visual language became paramount when Romeo and Juliet embraced and an image of La Virgen de Guadalupe appeared on the upstage wall. Most notably it was the appearance of Day of the Dead skeletons, or *calacas*, during key moments that enriched the representation of Spanish colonial culture interfacing with Indigenous populations through Aztec religious references. When Romeo and Juliet part for the last time, after they awake from their matrimonial bed, Juliet asks him, "O, think'st thou we shall ever meet again?" and he replies, "I doubt it not, and all these woes shall serve / For sweet discourses in our time to come."[64] At this moment, two actors dressed as *calacas*, in all-black bodysuits with white skeletons painted on the body and face, walked quietly on stage. They took hold of Romeo and pulled him offstage, foreshadowing Romeo's death. Another *calaca* made an entrance in the tomb, and simply stood in the back, watching the killing of Paris and the suicides of both Romeo and Juliet. These silent actions connote a wider conception of language, one that includes "gesture, costume, makeup, scenery, or architecture" plus "'stage language.'"[65] Indigeneity became the cultural and linguistic bridge between the Californio culture, the Spanish and English languages onstage, and the predominantly white and English-speaking audiences; in this scene, the linguistic marker of culture was not sound, but silence.

As the aural soundscape invoked ethnicity, the flashback concept reworked the idea of who gets to tell the story. For this OSF production of *Romeo and Juliet*, the soundscape ultimately served as the connective tissue and the vehicle of memory, facilitating an engagement with a time period and a history of mestizaje that are not often staged in American theater. Playwright and feminist scholar Cherríe Moraga discusses the Chicana need for the act of remembering, but warns against nostalgia.[66] The emphasis on memory as a necessary act becomes complicated with the project of doing so through Shakespearean language at a predominantly white theater. The flashback narrative personalized the story so that it did not attempt to stand in for a history of the Californios per se, which is a risk of false historicity that cultural adaptations take, especially when depicting a less-familiar time period.[67] For Williamson, the trope of remembrance fostered an affective precision in feelings, not historical or linguistic accuracy. But Hispanic culture presented a desire and ability to "conjure" up its own past through the invocation of language, with reliving pain as part of the process of healing. The Nurse spoke the last two lines of the play, which in Shakespeare's script belong to the Prince, "For never was a story of more woe / Than this of Juliet and her Romeo,"[68] as a final reminder to the audience that she was the storyteller. OSF not only staged an ethnic concept setting and cast the lead roles with Latinx actors, but also shifted the narrative perspective to a woman of color, through the act of conjuring (invocation), and did so through auditory elements.

SOUNDING ETHNICITY

What resulted from OSF's concept stagings of both plays was a disjunction between the strategies for the visual and aural experience of Latinidad and Hispanidad. In *Measure for Measure*, the Latinx characters all spoke English with scarcely or no Spanish accent, and they all spoke Spanish as well; every Latinx character was portrayed by a Latinx actor, thus permitting Latinidad to be discerned aurally as well as visually. In *Romeo and Juliet*, Molina and Escalante likewise did not utilize a Spanish inflection to signal ethnicity or culture, yet other Hispanic characters, played by both Latinx and non-Latinx actors, did do so. The audience was thus asked to note ethnicity through visual signifiers for some characters and through aural signifiers for other characters, and was asked to determine which signifiers to use for each character/actor. Indeed, at the Capulet ball, Tybalt's statement that he recognizes Romeo—"This, by his voice, should be a Montague"[69]— was changed to "This, by my soul, shall be a Montague."[70] This change to the script signals for the audience that there is no aural distinction between Tybalt and Romeo, that they are unified aurally through their Hispanic heritage and ethnicity. In Shakespeare's play, the two young men are both Veronese but reveal an aural differentiation, an individuality permitted within a racially and ethnically homogeneous upper-class society. In OSF's production, the soundscape dominated throughout, invoking an affective ethnicity through various aural features.

Ultimately, auralidad functions as an affective register for Latinx agency to subvert Shakespearean linguistic hegemony. Accents and the Spanish language were used to signal a shared cultural background and to demonstrate familial ties in *Measure for Measure*; in *Romeo and Juliet*, they marked generational change, the Montague boys' knowledge of bawdy slang, and intimate moments between the lovers. In foregrounding the aural as a marker of difference, between the Latinx characters and the multicultural society in the former and between the houses and the white government and military officers in the latter, Latinx Shakespeares enact a seismic shift in theatrical performance. Stuart Hall describes the "whole repertoire of imagery and visual effects through which 'difference' is represented at any one historical moment as a *regime of representation*."[71] Like Hall, with his focus on visual effects, most Shakespearean (and most theatrical) representations have traditionally employed visual semiotics. For example, Barbara Hodgdon notes that in Janet Suzman's famed 1987 *Othello*, the lead character was made "Black" through his gestures, as much as his color and attire.[72] Likewise, Margo Hendricks argues that racial identity has more to do with gesture than with language in her assessment of contemporary Shakespeare films.[73] But with Latinidad, the regime of representation is tied to the affect that is invoked through the auditory, including the wide scope of the soundscape. In *Measure for Measure*, Shakespeare's words in English proved unnecessary to conveying the given circumstances of several scenes, and in *Romeo and Juliet*, the exchange for his words with modern-day Spanish slang gave resonance to humor that is otherwise barely discernible to modern audiences. Staging Latinidad, which always includes an excess of the aural, subverts a dominant theatrical language that does not include words or ideas to depict Latinx: the language of Shakespeare.

In casting Latinidad in opposition to white Americans (*Romeo and Juliet*) or to a diverse society (*Measure for Measure*), these two OSF productions used the soundscape to foster a discernibility of Latinidad. For decades, the sound of Spanish and the Latinx body were perceived as disjunctive to Shakespearean language and stories. Any notions of a fixed Latinx identity to represent through Shakespeare, or through language from two distinct periods, confounds the possibilities of mimetic representation. It is through this linguistic impossibility of mimesis in Latinx Shakespeares that both productions engaged the soundscape to make Latinx recognizable for all audiences. Aural excess and a Latinx acoustemology for Shakespeare make evident that the soundscape is cross-temporal, and therefore Latinidad is too.

The unification of Latinx and Shakespeare demonstrates not just their compatibility, but a better understanding of both. Latinx, as a culture, temporality, and acoustemology is the narrative device that Shakespeare does not offer but that OSF staged via Las Colibrí in *Measure for Measure* and the Nurse's conjured flashback frame in *Romeo and Juliet*. Shakespeare's plays have the capacity to integrate with Latinidad in all of these ways due to the spaces in the poetry, or what Paula Vogel describes as an epic form, or "linear with gaps," and scholar Emma Smith calls "gappiness."[74] This openness permits space for the very liminality that is necessary for Latinidad to be present. The back-to-back productions at OSF demonstrate how Shakespeare can be interpreted with, not simply for, Latinx culture; they illustrate Latinidad as a method of interpretation.

HEARING ETHNICITY

While there are never cohesive viewing experiences across audience members, Latinx Shakespearean productions offer an example of how varied experiences with the soundscape can challenge the visual strategies of theater for the theatrical recognition of race and ethnicity. For audiences to attune to Latinidad, they must negotiate their experience with Latinx cultures and the Spanish language with their own experiences and position. Jon Rossini attests that ethnicity is constructed by the spectator,[75] and the dramaturgical elements used to foster the perception and discernment of Latinidad vary across theaters and audiences. How we hear is subjective and based on numerous factors outside what is presented on the stage. Sound theorist Ross Brown notes, "The categories of aural dramaturgy . . . are not fixed but determined in the cultured ear of the listener. Here, then, we come to aurality, the subjective phenomenology of hearing."[76] Audience members bring with them their cultural backgrounds, experiences, biases, and corporeal abilities for listening. The concept of aurality points to one of the underlying questions of Latinx Shakespeares: who is Latinidad being performed for, and to what effect on the Shakespearean stage? At Oregon Shakespeare Festival, the audience was wealthy and highly educated, but this does not equate to fluency in Spanish, familiarity with semibilingual theater, or recognition of nonwhite cultural references.[77] For the monolingual English-speaking audience, the dialogue in Spanish could become a form of white noise, or rather a Brown noise—the reprieve granted by an unfamiliar foreign language spoken by Latinx and Hispanic characters that offers an aural respite from the taxing high poetry in English of Shakespeare. For audience members conversant in Spanish, Spanish offered greater access to points of humor, intimacy, and tertiary characters. Alicia Arrizón notes, "In society as a whole, language serves both to differentiate power from culture and to interweave the two."[78] The soundscape of Latinx Shakespeares exemplifies this for the theater.

Shakespearean actors are known for their virtuosity of speech, and Latinx language play is key to identity. These two productions, staged back to back at the country's largest repertory theater, depicted American culture at two distinct periods, 130 years apart. More importantly, they represented the United States as it is and has always been: multilingual. Because representations of Latinidad are so heavily marked by language, they make for a ripe encounter with Shakespeare. The mixing of Elizabethan English and modern-day Spanish makes a crack in the temporal border, creating a liminal space that allows an opening for language justice, or "the right everyone has to communicate in the language in which [they] feel most comfortable."[79] The language play and the foregrounding of Spanish alongside Shakespeare foster this sense of justice because, in the words of Alfred Arteaga, the Spanish "undercuts claims of prevalence, centrality, and superiority, and confirms the condition of heteroglossia. It draws the monologue into dialogue. In short, it dialogizes the authoritative discourse."[80]

The aural pathway fights linguistic hegemony and expands ideas about identity, and it does so through the creativity of the theater. Because Latinx Shakespeares involve a soundscape, and therefore an ethnicity, outside of a singular temporality, the audience must use creativity to make meaning.[81] Ross Brown writes, "If sound is elemental to theatre, as a building and a live event, then acoustemology is fundamental to dramaturgy, which deals with meaning and must therefore understand that audiences *know* sound only as they are culturally equipped to."[82] If the predominantly white audiences at OSF were new to attending to a Latinx soundscape, both productions accentuated the aural with the more theatrically familiar visual language of Catholic and Indigenous religiosity. After *Measure for Measure* and *Romeo and Juliet*, OSF would not return to Latinx Shakespeares until 2019 with *La Comedia of Errors* (see chapter 5), but the sound, the visuality, and stories and histories of Latinidad permeated their theaters. As Latinx Shakespeares are mounted more at smaller theaters and Latinx theaters, the emphasis on auralidad expands to be more inclusive of Indigenous and other languages, amplifying the aural excess, and in other instances is integrated with an acoustic that extends Latinidad to wider conceptions of Brownness. It is auralidad that opens up the policed category of Latinx to wider communities. Our means for hearing Latinidad change through the very action of challenging the parameters that define it. The next chapter explores an expansion of Latinx into Brownness and what conceiving of community beyond the government-based parameters of race and ethnicity means to Latinx cultures, and for the very notion of identity categories.

THREE

Identity

Remapping Latinidades

In 1997, *Icarus and Aria* (dir. Aaron Beall), Kirk Wood Bromley's adaptation of *Romeo and Juliet*, premiered at the Nuyorican Poets Café at the first Fringe NYC. The play makes Icarus Alzaro (Romeo) a wealthy and successful Latino quarterback for the Arizona Aztechs, while Aria (Juliet) is the white daughter of the owner of the team. The role of Icarus's brother Primalo— whose nickname, Cochise, recalls the Chirichua Apache leader of the same name who fought bravely in the Apache wars—was notably played not by a Latinx actor but by Filipino actor Joshua Spafford, whom the *New York Times* later described having "a mania, mordancy and merriment unseen since the death of Raul Julia."[1] Three years after this premiere, Spafford was cast as the lead in a production of *Othello* (dir. Jonathan Bank) for the National Asian American Theatre Company (NAATCO). Spafford, who can read as white to many audiences, was visibly set apart from Filipino Joel de la Fuente (Iago), Hawaiian Tina Horii (Desdemona), and the remainder of the diverse Asian cast. Spafford's "ethnic ambiguity," a term overused and underinterrogated in casting practices, has thus resulted in his portrayal of a range of characters from ethnic and racial backgrounds. As Anthony Christian Ocampo writes in his book *The Latinos of Asia*, Filipinx occupy a state of in-betweenness much like that traditionally assigned to Latinx: "They are neither black nor white; rather, they have vacillated between identifying with Asian American and Latino communities. Filipinos know they are considered Asian, but the cultural residuals of their Spanish colonial past—their surnames, their foods, their strict Catholicism— cannot be ignored either."[2] Spafford can play both an Indigenous-Latinx character in a Latinx Shakespearean production and the foreign and Othered Othello in an Asian American Shakespearean production. Such vacillation and casting flexibility raise the question of how racial and ethnic categories intersect if some can be so easily traversed.[3]

Latinx theater and performance scholars theorize Latinidad as a network of relationships grounded in heritage and an aesthetic rooted in certain creative practices, modes of engagement, and perspectives rather than a fixed identity to be represented through such signifiers as the Spanish language, life on the border, and assimilation motifs. Jon Rossini argues, "If we understand ethnicity not as a category of representation, but, rather, as a process or mode of thinking and creative activity, then we have to shift the very terms through which we take the idea of identity for granted."[4] Likewise, playwright Georgina Escobar—whose oeuvre includes both Latinx and non-Latinx themes and characters—details the "harmony of spirit, global mindfulness, acute body politic, and a fully human approach to otherness . . . [that] makes up my Mexican aesthetic—and perhaps, that is what makes my work Latinx."[5] Such understandings of Latinidad are ambiguous and elastic, resisting easy categorization or compartmentalization. This elasticity can simultaneously prove productive for artists and uncomfortable for audiences who have certain expectations of theatrical and mimetic representation of Latinx.

In contrast to Rossini and Escobar, José Esteban Muñoz shifts his focus from the unifier of Latinidad to one of "brownness." Like Rossini, Muñoz looks to Latinx-authored and Latinx-themed theater and performance as case studies, but he imagines parameters that extend beyond the limitations of given categories. Muñoz distinguishes between "feeling brown," a way of living (*manera de ser*), and a "sense of brown," or the recognition of the commonality of subjugated people. For Rossini, Escobar, and Muñoz, the emphasis on process, aesthetics, and affect, respectively, is not a call for redrawing parameters of ethnic categories but rather a challenge to the very use of identity as a category.

In this chapter, I examine three Latinx Shakespearean adaptations that center Filipinx, Afro-Latinx, and Indigenous characters and dramaturgically incorporate themes of immigration, anti-Blackness within Latinx communities, and colonialism, respectively. Coeurage Theatre's 2016 production of *Twelfth Night* (dir. Kate Jopson) included Tagalog-speaking Filipinx Viola and Sebastian as new immigrants to Los Angeles. Alex Alpharaoh's 2019 *Othello* adaptation, *O-Dogg: An Angeleno Take on "Othello"*, positions the story within the 1992 Los Angeles uprisings, with the Othello character as Afro-Latinx and Desdemona as the daughter of a Korean shopkeeper. In José Cruz González's *Invierno*, an adaptation of *The Winter's Tale* that premiered in 2009, the action shifts between two nineteenth-century Californio ranches, with Paulina and Hermione as members of the Indigenous Chumash tribe who speak Samala. All three plays are set in and were first performed in California, a state that, as of 2020, was 39 percent Hispanic/Latinx.[6]

These adaptations extend beyond merely serving as vehicles for a desired mimetic representation. Together, they force a critical conversation about Latinx *culture*—both the way of life of Latinx and the artistic practice and intellectual activity of Latinx[7]—and an expanded idea of Brownness. "Brownness," as theorized by Muñoz, is not a culture but a wider network of feeling and way of life within a culture that values whiteness.[8] The distinction between Latinidad, indicative of the heterogeneous cultures of those in the United States who share political and social histories, and Brownness, suggestive of the relationship of those who experience a similar unsettled relationship to whiteness, illuminates the aesthetic differences and activist consequences between integrating Latinidad, versus Brownness, into Shakespeare. While each of these adaptations builds on specific ethnic and geographic histories, I am interested in their potential to communicate Brownness: how they are both generative of categorically discrete Latinidades, and how they speak to one another within the network of Brownness.

I will address the Latinx thread within these productions where multiple cultures encounter each other in order to parse out how Brownness can function within the diverse environments of each play. I argue that by drawing on canonical stories that exclude Brown people—in this case, Shakespeare—these productions offer the possibility not just of remapping Latinidad for the theater, but of remapping the very parameters by which Latinidad is defined. The process of remapping is key to shifting from a representation of a cohesive identity category to an exploration of Brown aesthetics and affect, from a perceived genre of Latinx storytelling to a process or way of being.

Brown aesthetics and affect move away from mimesis to offer a relational network of Brown peoples. Because Brownness is relational, it is in flux, elastic, and therefore not monolithic in opposition to whiteness. Brownness as frame of reference permits an evaluation of the historical relationship of Brown peoples to each other, and to whiteness, that is older than Latinx as a category and community. In most of Shakespeare's plays that contain an ethnic or racial Other, the character is isolated, such as Othello, Aaron the Moor in *Titus Andronicus*, the Welsh Lady Mortimer in *Henry IV, Part I*, and the suitors Morocco and Aragon in *The Merchant of Venice*. These individual representations enable stereotypes and cannot depict the shared experience of feeling Brown. The three Latinx Shakespeares in this chapter offer community and commonality where Shakespeare does not, remapping several Othered characters to a wider scope of Brownness. This collectivist logic pushes against Shakespeare's character-based individualism to depict Brown communities. Brownness functions as a form of activism to remap the racial categorization that offers Black and white as discrete poles and make an Other of Brown.

A FILIPINX *TWELFTH NIGHT* IN LOS ANGELES

Coeurage Theatre in North Hollywood advertises itself as "LA's Pay What You Want Theatre," and its vision statement describes a theater that "continually lifts up artistic voices from the global majority, provides equitable access to theater, reaches traditionally underserved audiences and explores new storytelling languages."[9] It is perhaps no surprise, then, that for Coeurage Theatre's 2016 production of *Twelfth Night*, director Kate Jopson chose to focus her adaptation on themes of immigration, linguistic isolation, and violence toward people of color, centering Filipinx characters in a play that also encompasses Latinx. Jopson's production takes story lines that audiences might expect to see with Latinx characters and instead centers Filipinx. In a 2009 report on language diversity in Los Angeles County, 4.0 million people stated that English was their primary language, 3.3 million claimed Spanish, 288,000 Chinese, and 196,000 Tagalog.[10] Although the drop-off from English and Spanish to Chinese and Tagalog is steep, Tagalog is the fourth most-spoken language in Los Angeles, and the Filipinx population comprises more immigrants than does Los Angeles's Latinx population, making Jopson's concept apropos of a cultural group that often gets overshadowed by Latinx but shares experiences of colonial histories, immigration, and racism.[11] Oftentimes when Brown characters are depicted, they are homogeneous in background and language; here Jopson created what could be considered a multicultural Shakespearean production but what I deem a Latinx Shakespearean production because of the deliberate extension of Brownness in a Los Angeles setting.

For Shakespeare's tale of the washed-ashore Viola, who must disguise herself in a new land, Jopson chose to accentuate the feeling of being lost as the root of the piece, and she began developing her concept with the Viola and Malvolio characters.[12] The former was portrayed as Filipina, her desire to find a new life tied to the statistics of the high rate of female indentured servitude as an export of the Philippines.[13] Malvolio, the social-climbing servant to Lady Olivia, was portrayed as a first-generation Brazilian, a character attempting to erase his own culture, by an actor who had just come to Los Angeles from Brazil a few years earlier. Count Orsino, who is infatuated with the idea of love, was portrayed as a first-generation Indian, "the son of immigrants who pushed him to succeed" and an admirer of the white, paparazzi-hounded blonde Olivia.[14] Antonio, the man who cares for Viola's thought-to-be-deceased twin brother Sebastian, was depicted as a Black Jamaican fisherman with a thick accent, "who has been branded a Pirate by the Illyrian government."[15] Olivia's serving-woman Maria was Black and "came to Illyria as an adult to escape a bad marriage and make money,"[16] and the foppish character Andrew was white and had a gay affect, replete with an effeminate exit and hand wave. The diversity of Los Angeles and the large number of people in the entertainment industry meant that Jopson was able to develop the theme and dramaturgy even before she had cast the play. Her production was not intended to be an "accurate" depiction of Los Angeles, but it did reflect some of its demographic diversity; like many contemporary Shakespearean productions, it offered a mirror to the audience through a familiar story. The production adhered to Shakespeare's text with little modification throughout.

Performances of *Twelfth Night* began outdoors, outside of the theater space, with the audience standing near a nighttime baseball field with a game in progress. A yellow Volkswagen bus pulled up, and a woman and man had a quick exchange in Tagalog. Then the woman said, "And what should I do in Illyria? / My brother he is in Elysium."[17] After this moment of English-language dialogue, Viola immediately returned to speaking Tagalog with the Captain and paid him for the transport. At that point, he violently pushed her against the van and himself against her, although she was able to fend him off. Moments later, while she was still shaking, a man with a music case and harmonica began to speak with her. The production, then, began not with Orsino's excess but with Viola's dislocation, and the Sea Captain—the character who, in Shakespeare's play, finds Viola on the shore and kindly offers to disguise her—is now the trafficker who has brought Viola to this country. Feste, the Fool (and the approaching musician in this opening scene) takes on the Captain's role of aiding and disguising Viola.

After Feste agreed to conceal her, she offered to sing, and he handed her a guitar. She played and sang the chorus and one verse of Jason Mraz's song "Plane," conveying through the lyrics her love for her lost brother and, through extended lines in English, her character's bilingualism. This sequence made clear to the audience that this Viola will demonstrate her musical ability, unlike in Shakespeare's play, offering another affective mode for communication and character. After the song, the audience was escorted by Feste toward the theater. As attendees headed toward its doors, Olivia, a thin blonde woman followed by a crowd of gawkers and the press, made her way through the crowd as her handlers, including Malvolio, shooed people away. As the audience entered the dark indoor theater, Feste sang in Spanish, while Viola accompanied him on guitar; Orsino's voice began, "If music be the food of love, play on," and the lights came up onstage.[18]

Music became the affective medium for a network between the linguistically diverse characters, and Feste, Shakespeare's most musical Fool, its arbiter. Music ran throughout, from Feste's and Viola's acoustic rhythms to prerecorded sounds, Andrew's and Toby's electric guitar riffs inspired by The Clash, songs in Spanish and piano playing from Feste, and French background music in one scene. Feste is described as "Androgynous. Likes to keep his/her origins unknown,"[19] and "a conduit between cultures and classes, slipping into different languages as needed."[20] This easy shifting between musical styles was emblematic of the linguistic shifts onstage where the characters could switch languages and understand others with ease. The language and accents were just as varied as the musical styles.

The adaptation included a total of seven languages to mirror the complex aural experience of Los Angeles's diversity. The actor playing Malvolio helped Jopson translate the Portuguese passages, and her Filipina relatives helped with the Tagalog. While recognizing that no single individual contains sufficient linguistic fluency to negotiate this adaptation, the desire for linguistic multiplicity reflects the larger heterogeneity of Los Angeles's existence. When I asked her why there was one phrase in Swedish, Jopson responded as those of us who live in between languages do: "I'm Swedish." This sense of existing between languages provides a crucial framing of the immigrant experience as in-between and reflects how that paradigm frames a city such as Los Angeles, in which 34 percent of the population is foreign-born.[21] At the same time, language becomes a means of both real and manufactured connection. When Feste as Sir Topas visited Malvolio in the makeshift prison, Feste spoke Portuguese to him, which, when the deception was later revealed, created a sense of deep betrayal for Malvolio at the way his home language was used against him. When Viola and Sebastian reunited, they shifted to their home language of Tagalog to signal their connection.[22]

While Jopson largely retained Shakespeare's text, she did make two significant alterations at the end of the play, not only tempering the joyous resolution of the comedy, but insisting on the vulnerability that accompanies immigrant status. First, in a striking departure from both Shakespeare's play and performance traditions, Orsino did not propose to Viola after she revealed that the male Cesario was a disguise. Instead, he sat alone for several minutes, contemplating this discovery. The burden of that information physically weighed on him, but eventually he approached

Viola and chatted with her, and the two left holding hands, suggesting that they might still find happiness together, albeit not the immediate and unreserved happiness of Shakespeare's play. And in so doing, they implicitly reminded the audience of the contingent power of a marital contract to advance an immigrant's quest for citizenship. More dire was the fate of Antonio, Sebastian's friend, who ends Shakespeare's play isolated from the couples and oftentimes staged as an outsider to society, but free from imprisonment. In Jopson's play, actors dressed as US Immigration and Customs Enforcement (ICE) officers entered from the back of the theater through the audience and escorted Antonio offstage in handcuffs, and seemingly out of the theater to prison. This was immediately followed by Orsino and Viola leaving, and the play ended as Shakespeare's does, with Feste on stage alone singing, "But that's all one, our play is done, / And we'll strive to please you every day."[23] The violence that bookends the play, Viola's arrival and Antonio's arrest, demonstrates immigrant precarity as it intersects with race, nationality, immigration status, gender, and sexuality. Shakespeare's Viola can safely arrive in a distant land and be aided by a man without an intended assault, and Antonio may engage in a strong homosocial, or perhaps homosexual, affection with Sebastian. But in Jopson's play, their status as immigrants makes them susceptible to sexual violence for the former and physical violence for the latter, even among a racially and ethnically diverse community of characters.

While the production's final moments were poignant for the Los Angeles audience, the choice to center Filipinx characters as immigrants and deport a Jamaican character challenges the dominant conversations in Los Angeles about immigration, nearly all of which are associated with Latinx. Jopson invoked Brazilian, Filipinx, and Jamaican characters to create a story about immigration that dramaturgically and affectively invokes a wider network of Brownness; by extending the soundscape to seven languages and a vast range of musical styles and the often-dramatized Latinx experience of immigration to other Brown and Black characters, Jopson invoked a sense of Brown.[24] A sense of brown is not about "enacting a brown commons but rather of knowing a Brownness that is our commonality."[25] This Brownness cuts across ethnicity, race, language, and national origin to reveal the shared experience of violence that unites the characters.

O-DOGG: ETHNICIZING A "RACE" PLAY

In 2019, spoken-word artist Alex Alpharaoh began staged readings of his new play *O-Dogg: An Angeleno Take on "Othello"*, which he describes as an "ode to street culture of the city of LA, that is diminishing."[26] *O-Dogg* is written in verse, with some rhyming couplets and plenty of slang and profanity. The play, which is set during the six days of the 1992 Los Angeles uprisings—traditionally referred to as the LA Riots, following the Rodney King verdict—employs hip hop rhythms and style, street language, and a diverse cast of characters in order to explicitly take up intra-Latinx colorism, anti-Blackness, and misogyny.[27] *O-Dogg* dwells on how feeling Brown (having a shared experience of street culture) did not give way to a sense of Brown (community-based on the commonalities of oppression) during a heightened moment of racial relations.

Unlike in *Othello*, all the characters in *O-Dogg* occupy positions of precarity and are threatened by the dominant culture, a threat of violence that plays out when Eye-G and Cash-O are chased by police dogs and then pressure hosed.[28] O-Dogg is the Afro-Latino leader of a street graffiti crew, and Eye-G (Iago) is the racially Indigenous Latinx shot caller of the group. O-Dogg has just married Da-Eun Pak (Desdemona), or Desireé "Dez" Park, a Korean American who is the daughter of the owner of a local liquor store in Koreatown. Cash-O (Cassio) is Muslim, Rowdy (Roderigo) is a Latinx entrepreneur from a wealthy area, and the additional character, Donna Jones, is an African American radio personality who narrates the progression of the uprisings throughout.[29] In the play's centering of an Afro-Latinx character and relegating of non-Latinx Blackness to the auditory periphery through Donna's radio broadcasts, the sense of Brown of street culture that is depicted includes a diverse group of people of color outside of the Black (here African American) / white binary that dominates much of US culture and history. The interracial relationships within Los Angeles also play out when Jay Park, or Ye-Jun Pak (Brabantio, Desdemona's father), blames the death of his wife on O-Dogg: Jay (who plays a much larger role in this play than in Shakespeare's) had left his store to spend time with the racially Black O-Dogg, and during that time, she was killed by a Black man who robbed the store.[30]

Alpharaoh's play can be historicized through the genealogy of Los Angeles's 1943 Zoot Suit Riots, which were largely based on the Sleepy Lagoon murder trial, in which Latinos were incarcerated en masse, and the 1965 Watts Rebellion (or Watts Riots), which primarily focused on white violence and oppression toward African American communities. By the time of the staged readings in later 2020, *O-Dogg* was also communicating across temporal moments by speaking back to the uprisings that had taken place throughout the country in response to the May 2020 murder of George Floyd and the centuries of violence faced by Black and Indigenous communities and people of color (BIPOC). The Rodney King beating was one of the first video recordings of police brutality to "go viral," before going viral was made possible by the internet and social media. Alpharaoh includes a voice-over of Rodney King's now legendary call for unity, "Can we all get along?"[31] to call for peace in Los Angeles after the verdict acquitting the white police officers who beat him. The cyclical pattern of racism, violence, uprisings, calls for peace, and more police brutality continues through today, and Alpharaoh's play is simultaneously enmeshed in a specific historical event and set within the lengthy narrative of racism.

The Los Angeles uprisings led to widespread damage to property: the more than two thousand Korean-owned businesses that were damaged accounted for more than 40 percent of the total one billion dollars' worth of damage during the six days of uprisings.[32] Relations between the Black community and Korean shopkeepers had intensified with the death of fifteen-year-old African American Latasha Harlins, who was shot in 1991 by a Korean American convenience store owner who perceived that she was stealing. The videotape of the shooting was shown widely on television networks, and although shopkeeper Soon Ja Du was convicted of voluntary manslaughter, she was only sentenced to probation and a fine. Alpharaoh's choice to make Desdemona Korean American and the daughter of a shopkeeper forces not just racial division but a contemporary economic and violent context into Othello's marriage. Along with other incidents and killings in this vein, tensions were amplified by the recession of 1991 that hit the African American community much harder than the Korean American community and by the high number of stores owned by Koreans and Korean Americans in an area that was predominantly Black. During the Los Angeles uprisings, much as would be done years later after George Floyd's murder, stores were painted with the designation "Black Owned" as a signal for BIPOC communities to protect them from theft and damage from looters, and from damage by the police. O-Dogg offers to protect Jay's store by marking it "Black Owned," but La Patí (a female Lodovico) replies, "You know you can't make that call, you ain't black." O-Dogg responds, "What'chu know about Nicaraguans?" and she replies, "Nothing. 'Cept, they ain't Black Americans. / Even if they did come here as a kid."[33] Her viewpoint encapsulates intra-Latinx anti-Blackness.

While La Patí views O-Dogg as insufficiently Black, Eye-G takes the opposite perspective, seeing O-Dogg's Latinx identity as not authentic because of his Blackness. Eye-G, whose skin color is Brown, refers to O-Dogg as "the Negro"[34] and says to Rowdy: "I hate fake raza much as you love Dez."[35] O-Dogg, who describes himself as a "latino-negro," sums up his racial and ethnic in-betweenness when he tells La Patí, "I'm too black to run latin crews, although / Now i'm not black enough to claim 'Black Owned'?"[36] O-Dogg's Afro-Latinx heritage leaves him in between the politics of Black and Latinx, informed by a societal lack of understanding of the heterogeneity of Latinidad, a political landscape that pits people of color against one another, and racial and ethnic categories that are viewed as distinct. Afro-Latinidad is rarely represented onstage because Black Latinx contrast with mainstream and Hollywood conceptions of both Latinx and Black cultures. This is a problem of both representation and identity categories, and it is true not just within theater but in the arts writ large.

Dominican studies scholars have addressed and theorized Latinx anti-Blackness for decades,[37] arguing that anti-Blackness is systemic and historical, key to the formation of a Latin America in response to the imperialism of the United States.[38] Lorgia García-Peña states, "In the diaspora, the logic of colonial racial capitalism divides Black people based on national and ethnic identities. . . . It obliterates the fact that Blackness and anti-Blackness transcend national identity. . . . It divides and it reproduces oppression."[39] This is a key part of the critique of unifying ethnic categories such as Latinx and Latinidad (see the introduction): "Like the colonial project of mestizaje, 'Latinidad' reinforces a commonsense of whiteness that omits Blackness from the Latinx experience."[40] Only since the murder of George Floyd in the summer of 2020 has anti-Blackness within Latinx communities been addressed on a more public scale. To address Brownness is to confront the colorism that informs white Latinx as the standard image of Latinx peoples, and it acknowledges Indigenous and mestizo heritage. Alpharaoh transposes the experience of the liminal Othello, who is both Othered and a general, Moor and converted Christian, to O-Dogg, who is Black and Latinx, an Angeleno and a foreigner, to theatricalize how society is constrained by and dependent upon these categories.

Because of his in-betweenness, O-Dogg attempts to call on a sense of Brown within the BIPOC community. Unlike Shakespeare's Othello, O-Dogg is surrounded by ethnic and racial Others, and he attempts to cross these categories in the name of community. He tries to relate to Jay through their respective pasts, saying, "Jay, we're both kids of mistresses / Who lost our mothers after they got sick. / We both immigrated, built businesses."[41] But the similar experiences cannot overpower Jay's internalized racism. Once he becomes aware of Jay's animosity toward him, O-Dogg fears that his wife might be anti-Black like her father: "Maybe Eye-G is right. Maybe she would / Play me without hesitation because / I'm dark and remind her of the man who / Killed her mother."[42] Anti-Blackness is something he has

Figure 5: Luis Kelly-Duarte as O-Dogg and Hester Jean Lee as Dez in *O-Dogg, an Angeleno Take on "Othello"* by Alex Alpharaoh. Photo by Julianna Stephanie Ojeda. Courtesy of Alex Alpharaoh.

encountered within the Latinx community through Eye-G and La Patí, from his own father-in-law, who is a person of color, and in society; in this context, it is not a surprising leap for him to question whether his wife harbors anti-Black sentiments as well. Aside from being Latinx and currently living in downtown Los Angeles, the members of their crew are not especially bonded. O-Dogg emigrated from Nicaragua, Cash-O is "south-side / Went to Venice High,"[43] and Rowdy is the "rich kid from Arlington Heights"[44] who went to college with Dez. *O-Dogg* initially calls on a wider notion of a sense of Brown extending across the diversity of BIPOC; but as the story line unfolds, it is clear that there is none of Muñoz's "feeling brown" here, merely further ethnic and racial strife.

But Dez doesn't inherit her father's racism. In fact, she is the only character who consistently addresses racism head on. When the radio announcer says, "I guess enough / Is enough when asians kill others asians, / But black and brown boys get hunted daily,"[45] Dez says, "Donna should be careful with that bias / Bullshit."[46] Dez is the most honest character in the play, but she is always silenced, a subordinate figure in an oppressed community. When Dez enters the liquor store with her father and O-Dogg, the stage directions specify that "neither men [sic] acknowledge her."[47] As an educated, light-skinned Asian woman, she is able to maneuver within the diversity of the Latinx street crew, but she is still subject to misogyny and is suspected of being anti-Black. Alpharaoh's decision to have the Brabantio role throughout the play permits O-Dogg's descent into isolation to be traced through the loss of rapport with a non-Latinx, non-Black male of color. It also contributes an added force to Dez's isolation from the (male) world. Shakespeare's Desdemona, as the daughter of a senator, speaks confidently and is regarded highly by the outer society at the start of the play, making her transition into an obedient wife, one who is slapped and then strangled, all the more marked. Alpharaoh's Dez never holds a central position in society.

In opposition to Dez, who is educated yet consistently disempowered, the fully white-passing Lourdes owns her own business, a bar, and acts as mentor to her. Dez reminds her father of his own prejudice, saying,

> You approved of my friends if they were white,
> But the only white people here are cops.
> You didn't give me a hard time with Lourdes,
> Because you assumed things based on her looks.
> She's latina, Appa.[48]

Lourdes (Emilia) is a white Latina, with blonde hair and blue eyes, the sister (rather than wife) of Eye-G. Her ability to "pass" for white (non-Latinx) allowed her to be welcomed into Jay's circle of aspirational white adjacency. While Lourdes meets the same fate as her Shakespearean counterpart, Emilia, Alpharaoh's adaptation makes Lourdes a successful, independent, legitimate business owner to comment on the power of whiteness, or the perception of whiteness, over education as means for social mobility. Lourdes suggests a short trip for her and Dez so that Dez can get away from the uprisings and O-Dogg's sudden change of behavior and jealousy toward her. O-Dogg sees Dez packing her clothes and assumes the action to be confirmation of her infidelity. He strangles and kills her, and Eye-G shoots and kills Lourdes after she reveals his role in giving the bandana (Othello's handkerchief) to Cash-O and therefore his plotting against O-Dogg. O-Dogg goes to Jay's store, which Jay himself has marked "Black-owned," not to show unity with the Black community but to align himself with a racial group that has achieved power in the current moment. O-Dogg makes his peace with Jay and then strangles him to death. Shakespeare's Brabantio is disappointed in his daughter's choice of spouse and then disappears for the remainder of the story; here Jay survives her and is killed in the same way by her spouse at the play's end, making O-Dogg doubly murderous and affirming Jay's death through violent racism, whereas in Shakespeare's play it is merely referenced that Desdemona's "match was mortal to him."[49] The play closes with O-Dogg setting fire to Jay's store and then remaining in the store to defend it—or perhaps himself—and failing in his retaliation. He fights to the end: "Banging on the door of the liquor store / can be heard with sounds of sirens and a megaphone / yelling commands. The door bursts open, O-Dogg picks / up his 45 and begins to shoot."[50]

The first reading of *O-Dogg*, in August 2019, was directed by Julianna Stephanie Ojeda for A Noise Within theater in Pasadena for its New Original Works (NOW) festival. Ojeda wanted to convey a sense of the chaos from 1992 through theatrical form; she had the actors throw each page after they read it, so there was paper all over the stage by the end of the reading.[51] As each character died, the actor put their music stand horizontally on the floor. A series of readings followed: in September 2019 as a collaboration with SP!T: Spoken Word Theatre (Los Angeles), Atlantic Pacific Theatre in New York, and Hi-Arts NYC in Harlem; in September 2020 via Zoom through the Garry Marshall Theatre for its New Works Festival Series in Burbank; and in October 2020 via Zoom as part of the New Works Festival at Roy and Edna Disney / Cal Arts Theatre (REDCAT) in Los Angeles.[52] The intersecting pandemics of Covid-19 and racial inequality affected, respectively, both the possibility of staging the show and its poignancy. During the REDCAT production, toward the end, director Brisa Areli Muñoz lit a Virgen of Guadalupe candle. She spoke of healing as the camera panned to each of the actors, lighting their own candles.

Alpharaoh's goal was to use language and concept to make Shakespeare accessible to people of color and people of various languages: the demography of Los Angeles. Access here means exploring a wider scope of feeling Brown, a way of living and speaking that is realized in Los Angeles street culture. What the crew has in common is a counterculture stance toward white hegemony, expressed through graffiti, a visual art form that uninvitedly (and often illegally) changes the aesthetics of public space. It is a shared visual language, and their shared verbal language is the street slang they speak, which includes Korean, Spanish, and contemporary English. *O-Dogg* is a trilingual play, and one that depicts a community predicated on a visual art form to claim space in white US society. Shakespeare becomes accessible not just through Alpharaoh's English-to-English translation, but through the creation of characters who employ visual language the way Alpharaoh adapts Shakespeare.

Similar to Georgina Escobar, whose sense of the acute body politic of Mexican heritage informs her work, Alpharaoh draws from his experience in Los Angeles street culture to inform his dramaturgy, not just the setting of the play. Linguistically, this means that he found an entry point through Shakespeare's poetry as street slang and through the intersections of languages in Los Angeles; Alpharaoh is unapologetic about writing characters faithfully to how they speak.[53] O-Dogg and Dez affectionately refer to each other as "Mi Reyna de Los Angeles" and "Mi Rey,"[54] and Dez and Jay speak Malay for a moment and say farewell with "Salanghae."[55] Culturally, this means the people he depicts in the play are a heterogeneous group who are brought together at times through the way of living that is feeling Brown in white culture but who are not always connected otherwise. Their shared sense of Brown, of a commonality of subjugation, cannot be felt within the category of Latinx, as it is fractured based on skin color and race. The visual of color is a key element that separates Latinx from a shared experience, so that linguistic code-switching can function as the aural connective tissue. Outside of the story of the play, as people of color, his ensemble of spoken-word artists were not getting cast in Shakespeare, so he created the opportunity himself. For Shakespeare to be accessible to Alpharaoh as one who is Brown and Latinx, he had to remap it outside of identity categories linguistically and geographically, to Brownness.

Alpharaoh's *Othello* adaptation offers a theatrical closure similar to Shakespeare's play, but it leaves an unsettled identity resolution. Recognizing the character of Eye-G as an appreciation of a street life that Alpharaoh overcame offers a portion of that understanding; Alpharaoh was writing a show for his friends and about how theater saved him. But the world of interracial violence destroys not just O-Dogg, but everyone, and allows for the space to redraw the connective tissue between communities of color that have sometimes shared, and sometimes had distinct, experiences of being subjugated. As positions of power and familial relationships change throughout *O-Dogg*, the elasticity of Brownness does as well.

INVIERNO: A CENTRAL COAST VERSION OF THE WINTER'S TALE

As part of its 2009–10 season, PCPA Theaterfest Santa Maria (now PCPA Pacific Conservatory Theatre) presented an adaptation of *The Winter's Tale* called *Invierno*.[56] The play, which was directed by Mark Booher, is set in California's Central Coast, the same region where PCPA is located. Booher commissioned José Cruz González to write the adaptation.[57] Unlike *O-Dogg*, which challenges identity categories through racial differentiation among today's Latinx and Brown peoples in Los Angeles, *Invierno* turns toward the distant past, redrawing connections to the land and the layers of historical claims to it by depicting the diverse peoples of colonial California and recovering the Indigenous Samala language onstage. *Invierno* remaps Brownness across linguistic histories, through the invocation of Indigenous temporality, and through a connection to the land and the palimpsest of peoples who feel a tie to it.

The prelude to *Invierno* begins, "A winter night. A low fog hovers over the ground. A giant oak tree remains on stage. It is a sacred site. Carved into the tree is the shape of a woman. Old bottles hang from the tree's branches. A long red rope hangs from a branch."[58] The tradition of hanging bottles from a tree was brought to the Americas from Africa.[59] Although legends vary, it is generally thought that the bottles will catch evil spirits and trap them, that "Cobalt or multi-colored bottles were hanged on trees to reflect the sun's light and were believed to attract, capture, and contain evil spirits."[60] Their presence from the play's outset signals both the layers of colonization and oppression of various groups and the complicated heritage of the specific California locale. A woman is heard offstage, singing in Samala, the endangered language of the Chumash tribe whose land the modern-day town of Santa Maria was founded on.

The lights come on. A Young Woman is attempting to hang herself from the rope in the tree, but her boyfriend enters and stops her. She tells him that she is pregnant, he offers to marry her, and they argue. Then "a mysterious figure passes along the adobe walls."[61] When the Young Man asks, "Who's there?"[62] echoing the opening line of *Hamlet*, the Indigenous woman Paulina appears behind him. Frightened, he runs off, and Paulina replies, "No' ka 'eneq a saxtakʰiṭ" (I am Wind Woman).[63] Paulina informs the Young Woman that they are standing on sacred ground, where the "blood of the true and innocent" has been spilled.[64] When Paulina tells the Young Woman that she must awaken her faith through courage, the audience begins to hear Don León (Leontes) and Hermonia (Hermione) from offstage, and Paulina says, "The madness begins."[65]

Invierno is set in the early to mid-nineteenth century: the first half begins in 1831, the second half in 1848, on the precipice of the California Gold Rush.[66] It is written for a company of nine actors, seven of them doubled or tripled across roles. The Young Man and Woman double as Florentino and Perdida (Florizel and Perdita), the young lovers in the second act, respec-

tively, and the actress playing the Young Woman also plays the male character Maximino (Mamillius), the son of Don León (Leontes) and Hermonia
(Hermione). The doubling and tripling of parts allows the audience to
make connections between characters and across eras, from the past to the
present day. It also allows González to interweave races and ethnicities; the
Young Woman is designated by González as Latina, descended from but
not one of the Indigenous and Spanish peoples represented in the action of
the play. The character doubling, then, facilitates a meditation on the layers
of Latinx identity today and the irony of double colonization, by the Spanish and then the white settlers.[67] The changing notion of Latinx or Chicanx
is encapsulated in Luis Valdez's comments on Chicano: "It was a term that
referred to people on the wind, who were migrants. It was a transitional
reality, if you will. There's no nation, no Chicano nation so to speak."[68] The
ethnic group of Latinx and of Chicanx is in flux, and *Invierno* depicts both
its circularity and its evolution.

González's adaptation contains the same primary characters and plot as
Shakespeare's play: *The Winter's Tale* begins when Leontes, king of Sicily,
suspects that his wife, Hermione, has had an affair with his friend Polixenes, king of Bohemia. Leontes orders Camillo to poison Polixenes, but
Camillo warns him of Leontes's plot and rage, so they flee instead. Hermione is jailed for her supposed infidelity and gives birth to a baby girl,
which her friend Paulina brings to Leontes. The oracle decrees that Hermione and Polixenes are innocent, but Leontes holds to his belief. Mamillius,
the son of Leontes and Hermione, dies, and Hermione falls in a swoon and
is reported dead. Leontes abandons his new daughter, and Antigonus, Paulina's husband, leaves the baby Perdita in Bohemia. The baby is found by a
shepherd and his son. Time, as a character, enters to announce that sixteen
years have passed, and Polixenes's son Florizel will be wed to Perdita. Perdita comes to discover her birthright, and the statue that Leontes had commissioned of Hermione comes to life, restoring her and her union to a
repentant Leontes.

Invierno depicts the heterogeneity of cultures through its use of language, just as it does through its characters. There are song lyrics and dialogue in English, Spanish, Russian, and Samala, the ancient language spoken by the Santa Ynez Chumash Indigenous tribe. The play itself is an act
of recovery of an Indigenous language: "it was the first time that the language had been spoken in about one hundred years,"[69] and it may be the
first full-length play to feature Samala. González wanted the language
within the play to align with the communities he represented; he contacted
the cultural director at the Santa Ynez Band of Chumash Indians, Nakia

Zavalla, who translated González's dialogue from English to Samala. Although Leontes is Spanish and uses Spanish words, most of the dialogue is in English. Hermonia is Spanish and Chumash and speaks a few words in Samala, much more Spanish, and mostly English, but gives her baby a Spanish name, Alegría.[70]

At the outset, Don Patricio (Polixenes) has been at Don León's ranch but sets out to return to his own on the anniversary of his wife's death; Don León asks him to stay, but he declines. Yet when Hermonia immediately afterward convinces Don Patricio to stay, they speak entirely in Spanish. Don León interprets this shared linguistic moment as intimacy and becomes immediately jealous. The Irish Don Patricio has otherwise been welcomed into Californio culture, but when he uses the Spanish language as means of connectedness and calls Don León "hermano," León becomes even more suspicious of him. Hermonia's immediate support for Don Patricio causes a jealous man such as Don León to become more jealous; it is the additional layer of intimacy that Spanish provokes that wrongly solidifies Patricio's guilt. In Latinx Shakespeares, or any bilingual staging of English-dominant classics, the Spanish language may be used for humor, to designate generational change, ostracization, or in this case, intimacy.[71] Because Don Patricio is an Irishman who has learned Spanish, his use of language is both a product and a cause of his close relationships with the Spanish-descended rancheros, making it easily misinterpreted.

González remaps Brownness across diverse linguistic histories, making explicit the work of cross-temporal code-switching, or shifting between two distinct languages from different eras (see chapter 2). When Padre (a priest) attempts to speak to Don León with his findings of Hermonia's guilt, he speaks in Latin. Don León exclaims, "I don't speak Latin!" but the Young Man chimes in and becomes momentarily part of the action, saying, "I know some" and the Young Woman responds, "Altar Boy."[72] The Young Man translates for Don León, suggesting León's inability to speak Latin signals a waning of Catholic traditions and European heritage; by contrast, generations later, Latin is still associated with the church and studied by the Young Man for its very association with European white religious tradition. Yet to create a sense of continual, rather than linear time, the narrative perspective of the story comes from an Indigenous woman, Paulina, who crosses in and out of the action, from English to the extinct language of Samala.[73] She is given top billing in the list of characters and described as "our storyteller. A healer woman. Older half-sister of Hermonia."[74] At various moments, she (along with the Young Woman and the Young Man) watches the action from the present day rather than taking part in it[75] and

Figure 6: Cody Craven as Florentino, Leo Cortez as Afilado, and Sabrina Cavaletto as Perdida in *Invierno* by José Cruz González (dir. Mark Booher, 2009). Photo by Luis Escobar. Courtesy of PCPA—Pacific Conservatory Theatre.

has the ability to enter into the story at crucial moments. Paulina moves fluidly across time, demonstrating Mark Rifkin's claim "that Indigenous forms of time push against the imperatives of settler sovereignty."[76] Present and past weave throughout the play. After Maximino dies (and his mother, Hermonia, supposedly does too), León wraps the red rope from the tree around his own neck in the same manner as the Young Woman at the outset of the play but is prevented from committing suicide by the Young Woman's intervention. Indeed, chronological time differs from the Indigenous sense of the continual.[77]

Although Shakespeare writes a character named "Time," the presence of the character and the large leap forward in years do not complicate the linear narrative. By contrast, in González's play, Indigenous presence serves as a necessary shift in conventional storytelling and history. After Don León holds a pistol to Caspian's (Camillo's) head, ordering him to give Don Patricio a glass of wine that Don León has poisoned, the Young Woman crosses into the action to warn Don Patricio. It is through the Young Woman's interjection that his life is spared (though he will be exiled), and Caspian begs Don Patricio's forgiveness and tells him that Don León suspects that Don Patricio had an affair with Hermonia. Since the actress plays three roles—Young Woman, Maximino, and Perdida—it is unclear from whom Don Patricio receives this warning, as if the Young Woman descendent of the future is able to change her family's historical past.[78] At the end of the scene, Caspian directly addresses the Young Woman, asking, "How did you know?" to which she replies, "The eyes of men never lie."[79] In the following scene, Paulina and the Young Woman speak as narrators of the future, but Paulina folds into the past and speaks with her sister Hermonia. When Hermonia addresses the Young Woman as Maximino, it becomes clear that the character is simultaneously both the Young Woman and Maximino, but not either in full. When Hermonia addresses the Young Woman as Maximino, Paulina interjects, "Answer her." The Young Woman says, "She's not my mother"—making clear that in this moment she is *not* Maximino—and Paulina responds, "She needs you . . . and so do I."[80] The clear biological tie is not the point; rather, the audience must consider the coeval presence of Indigenous peoples simultaneously in the present and the past. According to Rifkin, "Employing notions of temporal multiplicity opens the potential for conceptualizing Native continuity and change in ways that do not take non-native frames of reference as the self-evident basis for approaching Indigenous forms of persistence, adaptation, and innovation."[81] Indigenous time elevates the importance of relationships across temporalities and locations, as evidenced here in the perpetuity of connections between the characters, and *Invierno* indicates how circular logics of time can be effectively syncretized into a Shakespearean play.

Shakespeare's play anthropomorphizes Time in order to explain its passage: the character Time speaks at the beginning of act 4, announcing that sixteen years have passed. Rather than resort to such means, González dramatizes this transition at the opening of his second act with a scene between the Young Woman and Paulina that conveys the layered temporalities of the play. At the start of the second act, Paulina asks the Young Woman about a necklace that she wears, and the latter replies, "How did this get on me?" as it was the necklace Hermonia put on her baby Alegría (later Perdida) when she was abandoned. Paulina says, "It's happening. We move forward. The past and the present become one."[82] The temporal space for Latinidad to connect with its past is actualized through González's recovery and inclusion of Samala in the play, more so than through the English and Spanish from different time periods. Not only is Samala included in the play, but it was the first time it was spoken onstage;[83] the creation of this Latinx Shakespearean adaptation served as an act of its recovery and revitalization of an extinct language. The doubling of temporal recovery that occurs in Shakespeare's play with Time's appearance and Hemione's revitalization occurs in a different and intimately connected way in Latinx Shakespeares: the auditory becomes the presence of Time. Rather than creating Time as a visual, embodied person onstage, language recovery, actualized through cross-temporal code-switching, interweaves time through language to enable its mobility.

If time has a circular logic with overlapping generations, the direction that steers life events can seemingly come from out of nowhere, or here, in another country offstage. González intermixes happenstance and settler-ism and delivers the news of how the characters' identities have been remapped as a result of colonialization through the character of the clown. When Afilado (Clown), the comedic character and Perdida's brother-by-adoption, breaks the news of the Anglo takeover, he says, "*México* signed a treaty making us citizens of the United States," and Perdida's adoptive father, Vaquero (Shepherd), replies, "We're '*Yanquis*'?" Afilado continues, "Sure looks that way, *compadre*. Better learn English. Besides that, gold's been discovered up north at Sutter's Mill. Once the word spreads[,] everyone and his cousin will be coming to *California*. Competition is going to be fierce."[84] In this way, it is the clown who aptly anticipates the dominance of English in the agrarian capitalism that would shape California's politics and economics. Although Clown in *The Winter's Tale* provides light comedy as a country bumpkin, as does Afilado for most of *Invierno*, here González invokes the cleverer fools of Shakespeare's earlier plays, such as those in *King Lear* and *Twelfth Night*. The other characters have been focused on their personal relationships and the politics of the moment, but here Afilado clearly sees outward; the path forward for the state and its peoples is changed by a treaty created and signed offstage and never mentioned previously. Indeed, outside actions shape identity categories and economics; the people already inhabiting the land are immediately categorized to fit these new formations.

Invierno depicts the repercussions of Californio society when it devalues or disregards the relationship to the land, but nature is given a prominent role in the play. The wintertime setting includes consistent stage directions about the wind, thunder, and other nature sounds. These sounds emphasize the aural, and well beyond merely English-Spanish code-switching; here Samala and the sounds of nature are given equal footing with the colonizing languages of Spanish and English. *Invierno* gives voice to nature, indicating the generative experience of listening to the earth. The question of shape-changing and transformation offers different possibilities as to when Don León carved Hermonia into a tree (rather than her turning into a statue), and the famous stage direction "Exit, pursued by a bear"[85] occurs when an oak tree transforms into a bear.[86] Paulina invites the Young Woman to kneel; the wind is heard, the tree glows from within, and Hermonia comes to life. The desire for equal access to white space (the early Latinx Shakespearean *West Side Story* trope) is replaced with a larger environmental claim: the play ends with the young couple and the tree blooming "with light,"[87] and nature serving as a life-source for each generation and the young couple's unborn child. These Indigenous cosmologies operate as potential Others to colonial thinking and Gold Rush–style capitalism, and in so doing, create a tension in Latinx Shakespeares that reveals the extent that Latinidad, despite its marginalization within the US context, is still caught up with Spanish colonialism and hegemonic economic practices.

If González shifts the play from linear to continual time to depict a history of California Chicanx, he does so by reclaiming the interpersonal pastoral tale of *The Winter's Tale* to *Invierno*'s specific time of year, winter. The story begins on "A winter night"[88] and anchors the play in a season that is part of the annual cycle, a familiar theatrical affective entry-point for a feeling of the past and of bleakness. González depicts the changing position of Alta California (today's area from California to Texas) and Baja California (now Mexico) within New Spain in the 1840s. As New Spain was losing Alta California to a new group of white settlers, the Californios shifted their geographic center, and their resources, to Mexico. Despite the layers of colonization that contribute to Latinx, it is this shift toward being subjugated by white settlers that remains in the marginalized position of Latinx in the United States today. Like the other Californios in the play, Don León recognizes that they cannot hold on to the land in the face of white European colonialism, especially when they themselves have taken the land from the Chumash. With the burgeoning threat of the "Bear Flaggers," who are white settlers, Caspian laments the imminent loss of Californio ranchera life, saying, "This way of life will disappear like the natives and the animals we slaughtered for pelts," relating his feeling of dislocation to those who were disenfranchised or killed in order to make his way of life possible. Don León becomes one of the those left behind as that happened.

> JAILER: Don León, the priest has arrived from Mexico City.
> DON LEÓN: A priest? I requested a bishop!
> JAILER: That's who they sent.

DON LEÓN: This is how we *Californios* matter to Mexico City? Is this what my grandfather fought and died for? He curses them from the grave![89]

At the beginning of the second act, Caspian reports that a revolt has started and that the "*Californios* are mustering a militia," and Don Patricio confirms that it means war: "The United States invades *México*."[90] González reminds the audience of who the new immigrants are: the "Bear Flaggers." At the end of the play, Don León himself reveals that he knows this to be true, after they set his ranch on fire. Paulina tells him, "Your *rancho* is in ruins," and he replies, "It was never truly mine."[91] Rather than the smooth ending of reunion that Shakespeare's play invokes, the double displacement of an entire group of peoples in *Invierno* extends the pathetic fallacy of winter to the loss of land and culture for the Californios. González's play is titled "Winter"; it is a history, not a tale.

A lack of connection between the land and the people is evidenced in the treatment of Paulina's role as a medicine woman. Despite Paulina's medicinal and spiritual powers, which the society acknowledges and depends on, she is still shunned for them; in this societal distrust, the natural world is aligned with aural culture and women's voices. Don León associates Catholicism with truth and Indigeneity with witchcraft, which he deems untrustworthy. He calls Paulina a "*bruja india*,"[92] and refers to her as Alejandro's "witch wife."[93] When the Jailer attempts to keep Paulina from entering Hermonia's cell to assist her while she gives birth, she threatens to put a curse on him. He responds, "*Crazy india*. My grandfather served the Spanish crown. Your ways mean nothing to me!"[94] but then allows her to enter the jail cell. Paulina's Indigenous knowledge comes from the earth, whereas Don León's power comes from the paternal linear line connected to the Crown, and therefore a monotheistic (male) God. *Invierno* presents this confrontation between knowledges to dramatize how hegemonic principles—religious, national, masculinist—denigrate the relationship to the earth.

Throughout, the characters have a larger conversation about ties, ultimately challenging and shaping who is viewed as "Brown" and who feels "Brown." After Don León attempts to murder Don Patricio, he challenges Alejandro (Antigonus) to convict Hermonia of infidelity. In order to attempt to convince him to do so, he brings up their familial connection as brothers-in-law through their marriages to the half-sisters Hermonia and Paulina, Alejandro says,

ALEJANDRO: No, we are blood.

DON LEÓN: We are not blood! I've never trusted that witch wife of yours or you for that matter! We are not blood!

ALEJANDRO: The natives who are her blood will ask what proof you have.

DON LEÓN: Proof? I've sent for a bishop from *México*. He will get a confession out of her and when everyone learns the truth, she will hang. See that no one visits her![95]

Don León and Alejandro are united by ancestry and related through marriage, but Don León's racism and misogyny toward Paulina break those relational ties. Hermonia and Paulina are half-sisters, with a Chumash mother, but it is revealed that Hermonia's Spanish father raped their mother.[96] While both sisters speak English and Spanish, Hermonia speaks Spanish often and fully and Paulina speaks it sparingly in short phrases; Paulina speaks Samala fluently and Hermonia speaks it sparingly. The question of community is both shaped and broken through the Spanish language, as well as through marriage (Don León and Alejandro) or sibling ties (Hermonia and Paulina). Among the multicultural and multilingual Californio society, community is created differently by each person, and the commonality of Brown is too. Caspian's Russian heritage, as racially white yet also an outsider, makes him unthreatening to the Indigenous and the Californio populations. Don Patricio tells him, "Very well. If this is any comfort, both the *Californios* and the *Yanquis* see you as one of their own. That is your advantage. You will survive because of it."[97] Russians and other northern and eastern Europeans such as Caspian have the fluidity to be welcomed by the current Spaniards and Indigenous Californio, as well as the incoming "Yanquis" due to whiteness. As Spain's colonial expansion in the Americas involved the intermixing with Indigenous peoples, the association of southern European Catholicism and Brown skin color cohered with Indigeneity—inclusive of spirituality, temporality, skin color, and non-European phenotypes. Spain ceded its land to whiter (both in power and skin color) settlers, shifting Brown peoples to a subordinate position politically and culturally. González's play illuminates that Brownness is part of the shaping of California's cultural identity and its elasticity key to the path to statehood.

FROM REPRESENTATION TO REMAPPING

These three productions, and many others like them, depart from a mono-lithic representation of Latinx culture for consumption, treating culture instead "not as a given but as socially constituted, objectified, and mobi-lized for a variety of political ends."[98] These productions push on what can be considered Latinx Shakespeares versus multicultural Shakespeares: they offer a deliberate extension of Brownness in a Brown setting and locale. Each was staged in the location of the story; Los Angeles is 28.5 per-cent white alone (non-Hispanic/Latinx),[99] and California is 36.5 percent.[100] These productions move outside the story of any one specific Brown cul-ture, and they do so through plays that do not depict Brown cultures, his-toricizing the interplay to move outside of racial and ethnic stereotypes of California and Los Angeles. Oftentimes in Latinx-themed adaptations or productions of non-Latinx-authored plays, the theatrical signifiers of Latinidad—the soundscape, Catholicism, Indigenous celebrations, belief in ghosts, and more—unite in an attempt to empower and represent a culture that is often ignored on American stages. Yet Jon Rossini considers "a fun-damental problem within the thinking of theatre historiography: an inevi-table, even desired, slip into the language of representation."[101] While rep-resentation empowers, it also solidifies the idea that ethnicity can be a unified construct.

What if identity categories and their resulting signifiers remain largely appropriative? Muñoz instead attempts to draw commonalities across cul-tures that have been made Brown, including Asian and Indigenous cul-tures, and describes this as a "being-in-common."[102] Just as Jopson's Filipinx-based *Twelfth Night* depicts a national group that is also made a linguistic and racial Other, she depicts a Los Angeles story that decenters Latinidad yet has the affect heavily associated with Latinx stories of immi-gration and dislocation. *O-Dogg*'s ode to Los Angeles street culture addresses the commonalities and divisions of intra-street crew politics, and González's historiographic play about California's Central Coast offers both a feeling and a sense of Brown among the characters that extends across time.

What an affective idea of Brownness[103] offers to Latinx Shakespeares is a way of remapping not just Latinx relationality to the Browning of the United States, but also contesting the possible sites of Shakespearean per-formance that can account for that demographic change. Only through understanding Latinx as a feeling of Brown, rather than a culture to be represented, can Latinx Shakespeares move outside of the counterstance of

Latinx-white solidified by *West Side Story*. The affective idea of Brownness that each of these productions conveys allows for a more nuanced exploration of colorism and anti-Blackness and exemplifies how *West Side Story*'s problematic opposition of Puerto Ricans to the not-quite-right whites is replaced by the networks, aesthetics, and affect that create and connect Brownness. It is through this action, through the larger Browning of Shakespearean performance, that these productions' historiographic versions of California and Los Angeles society are as such: Brown.

The dramaturgical means for negotiating a sense of Brown and feeling Brown occur through movement and mapping. Movement is a key theme in each of the adaptations: Viola begins the play having emigrated to a new country, and the story ends with Antonio being deported; O-Dogg and Dez wish to move out of Los Angeles to start a new life, and the characters in *Invierno* shift not only between Californio ranches (Shakespeare's Sicily and Bohemia) but across time. The movement within each play—Jopson's immigrant narrative, Alpharaoh's historically accurate geographies, González's depiction of the redrawing of national borders and identity categories—remaps Brownness as a feeling of commonality within Shakespearean plays that do not include these cultures. Each production depicted the movement of Latinx positionality toward a relational tie to other Brown peoples, challenging the boundaries and biases of identity categories and modeling how change can occur.

This theme of movement and migration is also evidenced in staging techniques. In Jopson's *Twelfth Night*, the production started outside and then remained indoors until intermission, when the audience returned outdoors to see Antonio and Sebastian for the first time and then was brought into the theater again. Antonio's imminent incarceration was staged by actors dressed as officers who entered from outside the theater and then signaled his deportation by removing him forcibly from the theater. For *O-Dogg*, the reading intended for REDCAT's 2020 festival became more constrained due to Covid-19 protocols, so the video presentation via Zoom ultimately included images from the 1992 uprisings, as well as shots of the actors, playwright, and director at the corner of Florence and Normandie and other locations of the uprisings. They were filmed driving, moving outside the building and inside the theater, socially distanced and with masks. In this way, their movement across downtown Los Angeles mirrored the spread of the uprisings and the varying locales of the scenes of the play. And through the doubling and tripling of actors' roles, González suggests the fluid movement between time periods and identities. His partnership with a historical society to revitalize an extinct language extends the work outside the context of the play, and the play itself revitalizes Chumash history.

Rossini wants to think of "ethnicity as fundamentally spatial" in order to move away from "the desire to chart manifestations of agency and to give voice to the marginalized."[104] And perhaps the problem is not how to think of ethnic categories, per se, but rather the very way identity is constructed politically and, at times, dramaturgically. For Muñoz, "Ways of being in the world . . . are organized by feeling."[105] What these productions reveal is how Jopson, Alpharaoh, and González utilize diverse modes of remapping to connect characters through movement and ultimately re-network a wider scope of Brownness. This shift from centering a metonymy of identity signifiers to centering spatiality and feeling as communities expands Brownness and breaks open a theatrically established notion of Latinidad.

Beyond a challenge to identity categories, these three adaptations counter dominant narratives of California history. In Jopson's Los Angeles *Twelfth Night*, the immigration narratives applied to Latinx are mapped onto Filipinx. In 2016, when the play was set and staged, "Five of the 20 metros with the largest unauthorized immigrant populations [in the United States] are in California: Los Angeles, Riverside-San Bernardino, San Francisco, San Diego and San Jose."[106] California is an immigration state, and over 50 percent of the unauthorized population of Los Angeles report their country of birth as Mexico.[107] The assumption that immigration overflow and ICE arrests are likely about undocumented Mexicans has some credence, based on these statistics, but Jopson's repositioning of Filipinx, especially the Filipina domestic worker that Viola becomes, elevates another prominent and important narrative. In Alpharaoh's story of the LA uprisings, he centers Korean characters, a narrative included in some early scholarship on the uprisings but little within the popular consciousness.[108] Only in the last fifteen years has the importance of the racial interplay with Korean shop owners become more well known through a series of news reports for the twenty-fifth anniversary in 2017,[109] and a meme of "Rooftop Koreans," or Korean Americans who armed themselves to protect their property, that became popular in 2020 alongside the rise of mass Black Lives Matter (BLM) protests, reinforcing the circularity of protests against racist police violence.[110] González's *Invierno* remapped the history book legends of Spanish Californio life, making connections between Spaniards, other European settlers, and Indigenous peoples, depicting the interweaving of Indigenous religiosity and a weakening of the tie of Spanish-Americans to European-centered Catholicism.

Theatrical mimesis typically elides the complexity of colonial histories, and these three productions advocate for a critical exploration of today's identity categories. Categorizing Latinx as an ethnicity shifts it away from histories of race that have persisted for centuries and were tied to the corporeal through pseudoscience. Recently, ethnicity has been "defined as cultural traits . . . utterly divorced from the workings of the physical body, defined as 'race.'"[111] Henry Yu argues that this was a progressive stance, to move away from the earlier "science" of bodily difference, but by the end of the twentieth century, the "commercialization of ethnicity also allowed those who were identified as different to turn that identification into an object with value."[112] One of the activist consequences of Brownness is that it makes objectification less viable. The movement away from representation reshapes the very category of identity. The next chapter addresses dramaturgical strategies for how Latinx can address layers of colonization and various relationships to colonial histories.

| Decoloniality

Theatrical Bilanguaging

In 2013, Lean & Hungry Theater Company in Washington, DC, hosted a one-night live recording of *The Taming of the Shrew* in partnership with the Women's National Democratic Club. Lean & Hungry is "a professional audio theater company . . . [that] creates one-hour, audio versions of English language classics in established or improvised venues throughout the capital region."[1] Artistic director Jessica Hansen, who works for National Public Radio, wanted to invoke a Latinx theme; therefore, she hired Puerto Rico–born, bilingual director Javier Rivera. Having worked with GALA Hispanic, INTAR, and Repertorio Español, Rivera was excited for the opportunity to work on a radio show for the first time, and one reality of American theater is the limited number of paid opportunities to do so.

The audio adaptation was advertised with both the title in English printed in small font and the title in Spanish, *La Fierecilla Domada*, in larger font, with a close-up, retro-style image of a beautiful woman in a strapless bikini on a beach. Rivera said that he immediately knew that at the core of the production was a desire to capitalize on "the Latinx craze" and felt that Hansen (who is white) hired him because she needed a Latinx person to validate her problematic concept.[2] It was marketed as a "Spanish-infused adaptation . . . set within a radio-novela [*sic*] in Mexico," but nothing specific to Mexico or any key convention in Latinx theater was integrated into the storytelling.[3]

Lean & Hungry sought Spanish-speaking actors for the production, but few auditioned. With a cast of six actors each playing multiple roles, half were Latinx, and Spanish words were added into some of the dialogue. Rivera worked within these constraints and never asked the actors who did not speak Spanish to feign an accent. The means of conveying a Mexican aesthetic were limited within an auditory genre and with non-Latinx actors in the roles of Kate and Bianca. Rivera felt that the concept production was an interesting proposition, but that it was "pandering" and "not organic" and, ultimately, "a flawed experiment when the artistic director was trying to make a deep statement."[4]

Despite the support of the Women's National Democratic Club and a production team that was female (though the director and dramaturg were males), Lean & Hungry advertised the radio play as "A Red Hot Radio Novela [*sic*]"[5] and, in so doing, failed to offset the misogyny in Shakespeare's script and the ethnic stereotypes embedded in the adaptation. The location of the performance was at "Whittemore House, the historic home of Eleanor Roosevelt"[6] and the setting of the radio play remained nonspecific Latin/Mediterranean even though it was inspired by the telenovela, a Mexican dramatic form. It was after this experience that Rivera chose never to compromise his artistic integrity again. He felt used by the artistic director, and in turn, it was not fair to the actors. He comments about Hansen, "She was trying to colonize me."[7] Latinx Shakespeares conceived and promoted through white artists can result in cultural appropriation, even if Latinx artists and auralidad (see chapter 2) are involved.

Although *La Fierecilla Domada* is an example of a culturally insensitive Latinx Shakespearean production, the concept involved bilingual and semi-bilingual characters. But culturally sensitive Latinx Shakespeares reveal that characters and actors are not merely bilingual or multilingual; they live between languages. To explore life between languages, I draw on Walter Mignolo's distinction between bilingualism, the ability to communicate in two languages, and bilanguaging, "that way of life between languages: a dialogical, ethic, aesthetic, and political process of social transformation."[8] Mignolo's concept of bilanguaging attempts "to draw in something that is beyond sound, syntax, and lexicon, and beyond the need of having two languages."[9]

Latinx Shakespeares that fully integrate Latinidad into the play and production achieve this type of bilanguaging—a *theatrical bilanguaging*—that involves more than the staging of bilingual theater or a desire for it; together, the characters within the play and the audience's experience of attending the production constitute this process, which Mignolo argues results in "liberation of colonial and national (official, hegemonic) discourses and epistemologies."[10] Theatrical bilanguaging occurs with a liberation from discrete genres of theatrical storytelling as well as Shakespearean English and pushes against the idea of universality to expand theater communities for a specific locality. The Latinx Shakespeares in this chapter are works of theatrical bilanguaging; they appropriate a space for Latinx subjectivity and interiority through a play that otherwise does not offer that space.

The borders between interior identity and exterior presentation run adjacent to those between interpersonal, familial, and larger national conflict. A borderland, as defined by Gloria Anzaldúa in her foundational book *Borderlands / La Frontera*, "is a vague and undetermined place created by the emotional residue of an unnatural boundary."[11] Thus, a borderlands epistemology, or border thinking, is a method and practice begun by countering hegemony to negotiate identities that have been informed by colonial histories. Border thinking is described by María Lugones as "a decolonial method that is the spatial connector between local knowledges with a history of colonial subjection."[12] Lugones, Mignolo, and others look to local histories as means to disable monolithic notions of individuated peoples, to break down hegemonic thinking that results in pejorative ideas of an Other. Border thinking is necessary for the process of decolonization and "offers a different perspective to human and civil rights based approaches to justice, an unsettling one, rather than a complementary one."[13] The concept of decolonizing is not without its challenges: decoloniality is a process that cannot be practiced solely by using the tools of the oppressor,[14] a theoretical claim actualized in practice through Rivera's reflection that Hansen was trying to colonize him. This notion, that Latinx are largely trapped in linguistic, political, racial, and other power systems that cannot be challenged from within, plays out in Latinx Shakespeares, which take up a canon that is a tool of colonization and emblem of English-language dominance.

And yet the Shakespeare canon is also an inspiration for Latinx adaptation and decolonial appropriations that weave Shakespearean storytelling with Indigenous theatrical and ritual practices. Mignolo proposes "delinking," thinking antithetically to the norm, as a necessary step toward decolonization, one that is indicative of "interculturalidad," having two distinct thought patterns at work simultaneously.[15] Like the *West Side Story* effect (see chapter 2), delinking is a process of opposition and division, changing not just the parameters of a play but also its entire ecosystem, staging, and audience. Latinx Shakespeares make clear that Mignolo's praxis for countering hegemony, that is, to "build decolonial local histories,"[16] can be reconfigured for theatrical practice.

This chapter applies a borderlands epistemology to three adaptations of *Hamlet*, exploring theater practices that intersect with linguistic and theatrical borders to both dramatize and enable a critique of colonization; Latinx Shakespeares' theatrical bilanguaging causes us to rethink how staging methods and themes can cross dramaturgical borders as well as linguistic and ethnic ones. *Hamlet*, with its focus on the individual through theme and structure—Hamlet's soliloquies about his inner feelings pause the forward action of the play—is a vehicle for exploring the border space of identity, between interior and exterior. I begin with a non-Latinx themed Shakespearean production that includes one Latinx character: Joseph Papp's 1968 *Naked Hamlet,* a dramaturgically and textually stripped-down production starring half-Spanish actor Martin Sheen in both the lead role and that of Hamlet's Puerto Rican alter ego, Ramon.[17] From there, I turn to Asolo Repertory's 2012 *Hamlet, Prince of Cuba,* which had the cast perform entirely in English for twenty-six shows and then entirely in Spanish for ten shows to audiences in Sarasota and Miami, Florida; and lastly, I attend to Tara Moses's 2018 *Hamlet: El Príncipe de Denmark,* which was adapted for telatúlsa, the only Latinx and Native American theater in Tulsa, Oklahoma, and staged during the Day of the Dead festivities.[18]

These adaptations address coloniality and the resulting crises of the self through multiple border crossings: linguistic and cultural, religious and ritualistic, within the play and without.[19] All three included auralidad and experimented with theatrical (if not also ritual) form. Importantly, each presents different strategies for addressing coloniality by experimenting with theatrical adaptations of Shakespearean performance, bilingual theater strategies, and the narrative structure of the play. While Papp's adaptation from more than fifty years ago foreshadows the later Latinx Shakespeares in this chapter, the production was largely *anti*colonial; it attempted to subvert colonialist frameworks by portraying the colonizing forces as oppressive, but it did not achieve a decolonial praxis. Asolo Repertory's adaptation, in contrast, was *post*colonial: addressing the cultural legacy of colonialism within the world of the play and by proxy, for audiences today. Finally, at telatúlsa, theatrical bilanguaging was actualized through intermixing ritual practices with a *de*colonial *Hamlet,* one that incorporated ceremony with theater, fully delinking Shakespeare from his narrative structure to create a new order of events, one that is "accountable to Indigenous sovereignty and futurity."[20] While this trajectory suggests a kind of progression toward the practice of decoloniality, each adaptation utilizes different modes to critique coloniality, slipping between the borders of anticolonial, postcolonial, and decolonial praxis. All three engage in decoloniality, a way of thinking or doing, that critiques Western hegemony.[21]

My discussion of these adaptations includes a focus on the rehearsal process and serves to validate individual language approaches to Shakespeare that are in direct resistance to the colonial weight of hegemonic speaking traditions, including British Received Pronunciation (RP), which was "the dominant voice of British theatre . . . [and] also the voice of the BBC."[22] The liberation that the adaptations achieve functions on multiple levels, including resistance to the linguistic policing in historical Shakespearean performance.[23] As Sonia Massai notes, "The use of anything but an educated, Southern [English] accent is still problematic when deployed on the [British] Shakespearean stage."[24] This historical rigidity of what constitutes acceptable speech extends outside RP to predominantly white theaters in the United States when a diverse cast comes together in the rehearsal room for a concept production/adaptation.

The adaptations detailed here illuminate how the legacy of coloniality in the United States manifests as a crisis of the self. They actualize a type of border thinking that includes a fluid embrace of the precolonial as well as the postcolonial while acknowledging the persistence of cultural vestiges such as Shakespeare, Catholicism, and the Spanish language. Latinx *Hamlet*s reconfigure the emphasis on interiority to engage ethnicity and prompt a conversation about structure and theatrical form. This is a decolonial praxis for the theater because it prioritizes inner conflict caused by the effects of colonization and leads to a reconfiguration of the structure/narrative.

HAMLET IN NEW YORK: JOSEPH PAPP'S *NAKED HAMLET*

In 1968, Joseph Papp directed a now-notorious production of *Hamlet* that he developed and later published under the title *William Shakespeare's "Naked" Hamlet*, more commonly referred to as the *Naked Hamlet*. For the production—which starred Martin Sheen as both the title character and his alter ego, the Puerto Rican Ramon—Papp cut the text significantly and pared down the set and dramaturgy, leaving a "naked" play and performance. Nobody was actually naked on stage, but that scandalous notion has stuck with this production all the same, in part because of the scathing review from *New York Times* critic Clive Barnes, who saw the production as "an almost pitiful attempt at avant-garde theatrical devices," and who wrote with disdain that "the play opens with Claudius and Gertrude in bed, and Hamlet, seemingly naked and clearly handcuffed, trapped in a coffin at their feet."[25]

Papp's production crossed linguistic, cultural, and theatrical borders to address the crisis of the self, brought on by coloniality and racism.[26] For Papp, *Hamlet* was not simply a story focused on Hamlet's interiority but rather one that must be viewed through multiple perspectives. In Papp's handwritten notes to develop the play, he wrote, "During the years in which Picasso and Kandinsky shattered the SINGLE FOCUS PERSPECTIVE in painting, Schoenberg and Varese shattered the SINGLE FOCUS OF TONALITY in music."[27] The pairing of Hamlet and Ramon allowed Papp to follow suit, "shattering the single focus" in Shakespeare's text. Sheen—who was born Ramón Antonio Gerard Estévez and is of Irish and Spanish descent—switched into Spanish or a Spanish accent to play Hamlet's alter ego, "Ramon the janitor."[28] In this act of cultural and linguistic code-switching, Ramon was ethnicized as Puerto Rican to make Hamlet "the man of the people,"[29] in contrast with Hamlet, who read as not Latinx and who retained his white identity.

Ramon makes his first appearance in the second act—suggesting that the intermission function as a type of borderland crossing—after Polonius insinuates that Hamlet might be mad. Unlike Hamlet, who wore a "white linen double-breasted suit, rumpled, with a mourning band on one arm" and "a polo shirt and a black tie, a black beret and horn-rimmed glasses," Ramon wore "baggy gray pants held with loose suspenders, a leather jacket, a worker's hat, a black wig, and a false nose with glasses attached."[30] Hamlet was thus not just white but visibly upper class; Ramon was not just ethnic but visibly working class. More than that, he was portrayed as comical or clownish, switching out effete horn-rimmed glasses for plastic ones with a nose attached.[31] Ramon first appeared from offstage already in his disguise, but later in the play he has his disguise removed slowly by both Rossencraft and Gilderstone until Ramon finally tears off his mustache "and dances away in delight at his joke."[32] Several times he entered with the disguise already on.

The use of the Puerto Rican accent arose in large part because Papp was attuned to the language politics of the day and sought to juxtapose Spanish and English onstage while still allowing the audience to follow along. Nuyorican identity and aesthetics were taking shape at this time; "Nuyorican" is a portmanteau of "New York–Puerto Rican," but as Patricia Herrera attests, for Miguel Algarín, cofounder with Miguel Piñero of the Nuyorican Poets Café, the term "means much more than 'a Puerto Rican born and/or living in New York.' It is a way of being."[33] Papp, Shakespeare, and Nuyorican culture intersected when by 1970, Algarín, a scholar and professor at Rutgers, had established a workshop for playwrights and actors in Papp's 4 Astor annex by the Public Theater that gave way to the founding of the Nuyorican Poets Café in 1973, where Algarín was "teaching—among other things—Shakespeare."[34]

While early efforts of the famous "To be or not to be" soliloquy involved "Hamlet speaking entirely in Spanish, and with the Ghost added into the scene and translating for the audience's benefit," such a choice obscured "the action of the scene and also many of the jokes."[35] Not wanting to lose comedic lines to translation for an assumed monolingual English-speaking audience, Papp struggled with how to negotiate representations of identity with various strategies of integrating a foreign language into a canonical text.[36] "To be or not to be" was ultimately delivered by Sheen as Ramon in English but in a Puerto Rican accent, with limited phrases and words in Spanish.[37] The notion that an American actor in a lead Shakespearean role would speak in a language other than English was profound for theater at the time. Even so, the ending of *Naked Hamlet* reveals an uncomfortable privileging of whiteness over ethnicity. In the final scene, titled "The Great Revelation," Hamlet "continues to speak in his Puerto Rican accent as the other characters try to ignore him";[38] this is the only instance in the play where Hamlet, and not Ramon, speaks with an accent. He then strips "off the last of his Ramon clothes, stands on the third level and speaks in his normal voice."[39] Papp, who was still at the beginning of his efforts to diversify American Shakespeares and experiment with race and ethnicity through Shakespearean performance, refers to unaccented English as "normal" in comparison to a Spanish accent. Hamlet says, "What is he whose grief bears such an emphasis? This is I, Hamlet the Dane."[40] He truly is Danish (read: white) at heart. Ultimately, audiences were given to understand that Hamlet is white (non-Hispanic/Latinx) and that his greatness equates to the whiteness unveiled as the character's true identity.

The rehearsal process was key to the development of Ramon, and if another actor had played Hamlet, the alter ego would not have been characterized or developed in the same way. Although Papp wrote and directed the play, Sheen contributed his own ideas about how Hamlet should be interpreted.[41] Sheen recollects, "The Puerto Rican idea was—my real name, as you know is Ramón Estevez; I'm half Spanish. And we decided to disguise Hamlet in several scenes as a Puerto Rican janitor."[42] Papp's goal was to break down the play into vignettes and reorganize it; it was Sheen who created the roles of Hamlet and Ramon in rehearsal. Ultimately, the show was partly modern-dress Shakespeare, rock musical, avant-garde performance, and social commentary, all created through a collaborative process with Papp at the helm. Papp writes, "Rehearsals were a process of unraveling and reweaving the text and the business of the play until the form which you see here was reached. This process continued when the second and then a third production were mounted as new actors and new ideas reshaped the play."[43] The process of exploration continued into the performance itself, with actors given the opportunity to ad-lib and improvise. After Clive Barnes called the show *Hamlet* for "Philistines,"[44] in his review during previews, Sheen gleefully recollected his improvised response: "Opening night I took his pen away from him."[45]

In Papp's concept for his *Naked Hamlet*, "Every scene is a play within a play,"[46] and the "play within" offered a key way to explode the number of perspectives being engaged in the adaptation. The play within is a site of action in Shakespeare's play: the Players' performance of "The Mousetrap" causes Claudius, the king, to rise, revealing his guilt in fratricide/regicide. For the play within, Papp staged Claudius as in fact playing one of the roles along with the players, causing him to implicate himself. The audience became participants in this chaos as well, able to read the lines of Claudius's guilt by holding scripts in their own hands. Sheen recalls, "We threw a party for the King, and I'm handing out scripts for everyone and filming it with a 16 mm camera, getting the King to play one of the roles, drunken and disorderly as he is, and he recites his own indictment."[47] In this staging of the play within, Papp transformed the spectator into reader of the dialogue, observer of the actors' performances in character, witness to Claudius's admittance of his own guilt, and audience to Hamlet as a documentarian of the action through the medium of film. The meta-mediatization of Hamlet as a filmmaker caused the audience to understand that what it was watching would be (supposedly, in the world of the play) available to other audiences at a later time through the point of view of Hamlet as director.

After the run at the NYSF, Papp toured his *Naked Hamlet* to over fifty high schools, with one key change: African American actor Cleavon Little played the title role and the alter ego, with the latter now named Rastus.[48] This suggests that the Latinx character was not important to the adaptation, but an ethnicized or racialized alter ego was key to shattering of a singular (white) perspective. Whereas "Ramon" is the given name of Martin Sheen, "Rastus" is a historical stereotype of Black servitude; the image is an offensive caricature, much like Aunt Jemima and Uncle Ben. Rastus is the name of the chef on the Cream of Wheat packaging, first designed around 1890 by Emery Mapes for the new-style breakfast porridge. The trademark image was replaced in 1925 by one modeled after a Chicago restaurant worker, Frank L. White.[49] Rastus was not merely an image, but a portrait of a presumed former slave who is nearly illiterate.[50] Whereas Ramon showcased Sheen's identity and linguistic ability, Rastus called on pejorative tropes of Black people and was applied to Little's portrayal as his alter ego.

In making this change, Papp fundamentally shifted the play from a focus on ethnolinguistic relationships (as conveyed through Hamlet and Ramon's split and particularly their relationship to the Ghost, who also spoke Spanish but to a lesser extent than Ramon) to one of the visual, racially inflected politics of era. Papp wrote, for example, that "the Ghost was replaced by Claudius in the gravedigger scene. Claudius was a cop harassing a poor Negro janitor whose trash basket seemed to be a grave."[51] While the dramaturgical choices accompanying this change rightfully drew criticism for their essentializing and stereotyping of Blackness, they reveal a distinction in how Papp viewed Blackness and Latinidad. For him, Blackness was visual, "a symbol of change—it is the eye that focuses on all injustice and corruption and authorized legal violence,"[52] but Latinidad was linguistic.

Ramon at times does not understand, or pretends not to understand, English. When a character named Rachel asks Ramon to give Claudius some money, Claudius approaches Ramon and says, "Thank you very much," to which Ramon replies, "Que?" Claudius responds, "Gracias, gracias" and Ramon says, "Por nada."[53] By contrast, as a Black man at the height of the civil rights movement, Cleavon Little's Rastus had to negotiate racism based on his culture and the color of his skin. For example, Polonius's question "What do you read, my lord?" was met not with the response "Words, words, words," as in Shakespeare's play, but rather, simply, with "the program"; Sheen's Ramon read the theater program, and after the "scathing review in *The New York Times*, Hamlet was reading that newspaper for a while," but Little's Rastus read *Ebony*.[54] The racially white Puerto Rican character thus held a document directly related to the arts or a prominent national newspaper, while the racially Black character held a magazine about Black culture. Ultimately, Sheen's Ramon was subject not to visual but linguistic racism. And the Spanish language enabled the half-Spanish Sheen to embrace his alter ego, the Nuyorican Ramon, with costume changes to signal class status as a comical addition versus the tragic "poor Negro" Rastus.

Papp's idea to "strip down" the play and use casting, language, and accent to amplify ideas of interiority decentered traditional and hegemonic ideas about Shakespearean performance and monolithic notions of identity. His script and production, however, were *anti*colonial: they invoked a negative portrayal of colonizers that was predicated on the notion that colonialism was still in process, something that the civil rights movement at the time was highlighting.[55] For example, the idea of Denmark as a prison was inspired by contemporary political regimes, that Claudius had "staged a military coup in the manner of certain modern Latin American or Mediterranean countries . . . [Yet] [t]he character of Hamlet's mind—as it developed in Martin Sheen—became more important than the external political situation."[56] International politics were secondary to the characters' inner conflicts. Papp repurposed the emphasis to the American context, and Sheen notes the shift he felt, both as an actor and in his observation of the audience's response and resonance in "To be or not to be" when the soliloquy addresses cultural oppression. "Because who were the doormen in New York? Who was washing the dishes? Who was cleaning the garbage? . . . The Puerto Ricans."[57] It is noteworthy that Sheen's Hispanic heritage and ability to speak Spanish informed his ability and desire to shape and portray a Puerto Rican (Latino) character though he did not elide the distinctions between cultures. Spanish was the theatrical enabler that permitted Sheen to cross the border from Hispanic to Latinx.

Even though the anticolonial element of his stripped-down adaptation was somewhat ethnically and racially motivated, Papp's target was not white hegemony but rather traditional, British-based Shakespearean performance genres and a reverence for the text. Papp's significant cuts, added dialogue, and avant-garde staging pushed against theatrical form through one of the most famous Shakespeare plays, in the most renowned Shakespeare theater in the United States at the time. J. Daniel Elam notes that anticolonial thinkers "often debated the necessary aesthetic forms that should accompany (or inspire) political activism."[58] These anticolonial efforts were met with significant resistance: not just from critics such as Clive Barnes but from educators. Concerns about the suitability of *Naked Hamlet*'s "adult themes" for young people led the NYSF to perform a matinee for students and teachers that was followed by what we would now call a contentious talkback session to discuss whether the production should even be permitted to tour to schools (the problematic stereotype of a Puerto Rican janitor was not raised).[59] Such was the level of resistance, from outrage about the aesthetic style to concern about adult themes and rock music, that Papp faced for his transformational staging.

Even so, the production was a successful step toward the democratizing of Shakespeare. Papp stated that "the Public Theater was jammed every night for the run of the play, attracting audiences predominantly in their teens and early twenties."[60] Reviews, including excerpts that Papp reprints in his published script, indicate that older audiences (and critics) didn't like the play due to a feeling of infidelity to the text, but that younger New York audiences did. It was those younger and more diverse audiences that Papp was courting. Performances ended by visibly displacing Shakespeare and critics in their roles as author or interpreter of the play, with a gravestone carried onstage that read, "RIP Will Shakespeare."

HAMLET IN FLORIDA: *HAMLET, PRINCE OF CUBA*

Almost forty-five years after Sheen portrayed Hamlet, actor Frankie J. Alvarez became the first Latinx actor to perform Hamlet *as* Latinx or Latin American in a US production or adaptation of the play, doing so in the 2012 world-premiere adaptation *Hamlet, Prince of Cuba* at Asolo Repertory Theatre in Sarasota, Florida. This production, which was directed and adapted by Michael Donald Edwards, had separate runs in both English and Spanish languages, with Pulitzer Prize–winning Cuban American playwright Nilo Cruz penning the Spanish-language version. The play included production elements and staging techniques that encompassed a postcolonial critique, acknowledging the legacy of colonialism and attempting to reclaim land and aspects of culture of the previously colonized. Whereas Papp created an alter ego to comment on inequities, Edwards created a setting and characters that were both colonizers and colonized, and he invoked language as a leveling agent and access point for both characters and audiences.

Papp's adaptation was motivated by a desire to shatter the structure of the play, but Edwards's was informed by the linguistic dexterity of the actors in the local community.[61] As an Australian American, Edwards stated at the time that he knew nothing of Hispanic or Cuban culture before his six years in Florida, but was inspired by the wealth of talented bilingual actors he met. After over twenty-five years of primarily directing Shakespeare, Edwards was interested in directing a new production of *Hamlet*. He said that "the idea of setting it in Cuba came after the idea of doing the play at all."[62] Edwards chose a historical event that resonated with Floridians, especially with the Cuban population: the 1898 sinking of the USS *Maine* in Havana Harbor, which prompted the Spanish-American War.[63] The dramaturgy was primarily linguistic and the concept setting provided a context.

In *Hamlet, Prince of Cuba*, rather than starting with Shakespeare's night watchmen speaking of a Ghost they have recently seen or Papp's extratextual scene of Gertrude and Claudius in bed, the action began with an already deceased Hamlet onstage, dressed in a late nineteenth-century black suit and accompanied by the sound of acappella music in Spanish. This convention set the whole story of *Hamlet* as a flashback, an unusual construct for the play. Hamlet then stepped into a tableau vivant of his mother's wedding to Claudius, which is a scene that precedes the action in Shakespeare's script. By beginning with the deceased Hamlet and this silent marriage scene, the adaptation displaced any sense of a traditional linear narrative from the outset. It also further centered both Hamlet and the theme of interiority in a play that traditionally begins not with the titular figure but with minor characters.

Edwards made numerous cuts to Shakespeare's text but retained the verse for the English-language performances—a more traditional Shakespearean dramaturgy—while Cruz's translation also stripped away the verse rather than attempting to reproduce iambic pentameter in Spanish, ultimately altering the language in the process. Performances ran in English for the first month, after which a short run in Spanish (with English supertitles) picked up, overlapping with the run in English. The show then moved to Miami for a weekend of additional monolingual performances in both languages.[64] Costuming, set design, casting choices, and other aspects of the mise-en-scène were largely consistent across both versions. That said, the feel differed between the English and Spanish performances, with Alvarez's voice dropping nearly three octaves in the Spanish version, due to his guttural relationship with Spanish as his first language and his use of his upper register for Shakespeare.[65] Although Cruz translated from Edwards's cut of Shakespeare's play, he interpolated images, just as must happen with any act of translation. For example, Hamlet's "I know a hawk from a handsaw,"[66] which signals his powers of discernment, becomes "sé distinguir muy bien el vuelo de un halcón de una urraca" (I can distinguish quite well the flight of a hawk from a magpie).[67] Such a move changes the image for both the audience and the actor, as Alvarez notes: "If the image is different, the language is different, then the impulse is different."[68] Further, while most of the cast appeared in both versions, two of the English-speaking ensemble actors (playing the three smaller roles of Polonius, the Player King, and the Gravedigger) were replaced for the Spanish-language performances. Alvarez notes that when he was performing the two versions in rep, "I found that my performances were in constant conversation, and I would learn something from the Spanish version that would prove useful to me in the English version, and vice versa."[69] Alvarez, and most of the cast, embodied a form of theatrical bilanguaging rarely accessible to performers, of two linguistic lives in the same performance run.

The dual languages meant many unique challenges for the creative team. Edwards, a monolingual English-speaker, did not have the training to direct Spanish-speaking or Spanish-accented characters. The multiethnic cast, too, had not been trained with bilingual acting methods. Not all the actors spoke Spanish, fewer still were truly bilingual, and only one or two had ever performed Shakespeare in Spanish. To help overcome these challenges, Asolo Rep employed vocal coach Antonio Ocampo-Guzmán, who worked with the actors in both English and Spanish to develop speaking

Figure 7: Mercedes Herrero as Gertrude and Frankie J. Alvarez as Hamlet in *Hamlet, Prince of Cuba* (dir. Michael Donald Edwards, 2012). Photo by Gary W. Sweetman. Courtesy of Asolo Repertory Theatre.

skills in both languages.[70] Accents were not employed beyond the actors' natural voices; the English-language version was performed without Cuban/Latinx accents.

With a cast from linguistically and ethnically mixed backgrounds (including Cuban and Cuban American, Mexican, Spanish, Brazilian, Ecuadorian American, and more) rehearsing a bilingual production, the rehearsal room became a site for exploring the different experiences of cultural adaptation and translation. Rehearsals in Spanish began after the play had already opened in English and took place over a condensed, ten-day period (the English version had been rehearsed for six weeks). Despite being bilingual, Alvarez had no acting training in Spanish; Alvarez's father flew to Sarasota to help Alvarez run lines in Spanish.[71]

These Spanish-language rehearsals were liberating for some actors and daunting for others. Brazilian actress Gisela Chípe, who played Ophelia, spoke at length during a talkback session about the process of healing that she encountered when rehearsing in Spanish. She said:

> I grew up speaking mostly Portuguese, and so there was a part of my character, my being, that was defined by that language. And when I

was eight, my parents said we want you to learn English, we want you to be immersed and do that, so we rarely spoke Portuguese . . . after that point. And I found that even speaking in Spanish, as close as that is to Portuguese, it was like I was saying hello to my young self. . . . And so I think there is incredible potential for healing.[72]

Chípe's experience with Spanish paralleled something that Edwards had felt when first encountering Shakespeare. Edwards felt dislocated from Shakespeare due to the constraints of British Received Pronunciation and the linguistic bias against his Australian accent. Sonia Massai notes that the establishment of Standard English pronunciation in the mid-eighteenth century coincides "with the rise of English as the language of Empire."[73] Even though Edwards eventually made a career as a Shakespearean director, he first regarded Shakespeare as "an act of imperialism."[74] For Ocampo-Guzmán, Chípe, and Edwards, the Shakespearean dialogue initially meant exclusion and dislocation, but the language became freeing when the demand to perform it broadened to include other accents and languages. But with *Hamlet, Prince of Cuba*, it was in the space of the rehearsal room where Latinx and Spanish-speaking practitioners worked in tandem with a white director in developing Latinx and non-Latinx actors for these roles. The linguistic agency, as a result of the rehearsal process that Chípe, Alvarez, and other cast members achieved, validates individual language approaches to Shakespeare and serves as a direct resistance to the colonial weight of hegemonic RP.

The embodied interiority that the production enabled was perhaps most apparent in performance in the handling of the Ghost of Hamlet's father. Hamlet, Marcellus, and Horatio visit a Santero priest, who "begins to perform a cleansing ritual by thrashing healing herbs against HAMLET's body and blowing smoke around his aura, to remove all malignant energies."[75] The priest blew the smoke into Alvarez's face as part of a cleansing tradition; it is only then that Hamlet recites his "To be or not to be" speech, and immediately following, the Santero lights a match, and Hamlet becomes possessed by his father's spirit. Hamlet convulses on the floor of the stage, to then sit upright in a controlled manner as stark lighting indicates that the spirit has taken over Hamlet's body. Alvarez recalls, "I had a mic on me for this scene that allowed the sound engineer to amplify and modify my voice in the moment when the ghost assumes control over my faculties and issues his challenge."[76] The Ghost does not explicitly seek Hamlet out, rather, Hamlet goes to a healer to rid himself of his impure thoughts and only then becomes embodied by the Ghost.

In the English-language performances, the role of the Ghost was performed by white actor James (Jimmy) Clarke, who wore an Afro-Cuban mask. But in the Spanish-language performances, racially white Cuban American actor Gonzalo Madurga performed the role without a mask. With a Latinx actor, the Spanish language was enough to connote Indigeneity, but with a white actor, Indigeneity was represented through the visual of Blackness, performed through a mask. This difference in costuming based on an actor's ethnicity resonates with how a white director can imagine and stage Latinidad problematically. Additionally, Edwards scheduled no extra time to learn the play in Spanish but prioritized one extra week of rehearsal between Alvarez and Andhy Mendez (Laertes) before the other actors arrived to learn the fight choreography, making clear what the priorities were for the show.[77]

The Ghost wore an Afro-Cuban Santería mask and tribal costume and spoke through Hamlet's body, drawing on the (Yoruban) Santería tradition in which a devotee is "mounted" by an Orisha, inhabited during a dance or ritual.[78] Hamlet's deceased father was not only thus associated with an Indigenous culture hailing from (Black) Africa, but was portrayed as from a different religion than Hamlet himself, who was of white Spanish descent (and was thus presumably Catholic). Alvarez notes, "From this point, my performance awakens, as Hamlet's life has a renewed purpose."[79] It is through the physical embodiment of his father and the embrace of Black and Indigenous religiosity that Alvarez's Hamlet can take action.[80] Although the actor still performed in the colonizing languages of English and Spanish, the character was motivated by his previously lost relationship with his father and the latter's African Indigenous roots, rather than by the colonizing religion of Christianity or Catholicism.

HAMLET IN OKLAHOMA: *HAMLET: EL PRÍNCIPE DE DENMARK*

In contrast, Tara Moses's (Seminole Nation of Oklahoma, Mvskoke) 2018 production of *Hamlet: El Príncipe de Denmark* at telatúlsa in Tulsa, Oklahoma, encompassed a decolonial praxis for the Latinx Shakespearean stage. A decolonial praxis involves a reclaiming of land and space; physically, the space of the stage was given to Indigenous rituals and storytellers, and thematically, Hamlet's journey involved a move toward his Indigenous roots as the play progressed. According to Emma Pérez, the decolonial imaginary is "a rupturing space, the alternative to that which is written in history."[81] Breaking the play open from its contemporary performance history, Moses's version moved at a quick pace with no blackouts or intermissions, and her script includes detailed descriptions of the seamless transitions between scenes. Moses still has Hamlet die, but Ophelia lives, and it is Ophelia rather than Polonius who says, "This above all: to thine own self be true,"[82] which she addresses to the audience at the play's end to urge them to evaluate their own interiority. Whereas with *Hamlet, Prince of Cuba*, the rehearsals became a borderlands space for linguistic healing for the cast, for this telatúlsa production, healing began in the dramaturgy itself, specifically the interplay of theater and ritual, which shifted *Hamlet* from a revenge tragedy to communion with the dead.

As the play opens, three tombstones and three smaller altars are arranged onstage. Hamlet enters, alongside two women whose faces are painted like calaca skulls. They conduct a ritual for Day of the Dead, placing ofrendas (offerings) on the altars and lighting candles, all to the sound of "instrumental, Mexican music."[83] When Hamlet lights his candle, however, the music stops and the lights go out. The women run off, frightened, while Hamlet lingers, "perplexed,"[84] and then leaves. Bernardo then enters and speaks the first line of Shakespeare's play, "Who's there?"[85] Unlike Edwards's adaptation, this *Hamlet* begins with and centralizes Indigenous traditions and the dead, and it begins with women. In the scene that follows Bernardo and Horatio's conversation, "Music plays as OPHELIA, GERTRUDE, and another WOMAN enter in bright dresses and calaca makeup. They dance for the final day of celebrations."[86] Shortly thereafter, however, the king, who has been standing on stage, "hands GERTRUDE a wipe to clean her face of the makeup," and Gertrude complies, removing the physical makeup of the Indigenous ritual and thus stepping into her theatrical role.[87] This opening scene sets the tone for the centering of Indigenous ritual practice as a mode of transcendence. It also suggests that the interplay between ritual and theater will be a hallmark of the show; Gertrude can quickly wipe off the makeup from the Indigenous ritual and move immediately to portray a Latinx Shakespearean queen, and the wiping off of makeup suggests that her Indigenous roots are something that she wishes to erase.

Day of the Dead, or Día de Muertos, is a celebration held on November 1–2 each year, originating in Mexico and most likely coming from Aztec or Toltec origins.[88] For the last twenty-five years, Living Arts Tulsa has hosted a large Day of the Dead festival at the Guthrie Green open-air park in downtown Tulsa. Telatúlsa's 2018 production of *Hamlet*, a bilingual adaptation running ninety minutes with no intermission, was staged as part of these festivities, with the first two scenes (through Horatio telling Hamlet of the Ghost) performed in the round in the Living Arts museum and exhibition space as part of the festival; a full production was mounted later in November. Actors were costumed in a variety of styles, with Claudius and Gertrude in modern European business attire and Hamlet dressed more informally, wearing a T-shirt with an image of a kitsch item—a skull image overlaid on a beer mug. The costuming actualized a clash between characters who resist colonization (Ophelia and Hamlet, in a bright color palette) and those who represent it (Polonius, Gertrude, and Claudius, in neutral tones). The entire costuming scheme got darker as the play progressed, offering a visual manifestation of the play's impending tragedy. Moses designed the sound and translated portions of the script herself in addition to using the Spanish-language translation from Mexican publisher Editorial Porrúa, and her family members from Panama and Guatemala did the lighting. In terms of staging for the festival excerpts, the performance space was surrounded by seating, and around that, community altars.

The setting was adapted to colonized Mexico, though Moses made a deliberate choice to keep the references in the play to the original setting of Denmark.[89] The events take place on November 2, the last of the two-day celebration for the spirits of those who have departed. This setting lends the play a sense of urgency: the spirits of both King Hamlet and Ophelia will leave at the end of the festival, passing on to another realm, and a full calendar year will pass before another opportunity arises to revenge King Hamlet and let his spirit rest. There is also an amorphous idea of time and place, however, to signal both the continuing acts of colonization and the interplay of the worlds of the living and the dead. Despite the Indigenous ritual references, Moses wanted to make the setting both specific and ambiguous to illustrate that acts of colonization have not ended. For example, Bernardo tells Horatio of the Ghost, saying "O'er the sounds of celebrations / During Dia de Todos los Santos / The bell then beating one—"[90] and the Ghost enters. Horatio speaks to Bernardo in Spanish, "Calla; mírale por dónde viene otra vez" (Quiet, look where it comes from again), and just six lines later describes the Ghost as having "that fair and warlike form / In which the majesty of Denmark / Did sometimes march)."[91] This ambiguity functioned to keep the characters and audience in two locations (Mexico and Denmark), in two time periods (early modern and colonial Mexico), and in two languages (English and Spanish), as they attempt to speak across spiritual worlds (the living and the dead). The production thus marked a cross-cultural, temporal, linguistic, and spatial border experience.

All characters in the play are designated as Latinx, but their language skills vary: the Ghost speaks only Spanish, for example, while Hamlet and Ophelia are bilingual. The adaptation retains Shakespearean language, but Spanish is used intermittently throughout, including for some of the famous lines; Hamlet reveals himself throughout the play to be skilled at navigating between the two languages. At the beginning of the play, he speaks English exclusively, demonstrating that following his father's death he feels he must assimilate. Once he encounters the Ghost, Hamlet realizes that his father's death was not a natural passing. He begins to weaponize Spanish so that others will think that he is crazy, that he is resisting the colonizing force of English. For example, as the Players get ready to mount their performance, Claudius asks, "How fares our cousin Hamlet?" to which Hamlet responds, "Muy bien. Me mantengo del aire como el camaleón engordá con esperanzas. No podrás así a tus capones," (Excellent, i' faith; of the chameleon's dish: I eat the air, promise-crammed: you cannot feed capons so) and Claudius replies, "I have nothing with this answer, Hamlet. / These words are not mine."[92] Moses retains Hamlet's lines from Shakespeare's play, but his wordplay and puns are transposed to Spanish, to which Claudius cannot respond because he only speaks English. Claudius has fully embraced white colonial culture, as evidenced by his English-language monolingualism. Ngũgĩ wa Thiongo writes, "The bullet was the means of the physical subjugation. Language was the means of the spiritual subjugation."[93] This Hamlet is not actually mad, but he uses language to convince others that he is: accepting linguistic subjugation is code for accepting spiritual subjugation, and here, Hamlet does neither.

Key to Moses's decolonizing praxis is amplifying the role of Ophelia and reworking the play to grant her more agency. This Ophelia personifies resistance within a patriarchal society. Moses shifts the dialogue about how Ophelia responds to being told of her father's death to depicting that scene onstage, making clear that Ophelia's descent was not unintentional and was not madness. When Claudius tells Laertes and Ophelia that Hamlet killed their father, Laertes immediately states his intention to kill Hamlet, and Ophelia pleads with her brother: "Una vida no traerá otra. No tendré a nadie y estaré sola en tristeza por el resto de mi vida. ¿No soy importante para si?" (One life will not bring another. I will have no one and I will be alone in sadness for the rest of my life. For am I not important?)[94] Laertes does not heed her advice, and in the next moment, the audience watches Ophelia kill herself, a scene absent from Shakespeare's play. The stage directions read,

It starts to rain as thunder and lightning strike as OPHELIA walks up to the river. We can hear the rushing of the waters as soft, solemn music plays. She's sobbing. As she walks up to the bank, she pulls out her makeup. In a ritualistic motion, she attempts to paint her face like calacas one last time. She finishes, throws her remaining makeup into the river, and stands.[95]

Ophelia moves toward Indigeneity by painting her face as Gertrude at the outset moved away from it by removing her calaca makeup. Once Ophelia has become a spirit, she and the Ghost appear together during the scene with the Gravedigger, to see and hear the Gravedigger describe her death: "It must be *se offendendo*; it cannot be / else."[96] Ophelia has agency in the scene, and she hands Hamlet a skull and watches Hamlet and Laertes fight at the gravesite. Her choice to cross into the light at the play's end does not equate to her absence; she is an active presence that shapes and observes the action.

Moses's adaptation makes clear that even a patriarchal and colonial society needs Ophelia, and her spirit as well. Although both Hamlet and Ophelia are victims of colonization, Hamlet is still enmeshed in patriarchal discourse and actions and treats Ophelia as a subordinate. After he has just learned that his father was murdered, he is "still shaking from the anger of his discovery. . . . He grabs her by her wrist. It hurts. . . . He gets overwhelmed and shakes her, pauses, sighs, then lets her go."[97] At this moment, Moses seems to ask how we can resist assimilation without hurting others. All the men enact colonialist actions; Claudius is Latino and has been colonized linguistically and culturally, and he has killed his brother for power, which is a colonizing action.[98] The emphasis on Ophelia brings to light the space where patriarchal norms and coloniality intersect.[99]

Ophelia's deceased mother was Indigenous, but her father, Polonius, is Mexican. Although Polonius understands and speaks Spanish, he urges Ophelia to speak English to assimilate:

OPHELIA: ¡Papá!
POLONIUS: How now, Ophelia, what's the matter?
OPHELIA: ¡Que he tenido un susto muy grande!
POLONIUS: With what, i' th' name of God? In English, child![100]

Beyond this notion of linguistic assimilation, this exchange highlights the similarity between Ophelia and Hamlet. Hamlet's depression is rooted in a loss of culture and community; his father was his last connection to preco-

Figure 8: Xavier Santiago as Hamlet and María Carmona Hernández as Oph-elia in *Hamlet: El Príncipe de Denmark* by Tara Moses (dir. Tara Moses, 2018). Photo by Russell Mills. Courtesy of Tara Moses.

lonial life, as evidenced in the Ghost's inability to speak English. Ophelia's suffering is a direct result of colonization, and, like Hamlet, she has lost the parent who connects her to a precolonial Indigeneity. By juxtaposing Oph-elia with Hamlet, Moses does not make Hamlet a martyr but rather posi-tions him as someone who is deeply flawed and yet resists colonization. Ophelia's role in the play extends through to the end, positioning her as a model for Hamlet, someone who can help him transition to the next part of his journey, to the spiritual realm.

The play within functions similarly to how it does in Shakespeare's play, but here it is through the invocation of Indigeneity that Claudius is given to rise and affirm his guilt. The Players enter "in folk masks. They move around the stage in a traditional, physical manner,"[101] as they per-form their show without words. Here Shakespeare's dumbshow is trans-posed to the silencing of Indigenous languages but retains the visuality of costuming and choreography. Hamlet watches, speaking his asides in Spanish, distanced linguistically from the English-speaking (though Indigenous-masked) players but sharing his thoughts in confidence with the Spanish-speaking audience. For example, when the Player Queen says, "If, once a widow, ever I be wife," Hamlet replies under his breath, "Si ella no cumpliese lo que promete."[102] Indigeneity here is performed through movement and gesture, as linguistically Indigenous cultures have been silenced; but the Indigenous-themed dumbshow is also prologue to "The Mousetrap," which causes Claudius to rise and confirms for Hamlet that his uncle killed his father. The entire audience is privy to Hamlet's increasing revelation through his expression and gestures, but only the Spanish-speaking audience has the privilege of hearing his thoughts when he speaks Spanish in response to the performance, giving them the upper-hand to the English-speaking (white) audience.

The end of the play returns, in a way, to the beginning. In the final scene, calacas "perch on either side of the stage, awaiting what is to come."[103] After the killings, Fortinbras enters, and he speaks his lines in a British accent, signaling white coloniality as the political winner of the monarchy. The last lines, though, belong to Ophelia and the Ghost:

(They bend over to examine the bodies. Lights change and they freeze in tableau. Soft, Indigenous music plays. The spirits make their way downstage.)

OPHELIA: Pero ahora que los ánimos están en peligroso movimiento, no se dilate la ejecución un instante solo, para evitar los males que pudieran causar la malignidad o el terror. This above all: to thine own self be true. (But now that the spirits are in a dangerous movement, do not delay the execution for a single moment, to avoid the evils that evil or terror could cause.)

(The GHOST helps HAMLET up.)

GHOST: ¿Entiendes ahora? (Now do you know?)

(The three exit into the light. Blackout.)[104]

The last line of the play, "¿Entiendes ahora?" is the Ghost's response to the first line of the play, "Who's there?" The tableau, then, picks up where the opening Day of the Dead rituals left off, and Indigenous practices frame the theatrical event, in addition to being interwoven into the plot and dramaturgy of the play. Decoloniality involves creating borderlands spaces of the theater with identity performance, ceremony, and ritual. These spaces are both linguistic and aesthetic, "because the border is a space where English and Spanish compete for presence and authority."[105] Theatrical bilanguaging, telatúlsa's *Hamlet* makes clear, can be and must be part of the practice of decolonizing Shakespeare, illuminating how coloniality produces a crisis of the self that only begins to heal when borders are broken down between white and Latinx audiences, Spanish and English, theater and ritual, Shakespeare and Latinidad.

TOWARD A DECOLONIAL AMERICAN SHAKESPEARES

In all three *Hamlet* adaptations, the use of theatrical bilanguaging facilitated an explicit engagement with coloniality, linguistic hegemony, and cross-cultural power structures that resulted in an expansion of the theaters' communities, drawing in new audiences and attempting to democratize Shakespeare. None sought to tell a specific history, but each was entrenched in the cultural and theatrical politics of their locality.[106] The practice of decoloniality through Shakespeare was enabled through addressing the historical and geographic moments of each production: Papp's Nuyorican culture at the height of the civil rights movement, Asolo's Cuban Miami culture in a locale and moment with an increasing Latinx population that is not Cuban, and in the Mexican-Indigenous South/Southwest of teletúlsa's show. These breaks reveal a border gnosis in the Shakespearean ecosystem and lead to the possibility of a reparative future by integrating locally specific cultures.

Papp's inspiration to open up new perspectives in the play evolved "so that eventually no scene was allowed to carry the same significance it bears in the classical arrangement."[107] Part of that new perspective was hiring a diverse cast and listening to and engaging with the cast as collaborators. Sheen commented that "the cast literally contributed new ideas daily that became the production."[108] It was Sheen's heritage that prompted Ramon the Puerto Rican janitor, and his cultural identity and linguistic agency were both reflective of him as an actor within the character he portrayed. The purpose was to get the audience into the play, and outside of it too. The liberation from linguistic and stylistic norms for Shakespearean performance has remained a hallmark for the NYSF in the decades that have followed.

Hamlet, Prince of Cuba was part of Asolo Rep's forty-third season, and Michael Donald Edwards adapted and directed the play in his sixth season as artistic director. Located in Sarasota, Florida, over two hundred miles northwest of Miami, Asolo Repertory is "the largest professional not-for-profit theatre in the U.S. south of Atlanta."[109] While demographic statistics for Asolo's audiences are not published, the theater markets its audience to corporate sponsors as "culturally sophisticated, well-educated local residents, business professionals and seasonal visitors with high average household income."[110] Asolo advertised to its investors that the 2011–12 season would provide "outreach to the Spanish-speaking community,"[111] primarily through the Latinx *Hamlet*, which only contributed ten Spanish-language performances to its entire season.[112] Edwards included the regional tour and full Spanish-language production to draw in new audiences and reflect the Spanish-speaking communities in central and south Florida. The surrounding area is 19 percent Latinx,[113] and ultimately, setting the play in Cuba did attract a mixed local Latinx audience and offer the chance for some Spanish speakers, including student groups, to see Shakespeare performed for the first time.

Hamlet: El Príncipe de Denmark, the first Shakespeare play to be performed at telatúlsa, was a catalyst for both Moses and the theater. The company had been known as Tulsa Latino Theater Company (TLTC), staging works by Latinx people for Latinx people, and consequently, white audiences didn't attend. *Hamlet* offered a gateway for wider audiences, both wider Latinx audiences and white audiences, as it is a familiar story to many, but in fact not all; Moses said she told people who were unfamiliar with the play, "It's like *The Lion King*."[114] They reached out, literally, in part through the inclusion of talkbacks and a partnership with the Equality Center due to their DREAMers program. With *Hamlet*, then, telatúlsa attracted new audiences while also integrating Indigenous ceremony into a canonical text, challenging seeming borders between the living and the dead, and centering a female character in a play dominated by the male lead and male society. In 2019, Tara Moses was named artistic director, and the theater changed its mission.

While Papp's *Hamlet* included what was a problematic attempt at staging a lower-class and ethnicized interiority, both of the twenty-first-century productions invoked Indigenous rituals in a theatrical depiction of border gnosis, or border thinking that involves a knowledge of the spiritual. The border between English and Spanish (linguistic), Latinx and white (cultural), and Shakespeare and Latinidad (power relationships) cannot be negotiated without an exploration of interiority, and the two twenty-first century productions feature Indigenous characters and knowledge as essential—socially, spiritually, dramatically, structurally—to Latinx identities and stories. *Hamlet, Prince of Cuba*, actualizes this motif and stages Hamlet internalizing the shaman/Orisha to learn the truth of the past. Several years later, *Hamlet, El Príncipe de Denmark* interweaves Day of the Dead Indigeneity for Latinidad.

The case studies in this chapter are unique in part because ensemble plays dominate in the history of Latinx Shakespeares, due to a historical lack of Latinx actors being welcomed into the Shakespearean actor-training pipeline.[115] *Hamlet*, no matter how it is adapted, is no ensemble play, and so both Edwards's and Moses's adaptations helped rupture the notion that Latinx actors are not up to the challenge of leading roles, as well as the corollary notion that they have only limited opportunities before them. But in the last decade, these ideas have been clearly disproven. In 2011, Julliard-trained Frankie J. Alvarez was acting at OSF when he was cast as Hamlet at Asolo Rep, and in 2018, as casting was underway for *Hamlet: El Príncipe de Denmark*, the actor "who played Hamlet just showed up."[116]

The ecology of a borderland permits movement, confrontation, and intermixing; walls ruin the free-flowing ecosystem of the space of the borderlands. The walls that govern productions that adhere to the *West Side Story* effect as a trope for division are a detriment to the community of characters in the play. In productions of *Romeo and Juliet*, for example, the *West Side Story* construct ignores the community of men that permits Romeo to describe his competitor for Juliet's hand, Paris, favorably, as "Mercutio's kinsman, the noble County Paris!"[117] There is household division already in the text; the additional layers of ethnic and linguistic divide build a political wall between the two sides. And yet the *West Side Story* effect serves an essential role on the path toward decolonizing Shakespeares: it chips away at a (white, hegemonic) cultural ecosystem, even if this act of division can only take us so far. Frederick Luis Aldama and Christopher González argue that "Border Theory stresses the idea that the proximity of two cultures creates a permeable boundary that allows for movement, contestation, hybridity, and creation of something new altogether, among other things."[118] Decoloniality is not simply about opposition, but a counterstance (specifically that of division) is necessary to begin the process toward rebuilding and creating something new in the third space, the borderlands, los intersticios. These productions demonstrate three possible strategies for moving toward a decolonial, and perhaps reparative, future. It is the process of productive messiness within the imbrication of Latinx and colonialism with which these *Hamlet* adaptations engage; the process is part of the third space of the borderlands.

Chela Sandoval argues that "de-colonizing performatics generate a pause in the activity of coloniality; their activity discontinues its ethos.

Before clarifying their function further, we now break for a brief intermission."[119] This "brief intermission" is the space where change is possible, or as María Lugones phrases it: "The interstices are where the decolonial imaginary is at work."[120] It is this brief intermission, between Shakespeare and Latinx theater, between Hamlet's inner soliloquies and outer performance, between the rehearsal room and the public performance, that becomes a site of decolonizing one of the best-known plays worldwide.[121]

| El Público

Healing and Spectatorship

In 2004–5, the Old Globe in San Diego partnered with high school teachers and students on both sides of the US-Mexican border for its Bi-National Project, which presented a bilingual, large-cast staging of *Romeo and Juliet* under the title *Romeo y Julieta*. The cast included sixty student actors from ten high schools as well as adult actors, and it resulted in a total of five performances in San Diego, Chula Vista, and Tijuana after a series of rehearsals at an elementary school halfway between San Diego and Tijuana. Shakespeare's story was adapted to incorporate Mexican culture and youth culture, with the ball where the lovers meet transformed into a *quinceañera*, skateboards included in the fight scenes, and Latinx-style music ranging from cumbia and salsa to hip hop woven into the soundscape. The production was in fact trilingual, including Spanish, English, and Mixteco, an Indigenous language of Mexico. Performances catered to the local audiences. In Mexico, the play was performed as seventy/thirty Spanish/English, "with quite a few Mixteco words and speeches added" for the Tijuana performances.[1] For the shows in California, it was reversed, with a seventy/thirty English/Spanish mix. The project fostered cultural exchange between the high schools, theaters, and countries.[2] Translation services were employed, and the project crossed borders not only geographically and culturally, but also financially.[3]

This binational collaboration set the tone for subsequent initiatives from other companies and organizations, both because of its focus on the rehearsal and cultural processes to build bridges rather than solely on the final product, and because of its turn to Latinx Shakespeares as a way to help navigate the cultural and linguistic divide. For example, the 2019 Bridge Across the Wall Bilingual Theatre Festival—created by Bay Area company Symmetry Theatre in partnership with actors and theater spaces in San Miguel de Allende, Mexico—included a bilingual staging of *Much Ado About Nothing* (under the title *Mucho Ruido y Pocas Nueces*) as one of its two productions. American director Chloe Bronzan treated the creation process as collaborative, working with multiple Spanish translators and speakers to develop the script, and making further adjustments based on input from the Mexican actors.[4] In line with Symmetry's mission for gender parity in theater, Broznan changed Dogberry, Don John, and Leonato to female characters.[5] Some characters were expats and some Mexican nationals, some bilingual and some monolingual. Claudio was portrayed as a fraternity-type American who doesn't speak Spanish and Hero doesn't speak English that well, offering the *West Side Story* effect as a reason for their misunderstanding of each other. After the performances in San Miguel, the Mexican actors were able to travel to northern California for an encore performance.[6] Both of these examples of border-crossing productions illustrate how artistic expression and collaboration can cross borders of influence and generate new audiences.

While a number of theater companies now regularly cross the established border between countries for such outreach initiatives and festivals—and plays and theatrical concepts address life on the geopolitical border along the southern United States and Mexico—this chapter focuses on mobile theater of a different sort. Here I look at theater that moves within the United States, bringing Latinx Shakespeares to new audiences in big cities and small towns alike.[7] Such productions seek to transform both the politics of the stronghold of Shakespearean performance and that of ethnic theater. In Lee Bebout's analysis of whiteness on the border, he writes, "We do not need to accept contemporary racial politics as they are. Radical imagination is required."[8] The necessary radical imagination, when applied to theater, is the work of worldmaking.

Dorinne Kondo studies worldmaking in theater and performance, writing, "'Worldmaking' evokes sociopolitical transformation and the impossibility of escaping power, history, and culture."[9] This definition echoes Gloria Anzaldúa's call for community-based art and community activism, or "engaging in healing work."[10] But Kondo's theoretical framing is specific to theater and focuses on structures and processes for change. Kondo explicates the processes and possibilities of what she terms "*reparative creativity*: the ways artists make, unmake, remake race in their creative processes, in acts of always partial integration and repair."[11] The act of engaging Latinidad, auralidad,[12] and Shakespeare is in fact an act of radical imagination in the long history of Shakespearean performance. Yet the worlds that have been imagined in Latinx Shakespeares are something that conventional wisdom and the US media cannot seem to enable through their divisive rhetoric. My focus thus far has been mostly on worldmaking onstage and backstage. Here I push my attention to the collaborative work of the making of an audience for a new type of ethnic theater.

At the center of one of the powerful projects contained in Latinx Shakespeares is this fundamental consideration of reparation. Can engaging in a site through which so much colonial violence can be and has been enacted—one that insists on the real possibility of "our Shakespeare"—lead to healing? The adaptations discussed across this book signal different stages on a path toward transformation that results in new publics generated for and because of the intersection of Shakespeare and Latinidad, a space that offers keen potential for healing and worldmaking. This intersection generates new possibilities by productively bringing together two modes of thinking too often conceptually and politically separated. If, as Jon Rossini notes, "Thinking of the border as a theater provides a site-specific frame for understanding theatricality as a spatial practice,"[13] then the continuous creations of real and metaphorical borders that emerge in the movement of Shakespeares into new spaces and voices to craft new audience communities is an ideal form of worldmaking. In "explicating the relationship between space and the framing of ethnicity,"[14] Latinx Shakespeares can, at their best, force a reconsideration of exactly how we are situating Latinidad within the United States, fundamentally recognizing it as part of the larger US theater scene and not something apart from US theater. Kondo's model of reparative creativity provides a language to think through and with the theater of artists working in community to create new articulations. Articulations are the constructed practices and connections between seemingly different groups, objects, and ideas. Articulation theory, as developed by Stuart Hall, is an analytical tool to describe the process of connections and activism. It emphasizes that "positions are strategic and motivated, rather than arbitrary and free-flowing," but also stresses the exploration of possible alternative articulations. Worldmaking conceives of art-making as something that both represents and generates ideas about ethnicity and culture, and the possibilities generated by Latinx Shakespeares create new connections within art and audiences.

Latinx Shakespeares resist hegemonic and white traditional modes of Shakespearean performance and theater-making. All Latinx Shakespeares are intracultural theater, and some are in fact ethnic theater, theater by and for a specific community. The case studies in this chapter push on that definition; they are the collaboration between theater companies and communities that together advance both the dramaturgy and politics of performance and reception and, outside the scope of theater, challenge strongly held notions of American identity as well. The two productions I attend to in this chapter both engage a borderlands epistemology but do not cross a physical, geographic border. They are invested in worldmaking, the result of years of public engagement work by their respective theater companies, both of which have a mission to create art for their communities and create new publics for the arts. Oregon Shakespeare Festival's 2019 *La Comedia of Errors*, a bilingual adaptation, was performed in one of its primary theaters as part of the regular season, and it also was performed elsewhere on the OSF campus and toured throughout the region through a partnership with twelve Latinx community dramaturgs. Teatro SEA's 2015 *Sueño: A Latino Take on Shakespeare's A Midsummer Night's Dream* was performed entirely with puppets, and first staged in an outdoor parking lot in New York before traveling to Puerto Rico, Washington, DC, and back home to New York. Both productions fully integrated Latinidad—through the soundscape, casting, aesthetics, concept settings, and collaborative processes—into Shakespeare, creating design and production teams from a range of Latinx cultures and some outside of them, and staging work that was not "site-specific" but rather local to the communities they wanted to reach. Both productions were conceived and performed by mostly Latinx theater-makers, and for mostly Latinx audiences. But the diversity of peoples, the strategies for mobility, and the fundamental differences between work from a predominantly white institution (PWI) and from a Latinx theater all inform their possibilities as ethnic theater.

NEW MAPS OF HEALING: *LA COMEDIA OF ERRORS* AT OREGON SHAKESPEARE FESTIVAL

In 2007, Bill Rauch became artistic director of the Oregon Shakespeare Festival (OSF), beginning a trajectory that would change the face of American theater, including Latinx Shakespeares. Rauch, who had previously cofounded the community-based theater company Cornerstone, commissioned an internal audit of OSF by Carmen Morgan and ArtEquity, with a focus on the theater's commitment to diversity.[15] In 2008, OSF created a Festival Latino, whose offerings included bilingual backstage tours, Spanish captioning for six plays, and other cultural activities and performances. This one-time event helped shape a broader cultural outreach program, heralding a dramatic shift toward Latinx plays at OSF.[16] Before the Festival Latino, OSF sporadically engaged with Latinx playwrights or Spanish-themed plays. Every season under Rauch's tenure (2008–19) included a Latinx or Latinx-themed production, with these offerings beginning to feature Latinx Shakespeares starting in 2011. According to Trevor Boffone, "OSF has shown more of a commitment to supporting the work of Latinx theatre artists than have most regional theatres."[17] In fact, in the last several years of his time at OSF, Rauch hired Latinx directors to direct non-Latinx-themed Shakespearean productions, marking a Latinx integration into the pool of Shakespearean directors that did not require them to represent, or be representative of, their cultural backgrounds (such a level of integration is unfortunately still rare across American theater). For Rauch's last season at OSF, the mainstage season featured three shows that embraced and reflected Latinx aesthetics, culture, and dramaturgy: a new play from Octavio Solis (*Mother Road*), a Latinx-directed but non-Latinx-themed *Macbeth*, and the bilingual *La Comedia of Errors*. For the first time in OSF's history, it staged both a Latinx-authored play and a Latinx Shakespearean play in a single season (both directed by Rauch himself, in his final send-off to OSF).

From its text to its staging to its pre- and postshow framing to its touring plan, OSF's production of *La Comedia of Errors* was focused on fostering new audiences and building community. Rauch partnered with OSF dramaturg Lydia G. Garcia to adapt Shakespeare's play into the fully bilingual show. They began their process with an English-language translation of *Comedy of Errors* that African American playwright Christina Anderson had created for OSF's *Play on!* initiative (2015–18), which commissioned thirty-six playwrights to translate Shakespeare's thirty-nine plays into contemporary English. Garcia authored the Spanish translation, using Anderson's text (a line-by-line translation into contemporary English) to translate portions into contemporary Spanish, with Salvadoran, Mexican, Costa Rican, Puerto Rican, and more nationally specific Spanish languages included.[18] Characters shifted between languages and responded in one language to dialogue in the other:

> ANTIPHOLUS OF U.S.A.: Yo, open the door!
> DRÓMIO DE MÉXICO (within): Sí, cómo no, si me das una buena razón, por favor.
> ANTIPHOLUS OF U.S.A.: Por favor? Por my dinner: I have not dined today.
> DRÓMIO DE MÉXICO (within): Y aquí tampoco comes. Regresa otro día, güey.
> ANTIPHOLUS OF U.S.A.: What are you that keeps me out of the house I owe?
> DRÓMIO DE MÉXICO (within): El portero cuidando el arco, y mi nombre es Drómio.

DROMIO OF U.S.A.: O villain! You've stolen both my job and now my name. The one never got me credit, the other lots of blame.[19]

The act of clarifying language by modernizing it—the objective of the *Play on!* initiative that had led to the initial English-language translation—also functioned from Spanish to Spanish. The contemporary English translation facilitated more direct engagement with current political issues of immigration, and translation became thematic within the dialogue as well. For example, when The Guide / El Guía says, "Don't let anyone know you are illegal," Antífolo de México responds, "Ah, somos indocumentados, no ilegales."[20] Here El Guía uses the antiquated term "ilegales," and Antífolo modernizes and clarifies with "indocumentados." The text also highlights other aspects of Chicanx and Mexican cultures. In Shakespeare's text, the layers of plot and character confusion lead to Pinch's suggesting to Adriana that Antipholus and Dromio "must be bound and laid in some dark room" as a cure for their perceived insanity.[21] In the Garcia and Rauch text, this treatment for insanity becomes a jar of VapoRub, a substance with deep meaning in some Latinx cultures. VapoRub, or Vaporú, as it is affectionately called, is a nostalgic cure-all that "some telenovela actors even rub . . . on their eyes to bring about tears. Others scoop it into their coffee or their tea."[22] In performance, the jar was carried around the stage, and the audience was even invited to "join in the worship."[23] The specificity of this reference to Chicanx and Mexican culture invoked an immediate sense of community and provided a specific pedagogical moment for an audience unaware of this practice.

While largely adhering to Shakespeare's script, Garcia and Rauch added a character, La Vecina (the neighbor), who was played by Meme García (they/them) in the 2019 production. La Vecina begins the play "seated in the audience, as yet another audience member."[24] She speaks only from the audience, commenting toward and on the action of the play. A reviewer noted, "As La Vecina, Meme Garcia makes sure we understand that la tragedia of 'La Comedia' plays out daily on our country's southern border."[25] Her interjections, at first largely in Spanish but then in English as well, clarify the action for all audience members. She says,

Espera, espera, espera.

(to audience)

If you're not a Spanish speaker: apparently, the gringa house
    cook—who is wild about "Latin" dance—insists that Dromio

Figure 9: Caro Zeller as Luciana and Tony Sancho as Dromio in *La Comedia of Errors* by Lydia G. Garcia and Bill Rauch (dir. Bill Rauch, 2019). Photo by Jenny Graham. Courtesy of Oregon Shakespeare Festival.

here is her partner, and not just on the dance floor, if you catch my drift. She's been dancing him up and down Latin America all afternoon.

(to ANTÍFOLO and DRÓMIO)

Why don't you show us how? Adelante, caballeros.[26]

Like a Greek chorus, La Vecina speaks to both the audience and the actors in different moments, and she has the power to explain the action and propel it forward. In performance, after her invitation to Antífolo and Drómio, the two actors performed a comic-relief bit, dancing with each other to the various styles of Latin dance: la bamba (Mexico), salsa (Cuba), reggaeton (Puerto Rico), cumbia (Colombia), samba (Brazil), tango (Argentina), and even the dreadful Macarena (Spain). Through exposition, interjection, dance, and comedy, the audience follows the story and can engage a variety of Hispanic, Latinx, and Latin American cultures. The dance sequence could be perceived as solidifying stereotypes, but I argue here that it challenges them by showcasing a range of cultures often subsumed under the unifying banner of Latinidad and being performed by Latinx actors and under the explicit umbrella of high comedy. Cast and creative team members hailed from Latinx communities (Puerto Rican, Mexican, Nicaraguan, and Salvadorean, to name a few) from all over the United States. Further, it allows the audience to take in Shakespeare's comedy through a contemporary genre that is recognizable in the Latinx community that the play serves.[27]

La Vecina illuminates for the audience how to understand this early Shakespearean comedy by comparing the action to her "telenovela favorita"[28] and later says, "All we're missing in this telenovela is a case of amnesia, a faked death, or a nun with a past. We've already got plenty of twins."[29] Theater reviewer Maureen Flanagan Battistella notes that La Vecina "is a reminder that the telenovela form has both ridiculous and serious intentions."[30] This "neighbor," who speaks from the audience position both literally and figuratively as the voice of reason, functions differently than the Duke who opens Shakespeare's version of the play and other narrative characters such as Chorus in *Henry V* and *Romeo and Juliet*, Time in *The Winter's Tale*, and Hymen in *As You Like It*. La Vecina offers to the audience a metamodel for how to engage with Shakespeare and is positioned as a worthy interlocutor; she is bilingual.

La Comedia, from pre- to postshow, ran counter to previous Shakespearean productions within OSF, and within most PWIs. Just as OSF's programming strategies over the last decade slowly built to this fully bilingual production (see chapter 2 for OSF's initial Latinx Shakespeares), its theatrical strategies for *La Comedia* eased the audience into a bilingual show through direct civic engagement at the outset, physical theater at the start of the play, and community-building through shared experiences at the end. The show began with a thirty-minute pre-engagement between the actors (nine in total for the production) and the audience members, in order "to prep the audience and to own the space for the ninety-minute performance."[31] Community liaison Alejandra Cisneros states that this practice was a callback to shows on Spanish television stations such as Univision and Telemundo, where TV hosts such as the Chilean Don Francisco directly engage the crowd. The properties, costumes, and set were all minimal, with a movable door onstage that actors could use to enter from multiple directions.[32] Rauch purposefully turned to nonverbal forms of communication to bring all audience members into the story. For the first scene, for example, in which Shakespeare has the merchant Egeon deliver a series of monologues to the Duke about the two sets of twin boys and his family's shipwreck, the OSF version transposed the exposition to physicality and mime, with music, props, and bilingual placards used to "underscore" the action.[33] The birth of both sets of twins was comically portrayed by the actresses as they each pulled two bundles from underneath their shirts. This *acto*—a short, representational play, often in Spanish—included a storm created with the actors' bodies; one actor carried a small toy plane that is struck down in the storm, humorously accompanied by a doll dressed as a pilot made to "'jump' out of the plane with a toy parachute."[34] Everyone survived the crash, and then the actors created a sandstorm that separates the twins. This use of physicality rather than monologue to convey the backstory culminated when "the cast [led] the audience in applause,"[35] clearly signaling the end of their pantomime, and indicating that the actors are both performing for and in direct dialogue with the audience. In this way, the show bridged audience reticence about bilingual theater, the Spanish language, and/or Shakespearean plays, through visual excess: this demonstrates how auralidad and the visual excess of physical theater can work together to create ethnic theater from a nonethnic (Shakespearean) source. The postshow experience of the touring production included a shared meal and conversation between actors and audience members, in their local venues. Cisneros remarks, "After the show we break bread. We bring tamales, horchata, and share in discussion and get to know each other better and just eat some yummy food."[36]

Thematically *La Comedia* transformed the immigration story that Shakespeare wrote into a Mexican-US, Spanish-English, cultural-linguistic division via the *West Side Story* effect, but the production itself became a bridge to healing through the making of new publics for the theater. *La Comedia of Errors* not only generated new audiences who were previously unaccustomed to bilingual theater, but also remapped OSF's audiences through their first-ever combined repertory run and community tour.[37] OSF brought free performances of the production to local communities as part of "a nuanced community engagement plan that utilised spaces at OSF and the surrounding Rogue Valley in addition to digital spaces."[38] The show toured to mostly Spanish-speaking community centers in southern Oregon and was performed in different sites on the OSF campus, including the indoor Thomas Theatre and the Hay-Patton Rehearsal Center, as well as in a variety of time slots. OSF partnered with eighteen local organizations and created jobs for a group of twelve dramaturgs, a community liaison, and a producer. The dramaturgs were primarily Spanish-speaking, and OSF empowered them to share their voices and contribute suggestions to the play and production.[39] In this way, the play's theme of division and reconciliation maps the history of OSF in its surrounding area (a history marked by a long period of discreteness) and offers a theatrical template for the healing of that division.

PUPPETS AND PUBLIC SPACES: TEATRO SEA'S *SUEÑO*

Teatro SEA's mission to educate and entertain children, and their efforts to do so through puppetry, displace ideas about ethnic theater that position actors' bodies as central to the audience-performer connection. The Society of the Educational Arts (Teatro SEA), which was established in 1985 by Manuel Antonio Morán, is a New York–based theater company "dedicated to theater for children, youth, family, Latino and bilingual audiences."[40] SEA has been extraordinarily successful, with over thirty Association of Latin Critics (ACE) Awards, over twenty-five Hispanic Association of Latin Actors (HOLA) Awards, and several dozen more awards and honors, including the invitation to perform *Sueño* at the Dedication of the Fifty-First International Theatre Festival of the Instituto de Cultura Puertor-riqueña in San Juan, Puerto Rico, in 2015. It has a history of producing Latinx versions of a number of classics, including *Don Quijote, Cinderella, Goldilocks and the Three Bears, The Three Little Pigs, Pinocchio,* and others.[41] Teatro SEA uses children's stories and puppetry to address specific issues, a type of "cultural preservation."[42] For example, *A Mexican Pinocchio!* | *¡Viva Pinocho!* addressed immigration, and *The True Story of Little Red* | *La verdadera historia de Caperucita* took up the issue of children using technology.

Whereas Rauch used pantomime and physical theater to work along-side auralidad, Morán's use of puppetry provided the visual excess for monolingual Spanish, monolingual English, and mixed bilingual theater, all of which SEA produces. Morán notes that European classics and Disney stories are often performed in Latin America, and that he wanted "to edu-cate a group that didn't have the resources to bring their kids to the theatre. I did things they would recognize, children's theatre Latinized."[43] Although Teatro SEA has an indoor theater and often tours schools to perform for children, it created a show in which some of the puppets were taller than a room in a one-story building and the spectacle larger than life. In 2015, in collaboration with the Clemente Soto Vélez Cultural and Educational Cen-ter (the Clemente) and the Latin American Theater Experiment Associates (Teatro LATEA), Teatro SEA turned its attention to Shakespeare, creating an adaptation of *A Midsummer Night's Dream* titled *Sueño*. Morán directed and produced the show, which was performed at "La Plaza," the parking lot of the Clemente, with performances alternately entirely in English and entirely in Spanish.[44] Tickets were free with an option to donate, facilitating attendance for young people and families. Audience members brought blankets and lawn chairs, and there were inexpensive concessions for purchase.

For this production, the action was transposed to an Afro-Cuban carnival style, and the play text was written in prose, with only the Mechanicals, Oberon, and Puck speaking some verse directly from Shakespeare. Two actors narrated the story, standing onstage with exaggerated large folio books in their hands, one of the two on stilts. The remaining actors were dancers and puppeteers, and a live band performed below, in front of the stage. Puppet theater scholar Penny Francis writes, "Puppetry springs from two taproots: one nourishes its magic and illusion, its dramaturgy of ritual and religion, fairy tale, legend and folk memory, and the other nourishes the broad branches of its comedy, parody and satire."[45] *Sueño* captured the first of these "taproots," with heavy doses of magic, carnival, and folktales.[46] The casting call was advertised with dance as the priority, and the text was adapted by Cuban playwright Norge Espinosa and translated by Chicano actor Alan González, and the creative and performance teams included individuals from Uruguay, the Dominican Republic, the United States, Spain, Puerto Rico, El Salvador, Mexico, Peru, England, Cuba, Brazil, Colombia, Holland, Canada, and China.

The characters and story largely follow Shakespeare's play, with alterations to engage Caribbean culture and the production's concept. Morán "wanted that universe to be completely white—scenery, the props, costumes—everything as white as snow. The only exception would be the actors-puppeteers-dancers and the puppets, who would be mulatto or Black, representing the Afrodescent of the region."[47] Although the actors' bodies were not centered, Morán's concept depended on the specific casting of actors of color. The "skin color" of the puppets was akin to darker Brown or racially Black, and all puppeteers and puppets were costumed in white. Bright colors projected onto the backdrop gave each scene a new thematic sensibility, from bright hot pink as the actors held small puppets on sticks, to orange-yellow, when Bottom with both donkey head and hind legs confronts Oberon with his crown and bejeweled full-costume plush body. Morán notes, "The final production had over 65 puppets, masks, bigheads, 'vejigantes' and body puppets combined with actors, modern dancers and live music. Together they represented the story and additional dreams set in a Caribbean and Latin magical realism environment."[48]

In the parking lot where the show was staged, lighting, music, and the white fabric established the dream world at the top of the show. It was a spectacle, even by the standards of a night on the Lower East Side, with bright lights, warm blankets, and the hope that a summer rainstorm would pass. When the music began and lights came on, all of my senses engaged, from the feeling of close community with the people around me, hearing murmurings and expressions of excitement from children in Spanish, the smell of warm food on a cool post-rain summer night, and noting pass-ersby who stopped in their tracks when seeing bright lights and actors on stilts. The play begins with a prelude and dialogue between Oberon and Puck, the lovers having already appeared in the tropical forest. They both speak in verse, and Puck contextualizes the action within an atemporal set-ting, "It's a summer night, my king, a night which incites love! (*Moves for-ward.*) It all started when these lovers appeared. It all started, as in the beginning of time, with a pair of lovers."[49] Morán accentuated the dream and fantasy aspects of the play to make it suitable for children, and the use of puppetry, music, and dance was emphasized over the problematic sex-ual and power dynamics of Shakespeare's play.

Here the magic does not have its origins in a male god but in mythic women of the region in which the story is set; the sound effects, music, and rhythm are sourced from the magical world. The source of magic in Shake-speare's play comes from the place "where the bolt of Cupid fell: / It fell upon a little western flower"[50] that Oberon instructs Puck to fetch. In *Sueño*, Oberon recollects the "magic flower I found near the sea, that night when we heard the sirens," and Puck sighs, "Ah, sirens of the Caribbean."[51] Although Shakespeare sets up his play with a plot that is dependent on magic as an essential component, here Espinosa gives agency to the super-natural, to the fantastical, by making the fairy Puck the narrator who also opens the play.[52] Puck and Oberon's brief exchange in contemporary Span-ish prose (or contemporary English prose, on alternate nights) begins to shift as Puck narrates the tale of the lovers. The lights change, the music begins with drums and singing, and Puck begins to speak in verse, along with the rhythm of the music. In Shakespeare's play, the fairies speak in a range of meters; here Espinosa creates short lines of varying lengths, relax-ing the constraints of the verse but retaining the musical feel.

The variety of styles and sizes of puppets added to the affective quality of a carnival that the show celebrated. *Sueño* presents Oberon as the domi-nant force, and he opens the second act singing,

I am the night, I am the master
of each step within the forest.

Figure 10: Oberon and the fairies' carnival in *Sueño: A Latino Take on Shakespeare's A Midsummer Night's Dream* by Norge Espinosa (dir. Manuel A. Morán, 2015). Photo by George Riverón. Courtesy of Teatro SEA.

> I have within my hand, every mystery,
> And so, I have dominion over man and beast.[53]

Oberon was modeled "after Spain's 'gigantones' or giants: rigid and tall, worked much of the time by a single puppeteer. Titania, on the other hand, is a giant puppet with many articulations in arms, torso, head and legs, requiring six puppeteers."[54] In this way, Oberon's presence was more rigid and grand, and Titania was able to move more intricately due to the style of puppeteering. If the dominance of the male Oberon was conveyed through sheer size and immobility, the coordination of the female Titania contributed to the complexity of character and more nuanced physical movement. The four lovers were puppets nearly three feet tall, each held by actors from a stick underneath so that they appeared physically above the actors' heads. These puppets did not have body parts capable of movement, conveying their static position and shape even as their situation changed. By contrast, the Mechanicals were puppets of roughly the same size, but much fuller and with openings for the actors' faces. Each puppet was maintained by an actor and placed on a long table, with the actor directly behind it. This made the actor in fact the face of the character yet shortened the body to half of human size. Consequently, the dream world of the play was diverse in size, color, and shape, and characterization came through in differentiating puppetry styles.

During the intermission, *Sueño* offered an entremés-style entertainment, a short one-act interlude, that also explained a key literary reference in the play to those who might not be familiar with it—the story of Pyramus and Thisbe. With three actors/puppeteers, this interlude offered a break from the Shakespearean story that was being presented on the elevated stage and instead brought a different form of theater to the same level as the parking lot, with closer proximity to the audience. A presenter and two puppeteers directly addressed the audience to stage a brief puppet version of the story of Pyramus and Thisbe. The storytelling style was aimed at the children and young people in the audience, with hand-sized puppets and a playful atmosphere often employed with young audiences, and the dialogue was spoken entirely in prose:

PRESENTER. Ladies and Gentlemen!

PUPPETEER 1. Older Ladies and Older Gentlemen!

PUPPETEER 2. Children, Infants, babies . . . fellow country men [*sic*], lend us your ears and listen.

PUPPETEER. Listen to a story we are about to tell . . . a story so terrible, so sad . . .

PUPPETEER 1. . . . so painful is the unfortunate love of Pyramus the Brave and Thisbe the beautiful . . .

PUPPETEER 2. DON'T FORGET THE LION!!! Of course this tremendous show would have a Lion! Lets [*sic*] see, who can play the drums so we can continue with this story? You? You? How about you?[55]

This interlude, which took place without bold lighting or music, was both outside the play and within it; while it maintained the play's themes and provided some useful context for the upcoming act, it was not integral to the plot of the show. Some audience members took it as an intermission, eating, talking, and using the restroom, and the turn to less poetical language with the house lights up allowed parents and children to converse about the show while it was happening. People greeted one another, an experience fundamentally different from most indoor Shakespearean theater intermissions; the night I attended I met some people who were seeing the show for the second time.

At the end of the show, after the lovers were happily reunited at the command of Theseus, Puck closed out the night with a jubilant call to revelry: "Oh night, let us be happy, let us sing, let us dance, let us love. Let us love forever!"[56] The bright white lights set up in the outdoor space counteracted the colors of the show, and the audience awoke from the dream that they experienced that night. Postshow, many of the actors and the orchestra came into the audience to greet friends and members of the community; because the show was performed only at night, their all-white costumes starkly contrasted to the black sky and parking lot. Families with small children left for bedtime (the show ended at about 11:00 p.m.). All in all, the production was marked by high theatricality—puppets, music, dance, bold lighting, and unreliable weather conditions—and it was incredibly successful. While Morán and SEA's work had for years been specifically not just about, but for, the Latinx communities in New York, with *Sueño* they moved their performance outside, and showed New York audiences and passersby that theater for the community can be simultaneously professional, colorful, musical, freely accessible, cross-cultural, and linguistically varied. Morán served multiple audiences within the community with this production, including monolingual English speakers, monolingual Spanish speakers, children, adults, puppet enthusiasts, and those who wish to see Afro-Cuban culture and music celebrated. *Sueño* garnered rave reviews and a bevy of awards,[57] and as a result it traveled to Puerto Rico, serving as a bridge for Caribbean theater from New York to Puerto Rico. In 2018, it was produced by Teatro SEA and the MORÁN Group for the first International Puppet Fringe Festival NYC, and it was performed every night of the six-night festival.

THE PATH TO WORLDMAKING

Theater is an inherently public art form, and theater-makers always want to attract new audiences. This objective is perhaps even more prevalent among the theater-makers who take on the challenge of making Shakespeare for specific ethnic communities. Over the course of a decade, OSF prepared a predominantly white and monolingual English audience for bilingual theater and Chicanx cultural references and storytelling. Developing an audience was always just as important to Rauch as the development of theater; in 2009, Rauch asked, "'How much progress can we make in creating a theater that, in its work and in its audience, reflects our country?'"[58] Teatro SEA prepared communities unaccustomed to theater and stronghold myths of the Western canon for community-building through a shared family theatrical experience. Both trajectories challenge a traditional definition of ethnic theater and model how PWIs and theaters of color can create an audience over time.

This chapter demonstrates that theaters, centers for the arts, and other organizations can create movements toward theatrical bilanguaging (in its myriad of forms) and ethnic theater. But this can only be achieved through a long-term commitment and with the resources and desire to take risks. Rauch's annual commitment to engaging Latinidad within a PWI was in fact a multiprong approach: he integrated Latinx themes into Shakespeare and other Western canonical plays, commissioned and staged adaptations and appropriations of the Western canon, and he staged contemporary plays by and about Latinx.[59] Morán created works for a range of Latinx audiences, in both English and Spanish, and sought partnerships with arts organizations to create accessible theater that not only represents but celebrates the community. Rauch's tenure at OSF culminated in the season that included *La Comedia*, and Morán celebrated the thirtieth anniversary of his company by adapting Shakespeare for the first time and producing *Sueño*. They, and many other theater-makers, partnered with their communities to move art forward and help to create audiences and publics for it.

Unlike Joseph Papp at the NYSF decades earlier, who at first diversified Shakespeare and later came to produce and develop work by minority playwrights and practitioners, Rauch's artistic work in diversity grew out of devised and community-based processes and into his role as artistic director of the largest repertory theater in the United States, integrating diversity initiatives into Shakespeare.[60] What both OSF and SEA achieved was the integration of a movement toward linguistic, cultural, and theatrical diversity into the theaters. Social scientist Hildy Gottlieb offers clear definitions of movements versus organizations. She writes, "In movements, accountability is to a cause greater than any one individual. When it comes to making tough decisions, the cause is the top priority. In organizations, accountability is first to the organization; when leaders face tough decisions, their top priority is organizational sustainability."[61] Both Rauch and Morán were accountable to the cause; Rauch stepped into an already established repertory theater and integrated a movement toward diversity and community theater into the organization, and Morán was tasked as founder and artistic director of Teatro SEA to "expose a community, an immigrant community, to expose kids and families to these works" and create a theatergoing public.[62]

Each theater was also met with challenges to its movements. OSF focused more on Latinx plays about Latinx culture, and the number of Latinx actors, designers, and staff increased as well. But there is a recent history of resistance to this diversity work by OSF's white neighbors. When OSF staged *The Wiz* in 2016, a local bookstore placed a racist book next to a copy of *The Wizard of Oz* as a response.[63] Some even attributed lower financial revenue to more diverse programming rather than environmental factors such as wildfires that caused the theater to close for portions of multiple seasons.[64] More friction occurred when in 2020, OSF actor Tony Sancho, who played Dromio and Drómio in *La Comedia*, was detained by Jackson County police, which led to a lawsuit due to the way he was treated by white police officers.[65] Despite the successes of OSF's movement toward reparative creativity, the work of healing remains a process for which some were not yet ready.

Likewise, Teatro SEA faced challenges, but of a different sort. SEA regularly performed for schools by 1999, but due to the events of 9/11 a few years later, it lost almost three-quarters of its school contracts.[66] SEA's physical mobility is what makes it part of a community, and generative of a community. It set about to rebuild, shifting from a 50-seat theater to opening a 150-seat theater in 2011, which is often sold out for shows. And more recently, the puppets from *Sueño* suffered a Shakespearean fate: they were lost at sea in a tempest.[67] Less romantically stated, after the show ran in New York in summer 2015, all of the puppets were shipped to Puerto Rico (where they were originally designed and built) for the shows that fall. The puppets traveled back to New York in January 2016, but SEA's team did not open the boxes for several months. Upon so doing, they realized that not all of the puppets had made it back. This was devastating and costly, but it prompted the necessary rebuilding of the puppets, this time with cardboard and liquid plastic rather than the previously-used foam rubber that was expedient. The intricate detail met with Morán's vision: "I am very clear; I am not competing with Broadway. But we cannot just do children's theatre with a red nose."[68] Consequently, *Sueño*'s Titania's puppet was included as part of the 2021 exhibition titled *Puppets of New York* at the Museum of the City of New York alongside puppets from *Avenue Q* and Oscar the Grouch, and the Oberon and Puck puppets were also featured in a puppet exhibit at the Ballard Institute and Museum in Connecticut from November 2021 to May 2022, as part of an exhibition on Puerto Rican puppetry. The audiences that SEA cultivated for Latinx Shakespearean puppet performance extend beyond the theater and the local community.

THE TRANSFORMATIVE POWER OF COMMUNITY THEATER

Latinx Shakespeares demonstrate that ethnicity can permeate Shakespearean storytelling and aesthetics, and community theater can bring together audiences. Dorinne Kondo writes, "The work of creativity enacts reparative critique, challenging liberal ideology's split of aesthetics from politics: the liberal humanist subject, authorship as the work of the singular imagination, dramaturgy as polite suggestion, power-free conversation, and the audience as unified."[69] Both *La Comedia* and *Sueño* enact such reparative critique through culturally specific forms—the telenovela for *La Comedia* and carnival aesthetics for *Sueño*—and the liberal humanist subject transforms to physical comedy for *La Comedia* and puppetry for *Sueño*. They each are the result of extensive cross-cultural collaboration, and they integrate storytelling modes and specific Latinx communities beyond a superficial concept setting. The different forms of bilingual theater the plays exemplify showcase linguistic dynamics and possibilities for their community-specific yet heterogeneous audiences. By engaging storytelling genres and a visual excess to accompany auralidad, these two productions, and others like them, exemplify how Latinx Shakespeares can function as a mode of healing.

This type of collaboration extends beyond long-standing theaters such as OSF and Teatro SEA, suggesting that the communities, onstage, offstage, and in the audience, exemplified in this chapter can last beyond the event. For example, in 2018, artists from the Public, SITI Company, and Pregones Theater / PRTT's Raúl Juliá Training Unit collaborated to devise a piece called *To Be or Not to Be . . . A Shakespearean Experience* as part of the "Beyond Workshop" series. It was helmed by Puerto Rican Broadway actor, performer, choreographer, and director Luis Salgado and performed at the Harlem School for the Arts. Performers ranged in age, dance and acting experience, national background, and language. Jose Solís states that "the performances were warmly received by audiences who praised them for being reminders that the United States is a country where walls should be torn, not put up."[70] Salgado's work speaks to methods for creating community around creating new work through Shakespeare; rather than adaptation, the devised piece inspired by Shakespeare positioned collaborators as creators of the piece themselves. In 2019, Salgado directed a multilingual, multicultural version of *The Tempest*, performed at Pregones with a cast of twenty-two and a heavy amount of movement created by five guest choreographers. Both pieces were collaborations between Pregones/PRTT (a theater) and R.Evolución Latina (an arts organization). They both involved music, movement, and dance, artists from a variety of Latin American countries, seasoned and new actors, English and Spanish, Shakespeare's language, and Spanish Golden Age poetry.

Expanding dramaturgy to an excess of the visual—Rauch's physical comedy, Morán's puppetry, Salgado's choreography—marks the opportunity to counter Shakespeare's hegemony through the combination of auralidad and visual excess, making explicit the power dynamic of ethnicizing Shakespeare. The division that marked early Latinx Shakespeares is reframed in more current works as a mode of discovery. Long-term strategies for worldmaking can result in ethnic theater, both at PWIs and at theaters of color. This only becomes possible through the acknowledgement of an audience's heterogeneity and deliberate cultivation of a public for bilingual and semi-bilingual theater. Through collaborative processes, diverse casts and artistic teams, these productions force a reconsideration of how publics situate Latinx in the United States. Collaborative reparative work can transform the division of the *West Side Story* effect into a bridge.

six

Futures

Shakespearean Critical History

El Fausto (Falstaff) enters from the battle offstage, covered in red liquid and saying, "Chingao, bullets flying every which way, buey! A burrito, a burrito, my kingdom for a burrito! Shit! I don't need any lead in my panza. My gut is heavy enough" (89). Lives are being lost and bullets are flying, and El Fausto does not want to get killed. But the kingdom is today's city of San Diego and it is not El Fausto's to claim, making his expression that he would give it up for a burrito all the more comical. El Henry (Prince Hal) and Johnny (Lancaster) enter, and Fausto says, "Look at all the blood on me." When El Henry tastes the "blood," he says, "That's enchilada sauce!"[1] El Henry and Johnny do not have time for El Fausto's jokes; they return to the battle. El Fausto is scared he will be killed, fakes his own death to the sound of a Pavarotti aria, and falls to the ground "with a dramatic thud."[2]

This chapter centers on a single Latinx Shakespearean play, Herbert Siguenza's 2014 *El Henry*, a postapocalyptic adaptation of *Henry IV, Part I*.[3] *El Henry* moves away from modes of division and representation to serve as a speculative critical history, a style of play in which time overlaps in order to fold critical and creative praxis, Latinx and British history. This Latinx Shakespearean history play situates Latinx peoples in a narrative that precedes this identity construction and places them in a future beyond white settlerism. Whereas the productions and plays based on Shakespeare's comedies, tragedies, and romances in this book are recontextualized into the past and the present, they operate within the established ideologies of their formal genres. But a history play that is set outside any historical time period and does not include real-life characters involves layers of speculative imagination that do not exist within even a heavily fictionalized story of the past. As the culminating chapter of the book, this discussion of *El Henry* models how a futuristic concept adaptation of a Shakespearean history play offers a theorization of Latinx place and time, integrating Shakespeare and Latinx theater into a new historical configuration.

ETHNICIZING A HISTORY PLAY

But how can a history play be adapted to Latinx contexts? I turn to this play in this closing chapter in part because it directly contravenes the *West Side Story* effect. *Romeo and Juliet*—like many of Shakespeare's tragedies and comedies—is easily transposed to Latinx Shakespeares because it lacks a cultural specificity necessary to the action. The lack of anything Veronese about the two lovers of Verona makes their story an easy template for other, later stories to be layered onto. In contrast, history plays are chock full of historical detail (even if that detail is largely inaccurate). This historical detail makes the plays less viable for adaptation and, frankly, less appealing for production and study alike: US theater companies today produce the histories as rarely as high schools and universities address them in their curricula. For example, San Francisco's African-American Shakespeare Company, founded in 1994, has produced only one history play, *Richard III*, in 2018, and Classical Theatre of Harlem has produced one history play of the six Shakespeare plays in its more than twenty-year production history, *Henry V*, in 2011.[4] *Richard III* is the history play that figures most prominently for African American practitioners due to its historical theatrical legacy. The production of the African Theatre's first performance in 1821, of *Richard III*, becomes the subject matter for Carlyle Brown's 1988 historical play, *The African Company Presents Richard III*, commemorating the event. There is no Shakespeare history play that has a similar performance resonance for Latinx practitioners. Until 2014, with the production discussed in this chapter, no Latinx Shakespearean history play had been mounted at a regional or professional theater, and none has since.

Shakespeare's history plays are in fact no more historically accurate than Lin-Manuel Miranda's lauded 2015 racially and musically diverse hit, *Hamilton*. Alexander Hamilton, as the primary character, is made more palatable; his progressive views on slavery that likely involved his owning household slaves are reshaped to an abolitionist stance.[5] But whereas Miranda sacrificed accuracy in service of centering the story of a historical immigrant portrayed by a contemporary person of color, Shakespeare had no such decolonial vision. Instead, he fictionalized the love stories, dialogue, and defining historical moments of England's past for dramaturgical effect. Take, for example *Henry IV, Part I*. In Shakespeare's play, Prince Hal and his friend Falstaff take turns in a bar play-acting the role of King Henry IV, a fictitious scene that speculates about possible future events. In actuality, Shakespeare reshaped the character of Falstaff, an amalgamation of the real-life Sir John Oldcastle and other men, as a Lord of Misrule to heighten the comedy. For a dramatic duel scene between two factions, he staged Hotspur's death by Prince Hal's hand, even though historical accounts of Hotspur's death vary.

While both Shakespeare and Miranda adapt history to create plays, Siguenza uses a British history play to depict one possibility for the future of Chicanx (those in the United States who are Mexican, Mexican-American, and Mexican-descended) and Latinx. For his postapocalyptic adaptation, Siguenza transposes *Henry IV, Part I* to the year 2045, and to a place identified as "Aztlan City, Aztlan. Formerly San Diego."[6] The primary elements of the story remain the same, although now the royal houses lead rival Chicano gangs. These gangs exist as a powerful underclass in a San Diego that has been abandoned by the Americans and is now under the control of a white Hispanic government. El Hank (King Henry IV) is about to go to jail, and he worries about the future of his gang since his eldest son, El Henry (Prince Hal), spends his time partying at a tavern with his friends, including El Fausto (Falstaff) and the tavern owner, Chiqui (Mistress Quickly). The generals meet, El Hank and his rival, El Tomas (Northumberland), and El Tomas's son, El Bravo (Hotspur), but they do not arrive at a truce. The two gangs are at war, and El Henry joins his father's fight after learning that his father has been importing water and selling it at cost in the barrio; El Henry has a newfound respect for his father for this. El Henry challenges El Bravo to an individual fight to spare the lives of their gang members, but El Bravo declines. El Henry later kills El Bravo in action, and El Hank stays out of jail and retains his power. The play includes numerous additional characters in each gang. El Fausto provides the comedy and direct address to the audience, telling spectators: "There was a worldwide bank collapse and Mexico went completely bankrupt, fifty million Mexicans fled north, . . . [and] In 2035, the Gringos, the Negros, the Chinos even the Ethiopian cab drivers said 'Chale! Screw this! Too many Mexicans!—we're out of here.'"[7] With this as the pretext, all the characters are people of color. The only way for Siguenza to speculate an entirely Latinx future was to make it postapocalyptic, but even then, the Latinx characters are othered, subject to a ruling class of white European-descended Hispanics.

Siguenza engages a history play to speculate forward; the implied historical period is the present day, and his play cautions white and Latinx audiences about their complicity and current actions. His play is thus a work of speculative fiction that advances a critical approach to history. While historical fiction justifies and explains the route that led to the present, speculative fiction causes the audience to think critically about the present time and justifiability to a possible future. A critical approach to history involves interrogating the past in order to produce judgment about the present, assessing how power structures may have shaped our personal concepts of identity and ways of thinking, and incorporating one's identity and experience as tools of analysis of this past. This process may not lead to a final or singular conclusion about past events, but it does expose how the narrative of the past is shaped, by whom, and to what effect. Further, a critical reading of a historical fiction requires imagination that engages elements of myth, spirituality, and cultural consciousness, and with a burrito-like overlapping circularity of time, Siguenza folds Shakespeare as mythmaker of the historical past into Chicanx, Mexican, and Aztec myth to shape a historical narrative of the future. Notably, Siguenza's critical approach to history involves looking forward rather than looking back.

Siguenza uses the creative work of playwriting to generate a mode of historical criticism that is not dependent on Western dualisms, ethnoracial binaries, cultural division, or even a creative-critical split. In this, he participates in a practice that is both method and methodology for a Shakespearean critical history—a method for engaging with Shakespeare's history plays to develop new work as a methodology and dramaturgy for future history. While all Latinx Shakespeares are a creative-critical practice, the act of speculating forward through the genre and subject of a history play offers an intervention into both Latinx and Shakespearean histories and futures. I argue that Siguenza's *El Henry* models a Shakespearean critical history by overlapping British history with speculative Latinx/Chicanx futures, thereby forcing new questions about historicity, temporality, and identity. *El Henry* functions as a creative-critical investigation that uncovers, corrects, and revises the history of Hispanic and Latinx peoples, negotiating a history absent in Shakespeare's oeuvre through his story line. Rather than opposing the creative to the critical, or the historical to the futuristic, Siguenza's play reveals a praxis in which their overlap models a circularity of time that is necessary to intra-Hispanic/Latinx critique and to combat hegemonic narrative principles that will otherwise continue forward to the future. Shakespeare's historical fiction and Siguenza's speculative production overlap to rearticulate a physical (theatrical) connection between Shakespeare's revisionist history and Latinx/Chicanx practices for self-empowerment.

CHICANAFUTURISM AND LATINX SPECULATIVE THEATER

El Henry moves away from the dominant collective politics of culturally appropriative Shakespearean productions and adaptations that attempt a homogenized Latinx identity to represent onstage. Shakespeare's history plays allow for a variety of subject positions within one country's culture, gender, and race: other than a few French characters, the plays are dominated by English characters who share a country unity but range wildly in class, region of origin, language, accent, and at times, nationality.[8] Even minor British characters are individuated, antithetical to a monolithic representation of an Other, a theatrical consequence of having one or few characters from a marginalized group. Siguenza's critical meditation on *Henry IV, Part I* applies Shakespeare's same principle of individuality and differentiation within a cultural-national group in order to embolden Chicanx to claim their history and their own memorable (fictional) historical-futuristic characters. Here I turn to the theorization of Latinx speculative arts in order to situate *El Henry* within frameworks beyond Shakespeare studies.[9]

The speculative future is one possibility, one articulation, constructed from information available today. Stuart Hall's articulation theory moves away from binaries of performer-audience, sender-receiver, and colonizer-colonized.[10] Articulations are the constructed practices and connections between seemingly different groups, objects, and ideas. In this configuration, Latinx and non-Latinx theater practitioners, Latinx culture, physical theater spaces, and the economics, development, and marketing of Shakespearean productions all come together in various possible figurations. These connections are contingent and always in process, and, in fact, they may cause something to be lost in the process of connection-making.

In response to the exclusion of Chicanx, especially Chicanas, from histories and art involving science and technology, Catherine S. Ramírez coined the term "Chicanafuturism" in 2004 to describe "Chicano cultural production that . . . excavates, creates, and alters narratives of identity, technology, and the future."[11] She first formulated this concept to describe and theorize the work of female visual artist Marion C. Martinez, and she looks to the work of Gloria Anzaldúa and Octavia Butler, both of whom write extensively on women and queer sexualities. Ramírez applies her concept to all genders and people of color. For this reason, the term includes the feminine-gendered "Chicana" as part of its portmanteau, but its application extends beyond art made by and for women. Ramírez says that it applies to "Chicanas, Chicanos, and other people of color. And like Afrofuturism, which reflects diasporic experience, Chicanafuturism articulates colonial and postcolonial histories of *indigenismo, mestizaje*, hegemony, and survival."[12]

The term "Chicanafuturism" can be applied to non-Chicanx yet Latinx-related futurisms, but here I remain focused on *El Henry*'s specific portrayal of Chicanx and border issues to locate a specificity of setting, theme, design, cast, and audience that Siguenza's *El Henry* achieves. Chicanafuturist plays engage Indigeneity and nonlinear time rather than futuristic cyborgs. An example is Cherríe Moraga's *The Hungry Woman: A Mexican Medea* (1995), which is set in the then-futuristic second decade of the twenty-first century in the ethnically and racially divided spaces of Gringolandia and Aztlán, or what is today's Phoenix. Moraga's *Medea* moves backward and forward in time, includes a chorus of pre-Colombian Aztec warrior women, and explores the depths of maternity and humanity though a queer Medea who kills her son.

Chicanafuturism has roots in the speculative writing of Latin American authors such as Jorge Luis Borges and Gabriel García Márquez, both of whom imagine possibilities for the future that overlap with the present and the past. Numerous Latinx playwrights have embraced speculative aesthetics and forms, from Luis Valdez to María Irene Fornés to Caridad Svich to José Rivera to Georgina Escobar.[13] Cathryn Josefina Merla-Watson and B. V. Olguín argue that Latinx speculative arts "repurpose and blend genres of sci-fi, horror, and fantasy to defamiliarize the ways in which the past continues to haunt the present and future."[14] While some Chicanafuturist works may also be defined as Latinx speculative arts, *El Henry* does not meet this definition due to its lack of the supernatural and mixing of these genres.

According to Ramírez, Chicanafuturism "attends to cultural transformations resulting from new and everyday technologies (including their detritus)" and thus "redefines humanism and the human."[15] While technological advancement is often aligned with a notion of "progress," postapocalyptic art—visual, literary, dramatic—reveals how sophisticated technology (from cyborgs to genetically modified foods to artificial intelligence to advanced weaponry) often portends challenges and catastrophes to humans due to a lack of thought for the ethics and consequences of human invention. This is often done with "a vision of the future and past converging in the utopian possibility to reimagine the present as a world no longer conforming to heteronormative, patriarchal, and white supremacist patterns of thought."[16] So, for example, it's not uncommon for a futuristic story to be set after a nuclear war,[17] and this holds true in Siguenza's play, in which Lil Gus (Poins), El Henry's associate, tells El Henry, "The state of Oaxaca had a big nuclear explosion in the 20's and all the babies were born with one eye."[18] Oaxaca, known today as an American tourist destination, is the site of Siguenza's catastrophic disaster.

Postapocalyptic visions do not depict death to all. Rather, they fictionalize the stories of survival for those who pay the consequences of faulty human inventions. And in the Chicanafuturist world of Siguenza's play, those who pay the consequences are people of color. As the play opens, electronica music is heard,[19] and two homeless men search through "a collection of trash, old signage, tires and old television sets."[20] The two men are a nameless "Young Thug" and Tixoc, whose name is an Anglicized version of Tizocicztzin, grandson of Emperor Moctezuma of the Aztecs.

> YOUNG THUG: Tixoc!
>
> TIXOC: What is it, fool?
>
> YOUNG THUG: I found an iPhone 23!
>
> TIXOC: So what! That's old Gringo technology. It's worthless fool.
>
> YOUNG THUG: I know, huh. *The young thug throws the phone against the brick wall.*
>
> (*Sarcastic*) We're back to steam, coal and transistors. Yippee.[21]

From the outset, then, the audience learns that white, Western technology will not be of use in the Chicanx and Indigenous future. In this future, Chicanx are not the laborers and distributors of what is considered gold-standard technology, but rather the opposite: they rely on antiquated technology in order to survive. Siguenza's speculative *El Henry* opens with a popular device of connection and globalization, made in places throughout the world, discarded in a trash heap. The young thug is temporarily excited to find the iPhone, but the descendant of Aztec royalty quickly realizes the obsolescence of white, Western invention. The future, filled with people of color, is not in a new, ascendant stage of technology; instead, this post-tech future plays out the oppositional political forces that engage or squelch using basic technology such as electricity to give all peoples access to natural resources.

Chicanafuturist productions often include *rasquachismo*, or a making do, as they meditate on advanced technologies and position Chicanx more favorably in a future as users and creators (rather than distributors and manufacturers) of high technology. *Rasquachismo*, which Chicanx art scholar Tómas Ybarra-Frausto coined in his 1989 landmark essay to describe "an attitude . . . a visceral response to lived reality . . . an underdog perspective," manifests in an ability to make do with the materials available.[22] This attitude has also become an aesthetic, exemplified in the everyday, and in efforts that may be described today as "upcycling." A rasquache perspective is embodied in the early Chicanx theater of Luis Valdez and El Teatro Campesino,[23] who used minimal props and costumes to perform *actos* (short plays) from the back of trucks. Siguenza, who was trained by Valdez, utilizes rasquache aesthetics to build the world of his postapocalyptic Latinx Shakespearean play: "The Chicanos are still analog. I just find that funny. [They're] a lot slower."[24]

Rasquachismo manifests in *El Henry* in the characters' need to make do, and make better, with what they have. The characters' weapons, for example, range from rustic to advanced: a bow and arrow, futuristic rifles and handguns, knives, a walking stick with beer cans, a frying pan, car muffler, brooms, a baseball bat, a sickle, and a Japanese martial arts chuka stick. This is a world in which even the basic means of sanitation have been stolen from the Latinx characters, and so El Hank and others must forge their own way. El Hank succeeds in this task by dealing drugs and arms, for which his son, El Henry, condemns him:

> HENRY: Not my shit. Your shit. You're the drug dealer. You're the gun runner. That's your world, and I don't want any part of it.
> EL HANK: Don't be a pendejo, mijo! When the Gringos left, they took everything with them. *Everything!* The technology, the electricity, the cars, even the pinche plumbing! Then the Hispanics flew in like vultures gnawed on the carcass leaving the barrios nothing! Nothing! Nothing but drogas and guns and yes, that's what I do![25]

El Henry thus celebrates the rasquache preference for "communion over purity," or the hybridity and joining together in order to create over the virtue assigned to pristine aesthetics; it is the "high value [that] is placed on making do—*hacer rendir las cosas*."[26] More than that, though, the play demonstrates what Cathryn Josefina Merla-Watson calls "altermundos" or speculative rasquache.[27] She and B. V. Olguín define speculative rasquache as "blending the high and low, the modern and the so-called primitive, concatenating new chains of associations and meanings and going beyond Western dualisms."[28] Speculative rasquache in *El Henry* provides evidence that Chicanx are not dependent on Western inventions or governance for their future, but instead will select from their pool of resources to advance their culture, even if that pool is limited. This spirit of speculative rasquache, and the heart of Chicanafuturism, infuses *El Henry* and transforms it into a Shakespearean critical history play. Speculative rasquache consists of the "making do" under white and Spanish colonialist histories, the making absent of the technologies that depend on Latinx labor to build and distribute products but do not promise connection to the larger culture, and the creative interplay of old and new in *El Henry* to fold a Chicanx future over British colonial history without creating binary division between the two.

The next section looks to questions of spatiality, technology, gender, and economics to understand how rasquachismo works to foster a Latinx Shakespearean history play.

EL HENRY, A SPECULATIVE HISTORY PLAY

The original 2014 San Diego Repertory production of *El Henry* (dir. Sam Woodhouse) was an outdoor site-specific work.[29] No walls separated the audience or passersby from the fantasy, or the homeless people on the streets of San Diego from the homeless character of Fausto, whose make-shift residence is a truck. The production was staged at SILO in Makers Quarter, a dirt lot in San Diego's East Village that functions as an outdoor venue for festivals and gatherings but had never been used for a theatrical production. The site is part of a campaign of urban renewal, and it functioned as "a creative ground zero" for the set and theater design of the play.[30] The dramaturgical aesthetic included aspects of the graphic novel and Mexican vaudeville.[31] Stage manager Laura Zingle expressed concerns about the lack of toilets, running water, seats, electrical outlets, and theater stage, all of which were built and brought in for the show.[32] Graffiti artists were employed as part of the set design, adding to the already graffitied walls in the area, a palimpsest that served as a meta-metaphor for revision and adaptation; the physical space contributed to the aesthetic with "the full moon above stage right and the Hooters billboard above stage left."[33]

The production drew full audiences from within the community as part of the "Without Walls" (WOW) festival hosted by San Diego Repertory Theatre in conjunction with the La Jolla Playhouse.[34] Siguenza, who lives in San Diego, has had numerous shows commissioned by and produced at San Diego Rep since 1993. Siguenza wanted it to be performed outdoors, and first selected Chicano Park in Barrio Logan, "a park that Chicanos did take over,"[35] but it could not accommodate the theatrical setup. The long-standing relationship and Siguenza's community-engaged playwriting permitted Siguenza to draw from the larger area and diverse groups within it, including the lowrider community.[36] But the experience also included non-theatergoers, as Zingle notes, including patrons of the now-closed Monkey Paw Pub and Brewery, "who decided one night that if we could make loud sounds of revelry and war, then so could they."[37] The sounds of traffic, sirens, and nightlife enhanced the theatrical experience and made the production *of* the community. Although Shakespeare staged many of his plays in a large outdoor theater, Siguenza's site-specific location extended rasquachismo to a borderlessness beyond the stage. William A. Calvo-Quirós argues that "the power of a speculative production is not limited to its literary or artistic form, but also derives from its relationship with the community involved."[38] The theater space was not part of gentrification efforts within the East Village, the largest neighborhood in downtown San Diego, as Makers Quarter is described as "both a place and a collective ethos—a community of entrepreneurs, artists and makers."[39] It was a rasquache repurposing of public space that brought together a neighborhood by presenting a temporary possibility for that space, speculating a future for the physical site as well as for community-building.

Just as the rasquache transformation of the lot into a stage space claimed the land for the play, within the story line, the setting of Aztlán City reclaimed San Diego for its original inhabitants. The city's name is a reference to the mythical home of the Aztecs, which ranges from north Mexico to Oregon and Oklahoma (depending on legend) to shape Latinx identity. Scholar Matthieu Chapman, who served as script supervisor for the production, notes, "Through the use of Aztlán, Siguenza challenges his audience to suspend their disbelief in a way that accepts another's claim to the land . . . it becomes impossible to separate the imagined Aztlán of the play from the real Aztlán on which the performance space rests."[40] To create this setting of Aztlán City in a vacant lot in San Diego, the production made use of a digital rasquache, with video projections and lowrider cars driven onto the stage. Siguenza and the design team did not reject technological advancements; rather, they created a theatrical space with both sophisticated lighting and media but also portable toilets and defunct TVs. Frederick Luis Aldama describes a "digital rasquachismo" as one that mocks "the simplistic idea of 'connecting' in solidarity through technology."[41] Digital rasquachismo involves the use of everyday technology for satiric or subversive practice, and Siguenza's futurism offers antiquated technology such as brooms and frying pans as weapons of war. Just as Siguenza's audiences were not brought together by a theater season subscription or access to a theater house, *El Henry*'s characters are not bonded through white technologies, and it is not the sophisticated weaponry that leads El Henry to victory or connects or advances the characters within society. In a world in which iPhones are useless and even plumbing is nonexistent, the play shows how a functioning society can yet prevail.

Siguenza's play both reflects the early history of El Movimiento, the Chicano Movement that became prominent in the 1960s, in its heteronormative patriarchy, but also suggests a need to move beyond it into the future through characters who open up identity categories. According to

Cherríe Moraga, El Movimiento was "deformed by the machismo and homophobia of [the seventies] and co opted by 'hispanicization of the eighties.'"[42] Siguenza includes many seemingly pejorative stereotypes of women: Gata (Francis) is a sexualized woman whom Sir Blunt calls a "hood rat," Fausto grabs the unnamed "Hoochie" and places her on his lap, and El Bravo's girlfriend, Preciosa (Kate), is repeatedly described as an exoticized and ethnic Other, "a beautiful gypsy bohemian."[43] Importantly, however, Siguenza seems to establish such a pattern in the service of showing that machista characters such as El Fausto and El Bravo will not lead the future of Chicanx. The comical Fausto (played by Siguenza) lives to the end of the play, albeit in disgrace and covered in enchilada sauce after faking his death to avoid real death and falsely claiming to have killed El Bravo in the battle scene. El Bravo, who displays a desire to fight (to the death) rather than accept El Hank's "peace offering,"[44] also insults and condescends to Preciosa, who is part of an ethnic minority in Aztlán. When El Bravo seems more interested in plotting his fight than receiving a massage from his love, he barks at her, "You might be able to keep a secret, but you're still a haina [slang for 'chica,' girl], and hainas can't keep secrets."[45] Yet El Bravo's machismo that will literally cost him his life still permits him romance; at the end of this scene, he and Preciosa sensually dance to music from the 1950s, an era when normative gender divisions were not publicly challenged, illustrating El Bravo's outdated idea of masculinity (and his views on femininity), which dies in this futuristic Aztlán.[46]

Instead of reinforcing heteronormative and machista ideologies, the futuristic world embraces unisex and trans characters. Fausto's "partner in crime" is a character named Lil Gus.[47] The audience learns that Lil Gus has transitioned from male to female, a Japanese man who El Henry says to her, "You're the only Japanese man I know that had a sex change to become a woman and now thinks she's a Chicano Vato loco. You're alright with me you freak!"[48] Despite the teasing "you freak," El Henry and the rest of the characters respect and accept Lil Gus, who fights for El Henry's gang, and lives. Preciosa's bar, Club Thump, includes a scene with seven dancers, who wear "unisex costumes" and who are intended by Siguenza to be played by a mixture of male and female actors.[49] Although LGBTQ folx are not key to the primary storyline, their inclusion, acceptance, and survival to the story's end represent a progressive standpoint within an American play, especially one written by a veteran Latino playwright.[50]

One of the most salient characters from a gender standpoint in this play is the character of Chiqui, who both acts as "El Henry's confidante and organizes and trains a group of soldiers to fight for him."[51] With Chiqui,

Figure 11: Kinan Valdez as El Bravo and Robert Milz as Locos R Us in *El Henry* by Herbert Siguenza (dir. Sam Woodhouse, 2014). Photo by Jim Carmody. Courtesy of Jim Carmody.

Siguenza defies a Shakespearean convention noted by Phyllis Rackin, who argues that women in Shakespeare's history plays are either womanly or warlike, but not both.[52] Chiqui is a veteran with an eye patch, and a bartender, but also a friend and even maternal figure to El Henry. She willingly gives her life for his family, remaining committed to the cause even as she lies dying of wounds inflicted by El Bravo. In these last moments, she tells El Henry, "It's OK. I'm happy. (*cough*) I died for you Henry for your family's honor. I've loved you . . . I've always loved you . . . like a son. Now go kick some . . ."[53]

In her final moments, Chiqui embodies an observation that Georgina Escobar makes about women in postapocalyptic narratives. Escobar argues that the "way to start thinking about change is to introduce an end, an end to it, or a death to it. And so there is always a rebirth, and women function in that way of death and rebirth."[54] More than Chiqui, however, the character of La Mayan (associate to El Tomas, similar to Scrope in Shakespeare's play), a woman dressed as a futuristic Maya warrior, operates in this way. Part of El Bravo's camp, La Mayan uses both bow and arrow and futuristic rifles, and when Tomas suggests postponing the fight until they have fireworks and ammunition, she responds, "No need. Me and my girls got it covered."[55] She survives until the last moments of the play, when she and another one of El Bravo's soldiers are brought before El Henry. El Henry, to everyone's surprise, allows the prisoners to live. But the Duke of Earl (Westmoreland) takes them outside and kills them, and "No one hears the shots."[56] This establishes that the possible healing that could be achieved through El Bravo's death will not disrupt the cycles of power that will continue, and no life will be spared in the fight.[57] Both Chiqui and La Mayan die for a cause, but in this futuristic notion of rebirth, the audience understands that the unnamed female Maya warriors that joined the battle will continue to fight, pushing their historical noble warrior past into the future; Siguenza envisions that future through an unnamed army of women pushing against a singular man in power. Although West Side Story's Maria and Anita both live, there is no suggestion that women will lead a fight against systematic oppression in the years ahead; more than fifty years later and looking thirty years into the future, Siguenza's play fully disassociates from West Side Story's concept and tropes and offers that hope through female warriors of the Indigenous past.

A utopian rebirth of Aztlán would involve a return to the time before capitalism or an alternative to any of the economic systems that have been employed to colonize and subjugate people of the Americas. For Siguenza, whose plays explicitly engage history, "Almost every problem in the world right now has to do with colonialism."[58] Latinx are doubly colonized, first through the Spanish and then through white settlers. Therefore, Siguenza's Chicanafuturist play and Latinx speculative arts "remind us that we cannot imagine our collective futures without reckoning with the hoary ghosts of colonialism and modernity that continue to exert force through globalization and neoliberal capitalism."[59] These ghosts shape the events of El Henry. For example, when the white-Hispanic Navarro (El Hank's attorney) asks El Hank to buy tickets for his kids' Catholic school raffle, El Hank asks how much the raffle tickets cost. Navarro replies, "Two Cesar Chavez' each," which equates to $200, a sign that inflation has continued apace into 2045.[60] In the face of charging El Hank a fortune in legal fees so that El Hank can avoid jail time for the crime of stealing electricity to get water to the underclass, the Hispanic Catholic Navarro asks for his further participation in today's faulty economic system, including the opportunistic game of chance: a raffle. Although famed activist Chavez has replaced white, slave-owning colonizers on banknotes, the economic system remains the same, with costs for education of the elite being passed on to the people they subjugate politically and economically. Despite El Hank's wealth and status within his community, he is lured by the raffle's main prize, what Navarro describes as "the complete box set of Cheech and Chong movies on Beta." Hank replies, "Orale! I'm gonna need that in la pinta [jail],"[61] a signal that the incarceration system has prevailed as well and that El Hank believes he will be in jail for a long time for this petty theft.[62] Unlike Shakespeare's King Henry IV, who from the outset of the play is preparing for his eventual, natural death, El Hank prepares for a lengthy incarceration, a noncorporeal yet social death that disproportionately inhabits the American experience of people of color.

But the play offers some utopian elements as well—not least of which is the recovery of Aztlán by Chicanx and Mexicans and futuristic female Mayan warriors. *El Henry* is a postapocalyptic dystopia that, *because* of its rooting in Chicanafuturism, still has hope in it, and hope that is rooted in a communal/sharing economy. El Hank defies the problematic political and economic norms of the establishment, in favor of upholding an eco-consciousness and sharing economy that supplies basic needs. He is buying fresh water from north Aztlán and, in an anticapitalistic move, selling it at cost. It is for this crime, the disregard of a profit-motivated economy that withholds human needs (water) from the people, that the Hispanic authorities want to imprison El Hank for utility theft. Graffiti artist Fernando Martí explains that "different from technocratic futurism, a Latinx futurism would embrace the technologies and ancestral knowledges that will allow for our future resilience."[63] El Hank understands what the government sees as his real violation: "The Hispanics don't care if I'm dealing drugs and guns but once I got into legit water they had to get me on something and put me away."[64] In the play's Chicanafuturistic setting, Earth's materials that help sustain life are valued more than those that satisfy ego and material desires, as El Bravo reveals when he learns that El Hank is "dealing water" and exclaims, "Water? Well there you go . . . more valuable than gold."[65] In this dystopian future, water rights are still framed within a neoliberal system to disadvantage people of color (even though white people are gone, Chicanx are still subjugated by the Hispanic ruling elite). Only once his enemies are dead, in the end, does El Henry announce that he will make water free for all.[66]

While Siguenza upholds numerous aspects of Chicanx identity formation, he ruptures the American government-made ethnic category of "Hispanic/Latinx," which unites European (white) Spaniards with the peoples of the Americas into one homogenous group. "Hispanic" is a term based on language, describing peoples from Spanish-dominant countries, inclusive of Spain. But Latinx is a geographic term and describes the peoples of the

Americas, who share similar political and cultural histories and descend from Spanish and/or Indigenous peoples. While all of the plays and productions in this book include characters from a variety of regional and national backgrounds, and whose cultural specificity is more or less legible within the world of each play, Siguenza's futuristic history engages Southern California–Chicanx identity to illustrate how the unifying concept of the governmental category of "Hispanic/Latinx" becomes obsolete in the future. Further, the positive outcomes of community and activism enabled by today's concept of a collective Latinx identity no longer seem applicable to the Chicanx characters within the play. While both gangs are largely Chicanx, save the ancillary characters Chiqui who is Puerto Rican and Lil Gus who is a Chicana transitioned from a Japanese man, there is no larger intraethnic community. Mexicans having fled north to California, the New Aztlan has a division of race that is clearly a division of class: racially white Hispanics governing over the racially Indigenous, Chicanx, and Mexicans. *El Henry* offers the intraethnic tensions of Chicano gang against Chicano gang, and Hispanics whose white adjacency enables government power and economic success to rule over Chicano gangs. Fausto's direct address and comic subplot are enmeshed with his homelessness, echoing Papp's lower-class janitor alter ego to Hamlet, Ramon, more than forty-five years earlier (see chapter 4). Although comedic lower-class characters are a staple of Shakespearean plays, the Latinx Shakespeares explored in this book utilize such humor for a larger political critique. Further, the play exposes the fault lines within both "Hispanic/Latinx" and "Latinx" as categories and communities.[67]

In *El Henry*, the Hispanic politicians, including a male police chief and a female mayor, all resemble twisted versions of Reaganites: they wear "conservative 1970's polyester suits" and "white powdered half masks with pink cheeks and smile weirdly."[68] Siguenza noted that the partial masks were to signify their half-whiteness.[69] These politicians have also appropriated the United Farm Workers (UFW) symbol—a black eagle set inside a white circle, against a red background—taking an iconic Chicanx symbol of unions and labor rights for themselves, even though their agenda clearly disempowers the people. And the city seal itself is a duplicitous signifier, offering antithetical meanings to Siguenza's characters and his varied audiences: while the seal "looks like the Mayan calendar with the UFW eagle over it and says 'Aztlan,'" its color scheme and eagle both resemble the flag of the Third Reich.[70]

In this futuristic world, there are still "illegal" immigrants, but here they are white Hispanics and other gringos, coming into Aztlán to join the

Figure 12: Roxanne Carrasco as La Chicky and Lakin Valdez as El Henry in *El Henry* by Herbert Siguenza (dir. Sam Woodhouse, 2014). Photo by Jim Carmody. Courtesy of Jim Carmody.

ruling class. After the financial collapse of 2032, and subsequent "Gringo Exodus," Chicanx remained. In a mordant take on American immigration debates, there is no more border patrol, but a reporter asks the mayor about illegal whites, "What are you doing about the illegal Gringo problem?" to which the Hispanic police chief responds, "The Mayor will take no questions. Gracias."[71] If the white Hispanics and gringos are an immigration issue that the Mayor will disregard, then the Chicano gangs "are destroying the moral fabric of Aztlan," causing Mayor Alegre to declare, "Tonight, We Hispanics are declaring a war on Chicano Gangs."[72] In so doing, Chicanx and Latinx shift from their Third World position within white Western frameworks to the oppositional position from Hispanics as they hold noninstitutionalized power; in the future, white Americans are illegal.

The Hispanic/Latinx divide isn't just political but also societal; the Hispanics are depicted only as colleagues to one another, whereas the Chicanx structure their relationships through the fraternal and familial. These social structures are in parallel, though the Hispanics are united through educational and economic ties and the Chicanx through personal and biological relationships. El Hank has "Hispanic police on the payroll," and thanks to his "nerdy Hispanic attorney" he will eventually avoid imprisonment, leading him to give a check "for 10,000 Chavez's for [the Hispanic] Mayor Villa Alegre's re-election campaign."[73] El Hank cannot escape from the system; rather, he must work adjacent to and within it, and as a consequence, support it. He can buy influence with those in power, but he and his descendants will also remain part of a subculture.

CHICANX MASCULINITY: AESTHETICS, INDIGENEITY, AND HONOR

Crucially, *El Henry* represents a clear step away from the *West Side Story* effect, signaling a new direction in Latinx Shakespearean plays. While *El Henry* foregrounds two rival gangs, they share a place of origin, ethnicity, and class, and they are equally matched in numbers. Even their aesthetics are similar. The members of Barrio Hotspur (El Bravo's gang: his father Tomas, and his associates La Mayan, El Mago, Locos R Us) arrive in a low-rider, signaling their aesthetic style. In El Bravo's first appearance, he is described as "a mean street warrior with a Mohawk and wears football shoulder pads, a carrillera of bullets across his chest with punk and Aztec accessories."[74] El Henry is similarly described in terms of a futuristic but mythical warrior after he joins his father's cause. A soldier named Mr. V describes El Henry to El Bravo: "I hardly recognized the vato. He cleaned up. He stood under the streetlight, and I swear I saw an Aztec warrior ready for battle."[75] El Henry appears with his head shaved bald "and now wears a white tank top, a Pendleton shirt, high waisted khakis with suspenders, dark wrap around shades and shiny black Stacy Adams shoes . . . He looks like a brave Cholo warrior of the future!"[76]

Both El Henry and El Bravo draw on Aztec warriors and Chicano cholo aesthetics.[77] Their stylized yet similar appearance was made all the more apparent with the casting of Luis Valdez's sons in these two roles. Kinan Valdez, who is now artistic director of El Teatro Campesino and has codirected with his father, including the 2017 production of *Zoot Suit* at the Mark Taper Forum, played El Bravo. Lakin Valdez, an actor who has starred in Luis Alfaro's *Mojada: A Mexican Medea* at OSF and *Oedipus El Rey* at San Diego Rep, played El Henry. In my conversation with Siguenza, who trained with Valdez, he said that he did not write the show with these casting choices in mind.[78] But having real-life brothers in these roles—and more specifically Valdez's sons, who are active and prominent Latinx theater-makers—extends the story of Chicanx history and futurism to an overlapping of Chicanx theater history and its possible futures.

What ultimately distinguishes El Henry from El Bravo is their differing embodiment of masculinity and honor, and the value that El Henry places on human, especially Chicanx, life. Siguenza's adaptation thus comments on tropes of Chicanx machismo and masculinity. El Henry knows of El Bravo's reputation as a fighter; he tells his father, "In order to avoid muertes and restore my honor, I challenge him to a mano a mano combat."[79] When Locos R Us (similar to Shakespeare's Worcester) reports this to El Bravo, El Bravo becomes enraged.

> LOCOS R US: Nel, not at all. I swear I've never heard a challenge issued with such elegance.
> EL BRAVO: What the fuck?
> LOCOS R US: It was like a brother asking a brother to a friendly contest.[80]

El Bravo cannot accept El Henry's noble proposition; El Henry wishes to "avoid muertes" and spare the lives of many and accede to power not through lineage or advanced weaponry but through hand-to-hand "mano a mano" combat. El Bravo has internalized Western ideas of masculinity, and he attacks his subordinate Locos R Us to demonstrate his own aggression and strength, which he aligns with (heterosexual) masculine power. El Bravo says, "For a minute there, I thought you fell in love with El Henry. Did you fall in love, homes? Did he make you feel all funny inside? Sounds like you wanted to go down on him?"[81] After a few more lines of debasing and homophobic accusations, he then places a gun in Locos's mouth and kills him for bringing him El Henry's proposal.[82] Although Locos suffers this terrible fate, El Bravo and his homophobia do not survive either.

Once El Henry defeats El Bravo, Siguenza creates a climactic tableau that invokes Renaissance Catholic imagery, theatrical depictions of Latinx, and an image that is most often maternal, and recasts it through two real-life Chicanx brothers invoking Aztec-inspired warriors. The stage directions specify, *"El Henry holds the fallen warrior El Bravo like a Pieta sculpture."*[83] Michelangelo's famous *Pietà* depicts the Virgin Mary holding the deceased body of Jesus. This visual image is familiar to Catholics, and invokes the layers of colonization, both political and religious, that the futuristic Chicanx warriors still carry with them. But this position is also the blocking for *West Side Story*'s Maria as she catches her dying love, Tony, as he falls to the ground and "cradles him in her arms" at the musical's end.[84] Invoking the *Pietà*, the white Tony takes the place of the innocent Jesus, with Maria as Mary.[85] Yet here Siguenza plays with embodiment and images by staging them with Shakespeare's language: here he supplies dialogue directly from Shakespeare's play. El Bravo dies saying, "No homie, I am dust and food for . . . ," and El Henry completes his sentence: "Worms."[86] They are brothers in arms, literally, completing each other's thoughts, and the two sides in terms of honor and masculinity are fully stripped away in this image, offering the healing of two like souls. In tandem with Shakespeare's play, El Henry speaks honorably of El Bravo after his death. Warring Chicanx gangs hurt the Chicanx community, and the sentiment of loss was palatable in performance. As El Henry cradles El Bravo, Siguenza supplies a trifecta of theatrical legacies: Shakespeare's dialogue, the blocking from *West Side Story*, and the physical presence of Valdez's two sons onstage. But he also engages Chicanx-Indigenous bodies, the visual of Catholic imagery, and a speculative rasquache in the same moment.

SHAKESPEAREAN CRITICAL HISTORY

Shakespearean critical history understands that a linear historical narrative seemingly justifies (British colonialist) ethics but that futurisms demand a critical analysis of the present. Concept Shakespearean productions aim for specificity and historicity in time and locale, dramaturgically creating a setting that is recognizable to a contemporary audience. Siguenza's futuristic Shakespeare makes the setting precarious, destabilizing the binaries of creative/critical, historical/futuristic, Hispanic/Latinx, Shakespearean/Chicanx, high tech/rasquache. Moving away from divisiveness is key to building community, which is, as *El Henry* signals, the future for Latinx Shakespearean plays. Only through embodying Aztec mythology of the past as the technology of the future can Chicanx (and Latinx) move forward.[87] History plays do not require building community, but futures do.

El Henry as a critical reading of *Henry IV, Part I* displaces the subject of history—kings and royal descendance—in favor of a narrative of Chicanx/Indigenous warriors. Siguenza does not allude to historical Shakespearean performance but instead draws on theatrical representation of Latinx. His speculative history reveals that Latinx Shakespeares' initially dominant frame, the *West Side Story* effect, which contributed to hegemonic nation-building by reinforcing ethnic division, could function as a step toward healing and a new future history. In reclaiming Aztlán, San Diego, basic human rights, and Indigeneity, Siguenza's play not only speculates a different future but also questions the narratives of the historical colonial past. San Diego was in fact not home to the Aztecs, but to the Kumeyaay peoples when the Spanish settlers arrived in 1542,[88] and it is considered the "birthplace of California," as it was "the site of the first permanent Spanish settlement in California" in 1769.[89] Therefore, the reclaiming of the city for Aztlán is not intended to be theatrically cyclical to an actual historical past but instead is a folding or overlapping of times, both past and future. Fernando Martí describes this overlapping of times in his visual work:

> As I thought of a Latinx futurism, the cyclical nature of Mesoamerican time, cyclical, perhaps helical, expanding outward but always returning. Or perhaps it is a simultaneity of times, layered in parallel existences informing the present, accessible through ritual and ceremony. Mesoamerican time gave me a layering of myth and history and contemporary cultures and utopian visions.[90]

Shakespeare's histories helped affirm and consolidate British identity, based on a through line from the past to the contemporary audience. But Siguenza breaks down both time and history, leaving open the future and, in so doing, fractures a seeming cohesive politics of an ethnic identity category and human progress based on Western ideas. Luis Valdez argues, "Non-linear is one of those catch-phrases, like digital, that describes the future. It means non-sequential thinking, which gets us into poetry."[91] In this play, Siguenza shows that Shakespearean poetry and Indigenous temporality—not guns and warfare—are the technology of the future.

The nonlinear temporality pushes not just on history, but on the very concept of Western time that is marked by events in Christianity. It is this original colonization, the shaping of time based on one of the world's religions that would be used to build empire and to suppress Indigenous knowledges, that Siguenza responds to via a Shakespearean critical history play. Unlike Shakespeare's Prince Hal, who comes to understand his role in the future when he and Falstaff role-play his father, Siguenza's El Henry and El Fausto forego this exchange of acting out the future, and instead party in the bar and "Everybody parties and slam dances like theres [sic] no tomorrow."[92] But time continues, and the play ends with Henry on his throne. The cycle continues, but the historical narrative is forever changed by this critical futurism.

Epílogo

The history of Latinx Shakespeares is not a history of division, but rather a history of inclusion, with stops and starts, watershed theatrical productions, and theatrical practices with surprisingly long arcs, such as the *West Side Story* effect. Any study of performance must attend to these mainstay elements, as they reappear in particular moments to leverage dramaturgical strategies and political motivations. This familiar narrative will continue, and with each iteration, it advances a conversation about art-making and Latinidad.

Division is a necessary component in the process of healing fractured relationships within the United States, and early Latinx Shakespeares that are premised on this concept move one step toward creating a new theater public and therefore engage in the first steps of the process of reparative art-making. Creating theater that puts Latinx culture and Shakespeare in conversation prompts questions about American identity, its history and future. In so doing, the directors, actors, playwrights, and other artists that engage in this work contribute to reshaping the American theater through adaptive and appropriative strategies, shifting the landscape of access and labor for both Shakespeare and Latinx theater. This book chronicles how this movement became part of the organizations of the United States' most robust theaters and many of its smaller, local, and community theaters. As Shakespeare's plays are alive in the theater, education, and the cultural consciousness, new modes of storytelling and adaptation will continue to flourish.

The division, exchange, and seeming opposition of Shakespeare and Latinidad does not preclude a productive friction that is germane to Latinx theater. This aspect of Latinx aesthetics and dramaturgy extends beyond binaries of Spanish/English and white/Latinx. Georgina Escobar writes,

> The idea of the other as an active participant in the realization of a whole self is part of what makes Latinx Theatre a vibrant laboratory in the constant search for common meaning, and a common language. Latinx Theatre is not simply looking to identify itself within

the frame of the "Anglo-sphere" as much as it is a new form of theatrical language that seeks to create the best work of art possible."[1]

She conveys this position through metaphor, a rhetorical reflection of Latinx theater as a mode of engagement. Latinx Shakespeares are part of this conversation and cross borders, literal and metaphorical, linguistic and aesthetic, and pose crucial questions about how/why/where we are seeing and hearing Latinidad.

As a theater history, *Latinx Shakespeares* embraces the stories of how artists come to their work. For example, in 2010 when Herbert Siguenza was performing in Culture Clash's *American Night: The Ballad of Juan José* as the first production of OSF's "American Revolutions" cycle, he was cast as an understudy in *Henry IV, Part I*. He watched the show "twenty times but never had to go on stage . . . so it was just a coincidence," and he notes that, "This stuff sounds like barrio warfare to me. About loyalty, family, father-son relationships, honor. All the same things that people die for in the barrio."[2] Sources for inspiration also come from the opportunity that arises because of a talented actor (see Ocampo-Guzmán in chapter 2), a desire for access to certain roles that mainstream theaters do not envision for Latinx actors (see Alpharaoh in chapter 3), means to attract new audiences (see Moses in chapter 4), the use of familiar stories to engage children and audiences new to theatergoing (see Morán in chapter 5), and for Siguenza, learning multiple roles as part of a repertory theater (chapter 6).

It is also a history of the obstacles that theater-makers face. Although OSF's *Measure for Measure* (2011) and *Romeo and Juliet* (2012) were funded in part by Shakespeare for a New Generation, a national initiative sponsored by the NEA in cooperation with Arts Midwest, funding for new work by Latinx artists is often not eligible for substantial national grants. For example, the National Association of Latino Arts and Cultures (NALAC) NFA grant has for years been "open to US-based Latino working artists, ensembles and Latino arts organizations that demonstrate artistic excellence in pursuit of social justice through the arts,"[3] which makes Latinx Shakespearean productions most likely ineligible unless they have an explicit social justice component. Grantors like the New York Foundation for the Arts (NYFA) have changing categories each year, making it more difficult to ensure any consistent funding for a project or type of production from year to year. With granting agencies turning to emergency relief for theaters in the summer of 2020 and the effects of the Covid-19 closures and restrictions, there is hope that the parameters and possibilities for funding will change to encompass a wider range of art-making.

As a methodology for performance analysis, I have put forward artists' voices, focused on the processes and motivations for theater-making, and attended to the aural diversity of Latinx Shakespeares, which is fundamental to their crucial inclusivity. Auralidad will remain a key construct in the theatrical depiction of Latinidad, expanding ideas about sound and culture in the process. Theatrical bilanguaging transposes to bridging a divide by listening for commonality rather than difference across not only languages but dramatic narrative structures and theatrical practices as well, and the act of creating bridges is a look to the future for the new American theater.

The dynamics of theater-making today include a desire for ethical representations of a marginalized ethnic group, but they also include the choice to engage with art—inclusive of Shakespeare—for primarily aesthetic, dramaturgical, and linguistic purposes. Oftentimes, Latinx-themed productions of canonical (white) plays are staged and presumed to be social justice work. Theater for social justice is premised on the understanding that theater can evoke necessary change, and collective work through theater can lead to community-building. In short, it creates or uses scripts to drive political action. While this is a motivation on the part of some theater-makers, the assumption that the value of Latinx art is based in its overt politics elides its aesthetic, dramaturgical, and structural complexities. Cuban American performance artist Coco Fusco writes of this issue:

> The desire to restrict the validity of Latin American cultural production to its capacity to politicize the underprivileged is a symptom of the frustration of leftist intellectuals and a way of ghettoizing Latin American cultural production. It has also been turned in the US into an insistence that all "authentically" Latino artists perform this function. . . . Too many Latin Americans have suffered at the hands of authoritarian systems that reduce all forms of expression—public, private, religious or aesthetic—to a certain political value or meaning for there not to be an enormous amount of skepticism about such approaches to culture.[4]

The integration of Latinx bodies, auralidad, and Latinx cultures with Shakespearean stories does not necessarily connote an antiracist production or an explicitly political one. But the presence of Latinx bodies in theatrical spaces is an ideological stance, art-making is always engaged with the zeitgeist, and ethnicizing white canonical literature is sometimes overtly and always inherently a political act. But to Fusco's statement, now over twenty years old, reducing Latinx art to "the political" undermines and misunderstands its aesthetic and cultural value. In 2019, in a conversation with other BIPOC founders and artistic directors, artistic director of the Latino Theater Company and the Los Angeles Theatre Center José Luis Valenzuela regretted that many foundations "do not give money to art; they give money to social justice."[5] While theater for social justice is an important component of the theater community and an effective tool for engagement and advocacy, so is the recognition that people of color make theater for aesthetic and artistic purposes as well.

When art is judged based on social-political ideology, or determined as either a success or "failure," this simple binary invokes the us-them mentality that performance, and performance criticism, works against. Playwright Jorge Ignacio Cortiñas astutely asks, "What happens if we turn the prevailing ethos of our current moment that art should live up to our politics on its head, and instead insist that it is our politics that must live up to our art?"[6] *Latinx Shakespeares* is an example of the nuances of performance history, the range of factors and processes that go into theater-making, and the attention to detail that must be paid to theorize performance and tell the histories of theater. As the United States experiences internal polarization—political, economic, racial, ethnic—it becomes more and more important to attend to the sophistication of art as means to shape US identity rather than assume its simplicity as means to confirm our own complexity. Gloria Anzaldúa encourages just this, stating, "Intimate listening is more productive than detached self-interest, winning arguments, or sticking to pet theories."[7]

Shakespeare's plays have been taken up by social scientists, theater-makers, and critics to make claims about "universal" ideas of humanity and psychosis, which Latinx Shakespeares confound. The ideas about humanism that the plays portend reveal racialized tropes and the subjugation of women, religious minorities, and cultural Others. And not everyone makes theater to identify, or goes to the theater to identify. For some of the artists who make Latinx Shakespeares, the ethnic and racial issues in Shakespeare are important in fact *because* they are not explicitly tied to Latinx identity. David Lozano, artistic director of Cara Mía Theatre in Dallas, spoke about the process of a Latinx cast exploring the possibility of staging *The Merchant of Venice*, saying,

> in this predominantly Latinx cast . . . *The Merchant of Venice* isn't a play that our community of people of color, who are well-educated in the understanding of racial equity and racial justice—that's not a play that is easily digestible for us. So, there was a lot of questions, a

lot of wrestling with this play. . . . I'm curious if in a *Merchant of Venice*, we're going to find something more vital to our experience that
we may not be able to find in any other play.[8]

The exploration of other cultures, especially through performance, is a
well-known means for generating empathy, and as I have argued throughout this book, it is a strategy toward healing. Further, what is less often
discussed is the pleasure of not identifying, of staging lovers' quarrels or
political strife through stories that are so far removed from one's culture
that the pain is disassociated; it is poignant but not personal. Sometimes it
is in this distance that both artistry and healing flourish.

Latinx Shakespeares are not just part of American theater; they change
American theater. Even the übertext of *West Side Story* came to function as
the backdrop of a contemporary Latinx play—Matthew Lopez's 2011 music
and dance-based play, *Somewhere*, about a Puerto Rican family in love with
theater in 1959 New York. Further, Latinx-themed Shakespeare productions can positively contribute to diversifying the actor-training pipeline, to
non-Latinx-themed Shakespeare productions, and to the generation of new
plays. For example, Frankie J. Alvarez used the bilingual version of the
balcony scene from his undergraduate performance as Romeo (see chapter
2) as one of his audition pieces for the MFA at Julliard, to which he was
accepted.[9] During his third year at Julliard, Alvarez played Don Armado in
Love's Labour's Lost with a Castilian accent and blended some Spanish into
a production that otherwise did not contain aural elements that grounded
the setting or characters in a particular geographic locale.[10] It was this performance that playwright Ben Bartolone saw that was "the inspiration for
the tone of the character of Cardenio" in his 2010 play, *The Tragedie of
Cardenio*, for which he got Alvarez to play the role.[11]

The incorporation of the Spanish language into Shakespeare's plays
both mirrors the cultural rewriting of Spanish as a primary language in the
geographic United States and foregrounds the rise of language dexterity,
both onstage and off, in a country that has deep-rooted linguistic bias as a
measure for citizenship and belonging. The proliferation of Latinx Shakespeares signals a dramaturgy inclusive of the richness of auralidad that
artists will continue to hone and expand and, in the process, create new
strategies and opportunities for Shakespearean performance *as* ethnic theater. The diverse artistic practices and practitioners detailed on these pages
are evidence of a desire for a United States that is an intraculture, for creating inclusion from the categories, languages, and histories that seek to
divide. *Latinx Shakespeares* is a story of possibility.

Notes

INTRODUCTION

1. An outstanding exception is Lisa Jackson-Schebetta's essay about how the coaction of race with the Spanish Civil War played out through Robeson and Ferrer. For more on "stealth Latinos" in American performance, see Brian Eugenio Herrera's *Latin Numbers*.

2. Samuel Sillen, "Paul Robeson's *Othello* (1943)," *Shakespeare in America: An Anthology from the Revolution to Now*, ed. James Shapiro, New York: Library of America, 2014, 451–58, 457.

3. In the United Kingdom, the 1923 *Cymbeline* at Birmingham Rep was the first major production in modern dress, and the 1938 *Hamlet* at the Old Vic starring Alec Guinness followed. It would be another few decades before Peter Brooks's now legendary avant-garde *A Midsummer Night's Dream* (1970) at the Royal Shakespeare Company, with a set consisting only of a white box and with numerous clowning techniques as well.

4. In its first season in 1965, the Spanish Mobile Theater featured two plays by Spanish playwright Federico García Lorca, *La Zapatera Prodigiosa* (*The Shoemaker's Prodigious Wife*) and *Retablillo de Don Cristóbal* (*The Puppet Play of Don Cristobal*), both performed in their original Spanish and directed by Osvaldo Riofrancos.

5. Riofrancos had a repertory company, Primer Theatero en Español, that would make headlines the following year for performing at a club on the Lower East Side where "the privileged can't get in." See "Affluent Barred from Youth Club; Lower East Side Project Gives Poor a Theater," *New York Times*, April 6, 1964. Dr. Riofrancos was dean of the School of Drama at the North Carolina School of the Arts and often directed for Papp.

6. Juliá was to become the preeminent Latinx Shakespearean actor of his time, performing to great acclaim on both stage and screen in his decades-long career, but at this point he was still mostly an unknown. The year after this first experience in a Papp production, he recited a poem at a Puerto Rican poetry reading at the Delacorte and subsequently found himself cast by Papp as Demetrius in *Titus Andronicus* in 1967. But Juliá was still struggling financially after that, and he telephoned Papp to ask for a job. Papp made Juliá the house

manager for Papp's *Naked Hamlet* (see chapter 4) in 1968 (after Sheen left). Juliá's career would take off in 1971 when he starred as Proteus in the John Guare / Mel Shapiro / Galt MacDermott musical *Two Gentlemen of Verona*.

7. Mildred C. Kuner, "The New York Shakespeare Festival, 1966," *Shakespeare Quarterly*, 17, no. 4 (Autumn 1966): 419–21, 421.

8. "Proclamation of the State of New York Executive Chamber," July 13, 1989, New York Public Library, Billy Rose Theatre Division (hereafter NYPL).

9. In 1979 he played the role opposite Richard Dreyfuss as Iago, and in 1991 he starred opposite Christopher Walken as Iago; in both stagings he wore dark makeup to play the Moor.

10. Other early intersections of Shakespeare and Latinidad did not survive funding challenges as well. These include the San Francisco performance group Luminarias, which staged the first all-Latinx *The Winter's Tale* (1997) and disbanded shortly thereafter. Also, the New York–based Latino Shakespeare Company (2006), started by Alberto Bonilla and Roy Arias, "just kind of fizzled away." They were unable to attain grant money because they were not performing a play with a Latinx theme. Alberto Bonilla, personal interview, March 25, 2014.

11. Jens Manuel Krogstad and D'Vera Cohn, "U.S. Census Looking at Big Changes in How It Asks about Race and Ethnicity," *Pew Research*, March 14, 2014, https://www.pewresearch.org/fact-tank/2014/03/14/u-s-census-looking-at -big-changes-in-how-it-asks-about-race-and-ethnicity/

12. See Alan Pelaez Lopez, "The X in Latinx Is a Wound, Not a Trend," ColorBloq, September 2018, https://www.colorbloq.org/article/the-x-in-latinx-is -a-wound-not-a-trend; Rachel Hatzipanagos, "'Latinx': An Offense to the Spanish Language or a Nod to Inclusion?," *Washington Post*, September 14, 2018, https://www.washingtonpost.com/news/post-nation/wp/2018/09/14/latinx-an -offense-to-the-spanish-language-or-a-nod-to-inclusion/.   Merriam-Webster added "Latinx" to its dictionary in 2018. To note, while many also prefer terms based on region such as "Tejano," heritage such as "Chicano," or hyphenated terms such as "Nicaraguan-American," a larger ethnic category, no matter what it is called, remains prominent colloquially and for government purposes.

13. Douglas Lanier, *Shakespeare and Modern Popular Culture*, Oxford: Oxford University Press, 2002. 9.

14. See Carla Della Gatta, "Shakespeare, Race, and 'Other' Englishes: The Q Brothers' *Othello: The Remix*," *Shakespeare Survey*, 71 (2018): 74–87; Alexa Huang, "What Country, Friends, Is This? Touring Shakespeares, Agency, and Efficacy in Theatre Historiography," *Theatre Survey*, 54 (2013): 51–85.

15. The World Shakespeare Festival (WSF) was hosted by the Royal Shakespeare Company and offered twenty-nine productions throughout the United Kingdom, eleven by the RSC, six by the RSC in collaboration with international

theater groups, four by other British groups, and the remaining eight by international companies.

16. In Toni Morrison's *Desdemona* at the Barbican, Desdemona's speeches were given in a spoken-word style of delivery, in contrast to Rokia Traoré's voicing of the Black characters (including Othello, his mother, and his first wife). The absent Othello's Blackness came through the Black African female voice and body, and a white American woman voiced and embodied the character of Desdemona. The Q Brothers' *Othello: The Remix* at the Globe did not stage a biracial couple; actors played Emilia and Bianca, but Desdemona was portrayed only through the sound of her singing voice, prerecorded and played offstage. The RSC and Wooster Group joint production of *Troilus and Cressida* turned the warring Greeks and Trojans into British soldiers and Native Americans, respectively, with the Woosters donning redface makeup, muscular bodysuits, and using film and auditory tracks to reinscribe the sound of the Native American accent they attempted to portray. Will Tuckett's all-British production of *West Side Story* in Newcastle reset the action to a vague setting, but the dialogue, lyrics, and ethnic slurs remained. The Jets put on a New York accent, and most of the Sharks attempted a pan-Spanish inflection in their speech that could not be described as specific to New Yorkers or to Puerto Ricans.

17. I shift between "Latinx culture" and "Latinx cultures" as a reminder that identity terms homogenize and unite diverse peoples within one category.

18. *Cardenio* went largely unnoticed by academics until Charles Hamilton's 1994 book, *William Shakespeare and John Fletcher: "Cardenio" or "The Second Maiden's Tragedy"*, attempted to prove through Hamilton's knowledge of paleography that *The Second Maiden's Tragedy* was in fact the missing *Cardenio*. A brief scholarly debate ensued, with a reading hosted by Professor Hugh Richmond at University of California, Berkeley, in the 1990s to debate if the script were really Shakespeare's. Academics soon came to agreement that Hamilton's claims were not valid, and *Cardenio* slipped back into hiding for almost another decade.

19. Gary Taylor's version had several read-throughs beginning in 2006, followed by stagings in 2009 in New Zealand and in 2012 in Indiana. Stephen Greenblatt cowrote an entirely new play with playwright Charles Mee that opened at the Boston ART in 2008, and it was followed by an international adaptation project that prompted new work from playwrights in ten countries. Bernard Richards's version was staged in the United Kingdom in 2009, Ben Bartolone's version in New York in 2010 and 2011, Hudson Shakespeare's version in 2012, plus a number of productions of *Double Falsehood* during this period.

20. For scholarly interest in *Cardenio*, see Roger Chartier, *"Cardenio" between Cervantes and Shakespeare: The Story of a Lost Play*, Cambridge: Polity, 2013; Bar-

bara Fuchs, *The Poetics of Piracy*, Philadelphia: University of Pennsylvania Press, 2013; David Carnegie and Gary Taylor, eds., *The Quest for "Cardenio,"* Oxford: Oxford University Press, 2012; Terri Bourus and Gary Taylor, eds., *The Creation and Re-creation of "Cardenio": Performing Shakespeare, Transforming Cervantes*, New York: Palgrave Macmillan, 2013; and Arden Shakespeare's publication of *Double Falsehood*, 2010.

21. Neruda's translation garners attention because of his fame, but his translation is not the most widely circulated or performed; as of 2012, Juan Cariola and Luis Astrana Marín are more popular in Chile. Paula Baldwin Lind, "Chilean Translations of Shakespeare: Do They Constitute a National Shakespeare Canon?," *Tradução em Revista*, 12, no. 1 (2012): 61–80, 66. The Neruda translation would also greatly influence subsequent Latinx Shakespearean productions of *Romeo and Juliet* in the United States, as it was used in its entirety or for the Spanish-language portions of the production at Joe Papp's short-lived Spanish Mobile Theater (1965), productions at Repertorio Español in New York (1979), Teatro Brava in Tempe (2004), the Florida State University (2005) production in chapter 2, New Brunswick Theater Festival in New Jersey (2010), Miami Dade County Auditorium (2016), the staged reading starring Daniel José Molina (Romeo from chapter 3) as Romeo through the Public's Spanish Mobile Theater for its revival (2016), and Teatro Español en Mad Cow in Miami (2018).

22. The only exception was the casting of Cuban American actor Frankie J. Alvarez in Ben Bartolone's 2010 *The Tragedie of Cardenio* in New York. Bartolone's adaptation ran again the following year but with another (non-Latinx) actor in the lead role.

23. Jeff Biggers, "Who's Afraid of *The Tempest*?," *Salon*, January 13, 2012, https://www.salon.com/2012/01/13/whos_afraid_of_the_tempest/

24. See also Ruben Espinosa, "Chicano Shakespeare: The Bard, the Border, and the Peripheries of Performance," *Teaching Social Justice through Shakespeare: Why Renaissance Literature Matters Now*, ed. Hillary Eklund and Wendy Beth Hyman, Edinburgh: Edinburgh University Press, 2019, 76–84, 76–77.

25. Mari Herreras, "TUSD Banning Books? Well Yes, and No, and Yes," *Tucson Weekly*, January 17, 2012, https://www.tucsonweekly.com/TheRange/archives/2012/01/17/tusd-banning-book-well-yes-and-no-and-yes

26. John T. Reid cites the French Joseph Ernest Renan, French Alfred Fouillée, French Argentine Paul-François Groussac, and Argentine Vicente Gregorio Quesada (pseudonym Domingo Pantoja), along with Darío, as possible influences for Rodó. John T. Reid, "The Rise and Decline of the Ariel-Caliban Antithesis in Spanish America," *The Americas*, 34, no. 3 (January 1978): 345–55.

27. See José David Saldívar, "The School of Caliban," *The Dialectics of Our America: Genealogy, Cultural Critique, and Literary History*, Durham, NC: Duke University Press, 1991, 123–48; Irene Lara, "Beyond Caliban's Curses: The Decolonial Feminist Literacy of Sycorax," *Journal of International Women's Studies*, 9, no. 1 (September 2007): 80–98; Armando García, "Freedom as Praxis:

Migdalia Cruz's *Fur* and the Emancipation of Caliban's Woman," *Modern Drama*, 59, no. 3 (Fall 2016): 343–62.

28. The Caliban trope appears in works from Aimé Césaire's 1969 postcolonial play *Une Tempête* to Jamaica Kincaid's 1985 novel *Annie John*, Richard Rodriguez's 1982 influential autobiography *Hunger of Memory*, and as a character in Marvel comics, where Caliban is an albino mutant who speaks of himself in the third person. For how appropriations and adaptations work through the Caliban-Prospero-Ariel triangulation, see Thomas Cartelli, *Repositioning Shakespeare: National Formations, Postcolonial Appropriations*, New York: Routledge, 1999, 114–16.

29. Despite these nuanced adaptations, *The Tempest* does not recur in the history of Latinx Shakespeares due to its problematic depiction of Caliban, who is native to the island and associated with the Caribbean, and therefore typically considered Latinx and/or Indigenous. The twenty-first century has seen several plays based on Caliban's mother Sycorax as means to decenter the triangulation of Prospero-Caliban-Ariel. See Carla Della Gatta, "The Island Belongs to Sycorax: Decolonial Feminist Storytelling and *The Tempest*," Women and Power Symposium, Shakespeare's Globe, December 2021.

30. "Vilma Silva on Shakespeare's Work," Oregon Public Broadcast, season 10, episode 1001, video clip, October 18, 2015, Opb.org; emphasis added.

31. "Vilma Silva on Shakespeare's Work."

32. Marcos Gonsalez, "Caliban Never Belonged to Shakespeare," *Literary Hub*, July 26, 2019, https://lithub.com/caliban-never-belonged-to-shakespeare/

33. Joe Falocco, "Tommaso Salvini's Othello and Racial Identity in Late Nineteenth-Century America," *New England Theatre Journal*, 23 (2012): 15–35, 22.

34. Falocco, "Tommaso Salvini's Othello," 19. Falocco's essay is an exemplary model of how revisiting the constructs of historical racial categories sheds light on those of today, and how methods for performing the Other, from dark makeup to foreign actor status to language to a villain role, have changed little in nearly 150 years.

35. Tlaloc Rivas, "Directors' Panel," Latina Theater Today: New Voices, University of Notre Dame, November 17, 2011.

36. Cary M. Mazer, *Double Shakespeares: Emotional-Realist Acting and Contemporary Performance*, Madison, NJ: Farleigh Dickinson University Press, 2015.

37. Alejandra Escalante and Daniel Molina, "Diálogo: On Performing Shakespearean Characters as Latinx," *Shakespeare and Latinidad*, ed. Trevor Boffone and Carla Della Gatta, Edinburgh: Edinburgh University Press, 2021, 217–23, 221.

38. For varying theatrical strategies for integrating a foreign language into Shakespeare, and their consequences, see Carla Della Gatta, "Staging Bilingual Classical Theatre," *HowlRound*, September 15, 2020, https://howlround.com/staging-bilingual-classical-theatre

39. According to a 2018 Pew Research poll, "While 61% of Hispanic immigrants in the US are Spanish dominant (and another 32% are bilingual), the share who are Spanish dominant drops to 6% among second-generation Hispanics and to less than 1% among third or higher generation Hispanics." Mark Hugo Lopez, Jens Manuel Krogstad, and Antonio Flores, "Most Hispanic Parents Speak Spanish to Their Children, but This Is Less the Case in Later Immigrant Generations," *Pew Research*, April 2, 2018, Pewresearch.org

40. For representative plays with a significant amount of Spanish, see Dolores Prida's *Coser y Cantar* (1981), José Rivera's *The House of Ramón Iglesia* (1983), Cherríe Moraga's *Heroes and Saints* (1992), and Josefina Lopez's *Simply María, or the American Dream* (1996).

41. Latinx nominees and winners of the Pulitzer include Maria Irene Fornés's *And What of the Night?* (1990), Nilo Cruz's *Anna in the Tropics* (2003), Quiara Alegría Hudes's *Elliot, a Soldier's Fugue* (2007) and *Water by the Spoonful* (2012), Lin-Manuel Miranda and Hudes's *In the Heights* (2009), Kristoffer Diaz's *The Elaborate Entrance of Chad Deity* (2010), and Miranda's *Hamilton* (2016).

42. Ayanna Thompson, *Passing Strange: Shakespeare, Race, and Contemporary America*, Oxford: Oxford University Press, 2011, 17.

43. Thompson, *Passing*, 5.

44. James C. Bulman, "Introduction: Shakespeare and Performance Theory," *Shakespeare, Theory, and Performance*, ed. James C. Bulman, New York: Routledge, 1996, 1–11, 7.

45. Most of the Spanish translations used in Latinx Shakespeares are from Latin America (such as the popular Neruda *Romeo y Julieta*) or translated by Latinx artists for the productions and plays. US-based theater has a history fundamentally different from the tradition in Mexico of using translations from Spain. For more on translations used for Mexican productions, see Alfredo Michel Modenessi, "Of Shadows and Stones: Revering and Translating 'the Word' Shakespeare in Mexico," *Shakespeare Survey*, 54 (2001): 152–64.

46. Don Pedro, a "good" character, was also played by a Black actor.

47. Trevor Boffone, Teresa Marrero, and Chantal Rodriguez, "Introduction, Encuentro 2014: Encountering Latinx Theater and Performance," *Encuentro: Latinx Performance for the New American Theater*, ed. Trevor Boffone, María Teresa Marrero, and Chantal Rodriguez, Evanston, IL: Northwestern University Press, 2013, vi–xxxvi, especially xviii–xix.

48. Anne García-Romero, "Latino/a Theater Commons: Updating the U.S. Narrative," *HowlRound*, August 8, 2012, https://howlround.com/latinx-theatre-commons-0

49. Bruce Weber, "Stratford-upon-Main Street: Shakespeare to Tour, Thanks to N.E.A.," *New York Times*, April 23, 2003.

50. See Brandi Wilkins Catanese, *The Problem of the Color[blind]: Racial Transgression and the Politics of Black Performance*, Ann Arbor: University of Michigan Press, 2011; Angela C. Pao, *No Safe Spaces: Re-casting Race, Ethnicity, and Nationality in American Theater*, Ann Arbor: University of Michigan Press, 2010.

51. Examples of Latinx Shakespeares as outreach initiatives include Apollinaire Theatre Company's *Ay, Pobre Yorick* (2016) adaptation performed by three female actors entirely in Spanish as part of its Summer Shakespeare Intensive for urban youth in Chelsea, Massachusetts; Delaware Shakespeare's "Our America, Our Shakespeare / Nuestra América, Nuestro Shakespeare" (2016) presentation resulting from its playwriting workshop collaboration with the Latin American Community Center to coincide with its production of *The Comedy of Errors* in Wilmington, Delaware; and BYU's Young Company bilingual *Romeo y Julieta* (2018), which was workshopped with José Cruz González and toured throughout Utah. See also chapter 5 for mobile community Latinx Shakespeares.

52. Committee of the Jubilee, "Welcome to the Jubilee," *HowlRound*, October 17, 2015, Howlround.com

53. Some Latinx Shakespeares from this period include *Romeo and Juliet* riffs such as TEATRX's *Balcony Scene in Quarantine*, Elaine Romero's *Wetback*, which had a reading during the monthlong RomeroFest celebration, and the Public Theater's audio play of *Romeo y Julieta*. Others include Del Shakes's *Twelfth Night*, and Merced Shakespearefest's *Ricardo II*.

54. Even *The Guardian* reported on her heritage and her "Spanish lilt" in a press conference in 1967. See Amy Nicholson, "Interview: Olivia Hussey, Star of Zeffirelli's *Romeo and Juliet*: 'I Was Wild,'" *The Guardian*, August 1, 2018, https://www.theguardian.com/film/2018/aug/01/olivia-hussey-romeo-and-juliet-film-franco-zeffirelli

55. I was cast as a male—Tybalt in fact—because I was taller than everyone else in the group. Throughout high school, I danced in musicals and acted in tragedies; I played both Goneril and Medea my senior year.

56. Some interviews were not used for the final version of the book, but I wish to acknowledge here that so many artists kindly shared their thoughts and time with me.

57. Ric Knowles, *Reading the Material Theatre*, Cambridge: Cambridge University Press, 2004, 19.

58. David Román, *Performance in America: Contemporary U.S. Culture and the Performing Arts*, Durham, NC: Duke University Press, 2005, 30.

59. Catanese, *Problem of the Color[blind]*, 3.

60. Theater by Latinx practitioners predates Valdez, but this is the starting point for modern and contemporary Latinx theater. Immediately following was the establishment of International Arts Relations (INTAR) in 1966 and the Puerto Rican Traveling Theatre (PRTT) in New York in 1967. In 1971, El Teatro Nacional de Aztlán (TENAZ) became the first network of theaters for Latinos. Repertorio Español opened in New York in 1971, GALA Hispanic Theatre in Washington, DC, in 1976, Thalia Hispanic Theater in Queens in 1977, and Teatro Avante in Miami in 1979.

61. Jorge Huerta, "Introduction," *Necessary Theater: Six Plays about the Chicano Experience*, ed. Jorge Huerta, Houston: Arte Publico Press, 1989, 5–17.

62. The Latinx Theatre Commons was never an affinity space, and from the start it exemplified this type of community-building. It began with Latinx artists who formulated ideas for convenings and initiatives, and *HowlRound*, a theater organization that was also taking shape at the time and led by non-Latinx practitioners, provided the infrastructure.

63. Jorge Huerta, "Looking for Magic: Chicanos in the Mainstream," *Negotiating Performance: Gender, Sexuality, and Theatricality in Latin/o America*, eds. Diana Taylor and Juan Villegas, Durham, NC: Duke University Press, 1994, 37–48, 39.

64. Brian Eugenio Herrera, "Panel Discussion," Latinx Playwrights Project, Oregon Shakespeare Festival, September 26, 2015.

65. Georgina Escobar, "The Composition of Latinx Aesthetics," *HowlRound*, August 23, 2017, https://howlround.com/composition-latinx-aesthetics

66. Ric Knowles, *Theatre & Interculturalism*, New York: Palgrave Macmillan, 2010, 31.

67. Knowles, *Theatre*, 37.

68. Yong Li Lan, "Shakespeare and the Fiction of the Intercultural," *A Companion to Shakespeare and Performance*, eds. Barbara Hodgdon and W. B. Worthen, Malden, MA: Blackwell, 2005, 527–49, 533.

69. Rustom Bharucha, *Globalization*, New York: Oxford University Press, 2001.

70. Early examples include Luis Valdez's mitos (myths) including *Dark Root of a Scream* (1967), Jorge Huerta's *La Llorona* (1978), Carlos Morton's *La Malinche* (1984), and Josefina Lopez's *Unconquered Spirits* (1997).

71. There is an important and ongoing conversation about the relationship of Shakespeare's plays to adaptations and appropriations. For a sampling of these arguments, see Christy Desmet and Robert Sawyer, eds., *Shakespeare and Appropriation*, New York: Routledge, 1999, on appropriation, Graham Holderness, *Tales from Shakespeare: Creative Collisions*. Cambridge: Cambridge University Press, 2014, on "collisions," Matthew Kozusko, "Beyond Appropriation: Teaching Shakespeare with Accidental Echoes in Film," *The Routledge Handbook or Shakespeare and Global Appropriation*, ed. Christy Desmet, Sujata Iyengar, and Miriam Jacobson, New York: Routledge, 2020, 217–26, on "accidental echoes," and Valerie M. Fazel and Louise Geddes, "Introduction: Bound in a Nutshell—Shakespeare's Vibrant Matter." Variable Objects: Shakespeare and Speculative Appropriation, Edinburgh: Edinburgh University Press, 2021, 1–18, on networks.

72. This includes cultural adaptation (adapting for another culture), linguistic adaptation (or translation, which is a form of adaptation), appropriation (extending the characters or themes to a new story), and productions that integrate Latinidad as a concept for the show.

73. The Guthrie's 1969 staging of *Julius Caesar* had Latin American motifs. A Fidel Castro-like character appeared in a production of *Caesar* at the American

Shakespeare Company in Stratford, Connecticut, in 1979, and the 1989 production of *The Two Gentlemen of Verona* at Shakespeare Festival Dallas. An Oliver North-like character was in the 1988 staging of *Coriolanus* at the Old Globe, and a vague Latin American setting was the framework for *Julius Caesar* at the Philadelphia Drama Guild in 1988. These cultural adaptations were not without real-life consequences. During the run of John Briggs's *Julio Cesar*, produced at Florida Shakespeare in 1986, a planned publicity stunt in which the actor playing Castro/Cesar would be driven through Little Havana had to be canceled since several local leaders feared that people would think it was real, and feared for the actor's life. John Briggs, telephone interview, February 8, 2013.

74. Douglas Lanier, "Shakespearean Rhizomatics: Adaptation, Ethics, Value," *Shakespeare and the Ethics of Appropriation*, eds. Alexa Huang and Elizabeth Rivlin, New York: Palgrave Macmillan, 2014, 21–40, 29.

75. Cristina Beltrán, *The Trouble with Unity: Latino Politics and the Creation of Identity*, Oxford: Oxford University Press, 2010, 168.

76. Douglas Lanier, "Recent Shakespeare Adaptation and the Mutations of Cultural Capital," *Shakespeare Studies*, 38 (2010): 104–13, 106.

77. See Valerie M. Fazel and Louise Geddes, *The Shakespeare User: Critical and Creative Appropriations in a Networked Culture*, New York: Palgrave Macmillan, 2017; Thomas Cartelli, *Repositioning Shakespeare: National Formations, Postcolonial Appropriations*, New York: Routledge, 1999.

78. Stuart Hall, "Race, Articulation, and Societies Structured in Dominance," *Essential Essays*, vol. 1: *Foundations of Cultural Studies*, ed. David Morley, Durham, NC: Duke University Press, 2019, 172–221, 196.

CHAPTER 1

1. I refer to *West Side Story* cumulatively (book, musical, film, sound track, ballet, and opera) as a presence in the popular memory and as a cultural entity. All direct quotations are included in both the stage musical and the 1961 film unless otherwise noted.

2. William Shakespeare, *Romeo and Juliet*, *The Norton Shakespeare: Based on the Oxford Edition*, ed. Stephen Greenblatt, Walter Cohen, Jean E. Howard, and Katharine Eisaman Maus, 3rd ed., New York: Norton, 2016, 957–1036, Prologue 1–2.

3. Robert N. Watson, "Lord Capulet's Lost Compromise: A Tragic Emendation and the Binary Dynamics of Romeo and Juliet." *Renaissance Drama*, 43, no. 1 (Spring 2015): 53–83, 70.

4. Colleen Ruth Rosenfeld, *Indecorous Thinking: Figures of Speech in Early Modern Poetics*, New York: Fordham University Press, 2018, 138.

5. In competing narratives by each of the creators, details of the development of *West Side Story* rarely align. The four creators and multiple scholars

report different working titles for the project, from *East Side Story* to *Gangway* to *Romeo*. Whether in the original concept the male was Jewish and the female Catholic or the opposite is also contested.

6. "Telling the Story behind the Story behind *West Side Story*." *LA Times Blogs*, Los Angeles Times Media Group, February 27, 2012, https://latimesblogs .latimes.com/culturemonster/2012/02/west-side-story-inspiration.html. According to the *Los Angeles Times* in 2012, the newspaper clipping that inspired Laurents and Robbins to change the story to Puerto Ricans narrated this: "Two young Hispanic men fought outside a dance at a community hall in 1955. One of them died" ("Telling the Story"). Laurents recalls the article entitled "Six Jailed in Fight Death," about a street fight in San Bernardino, but this article ran a year later than Laurents's account of reading it ("Telling the Story").

7. For all the stock that Laurents (writer) and Robbins (choreographer) placed in the notion of a culturally or ethnically rooted divide, composer Leonard Bernstein saw the presence of warring sides as "much less important than the bigger idea of making a musical that tells a tragic story in musical comedy terms, using only musical comedy techniques, never falling into the 'operatic' trap." Nigel Simeone, *Leonard Bernstein: West Side Story*, Farnham, Surrey: Ashgate, 2009, 17. This hybrid genre of tragedy in a musical comedy form thus also furthered the affective quality of division.

8. *In the Heights* was written by Quiara Alegría Hudes, with music by Lin-Manuel Miranda. It had a workshop in 2005 in Connecticut, went Off-Broadway in 2007, and to Broadway in 2008. The 2015 musical *Hamilton* (book and music by Miranda) solidified new possibilities for casting and representation on Broadway.

9. Dramatists Guild Landmark Symposium, "*West Side Story* (1985)," *Shakespeare in America: An Anthology from the Revolution to Now*, ed. James Shapiro, New York: Library of America, 2014, 597–619. Crawford withdrew from the show before its premiere and was replaced by Robert E. Griffith and Hal Prince. Sondheim said, "[Cheryl Crawford] said the essential reason she was withdrawing from the show was, she wanted us to explain why these kids were the way they were. We are making a poetic interpretation of a social situation, but she wanted it to be more realistic" (606). Laurents also said, "I have a letter from her saying she wanted to see how the neighborhood changes from immigrant Jews to Puerto Ricans to blacks" (607). Then Robbins said, "My version of Cheryl's withdrawal is very simple: she couldn't raise the money" (607).

10. The four creators were Jewish and LGBTQ: playwright Arthur Laurents, choreographer Jerome Robbins, composer Leonard Bernstein, and lyricist Stephen Sondheim.

11. Arthur Laurents, "West Side Story," *Romeo and Juliet and West Side Story*, New York: Laurel-Leaf, 1965, 131–224, 167. The lyrics were written by Stephen Sondheim, who later changed this line and some others for the 1961 film version. This line became "My heart's devotion . . . / Let it sink back in the ocean." Jerome Robbins and Robert Wise, dirs., *West Side Story*, 1961, 50th Anniversary Edition, 20th Century Fox, 2011, DVD, 153 minutes.

12. Brian Eugenio Herrera, "Compiling *West Side Story*'s Parahistories, 1949–2009," *Theatre Journal*, 64, no. 2 (2012): 231–47, 241.

13. Laurence Maslon, "The Divided States of 'America'—Why Rita Moreno Objected to *West Side Story*'s Original Lyrics," *PBS*, October 8, 2021, https://www.pbs.org/wnet/americanmasters/the-divided-states-of-america-why-rita-moreno-objected-to-west-side-storys-original-lyrics/18671/

14. Keith Garebian, *The Making of West Side Story*, Buffalo, NY: Mosaic Press, 1998, 112.

15. *Look Up and Live: West Side Story*, hosted by Sidney Lanier, Jerome Robbins Collection, CBS, 1958, VHS.

16. Critiques of the representations of Latinx in *West Side Story* are plentiful and diverse. Alberto Sandoval-Sánchez, *José, Can You See? Latinos On and Off Broadway*, Madison: University of Wisconsin Press, 1999, addresses both the musical and film in his deconstructive analysis to establish how the (Puerto Rican) Sharks pose a threat to the spatial ownership of the (white) Jets. Frances Negrón-Muntaner, "Feeling Pretty: *West Side Story* and Puerto Rican Identity Discourses." *Social Text*, 18, no. 2 (2000): 83–106, levels several critiques of the film's depiction of Latinx, as well as commentary on how the Jewish and queer origins of the musical (and its creators) affect the portrayal of the Sharks. Regarding the film, Ernesto Acevedo-Muñoz, *West Side Story as Cinema: The Making and Impact of an American Masterpiece*, Lawrence: University Press of Kansas, 2013, argues that it offers a harsher view of the Jets than the Sharks, Deborah Paredez, "'Queer For Uncle Sam': Anita's Latina Diva citizenship in *West Side Story*," *Latino Studies*, 12, no. 3 (2014): 332–52, attends to Rita Moreno's Anita as a feminist and queer performance of the "affective *ambiente* central to Latina/o assertions of cultural citizenship" (333), Brian Eugenio Herrera, *Latin Numbers: Playing Latino in Twentieth-Century U.S. Popular Performance*, Ann Arbor: University of Michigan Press, 2015, examines the changes for the screen that heighten racist tropes applied to the Sharks, and Lauren Davine, "'Could We Not Dye It Red at Least?': Color and Race in *West Side Story*," *Journal of Popular Film and Television* 44, no. 3 (2016): 139–49, analyzes the use of color as part of racist tropes.

17. Walter S. DeKeseredy and Martin D. Schwartz, "Masculinities and Interpersonal Violence," *Handbook of Studies on Men & Masculinities*, ed. Michael S. Kimmel, Jeff Hearn, and R. W. Connell, London: Sage Publications, 2005, 353–66, 360.

18. Misha Berson, *Something's Coming, Something Good: "West Side Story" and the American Imagination*, Milwaukee, WI: Applause Theatre & Cinema Books, 2011, 138–41.

19. Laurents, "West Side Story," 152.

20. Laurents, "West Side Story," 156.

21. Laurents, "West Side Story," 199.

22. Shakespeare, *Romeo*, III.i.111–12.

23. The male physique is not on display in earlier 1950s musicals such as *Guys and Dolls, Singin' in the Rain*, and *A Star Is Born*. Bob Fosse, whose choreo-

graphic career began in the 1950s, would contribute greatly to this shift in his famous musicals in the 1960s.

24. Similarly, Maria is absent from "America," the Sharks girls' greatest song-and-dance number, and her only all-girls' number is in the scene in which she sings "I Feel Pretty." Tony and Maria dance together once, during the "Somewhere" ballet, which is placed outside the "reality" of the musical and is from a dance style that was associated with the feminine.

25. David Morgan, "Class and Masculinity," *Handbook of Studies on Men & Masculinities*, eds. Michael S. Kimmel, Jeff Hearn, and R. W. Connell, London: Sage Publications, 2005, 165–77, 170.

26. Jennifer Ludden, "1965 Immigration Law Changed Face of America." *National Public Radio*, May 9, 2006, https://www.npr.org/templates/story/story.php?storyId=5391395. It eliminated de facto discrimination in the form of quotas against southern and eastern Europeans, as well as Asians. Instead, it "gave preference to professionals with skills in short supply" and those with relatives who were US citizens.

27. In 1950, the three racial categories on the census were White, Black, or Other. In 1960, census takers were instructed to record people from Puerto Rico and Mexico, as well as other persons of Latinx descent, as White, unless they were visibly either Indigenous or Black. In 1970, a 5 percent sample of households was asked to indicate whether they were "of Spanish Origin." Hispanic (now Hispanic/Latino) identity was finally included as a census question in 1980, when it was added as an ethnicity question, separate from race. More recently, in 2013, the Census Bureau announced that it was considering including Hispanic as a racial (rather than ethnic) category for the 2020 census (Krogstad), but this change was not implemented. Jens Manuel Krogstad and D'Vera Cohn, "U.S. Census Looking at Big Changes in How It Asks about Race and Ethnicity," *Pew Research*, March 14, 2014, https://www.pewresearch.org/fact-tank/2014/03/14/u-s-census-looking-at-big-changes-in-how-it-asks-about-race-and-ethnicity/

28. Once they do speak, it is minimally, and after they have communicated through choreography. In the film, Wood's accent during this dialogue sounds more formal than it does Puerto Rican or Spanish-based.

29. "Hispanic or Latino Origin by Race," Data.Census.Gov, 2019, accessed October 7, 2020, https://data.census.gov/cedsci/table?q=HISPANIC%20OR%20LATINO%20ORIGIN%20BY%20RACE&t=Hispanic%20or%20Latino&tid=ACSDT1Y2019.B03002&hidePreview=false

30. Laurents, "West Side Story," 137. But the "anthology" had to be light-skinned. In a letter to Robbins about the division between the two gangs, Laurents writes, "Tonio should not be Italian but Irish or Anglo-Saxon: contrast between light and dark." Arthur Laurents, "Letter to Jerome Robbins," Billy Rose Division, MGZMD 182—Box 101, Folders 1–3, Series IV: Personalities—Arthur Laurents. Folder 1 (1952–55), NYPL. Note that in the original Broadway production, Maria was played by southern Italian American actress Carol Lawrence (née Carolina Maria Laraia). Although the contrast between Maria and

Tony was not based on race, colorism within whiteness was part of authorial intent and casting.

31. Birgit Brander Rasmussen, Eric Klinenberg, Irene J. Nexica, and Matt Wray, "Introduction," *The Making and Unmaking of Whiteness*, ed. Birgit Bander Rasmussen, Eric Klinenberg, Irene J. Nexica, and Matt Wray, Durham, NC: Duke University Press, 2001, 1–24, 8.

32. Richard Dyer, *White*, New York: Routledge, 1997, 57.

33. Laurents, "West Side Story," 139.

34. Laurents, "West Side Story," 138. In the film, the line is "But you ain't gonna do it on my beat!"

35. George Lipsitz, *The Possessive Investment in Whiteness: How White People Profit from Identity Politics*, Philadelphia: Temple University Press, 1998, 1.

36. Lee Bebout, *Whiteness on the Border: Mapping the U.S. Racial Imagination in Brown and White*, New York: New York University Press, 2016, 2.

37. Dyer, *White*, 12.

38. Laurents, "West Side Story," 161.

39. Laurents, "West Side Story," 183. Here Gayle Rubin's work on marriage as a kinship system in a patriarchal society gets the added element of a Latinx woman being welcomed into white ascendancy through marriage. See Gayle Rubin, "The Traffic in Women: Notes on the 'Political Economy' of Sex," *Toward an Anthropology of Women*, ed. Rayna R. Reiter, New York: Monthly Review Press, 1975, 157–210.

40. Officer Krupke and Lieutenant Shrank will assist them in elevating their status if the Jets side with the "white" officers over the "immigrant" Sharks, by saying, "I wanna help ya get rid of them!" Laurents, "West Side Story," 179.

41. Thomas M. Stephens, "Chino." *Dictionary of Latin American Racial and Ethnic Terminology*, Gainesville: University of Florida Press, 1989, 66–69.

42. Gustavo Arellano, "Ask a Mexican: Why Do Mexicans Call People with Curly Hair Chinos?," *Houston Press*, October 26, 2006, https://www.houstonpress.com/news/why-do-mexicans-call-people-with-curly-hair-chinos-6544916. Arellano writes, "Many blacks, of course, have naturally kinky hair, so at some point over the centuries, *chino* became an ethnicon (a term meant to comment on an ethnic group's prominent cultural characteristic that become popular shorthand for said characteristic) for both 'black person' and 'curly.'"

43. Laurents, "West Side Story," 199.

44. In the original Broadway run, only one other male Shark, Toro, was played by a Latinx actor: Erne Castaldo (who understudied Chino and played the role on the national tour). In the film, Mexican actor Rudy Del Campo played Shark "Del Campo." Along with Chita Rivera and Rita Moreno as Anita, on Broadway and in the film respectively, these were the only Latinx in the casts.

45. Shakespeare, *Romeo*, I.i.8.

46. In Eric Minton's documentation of over fifteen hundred professional Shakespeare productions (75 percent of them in the United States) from 2011 to 2016, *Romeo and Juliet* was second only to *A Midsummer Night's Dream*. But *Romeo and Juliet* comprised less than 6 percent of productions. See Eric Minton,

"Ranking the Bard's Plays by Stage Popularity," Shakespeareances.com, October 13, 2017, http://www.shakespeareances.com/dialogues/commentary/Bard _Board_Popularity-171012.html

47. In total, only four plays by Latinx playwrights made it to Broadway before the twenty-first century (all of which came after *West Side Story*): *Short Eyes* by Miguel Piñero (1974), *Zoot Suit* by Luis Valdez (1978), *Cuba and His Teddy Bear* by Reynaldo Povod (1986), and *Freak*, the one-man show by John Leguizamo (1988). Also, in 1966, María Irene Fornés debuted a play, *The Office* (dir. Jerome Robbins), that closed after nine previews.

48. The United States does not have a national reading requirement for secondary education, but Common Core requirements stipulate that high school students are assigned at minimum one Shakespeare play. In 2013, scholar Jonathan Burton surveyed four hundred high school teachers nationwide and determined that *Romeo and Juliet* was taught "in roughly 93% of all ninth grade classes." Jonathan Burton, "Shakespeare in Liberal Arts Education," *Rock Magazine*, Whittier College, Fall 2013, https://issuu.com/whittiercollege/docs/13-116 _wc_f13_mag_final_printer_fil

49. The facility of the play as an ensemble piece even affected Pablo Neruda's now-famous translation (see introduction). Neruda originally wanted to translate *Othello*, but it was felt that there was not a Chilean actor with the capacity for the title role. See David Schidlowsky, *Neruda y Su Tiempo: Las Furias y Las Pena*, vol. 2: *1950–1973*, Santiago de Chile: RIL, 2008, 1092.

50. Paz also problematically connects his notion of isolation as key to the contemporary Mexican psyche; he argues that the legacy of colonization left Mexicans with a feeling of loneliness due to not being either purely Spanish (European) or Indigenous. That said, social scientists have begun to utilize the construct of *fatalismo* to adjust mental and physical health services for Latinx, arguing that cultural differences need to be accounted for in order to make treatments effective. See Luis M. Añez et al., "Application of Cultural Constructs in the Care of First Generation Latino Clients in a Community Mental Health Setting," *Journal of Psychiatric Practice*, 2, no. 4: 221–30; and American Psychological Association Office on AIDS, *Resource Guide for Adapting SISTA for Latinas*, American Psychological Association, accessed July 2015, https://hiv.rut gers.edu/wp-content/uploads/2016/05/SISTA_Latina_Resource_Guide.pdf

51. Scholar Robert Sawyer has made a similar connection of the feeling of loneliness in both Shakespeare and the laments of country music. See also Yolanda Broyles-González on ranchera music. Gustavo Arellano examines the mournful singer Morrissey's large following in Mexico, as is evidenced in such Mexican Morrissey cover bands as Mex Moz. Arellano argues that the themes of Morrissey's music and persona relate to a feeling of isolation due to his northern English, working-class, and nondescript gender identity, through emotional music. See Gustavo Arellano, *¡Ask a Mexican!*, New York: Scribner, 2007.

52. The role of Bernardo was first played by a Latino only in 1980, with Puerto Rican dancer and actor Héctor Jaime Mercado. Bernardo was also performed by Venezuelan George Akram in 2009. In the 2020 Ivo Van Hove production, he was played by Amar Ramasar, who is of Puerto Rican and Indo-Trinidadian descent, and in the 2021 film by David Alvarez, who is Cuban-Canadian.

53. Moreno was the only Puerto Rican in the film's cast. She would later become the second Latinx actor, and also second Puerto Rican, to win an Oscar (Best Supporting Actress, *West Side Story*). The first was José Ferrer (who played Iago to Paul Robeson's Othello onstage; see introduction), for his work in *Cyrano de Bergerac* in 1950.

54. Rita Moreno, *Rita Moreno: A Memoir*, New York: Penguin, 2014, 187.

55. Steve Garner, *Whiteness: An Introduction*, London: Routledge, 2007, 46.

56. Frances Negrón-Muntaner, "Feeling Pretty: *West Side Story* and Puerto Rican Identity Discourses," *Social Text*, 18, no. 2 (2000): 83–106, 95.

57. Laurents, "West Side Story," 217.

58. These are canonical and award-winning performances for all. Although Ayala's portrayal was cut short due to the outbreak of Covid-19 in early 2020, she was cast as a Shark girl in Steven Spielberg's film remake, which premiered in December 2021.

59. Frances R. Aparicio, "Jennifer as Selena: Rethinking Latinidad in Media and Popular Culture," *Latino Studies*, 1, no. 1 (2003): 90–105, 91.

60. Allen and sister Phylicia Ayers-Allen Rashad spent time in Mexico when they were young. Unlike in the United States, where the sisters grew up with segregation, in Mexico they first experienced a society that interpreted their skin color as beautiful. Rashad said that Bill Cosby wanted her character Claire Huxtable to be bilingual, and that the time in Mexico was instrumental to her career. See Debbie Allen, Instagram, therealdebbieallen December 26, 2020. Allen in her role as Anita would have to speak some Spanish as well.

61. Ed Pilkington, "Latino Liberation: Sharks Sing in the Language of Their Streets as *West Side Story* Goes Bilingual on Broadway," *The Guardian*, March 19, 2009, https://www.theguardian.com/stage/2009/mar/20/west-side-story-on-broadway

62. Laurents's partner had seen a Spanish-language production in Colombia and reported back to Laurents that the language had transformed the show; the Sharks were the heroes and the Jets were the villains. Not accounting for the important role that a Spanish-dominant country played in this change in dynamic, Laurents translated this concept onto his new Broadway production.

63. In Puerto Rico in 1942, Spanish was taught in grades 1–2, English was a subject in grades 3–8, and English was primary (with Spanish as a subject) in grades 9–12. In 1947, Puerto Rico passed a bill for all-Spanish education, but President Truman vetoed it. From 1949 to the present, Spanish has been the

"medium of instruction at all levels with English as mandatory subject." See Alicia Pousada, "Being Bilingual in Puerto Rico," 2011, accessed October 1, 2021, http://aliciapousada.weebly.com/uploads/1/0/0/2/10020146/being_bilingu al_in_puerto_rico2.pdf

64. Qtd. in Julie Bosman, "Jets? Yes! Sharks? ¡Sí! in Bilingual West Side," New York Times, July 17, 2008, https://www.nytimes.com/2008/07/17/theater/17bway .html

65. Sondheim insisted that the translation adhere to strict rules regarding the need for rhyme and pacing when sung, constraining the ability for textual translation to contribute significantly to cultural translation. Sondheim instructed Miranda that the lyrics had to rhyme for the English listener. Ultimately, the production rested on the idea that the rhyming of the lyrics outweighed a straightforward linguistic translation of the original lines.

66. Arthur Laurents, Mainly on Directing: "Gypsy", "West Side Story", and Other Musicals, New York: Alfred A. Knopf, 2009, 172.

67. Arthur Laurents, West Side Story, bilingual version; unpublished script, 2009, NYPL. Note that "¡Oye Mamo!" translates to "Hey Cocksucker," "¡Mira! [sic] Maricones!" translates to "Look! Fags!" and "¡Polaco sangano!" to "Bloody Polack!" All translations are my own.

68. Dave Itzkoff, "Bilingual 'West Side Story' Edits Out Some Spanish," New York Times, August 25, 2009, https://artsbeat.blogs.nytimes.com/2009/08/25/bili ngual-west-side-story-edits-out-some-spanish/

69. Producing a bilingual show on Broadway is nearly unheard of, and it was felt that audiences were not yet prepared for this convention. Stuart Hecht writes: "Broadway's commercialism makes [the musical genre] generally slow to change, hesitant to get too far ahead of its audience's tastes or beliefs for fear of losing paying customers." See Stuart J. Hecht, Transposing Broadway: Jews, Assimilation, and the American Musical, New York: Palgrave Macmillan, 2011, 5.

70. Susan Stamberg, "A West Side Story with a Different Accent," National Public Radio, December 15, 2008, https://www.npr.org/templates/story/story .php?storyId=98207909

71. Marcus Center, email to the author, December 20, 2011.

72. Stamberg, "A West Side Story."

73. Herrera, "Compiling," 245.

74. Jorge Huerta also writes of this issue in his experience with Nilo Cruz's Anna in the Tropics, the first Latinx-authored play to win the Pulitzer Prize for Drama. Jorge Huerta, "From the Margins to the Mainstream: Latino/a Theater in the U.S.," Studies in Twentieth and Twenty-First Century Literature, 32 (2008): 463–52, 478–79.

75. See chapter 2 for how Latinx Shakespeares have prompted bilingual vocal methods. See also Della Gatta, "Afterword," Shakespeare and "Accentism", ed. Adele Lee, New York: Routledge, 2021, 198–208.

76. Laurents's desire for realism may seem disjunctive to storytelling in the

musical genre. In Derek Miller's review of the bilingual production at the National, he writes: "Such directorial choices aside, the major obstacles to realism were also the evening's highlights: the musical numbers. Singing and dancing subvert any musical's claims to being realistic." Derek Miller, rev. of *West Side Story* at the National Theatre, dir. Arthur Laurents, *Theatre Journal*, 61, no. 3 (2009): 480.

77. See Herrera, "Compiling." A flurry of articles and conversations emerged even before the film premiered. For an example of the divergent opinions, see this roundtable and the comments: "The Great *West Side Story* Debate," *New York Times*, December 1, 2021, https://www.nytimes.com/2021/12/01/theater/west-side-story-steven-spielberg-movie.html

78. Ashley Lee, "Commentary: Spielberg Tried to Save *West Side Story*, but Its History Makes It Unsalvageable," *Los Angeles Times*, December 12, 2021, https://www.latimes.com/entertainment-arts/movies/story/2021-12-12/west-side-story-puerto-rico-cultural-authenticity

79. For an analysis of the 2020 Broadway staging, see Daniel Pollack-Pelzner, "Why *West Side Story* Abandoned Its Queer Narrative," *The Atlantic*, March 1, 2020, https://www.theatlantic.com/culture/archive/2020/03/ivo-van-hoves-west-side-story-steeped-stereotypes/607210/

80. In the process of righting previous dramaturgical choices, they created new challenges, most notably making the new Puerto Rican character, Valentina, more aligned with Tony and the Jets rather than an elder and model for the Sharks.

81. Steven Spielberg, dir. *West Side Story*, 2021, 20th Century Studios, 2022, DVD, 156 minutes.

82. Choreographer Justin Peck altered Robbins's signature moves to have both male gangs dance more in plié, with rounded bodies, so that the movement was less ballet-like.

83. Spielberg, *West Side Story*.

84. Spielberg, *West Side Story*.

85. Spielberg, *West Side Story*.

86. Spielberg, *West Side Story*.

87. Carla Della Gatta, "*West Side Story*: A New Take on *Romeo and Juliet*, 60 Years Later," *Shakespeare & Beyond*, January 4, 2022, https://shakespeareandbeyond.folger.edu/2022/01/04/west-side-story-2021-film-romeo-and-juliet/

88. Spielberg, *West Side Story*.

89. Spielberg, *West Side Story*.

90. Spielberg, *West Side Story*. In addition, there are several moments where the actors perform to the audience not as characters, but to acknowledge a moment of self-aware theatricality. See Della Gatta, "*West Side Story*."

91. Spielberg, *West Side Story*.

92. Della Gatta, "*West Side Story*."

93. Chino ends the film headed to incarceration, which was not part of the

original 1957 stage script, though the 1961 film shifted this implication. In 2021, he is given over to the police by the Puerto Rican Valentina.

94. Spielberg, *West Side Story*.

95. Spielberg, *West Side Story*. Chino's asexuality is all the more evident in contrast to Maria's virginal readiness for sex. Tony and Maria meet in a pseudo-private space underneath the bleachers where she instigates through dance and makes an aggressive first move on Tony so much that he is taken aback. The next morning, she moves in sync to the music as she covers up the evidence that she has had a (yet unconsummated) illicit visit with Tony on the fire escape. At the end of "One Hand, One Heart," she says suggestively to Tony, "Come see me tonight," and they consummate their love.

96. "When Tony reacts to Maria's kiss, he says, 'You just caught me by surprise is all. I'm a by the book type, so,' to which Maria responds, 'By the book?' . . . And when they part on the fire escape, she calls him back. Maria says, 'I forgot why I call you,' and Tony replies, 'I'll wait till you remember.'" Della Gatta, "*West Side Story*." See Shakespeare, *Romeo*, I.iv.221 and II.ii.212–13, respectively.

97. Linda Saborío, *Embodying Difference: Scripting Social Images of the Female Body in Latina Theatre*, Madison: Farleigh Dickinson University Press, 2012, xxi.

98. It also satisfies this desire for a modern audience, updating Shakespeare's play through contemporary acting methods and storytelling styles. Aspects of Method acting based on Konstantin Stanislavsky's principles were interpreted, and misinterpreted, by his American successors such as Stella Adler, Sanford Meisner, Lee Strasberg, and others. Laurents said, "Like [producer] Hal [Prince], Jerry [Robbins] had been a George Abbott disciple. For *West Side Story*, he switched to Stanislavsky: he was going to direct the first Method musical." See Arthur Laurents, *Original Story By: A Memoir of Broadway and Hollywood*, New York: Alfred A. Knopf, 2000, 357.

99. The title of *West Side Story* in Spanish is *Amor sin Barreras*, or "Love without Borders." In translation, the "and" is nonexistent as well, and the title connotes that division can be surmounted by one thing: love.

100. Because of *West Side Story*'s influence as a musical, and an excessive aural soundscape as germane to theatrical depictions of Latinidad, oftentimes the cultural-linguistic divide manifests in the Shakespeare films addressed here through the musical soundtrack. Although Zeffirelli and Luhrmann did not direct "musical" versions of *Romeo and Juliet*, the musical scores were key to the success of their films (much as with *West Side Story*), both of which include Latina-inflected Juliets (in the casting of Hussey in the former and the affective ethnicity of the Capulets in the latter). The Love Theme from Zeffirelli "was issued as a single from the soundtrack album that accompanied the film's release." Robert Shaughnessy, "*Romeo and Juliet*: The Rock and Roll Years," *Remaking Shakespeare: Performances across Media, Genres and Cultures*, ed. Pascale Aebischer, Edward J. Esche, and Nigel Wheale, New York: Palgrave Macmillan,

2003, 172–89, 185. The Luhrmann soundtrack went triple-platinum in the United States, and Luhrmann sold a separate DVD of his film with three voice-overs about music, "William Shakespeare's Romeo + Juliet: The Music Edition."

101. For further reading on the Luhrmann film, see Phillipa Sheppard, "Latino Elements in Baz Luhrmann's *Romeo + Juliet*," *Latin American Shakespeares*, ed. Bernice W. Kliman and Rick J. Santos, Madison, NJ: Fairleigh Dickinson University Press, 2005, 242–61. See also Barbara Hodgdon, "*William Shakespeare's Romeo + Juliet*: Everything's Nice in America?," *Shakespeare Survey*, vol 52: *Shakespeare and the Globe*, ed. Stanley Wells, Cambridge: Cambridge University Press, 1999, 88–98.

102. Dennis Hensley, "Claire Danes: Teen Angst," *Movieline*, December 1, 1995.

103. He also played the Lord Capulet character that same year in *Love Is All There Is*.

104. Leguizamo identifies with his grandfather's Puerto Rican heritage, but in 2011 his father revealed that he was born in Bogotá. Despite his father's claim, Leguizamo retained his title of Global Ambassador of the Arts for the Puerto Rican Day Parade that year. Gisela Orozco, "John Leguizamo: Boricua o No, Presente en Desfile Nacional Puertorriqueño," *Chicago Tribune*, June 12, 2011, https://www.chicagotribune.com/hoy/ct-hoy-8007123-john-leguizamo-bo ricua-o-no-presente-en-desfile-nacional-puertorriqueno-story.html; "Despite Father's Claim, Leguizamo Asserts Puerto Rico Ties," June 13, 2011, *CNN*, http://edition.cnn.com/2011/SHOWBIZ/celebrity.news.gossip/06/13/leguizamo .puerto.rico/

105. In the voice-over to the music edition of the DVD, Luhrmann describes the Capulets as "Latin." Baz Luhrmann, dir., *William Shakespeare's Romeo + Juliet: The Music Edition*, 1996, 20th Century Fox, 2006, DVD, 120 minutes.

106. Similar to how Olivia Hussey's fair skin and blue eyes do not adhere to visual generalizations of Latin Americans, Mexican actor Rodrigo Escandón Cesarman, who played the little boy, has also been perceived to be white (non-Latinx / Latin American). Ruben Espinosa writes, "When he [Tybalt] finally draws his pistol, he aims it not at the nearby Montagues, but instead at a well-dressed, fair-skinned young boy, whose eyes, the close-up shot makes clear, are as blue as can be. Through this act, Tybalt, played by Columbian [*sic*] American actor John Leguizamo, stands as a threat not only to the white Montagues, but — as a Latino — to all white people" (48). Such colorism-based misidentifications reinforce a generic and homogeneous idea of Latinx and Latin American peoples. Ruben Espinosa, "'Don't It Make My Brown Eyes Blue': Uneasy Assimilation and the Shakespeare-Latinx Divide," *The Routledge Handbook to Shakespeare and Global Appropriation*, eds. Christy Desmet, Sujata Iyengar, and Miriam Jacobson, New York: Routledge, 2019, 48–58, 48.

107. Luhrmann, *William Shakespeare's Romeo + Juliet*.

108. Despite the film's Mexican locale for filming, Alfredo Michel Modenessi writes, "Luhrmann's rendering often foregrounds otherness and foreignness even to a native Mexican." Alfredo Michel Modenessi, "(Un)doing the Book 'Without Verona Walls': A View from the Receiving End of Baz Luhrmann's *William Shakespeare's Romeo + Juliet*," *Spectacular Shakespeare: Critical Theory and Popular Cinema*, eds. Courtney Lehmann and Lisa S. Starks, Madison, NJ: Fairleigh Dickinson University Press, 2002, 62–85, 72.

109. For more on the use of memory and flashback in Latinx culture and storytelling, see chapter 2.

110. Espinosa, "Don't It Make," 49.

111. Laurents, "West Side Story," 163.

112. Ben Brantley, "Such Sweet Sorrow: Orlando Bloom and Condola Rashad in *Romeo and Juliet*," *New York Times*, September 19, 2013, https://www.nytimes.com/2013/09/20/theater/reviews/orlando-bloom-and-condola-rashad-in-romeo-and-juliet.html

CHAPTER 2

1. The adaptation used the Pablo Neruda translation (see introduction) for the Spanish portions. About one-quarter of the production was in Spanish, including some of Romeo's monologues. Antonio Ocampo-Guzmán, telephone interview, November 21, 2011. Trained in Linklater Voice / Freeing the Natural Voice, Ocampo-Guzmán realized that a primary challenge that bilingual actors have is that acting methods are monolingual. He later became the first person to translate the Linklater method into Spanish, and he trains Spanish-speaking and bilingual Linklater coaches.

2. The actress playing Juliet was Nicaraguan, Romeo was Cuban American, and Lady Montesco was from Central America. According to Ocampo-Guzmán, Lady Montesco had a "bit darker complexion, Lord Montesco and Romeo were Cuban but looked white, Juliet looked more Italian" (telephone interview). The actor playing Benvolio was Central American and the actor playing Samson was Mexican; both spoke a "textbook Spanish" (telephone interview).

3. Antonio Ocampo-Guzman, "My Own Private Shakespeare; Or, Am I Deluding Myself?," *Colorblind Shakespeare: New Perspectives on Race and Performance*, ed. Ayanna Thompson, New York: Routledge, 2006, 125–36, 129.

4. Alvarez went on to star in several Latinx Shakespearean productions, cast as Claudio in OSF's 2011 *Measure for Measure* (discussed later in this chapter) and as Hamlet in Asolo Repertory's 2012 *Hamlet, Prince of Cuba* (see chapter 4). He also played Cardenio in Ben Bartolone's 2010 production of *The Tragedie of Cardenio* (see epílogo).

5. Alvarez, Skype interview, July 20, 2017.

6. Ocampo-Guzman, "My Own Private Shakespeare," 129.

7. Older translations can provide a greater cohesion with Shakespeare's English, so much that they can sound temporally similar. For example, a bilingual reviewer of Shakespeare on the Rocks' 2015 *Romeo y Julieta* misidentified the 1872 translation by Matías de Velasco y Rojas as "Renaissance Spanish." Estefania Seyffert, *"Romeo and Julieta* Opens Door to Future Bilingual Productions in the Borderlands," *Borderzine*, December 10, 2015, https://borderzine.com/2015/12/romeo-and-julieta-opens-door-to-future-bilingual-productions-in-the-borderlands/. This misidentification was repeated to further critique the show. See Katherine Gillen and Adrianna M. Santos, "Borderlands Shakespeare: The Decolonial Visions of James Lujan's *Kino and Teresa* and Seres Jaime Magaña's *The Tragic Corrido of Romeo and Lupe*," *Shakespeare Bulletin*, 38, no. 4 (Winter 2020): 549–71, 566.

8. Ocampo-Guzmán, "My Own Private Shakespeare," 135.

9. For bilingual staging practices and strategies, see Della Gatta, "Staging Bilingual Classical Theatre."

10. For exemplary studies of sound in the early modern theater, see Wes Folkerth, *The Sound of Shakespeare*, New York: Routledge, 2002; and Bruce R. Smith, *The Acoustic World of Early Modern England: Attending to the O-Factor*, Chicago: University of Chicago Press, 1999.

11. Diana Taylor, *The Archive and the Repertoire: Performing Cultural Memory in the Americas*, Durham, NC: Duke University Press, 2003, 6.

12. Lynne Kendrick and David Roesner, "Introduction," *Theatre Noise: The Sound of Performance*, eds. Lynne Kendrick and David Roesner, Newcastle upon Tyne: Cambridge Scholars Publishing, 2011, xiv–xxxv, xxv.

13. See Jennifer Lynn Stoever, *The Sonic Color Line: Race & the Cultural Politics of Listening*, New York: New York University Press, 2016; and Josh Kun, *Audiotopia: Music, Race, and America*, Berkeley: University of California Press, 2005 for sociological studies of sound. See Pao, *No Safe Spaces*, and Catanese, *Problem of the Color[blind]*, for theatrical studies. See George Revill, "Music and the Politics of Sound: Nationalism, Citizenship, and Auditory Space." *Environment and Planning D: Society and Space*, 18 (2000): 597–613; and Marcus Cheng Chye Tan, *Acoustic Interculturalism: Listening to Performance*, New York: Palgrave Macmillan, 2012, for an emphasis on music.

14. Kun, *Audiotopia*, 16.

15. Stoever, *The Sonic Color Line*, 19.

16. In *Keywords for American Cultural Studies*, for "Sound," Kun writes, "Yet the distinct sound of the founding of the United States as a nation was one that excluded African Americans, Native Americans, and women. 'Americans' made 'American' sounds; blacks and Indians made noise." Josh Kun, "Sound," *Keywords for American Cultural Studies*, ed. Bruce Burgett and Glenn Hendler, 2nd ed., New York: New York University Press, 2014, https://keywords.nyupress.org/american-cultural-studies/essay/sound/

17. Art M. Blake, *Radio, Race, and Audible Difference in Post-1945 America: The Citizens Band*, New York: Palgrave Macmillan, 2019, 6. Blake references Tony Schwartz's famous documentary sound recordings of New York at the time.

18. "Accent" describes pronunciation and emphasis, and "inflection" describes pitch and tone.

19. Switching between languages may include forms of bilingualism, interlingualism, languaging, code-switching, or more. "Bilingualism implies moving from one language code to another, while interlingualism implies the constant tension of two (or more) languages at once." Martha J. Cutter, *Lost and Found in Translation: Contemporary Ethnic American Writing and the Politics of Language Diversity*, Chapel Hill: University of North Carolina Press, 2005, 177. Code-switching, or shifting between languages, takes many forms of language play. Code-switching includes intrasentential switching, the repetition of phrases in another language; extrasentential switching, the completion of a thought in a different language than the beginning of the line; and tag-like switches, intermixing within one phrase. Languaging is the "thinking and writing between languages." Walter Mignolo, *Local Histories / Global Designs: Coloniality, Subaltern Knowledges, and Border Thinking*, Princeton: Princeton University Press, 2000, 226. For more details on these distinctions, see Della Gatta, "Shakespeare and American Bilingualism: Borderland Theatricality in *Romeo y Julieta*," *Renaissance Shakespeare / Shakespeare Renaissances: Proceedings of the Ninth World Shakespeare Congress*, eds. Martin Procházka, Michael Dobson, Andreas Höfele, and Hanna Scolnicov, Newark: University of Delaware Press, 2014, 286–95; and Glenn A. Martínez, "Mexican-American Code-Switching," *Mexican Americans and Language* Tucson: University of Arizona Press, 2006, 94–108.

20. Joseph Roach, *Cities of the Dead: Circum-Atlantic Performance*, New York: Columbia University Press, 1996, 11.

21. Folkerth, *The Sound of Shakespeare*, 106.

22. In George Home-Cook's work on theater and aurality, he writes, "Thus, in the theatre our ears *and* eyes can lead us astray. Yet, such unintended instances of audiovisual ambiguity and coincidence are not necessarily technical or perceptual problems to be 'solved' but rather are to be savoured, or even sought after." George Home-Cook, *Theatre and Aural Attention: Stretching Ourselves*, New York: Palgrave Macmillan, 2015, 45.

23. Tan, *Acoustic Interculturalism*, 45.

24. Gloria Anzaldúa, *Borderlands / La Frontera: The New Mestiza*, 3rd ed., San Francisco: Aunt Lute, 1999, 77.

25. Anzaldúa, *Borderlands*, 81.

26. Frances R. Aparicio, "On Sub-versive Signifiers: Tropicalizing Language in the United States," *Tropicalizations: Transcultural Representations of Latinidad*, ed. Susana Chávez-Silverman and Frances R. Aparicio, Hanover: University Press of New England, 1997, 194–212, 199.

27. Elena Machado Sáez, "Reconquista: Ilan Stavans Multiculturalist Latino/a Discourse," *Latino Studies*, 7, no. 4 (2009): 410–34, 416.

28. Ana Celia Zentella, "'José, Can You See?': Latin@ Responses to Racist Discourse," *Bilingual Games: Some Literary Investigations*, ed. Doris Sommer, New York: Palgrave Macmillan, 2003, 51–68, 58.

29. John M. Lipski, "Spanish, English, or Spanglish? Truth and Consequences of U.S. Latino Bilingualism," *Spanish and Empire*, eds. Nelsy Echávez-Solano and Kenya C. Dworkin y Méndez, Nashville: Vanderbilt University Press, 2007, 197–218, 198.

30. For more on the outcomes and consequences of Rauch's initiatives at OSF, see chapter 5.

31. Bill Rauch and William Shakespeare, *Measure for Measure*, DVD recording, 2011, Oregon Shakespeare Festival Archives, Ashland.

32. Bill Rauch and William Shakespeare, "Measure for Measure," unpublished script including prologue, 2011, Oregon Shakespeare Festival Archives, Ashland, Prologue.

33. In OSF's script, Isabella's name is spelled in Spanish as "Isabela" and Juliet is often referred to as "Julieta" by other characters to connote her ethnicity.

34. Julie Cortez, "Oregon Shakespeare Festival Reaches Out," *El Hispanic News*, August 11, 2011, http://www.elhispanicnews.com/2011/08/11/oregon-sha kespeare-festival-reaches-out/

35. Frankie J. Alvarez, "Passion's Slave: Reminiscences on Latinx Shakespeares in Performance," *Shakespeare and Latinidad*, eds. Trevor Boffone and Carla Della Gatta, Edinburgh: Edinburgh University Press, 2021, 45–56, 46.

36. The concept casting was a step removed from OSF's tradition at that time of colorblind casting; it was the first time that artistic director Bill Rauch directed a cultural adaptation, and the first time that OSF staged a cultural adaptation of Shakespeare.

37. Jane Hill uses the term "mock Spanish" to describe this type of "insertion of Spanish words and phrases like *mañana* [and] *Ah-dee-os*." Zentella, "José, Can You See," 52.

38. Tiffany Stern argues that "the idea of 'atmospheric' music had not yet come about" in Shakespeare's theater. See Tiffany Stern, *Making Shakespeare: From Stage to Page*, London: Routledge, 2004, 107.

39. Rauch and Shakespeare, *Measure for Measure*, II.i.

40. Escalante later played Isabella in a production of *Measure for Measure* at the Goodman Theatre in Chicago in 2013 (dir. Robert Falls). Isabella and Claudio were characterized as Dominican New Yorkers. For more on this production, see Michelle Lopez-Rios, "Shakespeare through the Latinx Voice," *Shakespeare and Latinidad*, eds. Trevor Boffone and Carla Della Gatta, Edinburgh: Edinburgh University Press, 2021, 117–22, 118–19.

41. Rauch and Shakespeare, *Measure for Measure*, III.i.

42. There are a range of dramaturgical effects that are produced by shifting between languages. Della Gatta, "Staging Bilingual Classical Theatre."

43. Alvarez, "Passion's Slave," 47.

44. Alvarez, "Passion's Slave," 47.

45. Rauch and Shakespeare, *Measure for Measure*, III.i.

46. *Measure for Measure* is the only Shakespearean play named for a biblical passage. "Judge not, that ye be not judged. For with what judgement ye judge, ye shall be judged; and with what measure ye mette, it shal be measured to you again." *The Geneva Bible: A Facsimile of the 1599 Edition with Undated Sternhold and Hopkins Psalms*, Buena Park, CA: Geneva, 1990, Matthew 7.1–2.

47. Laird Williamson, "Director's Notes," program for *Romeo and Juliet*, Ashland: Oregon Shakespeare Festival, 2012. Katherine Gillen and Adrianna M. Santos misread this comment of Williamson's to claim that the production was "complicit with Spanish fantasy narratives," but it refers to the flashback/ dream of the Nurse, which was made clear and explicit in performance and detailed in the archival theater ephemera. See Gillen and Santos, "Borderlands Shakespeare," 565–67.

48. Qtd. in "Show Introduction January 4, 2012," "Members Lounge Handbook, Oregon Shakespeare Festival," Oregon Shakespeare Festival Archives, Ashland.

49. Laird Williamson, "Romeo and Juliet," unpublished script, 2012, Oregon Shakespeare Festival Archives, Ashland. Gillen and Santos strangely categorize this production as set in "Borderlands spaces" though there is nothing to indicate a borderlands epistemology in the dramaturgy or script, nor a geographical adjacency to what is now the US-Mexico border; the wide geography of Alta California crossed seven (or 14 percent of) contemporary states in the United States.

50. Williamson, "Romeo and Juliet."

51. Courtney Elkin Mohler, review of *Romeo and Juliet*, directed by Laird Williamson at Oregon Shakespeare, *Latin American Theatre Review*, 46, no. 1 (2012): 207–10, 209.

52. Qtd. in "Show Introduction."

53. Mercutio sang the lyrics, "Maria, La Pastora," and the Nurse joined him for "mató a su michito." The popular story of La Pastora shifted in music from a romance to a ballad, with lyrics changing over time and region from Latin America to Alta California. See Vicente T. Mendoza, *El Romance Español y El Corrido Mexicano, Estudio Comparativo*, Mexico City: Imprenta Universitaria, 1939, 395–96. See also Carlos F. Ortega, "Romance," *Celebrating Latino Folklore: An Encyclopedia of Cultural Traditions*, ed. María Herrera-Sobek, Santa Barbara, CA: ABC-CLIO, 2012, 3:998–1000, 1000.

54. Lydia Garcia, telephone interview, February 4, 2012.

55. In *Double Shakespeares*, Cary Mazer argues that when stories are told as a flashback, it changes audience empathy (see Part III).

56. Language exchange and accents vary within ethnic groups and within families, and Williamson's production depicted this accurately. See chapter 1 for this discussion.

57. Spanishisms such as "¡Que divertido!" "¡Cuidado!" and "¡Mercucio está

muerto!" were not in the printed script but were given to the actors in lists of possible ad-libs once rehearsal began. "Prompt Book: *Romeo and Juliet* (2012)." Folder 1, Oregon Shakespeare Festival Archives, Ashland.

58. Shakespeare, *Romeo and Juliet*, II.iii.41–42. For more on macaronic theater, see Marvin Carlson, *Speaking in Tongues: Languages at Play in the Theatre*, Ann Arbor: University of Michigan Press, 2009, especially 41.

59. Escalante also played the monolingual Spanish-speaking Julieta in the prior year's *Measure for Measure*.

60. Alejandra Escalante and Daniel Molina, "Diálogo: On Performing Shakespearean Characters as Latinx," *Shakespeare and Latinidad*, eds. Trevor Boffone and Carla Della Gatta, Edinburgh: Edinburgh University Press, 2021, 217–23, 222.

61. Suzi Steffen, "A Fingernail Moon Honors a New Oregon Shakespeare Festival Season," Oregon ArtsWatch, March 10, 2012, https://archive.orartswatch.org/a-fingernail-moon-honors-a-new-oregon-shakespeare-festival-season/

62. Shakespeare, *Romeo and Juliet*, V.i.43.

63. Mohler, review of *Romeo and Juliet*, 207–9.

64. Shakespeare, *Romeo and Juliet*, III.v.52–53.

65. Carlson, *Speaking in Tongues*, 6.

66. Cherríe L. Moraga, *A Xicana Codex of Changing Consciousness: Writings, 2000–2010*, Durham, NC: Duke University Press, 2011, 85.

67. The flashback motif created a personal past narrative of the Nurse within a cultural past narrative of the Californios. Therefore, all characters and not just the Apothecary, as per the setting, were "relegated primarily to the past." Gillen and Santos, "Borderlands Shakespeare," 567.

68. Shakespeare, *Romeo and Juliet*, V.iii.309–10.

69. Shakespeare, *Romeo and Juliet*, I.iv.165.

70. Williamson, "Romeo."

71. Stuart Hall, "The Spectacle of the Other," *Representation: Cultural Representations and Signifying Practices*, ed. Stuart Hall, London: Sage Publications, 1997, 223–90, 232.

72. Barbara Hodgdon, *The Shakespeare Trade: Performances and Appropriations*, Philadelphia: University of Pennsylvania Press, 1998, 48.

73. Margo Hendricks, "Gestures of Performance: Rethinking Race in Contemporary Shakespeare," *Colorblind Shakespeare: New Perspectives on Race and Performance*, ed. Ayanna Thompson, New York: Routledge, 2006, 187–204, 187.

74. Emma Smith, *This Is Shakespeare: How to Read the World's Greatest Playwright*, New York: Pelican Books, 2020; "Paula Vogel on *The Baltimore Waltz*," Comparative Drama Conference, YouTube, September 26, 2012, https://www.youtube.com/watch?v=Mkj7NC9AU4w

75. Jon D. Rossini, *Contemporary Latina/o Theater: Wrighting Ethnicity*, Carbondale: Southern Illinois University Press, 2008, 10.

76. Ross Brown, *Sound: A Reader in Theatre Practice*, New York: Palgrave Macmillan, 2010, 3–4.

77. In 2012–13, OSF marketed its audience as affluent, loyal, educated, and urban, as 56 percent have a postgraduate degree, and the average household income is $120,000. See Oregon Shakespeare Festival, *Illuminations, 2012–2013*, Ashland: Oregon Shakespeare Festival, 2013.

78. Alicia Arrizón, *Latina Performance: Traversing the Stage*, Bloomington: Indiana University Press, 1999, 112.

79. Antena Books, "How to Build Language Justice," Antena Aire, antenaantena.org, 2020, accessed August 17, 2020, 2.

80. Alfred Arteaga, *Chicano Poetics: Heterotexts and Hybridities*, Cambridge: Cambridge University Press, 1997, 73.

81. Arteaga applies this practice as an ongoing part of Latinx identity. He writes, "Being 'chicano' is a process of continual remaking, a discursive process that is always negotiated within the context of the circumscribing discursive practices of the United States." Arteaga, *Chicano Poetics*, 75.

82. Ross Brown, "Towards Theatre Noise," *Theatre Noise: The Sound of Performance*, eds. Lynne Kendrick and David Roesner, Newcastle upon Tyne, Cambridge Scholars Publishing, 2011, 1–13, 3–4.

CHAPTER 3

1. Lawrence Van Gelder, "Theater Review; Zany Doings on a Ranch, All in Verse," *New York Times*, January 3, 2003, https://www.nytimes.com/2003/01/03/movies/theater-review-zany-doings-on-a-ranch-all-in-verse.html

2. Anthony Christian Ocampo, *The Latinos of Asia: How Filipino Americans Break the Rules of Race*, Stanford: Stanford University Press, 2016, 11–12. To note, the Delano Grape Strike where Luis Valdez's El Teatro Campesino was born was "started by heroic Filipino farmworkers," and Valdez's theater was bilingual from the outset for that reason. Luis Valdez, *Theatre of the Sphere: The Vibrant Being*, New York: Routledge, 2022, 38.

3. Filipino and mixed-race actor Lou Diamond Phillips is an example of this elision, becoming famous for his Chicano roles as the singer Ritchie Valens in the 1987 film *La Bamba* (dir. Luis Valdez) and as an LA high school student in 1988's *Stand and Deliver* (dir. Tom Musca).

4. Jon D. Rossini, "Thinking the Space(s) of Historiography: Latina/o Ethnicity Theatre," *Theatre/Performance Historiography: Time, Space, Matter*, eds. Rosemarie K. Bank and Michal Kobialka, 237–52. New York: Palgrave Macmillan, 2015, 243.

5. Georgina Escobar, "The Composition of Latinx Aesthetics," *HowlRound*, August 23, 2017, https://howlround.com/composition-latinx-aesthetics

6. US Census Bureau, *Annual Estimates of the Resident Population by Sex, Race, and Hispanic Origin for California: April 1, 2010 to July 1, 2019 (SC-EST2019-SR11H-06)*, accessed November 10, 2020, https://www.census.gov/data/tables/time-series/demo/popest/2010s-state-detail.html

7. George Yúdice includes a third inflection of "culture": "intellectual, spiritual, and aesthetic development" (68). George Yúdice, "Culture," *Keywords for American Cultural Studies*, eds. Bruce Burgett and Glenn Hendler, 2nd ed., New York: New York University Press, 2014, 68–72.

8. Whiteness refers not simply to skin color but to a set of power relationships (see chapter 1).

9. "About," Coeurage Ensemble, accessed October 12, 2020, https://www.coeurage.org/about

10. "L.A. Speaks: Language Diversity and English Proficiency by Los Angeles County Service Planning Area," *Asian Americans Advancing Justice Los Angeles*, 2009, accessed October 28, 2020, https://www.advancingjustice-la.org/media-and-publications/publications/la-speaks-language-diversity-and-english-proficiency-los-angeles-county

11. Sixty-six percent of Filipinx in Los Angeles County were born outside of the United States, compared to 49 percent of Latinx ("L.A. Speaks").

12. Kate Jopson, Zoom interview, September 8, 2020.

13. By the mid-1990s, "The Philippines [was] the largest exporter of domestic workers." Kristin Choo, "Indentured Servants," *Chicago Tribune*, June 23, 1996, www.chicagotribune.com/news/ct-xpm-1996-06-23-9606230346-story.html. In 2017, the posthumous essay "My Family's Slave" by Pulitzer Prize winner Alex Tizon brought to light the possibility of Filipina slavery within the homes of Filipinx Americans.

14. Kate Jopson, "Twelfth Night," unpublished script, 2016, 2.

15. Kate Jopson, "Theatre: Twelfth Night," accessed May 20, 2020, https://www.katejopson.com/12th-night

16. Jopson, "Twelfth Night," 2.

17. Jopson, "Twelfth Night," 4.

18. Jopson, "Twelfth Night," 9.

19. Jopson, "Twelfth Night," 2.

20. Jopson, "Theatre: Twelfth Night."

21. Hans Johnson, Cesar Alesi Perez, and Marisol Cuellar Mejia, "Immigrants in California," Public Policy Institute of California, accessed November 6, 2021, https://www.ppic.org/publication/immigrants-in-california/

22. This strategy was also used in Tim Supple's 2003 filmic version of *Twelfth Night*, starring Parminder Nagra and Chiwetel Ejiofor as Viola and Orsino. Viola and Sebastian (Ronny Jhutti) speak in Hindi when they reunite, and they are the only Indian characters in the film, distinct from the otherwise multicultural cast as per the *West Side Story* effect.

23. Jopson, "Twelfth Night," 72.

24. As of 2019, the city of Los Angeles was over 48 percent Hispanic/Latinx ("QuickFacts"). "QuickFacts: Los Angeles," Census.gov, accessed November 10, 2020, https://www.census.gov/quickfacts/losangelescitycalifornia

25. José Esteban Muñoz, *The Sense of Brown*, Durham, NC: Duke University Press, 2020, 2.

26. Alex Alpharaoh, Zoom interview, August 18, 2020.

27. Hip hop is strongly affiliated with African American culture, but it has diverse origins including Latinx rappers and DJs and an early prominent Greek-American graffiti artist. Della Gatta, "Shakespeare, Race," 77 n. 13.

28. Alex Alpharaoh, "O-Dogg," unpublished script, 19.

29. Donna does not take part in the action, performing a similar function to the African American news reporter who speaks the part of the Chorus in Baz Luhrmann's *Romeo + Juliet* film (see chapter 1).

30. Alpharaoh, "O-Dogg," 28.

31. "Rodney King's LA Riots Speech, May 1st 1992," press conference, You-Tube, accessed January 8, 2022, https://www.youtube.com/watch?v=tVidK2k agPA

32. Agnes Constante, "Years after LA Riots, Koreatown Finds Strength in 'Saigu' Legacy," NBC News, April 25, 2017, https://www.nbcnews.com/news /asian-america/25-years-after-la-riots-koreatown-finds-strength-saigu-legacy -n749081. Also, Kyung Lah, "The LA Riots Were a Rude Awakening for Korean-Americans," CNN, April 29, 2017, https://www.cnn.com/2017/04/28/us/la-riots -korean-americans/index.html

33. Alpharaoh, "O-Dogg," 14.

34. Alpharaoh, "O-Dogg," 18.

35. Alpharaoh, "O-Dogg," 18. "Raza" means "race" and signifies "the people" and a call for unity; while in use by the mid-1800s, it became popular and politically inflected during the Chicano Movement / El Movimiento of the 1960s and 1970s.

36. Alpharaoh, "O-Dogg," 15.

37. Lorgia García-Peña, "Dismantling Anti-Blackness Together," *The North American Congress on Latin America*, June 8, 2020, accessed November 7, 2021, https://nacla.org/news/2020/06/09/dismantling-anti-blackness-together

38. See Walter Mignolo, *The Idea of Latin America*, Malden, MA: Blackwell, 2005.

39. García-Peña, "Dismantling Anti-Blackness Together."

40. Julie Torres, "Black Latinx Activists on Anti-Blackness," *Anthropology News*, September 3, 2020, https://www.anthropology-news.org/articles/black-la tinx-activists-on-anti-blackness/

41. Alpharaoh, "O-Dogg," 28.

42. Alpharaoh, "O-Dogg," 58.

43. Alpharaoh, "O-Dogg," 3.

44. Alpharaoh, "O-Dogg," 4.

45. Alpharaoh, "O-Dogg," 49.

46. Alpharaoh, "O-Dogg," 49.

47. Alpharaoh, "O-Dogg," 10.

48. Alpharaoh, "O-Dogg," 33.

49. William Shakespeare, *Othello, The Norton Shakespeare: Based on the Oxford*

Edition, eds. Stephen Greenblatt, Walter Cohen, Jean E. Howard, and Katharine Eisaman Maus, 3rd ed., New York: Norton, 2016, 2073–158, V.ii.200.

50. Alpharaoh, "O-Dogg," 112.

51. Julianna Stephanie Ojeda, Zoom interview, August 17, 2020.

52. The presentation of "O-Dogg" by Ensemble Studio Theatre LA (EST/LA) was slated for March 29, 2020, was canceled due to the Covid-19 lockdown that began on March 13.

53. Alpharaoh's autobiographical work is forthright too; his solo show *WET: A DACAmented Journey* earned him two Ovation Award nominations and the cover for *American Theatre* magazine in 2018.

54. Alpharaoh, "O-Dogg," 21.

55. Alpharaoh, "O-Dogg," 35.

56. The play had a subsequent staging at the American Shakespeare Collective in Lansing in 2015.

57. González, who received an Emmy nomination for his writing for the children's show *The PAZ Show* and a Kennedy Center National Teaching Artist Grant, is an emeritus theater professor at Cal State Los Angeles and has written over fifteen plays. In 2022, he was named one of the "Next 50" by The Kennedy Center as one of "50 leaders who are lighting the way forward through art and action." "The Kennedy Center Next 50," https://www.kennedy-center.org/our-story/social-impact/next-50

58. José Cruz González, "Invierno," unpublished script, Draft 7, May 21, 2017, 4.

59. Robert Farris Thompson claims this tradition specifically hails from the Kingdom of Kongo (present-day Angola). Robert Farris Thompson, *Flash of the Spirit: African and Afro-American Art and Philosophy*, New York: Vintage Books, 1984, 143–47.

60. Richard M. Breaux, "After 75 Years of Magic: Disney Answers Its Critics, Rewrites African American History, and Cashes In on Its Racist Past," *Journal of African American Studies*, 14 (2010): 398–416, 401.

61. González, "Invierno," 6.

62. González, "Invierno," 6.

63. González, "Invierno," 6.

64. González, "Invierno," 6.

65. González, "Invierno," 10.

66. This is the same era of California history in which OSF set its *Romeo and Juliet* (see chapter 2). OSF uses the formation of California identity and US statehood as a premise for Shakespeare's play; González integrates this history into the action of his adaptation.

67. See chapter 4 for practices of decoloniality in Latinx Shakespeares.

68. Jorge Huerta, "Interview with Luis Valdez," Necessary Theatre: Conversations with Leading Chicano & Chicana Theatre Artists, San Diego, University of California Television, May 10, 1998, YouTube video, 57:35, https://www.youtube.com/watch?v=3-DaYL8cx9o

69. José Cruz González and David Lozano, "Diálogo: On Making Shakespeare Relevant to Latinx Communities," *Shakespeare and Latinidad*, eds. Trevor Boffone and Carla Della Gatta, Edinburgh: Edinburgh University Press, 2021, 154–59, 157.

70. González, "Invierno," 58. The Vaquero (Shepherd) who finds her renames her Perdida.

71. See Della Gatta, "Staging Bilingual Classical Theatre."

72. González, "Invierno," 49–50.

73. Samala is an attested language, one that is extinct but is documented.

74. González, "Invierno," 2.

75. González, "Invierno," 19, 25.

76. Mark Rifkin, *Beyond Settler Time: Temporal Sovereignty and Indigenous Self-Determination*, Durham, NC: Duke University Press, 2017, ix.

77. Margaret S. Bain, "'White Men Are Liars'—Another Look at Aboriginal-Western Interactions," booklet, Alice Springs, Australia: SIL Darwin, 2005, 23. In Leo Cabranes-Grant's study of intercultural performance in colonial Mexico, he argues that traditional models of interculturalism imply that newer cultures must live in the shadow of the past, but that all cultures are constantly being originated. Leo Cabranes-Grant, *From Scenarios to Networks: Performing the Intercultural in Colonial Mexico*, Evanston, IL: Northwestern University Press, 2016, 12.

78. González, "Invierno," 26.

79. González, "Invierno," 28.

80. González, "Invierno," 29.

81. Rifkin, *Beyond Settler Time*, ix.

82. González, "Invierno," 58.

83. "Shakespeare in Latinx Communities: José Cruz González and David Lozano," *Shakespeare Unlimited*, Folger Shakespeare Library, 2021, Episode 176, accessed November 12, 2021, https://www.folger.edu/shakespeare-unlimited/latinx-communities-gonzalez-lozano

84. González, "Invierno," 107.

85. William Shakespeare, *The Winter's Tale*, *The Norton Shakespeare: Based on the Oxford Edition*, ed. Stephen Greenblatt, Walter Cohen, Jean E. Howard, and Katharine Eisaman Maus, 3rd ed, New York: Norton, 2016, 3121–204, III.iii.57.

86. González, "Invierno," 56.

87. González, "Invierno," 112.

88. González, "Invierno," 4.

89. González, "Invierno," 44.

90. González, "Invierno," 59–60.

91. González, "Invierno," 99.

92. González, "Invierno," 32, 42.

93. González, "Invierno," 41.

94. González, "Invierno," 34.

95. González, "Invierno," 32.

96. González, "Invierno," 37.

97. González, "Invierno," 68.

98. Arlene Dávila, "Culture," *Keywords for Latina/o Studies*, eds. Deborah R. Vargas, Nancy Raquel Mirabal, and Lawrence La Fountain-Stokes, New York: New York University Press, 2017, 40–42, 41.

99. "QuickFacts: Los Angeles."

100. "QuickFacts: California," Census.gov, accessed November 10, 2020, https://www.census.gov/quickfacts/CA

101. Rossini, "Thinking the Space(s)," 237.

102. Muñoz, *The Sense of Brown*, 2.

103. Muñoz argues that brownness is an "affective particularity"—a mix of gestures, expressions, and emotion that can be conveyed through performance. Muñoz, *The Sense of Brown*, 101.

104. Rossini, "Thinking the Space(s)," 238.

105. Muñoz, *The Sense of Brown*, 62.

106. Jeffrey S. Passel and D'Vera Cohn, "20 Metro Areas Are Home to Six-in-Ten Unauthorized Immigrants in U.S.," Pew Research, March 11, 2019, https://www.pewresearch.org/fact-tank/2019/03/11/us-metro-areas-unauthorized-immigrants/

107. The cutoff drops significantly from there; 12 percent are born in El Salvador, 11 percent in Guatemala, followed by 5 percent and 4 percent from the Philippines and China, respectively. "Unauthorized Immigrants* California and Los Angeles County," Los Angeles Almanac, accessed November 6, 2021, http://www.laalmanac.com/immigration/im04a.php

108. See Nancy Abelmann and John Lie, *Blue Dreams: Korean Americans and the Los Angeles Riots*, Cambridge: Harvard University Press, 1995; Robert Gooding-Williams, ed., *Reading Rodney King / Reading Urban Uprising*, New York: Routledge, 1993.

109. See Lah, "LA Riots"; Constante, "Years after LA Riots." See also Karen Grigsby Bates, "25 Years Later, the Enduring Relevance of the Los Angeles Riots," *NPR*, May 2, 2017, https://www.npr.org/2017/05/02/526607419/25-years-later-the-enduring-relevance-of-the-los-angeles-riots

110. "Rooftop Koreans," *Urban Dictionary*, accessed November 6, 2021, https://www.urbandictionary.com/define.php?term=Rooftop%20Koreans

111. Henry Yu, "Ethnicity," *Keywords for American Cultural Studies*, ed. Bruce Burgett and Glenn Hendler, New York: New York University Press, 2014, 100–104, 100.

112. Yu, "Ethnicity," 103.

CHAPTER 4

1. "Home," Lean & Hungry Theater, accessed May 23, 2020, http://www.leanandhungrytheater.org

2. Javier Rivera, Zoom interview, August 27, 2020.

3. "Lean & Hungry Theater: Taming of the Shrew (Audio)," WAMU 88.5, American University Radio, accessed May 23, 2020, https://wamu.org/story/13 /02/07/lean_hungry_theater_taming_of_the_shrew_audio/

4. Rivera, Zoom interview.

5. "Lean & Hungry Theater Presents: The Taming of the Shrew," promotional video, YouTube, January 27, 2013, https://www.youtube.com/watch?v=K _npo25_glQ

6. "Lean & Hungry Theater: Taming of the Shrew (Audio)."

7. Rivera, Zoom interview.

8. Mignolo, *Local Histories*, 265.

9. Mignolo, *Local Histories*, 264.

10. Mignolo, *Local Histories*, 270.

11. Anzaldúa, *Borderlands*, 25.

12. María Lugones, "Decolonial," *Keywords for Latina/o Studies*, eds. Deborah R. Vargas, Nancy Raquel Mirabal, and Lawrence La Fountain-Stokes, New York: New York University Press, 2017, 43–47, 46.

13. Eve Tuck and K. Wayne Yang, "Decolonization Is Not a Metaphor," *Decolonization: Indigeneity, Education & Society*, 1, no. 1 (2012): 1–40, 36.

14. As famously stated by Audre Lorde, "For the master's tools will never dismantle the master's house." Audre Lorde, "The Master's Tools Will Never Dismantle the Master's House," *Sister Outsider: Essays and Speeches*, Berkeley, CA: Crossing Press, 2007, 110–14. More recently, rhetorician Victor Villanueva expresses a similar notion: "The indigenous, Latinxs, and Latin Americans of this hemisphere really do not have a *decolonial* option—in that we are subject to English or to Spanish, subject to racism, subject to world trade in what is essentially an oligopoly, and the like. Yet we cannot simply throw up our hands." Victor Villanueva, "Foreword," *Decolonizing Rhetoric and Composition Studies: New Keywords for Theory and Pedagogy*, eds. Iris D. Ruiz and Raúl Sánchez, v–viii. New York: Palgrave Macmillan, 2016, vii. For more on the many theorizations of decoloniality, see Amanda M. Smith and Alfredo Franco. "The Politics of Latinx Literature Today," *Chiricú Journal: Latina/o Literatures, Arts, and Cultures*, 2, no. 2, (Spring 2018): 5–19, especially 11, and Lugones, "Decolonial."

15. Mignolo, *Local Histories*, 117.

16. Mignolo, *Local Histories*, x.

17. The production began in previews in late December 1967, but it is widely referred to as the 1968 *Naked Hamlet*.

18. Telatúlsa was formerly known as Tulsa Latino Theater Company (TLTC).

19. Jon Rossini argues that the border can be thought of as a metaphor for the theater space because it involves the politics of crossing. See *Contemporary Latina/o Theater*, 114.

20. Tuck and Yang, 35.

21. While oftentimes these terms are used interchangeably, and scholars around the world define them differently, "decoloniality" is a way of thinking positioned against Western domination, "decolonialism" argues that colonial power structures remain in regions that are no longer colonized, and to "decolonize" is to liberate people (or a curriculum) from dominating forces, assumptions, and values.

22. David Crystal, "Early Interest in Shakespearean Original Pronunciation," *Language and History*, 56, no. 1, (May 2013): 5–17, 15. Received Pronunciation (RP) or the "Queen's English" is a standardized speech method dating back to the nineteenth century. The BBC adopted the accent as its broadcasting standard in 1922, and it was used in education and for Shakespearean performance in the United Kingdom throughout the twentieth century.

23. See Margaret Tudeau-Clayton, *Shakespeare's Englishes: Against Englishness*, Cambridge, Cambridge University Press, 2019, especially chapter 2; David Crystal, *Pronouncing Shakespeare: The Globe Experiment*, Cambridge: Cambridge University Press, 2005; Adele Lee, ed., *Shakespeare and "Accentism"*, New York: Routledge, 2021; Sonia Massai, *Shakespeare's Accents: Voicing Identity in Performance*, Cambridge: Cambridge University Press, 2020.

24. Massai, *Shakespeare's Accents*, 2.

25. Clive Barns, "Theater: Slings and Arrows of Outrageous Papp," *New York Times*, December 27, 1967. For more on this production, see Ruby Cohn, *Modern Shakespeare Offshoots*, Princeton: Princeton University Press, 1976, 221–27; and Philip Traci, "Joseph Papp's Happening and the Teaching of *Hamlet*," *English Journal*, 58, no. 1 (January 1969): 75–77.

26. The production was staged the same year as the assassination of Dr. Martin Luther King Jr. and the passage of the Civil Rights Act of 1968, more commonly known as the "Fair Housing Act." It was also the year that the Chicago street gang the Young Lords reformed to model themselves after the Black Panther Party. The New York chapter of the Young Lords would be founded in July 1969.

27. Joseph Papp, "For Program," typewritten notes, n.d., NYPL.

28. Sheen has intermittently embraced acting in Spanish. In 2016, he starred in the film *The Vessel* (dir. Julio Quintana). The film was shot entirely in both Spanish and English, so there was no need for subtitles. It is set in an unnamed Latin American country and was filmed in Puerto Rico. Sheen spoke the Spanish for his part well enough, and any flatness in his accent could be considered in character for his role as a visiting American.

29. Joseph Papp, *William Shakespeare's "Naked" Hamlet: A Production Handbook*, London: Macmillan, 1969, 33.

30. Papp, *William Shakespeare's "Naked" Hamlet*, 183.

31. Ramon was described by one scholar as "this Jose-Jimenez portion of Hamlet." Traci, "Joseph Papp's Happening," 77. Traci's reference invokes both an insult and a perceived threat in society. José Jiménez was a comical and later considered derogatory character played by comedian Bill Dana. Dana was

Hungarian-Jewish, and his Bolivian Jiménez gained popularity in the 1960s and appeared on several variety shows. José Jiménez was also the name of the leader of the Young Lords; in 1968, after Jiménez served time in jail and read the work of Malcolm X and Martin Luther King Jr., he publicly announced that he would reform the Young Lords to be modeled as a human rights group after the Black Panther Party, with whom they would later form the Rainbow Coalition along with the Young Patriots Organization, and soon after several other organizations. See "Young Lords," *Encyclopedia Britannica*, accessed December 8, 2021, https://www.britannica.com/topic/Young-Lords

32. Papp, *William Shakespeare's "Naked" Hamlet*, 80.

33. Patricia Herrera, *Nuyorican Feminist Performance: From the Café to Hip Hop Theater*, Ann Arbor: University of Michigan Press, 2020, 29. Karen Jaime uses a lowercase "nuyorican" to "refer to an aesthetic practice rooted in broadening the specific ethnic marker 'Nuyorican' to include queer, trans, and diasporic performance modalities." Karen Jaime, *The Queer Nuyorican: Racialized Sexualities and Aesthetics in Loisaida*, New York: New York University Press, 2021, 5. Papp met Piñero in 1973 and in 1974 produced his play, *Short Eyes*, which became the first play written by a Puerto Rican to appear on Broadway. In 1975, Papp invited the Nuyorican Poets to perform at the Delacorte in Central Park.

34. Helen Epstein, *Joe Papp: An American Life*, Boston: Little, Brown, 1994, 311–12.

35. Papp, *William Shakespeare's "Naked" Hamlet*, 143.

36. Likewise, the 2010 production of *Hamlet* (dir. Bill Rauch) at OSF included deaf actor Howie Seago as the Ghost. Hamlet (Dan Donohoe) spoke most of the Ghost's lines, leaving the audience without the full translation. For more on this production, see Lezlie Cross, "Speaking in the Silence: Deaf Performance at the Oregon Shakespeare Festival," *Shakespeare Expressed: Page, Stage, and Classroom in Shakespeare and His Contemporaries*, eds. Kathryn M. Moncreif, Kathryn R. McPherson, and Sarah Enloe, Madison, NJ: Farleigh Dickinson University Press, 2013, 7–18; Carla Della Gatta, "*Hamlet*: Oregon Shakespeare Festival 2010," *Shakespeare Bulletin*, 30, no. 1 (2012): 72–73; and Michael W. Shurgot, "Breaking the Sound Barrier: Howie Seago and American Sign Language at Oregon Shakespeare Festival," *Shakespeare Bulletin*, 30, no. 1 (Spring 2012): 21–36.

37. Half of Hamlet's famous soliloquies remained in the play, and they were abbreviated to make room for Papp's contemporary dialogue and plenty of pantomime, circus, and musical bits. "O, that this too too solid flesh" (I.ii.), and "O, what a rogue and peasant slave am I!" (II.ii.) were delivered by Sheen as Hamlet (sans accent). For "What a piece of work is man" (II.ii), Hamlet removed his Ramon clothes to deliver the speech, without accent.

38. Papp, *William Shakespeare's "Naked" Hamlet*, 147.

39. Papp, *William Shakespeare's "Naked" Hamlet*, 148.

40. Papp, *William Shakespeare's "Naked" Hamlet*, 149.

41. Martin Sheen, "Martin Sheen 1972 Interview about Joe Papp's 1967 *Hamlet*," WV State Archives, YouTube, accessed November 20, 2020.

42. Sheen, "Martin Sheen 1972 Interview."

43. Papp, *William Shakespeare's "Naked" Hamlet*, 31.

44. Barnes, "Theater."

45. Sheen, "Martin Sheen 1972 Interview."

46. Papp, "For Program."

47. Sheen, "Martin Sheen 1972 Interview."

48. Papp also shortened the production to ninety minutes and offered no intermission, in line with the length of other touring productions for schools.

49. Marilyn Kern-Foxworth, *Aunt Jemima, Uncle Ben, and Rastus: Blacks in Advertising, Yesterday, Today, and Tomorrow*, Westport, CT: Greenwood Press, 1994, 45.

50. Illiteracy was key to the shaping of the caricature and his name. The sign he holds in a 1921 advertisement reads, "Maybe *Cream of Wheat* aint got no vitamines. I dont know what them things is. . . . *Rastus*." General Research Division, New York Public Library, "Cream of Wheat," New York Public Library Digital Collections, accessed September 11, 2021, https://digitalcollections.nypl.org/items/88c29255-0ab0-a090-e040-e00a18065550

51. Papp, *William Shakespeare's "Naked" Hamlet*, 33.

52. Joseph Papp, "Art, the State and Illusion," Address, n.d., NYPL.

53. Papp, *William Shakespeare's "Naked" Hamlet*, 78.

54. Papp, *William Shakespeare's "Naked" Hamlet*, 73.

55. J. Daniel Elam writes that South Asian "anticolonial movements are generally considered to have taken place from the 1920s to 1947," although movements took place in different forms and times worldwide. I employ Elam's other conceptualization, as a "critical analytic." J. Daniel Elam, "Anticolonialism," *Global South Studies: A Collective Publication with the Global South*, December 27, 2017, https://globalsouthstudies.as.virginia.edu/key-concepts/anticolonialism

56. Papp, *William Shakespeare's "Naked" Hamlet*, 40–41.

57. Sheen, "Martin Sheen 1972 Interview."

58. Elam, "Anticolonialism."

59. The superintendent approved the performance because of agreement with suitably standards and because "he was not interested in denying a producer or director the right to put on what he wishes." Sam Zotolow, "School Aides Object to Papp's Modern Hamlet," *New York Times*, January 22, 1968.

60. Papp, *William Shakespeare's "Naked" Hamlet*, 9.

61. Frankie J. Alvarez was performing in *Measure for Measure* at OSF (see chapter 2) when he was cast as Hamlet for this production. Although he was not currently living in Florida, he is a Miami native who attended Florida State University in Tallahassee for his undergraduate studies, and his bilingualism exemplifies that of the actors Edwards met in Florida.

62. "Michael Edwards Talking about *Hamlet, Prince of Cuba*," video interview, YouTube, May 6, 2012, https://www.youtube.com/watch?v=jUgtTm5 2guk

63. As of 2013, Cubans were 29 percent of the Florida Hispanic/Latinx population, down as a percentage due to the growth of other groups. See Mike Vogel, "Snapshots of Florida's Hispanic Community," *Florida Trend*, April 30, 2013, https://www.floridatrend.com/article/15521/snapshots-of-floridas-hispanic-community. That said, 66 percent of the Cuban and Cuban American population in the United States live in Florida. See Luis Noe-Bustamante, Antonio Flores, and Sono Shah, "Facts on Hispanics of Cuban Origin in the United States, 2017," *Pew Research*, September 16, 2019, https://www.pewresearch.org /hispanic/fact-sheet/u-s-hispanics-facts-on-cuban-origin-latinos/

64. A similar construct of performing entirely in English or entirely in Spanish by the same cast was used by Los Angeles–based Will & Co. for its 1993 production of *The Taming of the Shrew*. Translated by Edgar Landa and directed by Benito Martinez, the production included Martinez's sisters, Benita and Patrice, who had previously gained fame as the sisters from the popular 1986 film *The Three Amigos*.

65. Frankie J. Alvarez, Skype interview, July 20, 2017.

66. William Shakespeare, *Hamlet, The Norton Shakespeare: Based on the Oxford Edition*, eds. Stephen Greenblatt, Walter Cohen, Jean E. Howard, and Katharine Eisaman Maus, 3rd ed., New York: Norton, 2016, 1751–906, II.ii.307.

67. Michael Donald Edwards, "La Tragedia de Hamlet, Príncipe de Cuba," trans. Nilo Cruz, unpublished script, January 3, 2012, 19.

68. Alvarez, Skype interview.

69. Alvarez, "Passion's Slave," 54.

70. Ocampo-Guzmán directed the bilingual *Romeo and Juliet* at Florida State University with Alvarez as Romeo in 2005 (briefly discussed in chapter 2).

71. Alvarez, Skype interview. In a similar vein, Lin-Manuel Miranda enlisted his father, Luis A. Miranda Jr., to help translate Stephen Sondheim's lyrics from English to Spanish for the 2009 *West Side Story*. The elder Miranda "acted as [Lin-Manuel's] thesaurus." See Patricia Cohen, "Same City, New Story," *New York Times*, March 11, 2009, https://www.nytimes.com/2009/03/15/theater/15cohe.html. See also Herrera, "Compiling," 239 n. 43. The growing number of bilingual theatermakers, of which Alvarez and Miranda are part, requires community and familial support as it continues to grow in advance of acting and vocal methods.

72. "Part II: *Hamlet, Prince of Cuba*," May 6, 2012, conversation at Asolo Rep, YouTube, March 7, 2014, https://www.youtube.com/watch?v=9tD_Jgqo3fQ. Alejandra Escalante expressed a similar thought about her role as the monolingual Spanish-speaking Julieta in OSF's 2011 *Measure for Measure* (see chapter 2). She says, "It was definitely the first time I had worked on a production that was almost entirely set within a Latinx community. I found a lot of happiness and

excitement in being able to represent that part of myself . . . I found a great sense of stakes in Julieta only being able to speak in Spanish. I felt her frustration and urgency in trying to communicate." Alejandra Escalante and Daniel Molina, "Diálogo: On Performing Shakespearean Characters as Latinx," *Shakespeare and Latinidad*, eds. Trevor Boffone and Carla Della Gatta, Edinburgh: Edinburgh University Press, 2021, 217–23, 220.

73. Massai, *Shakespeare's Accents*, 2.

74. Inside Asolo Rep, "Hamlet, Prince of Cuba." Asolo Repertory Theatre, YouTube, March 21, 2012, https://www.youtube.com/watch?v=L4vN8kLgeFI

75. Michael Donald Edwards, "Hamlet, Prince of Cuba," unpublished script, March 16, 2012, III.i.

76. Alvarez, "Passion's Slave," 50.

77. Alvarez, "Passion's Slave," 49.

78. Aisha Beliso-De Jesús, "Santería Copresence and the Making of African Diaspora Bodies," *Cultural Anthropology*, 29, no. 3 (2014): 503–26, 508–12.

79. Alvarez, "Passion's Slave," 51.

80. Sheen's Hamlet was also controlled by the Ghost to seek his revenge, yet the scene was played for laughs. Sheen sat on the Ghost's lap and imitated Charlie McCarthy, vaudevillian actor Edgar Bergen's ventriloquist puppet. The Ghost would speak the lines first, then Hamlet would repeat them as a puppet in a ventriloquist puppet's voice.

81. Emma Pérez, *The Decolonial Imaginary: Writing Chicanas into History*, Bloomington: Indiana University Press, 1999, 6.

82. Tara Moses, "Hamlet: El Príncipe de Denmark," trans. Editorial Porrúa, unpublished script, 2018, 77.

83. Moses, "Hamlet," 3.

84. Moses, "Hamlet," 3.

85. Moses, "Hamlet," 3.

86. Moses, "Hamlet," 7.

87. Moses, "Hamlet," 7.

88. The Toltecs preceded the Aztecs, and evidence of this ritual is found in both peoples. See Stanley Brandes, "Iconography in Mexico's Day of the Dead: Origins and Meaning," *Ethnohistory*, 45, no. 2 (Spring 1998): 181–218; and Rosa Isela Aguilar Montes de Oca, "The Day of the Dead: One Ritual, New Folk Costumes, and Old Identities," *Folklore*, 66 (2016): 95–114.

89. The term "colonial Mexico" designates the period from 1521 (the beginning of Spanish rule) to 1821 (the end of the Mexican War of Independence). Moses purposely left this specificity within the period open for interpretation. Tara Moses, Zoom interview, August 26, 2020.

90. Moses, "Hamlet," 4.

91. Moses, "Hamlet," 4.

92. Moses, "Hamlet," 44–45, translated portion directly from Shakespeare.

93. Ngũgĩ wa Thiongo, "Decolonizing the Mind," *Decolonising the Mind: The Politics of Language in African Literature*, London: J. Currey, 1986, 9.

94. Moses, "Hamlet," 63.

95. Moses, "Hamlet," 64.

96. Moses, "Hamlet," 65.

97. Moses, "Hamlet," 24.

98. Moses notes that the Ghost spoke Spanish, which is itself a colonizing language, stating, "In an ideal world, it should have been an Indigenous language" (Zoom interview). In this production, the age of the actors amplified the theme of coloniality. It was the casting of an actress who was sixty-eight as Gertrude, an actor who was seventy for the Ghost, and an actor who was thirty-five for Claudius that made it presumable that Claudius committed the murder for power rather than lust.

99. The actor playing Hamlet turned forty during the run, and Ophelia was twenty-five; their age difference enhanced his ability to dominate her.

100. Moses, "Hamlet," 24.

101. Moses, "Hamlet," 46.

102. "If she doesn't fulfill what she promises . . ." Moses, "Hamlet," 48.

103. Moses, "Hamlet," 73.

104. Moses, "Hamlet," 77.

105. Alfred Arteaga, *Chicano Poetics: Heterotexts and Hybridities*, Cambridge: Cambridge University Press, 1997, 70.

106. The title of the Asolo adaptation referenced Hamlet as "Prince of Cuba," but Cuba never had a monarchy, and the only monarchs to hold power in Cuba were kings, queens, and princes of Spain.

107. Papp, *William Shakespeare's "Naked" Hamlet*, 31.

108. Sheen, "Martin Sheen 1972 Interview."

109. "About," Asolo Rep, accessed June 10, 2015, https://www.asolorep.org /about

110. "Support Us: Corporate Sponsorships, 2011–2012 Season," Asolo Repertory Theatre, accessed June 28, 2015, https://www.asolorep.org/support-us/cor porate-foundation-sponsors/corporate-sponsors

111. "Support Us."

112. In the following 2012–13 season, this outreach to the Spanish-speaking community was eliminated from the theater's FactSheet and replaced with outreach to the African American community. As language is often conflated with culture, Asolo aimed its outreach at a language-specific audience one year and a racially specific audience the following year. To note, both seasons' Fact-Sheets mentioned outreach to the LBGT community, professionals age forty-five and under, and, in 2012–13, women's groups as well.

113. While Miami and other parts of southern Florida have large Cuban and Cuban American populations, the Latinx community surrounding Asolo Rep is predominately Mexican or Chicanx. As of the 2010 census, North Sarasota,

where Asolo is located, had an estimated population that was 19 percent Hispanic or Latino. Of the Hispanic population, 48 percent identified as Mexican or of Mexican descent, 15 percent Puerto Rican, 14 percent Cuban, 12 percent South American, and 7 percent Central American. "Local Data Search," North Sarasota, FL: Population and Races, USA.com, accessed February 1, 2014, http://www.usa.com/north-sarasota-fl-population-and-races.htm

114. Moses, Zoom interview.

115. It also has to do with the challenges Latinx actors face in being recognized as Latinx. Asolo's vocal coach, Antonio Ocampo-Guzmán, has black hair, fair skin, blue eyes, and a thick Columbian accent. He found difficulty in finding roles as an actor because his eye color did not fit the stereotype of someone who would have his accent. Tara Moses began as a Shakespearean actress but realized that she would never get cast, so she went into the offstage aspects of theater-making.

116. Moses, Zoom interview.

117. Shakespeare, *Romeo and Juliet*, V.iii.75.

118. Frederick Luis Aldama and Christopher González, *Latinx Studies: The Key Concepts*, New York: Routledge, 2019, 25. For a brief history of border theory, see Aldama and González, 23–26.

119. Chela Sandoval, Arturo J. Aldama, and Peter J. García, "Introduction: Toward a De-colonial Performatics of the US Latina and Latino Borderlands," *Performing the US Latina and Latino Borderlands*, ed. Arturo J. Aldama, Chela Sandoval, and Peter J. García, Bloomington: Indiana University Press, 2012, 1–30, 13.

120. Lugones, "Decolonial," 43.

121. *Hamlet*'s popularity is truly worldwide. From 2014 to 2016, Shakespeare's Globe in London toured a production of *Hamlet* to 197 countries. Although the reception and interpretation of the play vary widely, its status now includes its position as the Globe's primary theatrical export. In addition, per Eric Minton's database of Shakespeare productions, *A Midsummer Night's Dream* was/is the most performed in the United States and around the world. For a close second, *Romeo and Juliet* follows in the United States, but *Hamlet* is the most performed outside the United States. See Minton, "Ranking the Bard's Plays."

CHAPTER 5

1. Anne Marie Welsh, "This *Romeo* Will Cross Both the Borders of Love and of Life," *San Diego Union-Tribune*, July 10, 2005, http://www.utsandiego.com/uniontrib/20050710/news_1a10romeo.html

2. It also provided a means of connection for members of the artistic team. Peter Kanelos, who was involved with staging the production, did not speak

Spanish. He recalls taking on the project because "growing up in a Greek community, I was always aware of the interplay between Greek and English. And
so for me, Shakespeare is always a second language, and a point of conjunction
that transcends whatever linguistic differences there are." Peter Kanelos, personal interview, September 16, 2021.

3. According to the press release, the project was "made possible in part by
grants from Chairwoman Pam Slater-Price and the County of San Diego, U.S.
Bank, and other generous sponsors." See "The Old Globe Presents Finale of
Romeo y Julieta Bi-national Education Project with Free Performances in San
Diego, Chula Vista, and Tijuana," *Old Globe*, press release, San Diego, July 6,
2005. A newspaper reported that the City of Chula Vista's Office of Cultural
Arts also gave a grant that aided in the project's financing as well as the Globe
management. See Welsh, "This *Romeo*."

4. Chloe Broznan, telephone interview, August 25, 2020.

5. To achieve parity offstage, along with Shakespeare, they staged *Native
Gardens* by Karen Zacarías (dir. Mary Ann Rodgers) in English with Spanish
supertitles. There was also a reading of *Concepción*, a play by Rodgers; one of
Moscow! Moscow! (Idaho), an adaptation of Chekhov's *The Three Sisters* by Robert Parsons; and a one-man show of the already popular and toured *Richard III*
by Mexican performer Erando Gonzales, in Spanish with English supertitles.

6. Broznan gained money through a Kickstarter campaign and from the
Zellerbach Family Foundation; it was only due to the Zellerbach money that
the Mexican actors' travel could be funded. (Broznan, telephone interview).

7. For more on borderlands theater, see Iani del Rosario Moreno, *Theatre of
the Borderlands: Conflict, Violence, and Healing*, Lanham, MD: Lexington Books,
2015. See also Arturo J. Aldama, Chela Sandoval, and Peter J. García, eds., *Performing the US Latina and Latino Borderlands*, Bloomington: Indiana University
Press, 2012.

8. Lee Bebout, *Whiteness on the Border: Mapping the U.S. Racial Imagination
in Brown and White*, New York: New York University Press, 2016, 214.

9. Dorinne Kondo, *Worldmaking: Race, Performance, and the Work of Creativity*, Durham, NC: Duke University Press, 2018, 29. Like Muñoz's investment in
the psychoanalytic, Kondo's work has roots in the work of Melanie Klein and
Donald Winnicott. Yet Kondo is focused on the practice of theater, writing, "I
unmoor the reparative from its psychoanalytic origins to conceive productive
ways to repair the destructiveness of systemic inequality" (32).

10. Gloria E. Anzaldúa, *Light in the Dark / Luz en lo Oscuro: Rewriting Identity,
Spirituality, Reality*, ed. Analouise Keating, Durham, NC: Duke University
Press, 2015, 90.

11. Kondo, *Worldmaking*, 5.

12. Auralidad is the aural excess that theatrically connotes Latinidad
through the soundscape: languages, accents, music, sound effects, silences, and
noise. See chapter 2.

13. Rossini, *Contemporary Latina/o Theater*, 114.

14. Rossini, *Contemporary Latina/o Theater*, 114.

15. For more on this, see Trevor Boffone, "Creating a Canon of Latinx Shakespeares: The Oregon Shakespeare Festival's *Play on!*," *Shakespeare and Latinidad*, eds. Trevor Boffone and Carla Della Gatta, Edinburgh: Edinburgh University Press, 2021, 181–95.

16. Due to the success of the event, it morphed into CultureFest in 2010, which became a biannual event that is inclusive of other cultures. By 2015, the OSF website included synopses in both English and Spanish of all productions, and OSF hosted the first Latino/a Playwrights Project (LPP). See Trevor Boffone and Carla Della Gatta, "Introduction: Shakespeare and Latinidad," *Shakespeare and Latinidad*, eds. Trevor Boffone and Carla Della Gatta, Edinburgh: Edinburgh University Press, 2021, 1–20, 5.

17. Boffone, "Creating a Canon," 185.

18. In a savvy contribution to the staging of bilingual theater, Rauch color-coded the script to designate different types of Spanish and English. Red for text spoken in Spanish, blue for text in which a native Spanish speaker is speaking English, green indicates text in which a native English speaker is speaking Spanish, and black indicates text spoken in English (Garcia and Rauch). This facilitates work for a vocal coach to engage with the text and for future directors and theaters to stage the play. See Micha Espinosa, "What's with the Spanish, Dude? Identity Development, Language Acquisition and Shame While Coaching *La Comedia of Errors*," *Shakespeare and Latinidad*, eds. Trevor Boffone and Carla Della Gatta, Edinburgh: Edinburgh University Press, 2021, 224–33. Likewise, Edit Villarreal's unpublished 1991 script for *The Language of Flowers* (a *Romeo and Juliet* adaptation) underlined words to be pronounced in Spanish or with a Spanish accent. Edit Villarreal, "The Language of Flowers," music by Germaine Franco, Draft 6, unpublished script, 1991.

19. Lydia G. Garcia and Bill Rauch, "La Comedia of Errors," from the *Play on!* translation by Christina Anderson, unpublished script, July 2, 2019, 32.

20. Garcia and Rauch, "La Comedia of Errors," 12.

21. William Shakespeare, *The Comedy of Errors*, *The Norton Shakespeare: Based on the Oxford Edition*, eds. Stephen Greenblatt, Walter Cohen, Jean E. Howard, and Katharine Eisaman Maus, 3rd ed., New York: Norton, 2016, 745–97, IV. iv.93.

22. Esmerelda Bermudez, "Column One: 'Vivaporu': For Many Latinos, Memories of Vicks VapoRub Are as Strong as the Scent of Eucalyptus," *Los Angeles Times*, March 26, 2019, www.latimes.com/local/california/la-me-col1-vi cks-vaporub-20190326-htmlstory.html

23. Garcia and Rauch, "La Comedia of Errors," 60.

24. Garcia and Rauch, "La Comedia of Errors," 1.

25. Maureen Flanagan Battistella, "'La Comedia' Is a Play with Many Layers," *Mail Tribune*, July 8, 2019, https://www.mailtribune.com/tempo/theater/la -comedia-is-a-play-with-many-layers/

26. Garcia and Rauch, "La Comedia of Errors," 39.

27. As of 2019, Ashland itself was 85.8 percent white (non-Hispanic) and 7.1 percent Hispanic. This is in contrast to the surrounding Jackson County, which is 80.1 percent white (non-Hispanic) and 13.5 percent Hispanic. See "Ashland City, Oregon; Jackson County, Oregon," Census.gov, 2019, accessed November 21, 2019, https://www.census.gov/quickfacts/fact/table/ashlandcityoregon,jacksoncountyoregon/PST045219#qf-headnote-b

28. Garcia and Rauch, "La Comedia of Errors," 29.

29. Garcia and Rauch, "La Comedia of Errors," 48.

30. Battistella, "La Comedia."

31. Alejandra Cisneros, "The Community of La Comedia," Oregon Shakespeare Festival, YouTube video, 6:42, December 30, 2019, https://www.youtube.com/watch?v=M-D8bdYTBuE

32. *La Comedia* as a traveling show is akin to Joseph Papp's Mobile Theater, which was developed by The Public to travel to various communities (see introduction). In 2010, Joe Papp's Mobile Theater returned after a thirty-year hiatus, and in 2016, the Spanish Mobile was revived with a reading of the Neruda *Romeo y Julieta* (dir. Jerry Ruiz), starring Daniel José Molina as Romeo (also Romeo from chapter 2). In 2017, the Mobile offered a semi-bilingual production of *Twelfth Night* (dir. Saheem Ali), with Viola and Sebastian landing on the shores of Florida from their native Cuba.

33. Garcia and Rauch, "La Comedia of Errors," 2.

34. Garcia and Rauch, "La Comedia of Errors," 3.

35. Garcia and Rauch, "La Comedia of Errors," 4.

36. Cisneros, "Community of La Comedia."

37. The play continued to move outside the region; it was performed at Arizona State University in 2022, again with Micha Espinosa as the voice and text director.

38. Boffone, "Creating a Canon," 190. The website was designed as such that it presented information about the production in both languages in a visually equivalent format.

39. Cisneros, "Community of La Comedia."

40. Manuel Antonio Morán, "'Latinizing' Shakespeare," *Puppetry International*, 47 (Spring–Summer 2020): 18–21, 18.

41. For an excellent history of Teatro SEA through 2014, see Paul Eide, "The Story of Teatro SEA," *Puppetry Journal*, 65, no. 4 (2014): 2–6.

42. Manuel Morán, telephone interview, November 13, 2021.

43. Morán, telephone interview.

44. Since 2015, the Clemente has also hosted "Shakespeare in the Parking Lot" by the Drilling Company NY, which started in 1994 in a different location. After *Sueño* closed in June 2015, Shakespeare in the Parking Lot ran a steampunk *As You Like It* in the same site at the Clemente, followed by a Latinx-themed *Macbeth* (dir. Jesse Ontiveros) set in a banana republic; it ran for a month through the end of August.

45. Penny Francis, *Puppetry: A Reader in Theatre Practice*, New York: Palgrave Macmillan, 2012, 6.

46. Morán also writes shows that engage the second "taproot," offering risqué political and social critique through burlesque for adults, such as the "Bawdy, Naughty Puppet Cabaret/Puppet Slam" for the 2021 International Puppet Fringe Festival.

47. Morán, "Latinizing," 19.

48. Morán, "Latinizing," 19.

49. Norge Espinosa, "Sueño," La Sociedad Educativa de las Artes, Inc. (Teatro SEA), Unpublished script, 2015, 3.

50. William Shakespeare, *A Midsummer Night's Dream, The Norton Shakespeare: Based on the Oxford Edition*, eds. Stephen Greenblatt, Walter Cohen, Jean E. Howard, and Katharine Eisaman Maus, 3rd ed., New York: Norton, 2016, 1037–96, II.i.165.

51. Espinosa, "Sueño," 5.

52. Shakespeare's play opens at Theseus's palace, and the four lovers enter. The second scene involves The Mechanicals, and Puck first appears in act 2.

53. Espinosa, "Sueño,' 15.

54. Morán, "Latinizing," 20.

55. Espinosa, "Sueño," 12.

56. Espinosa, "Sueño," 23.

57. The production won fourteen awards from the Asociación de Cronistas de Espectáculos (ACE), the Hispanic Organization of Latin Actors (HOLA), and the Artistas de Teatro Independiente (ATI). Morán, "Latinizing," 21.

58. Qtd. in Kate Taylor, "Multicultural Stages in a Small Oregon Town," *New York Times*, August 14, 2009, https://www.nytimes.com/2009/08/15/theater/15oregon.html

59. From 2008 to 2019, OSF engaged with Latinidad every season. With Latinx-themed shows (*A View from the Bridge* in 2008, *Measure for Measure* in 2011, *Romeo and Juliet* in 2012, *La Comedia of Errors* in 2019), OSF began to cast a number of Latinx actors as Latinx characters when staging the classics. It staged adaptations and riffs of the Western canon (*Don Quixote* in 2009, *The Tenth Muse* in 2013, *Mojada* in 2017, *Mother Road* in 2019) and included other Latinx-authored plays (*Breakfast, Lunch, and Dinner* in 2008, *American Night: The Ballad of Juan José* in 2010, *Water by the Spoonful* in 2014, *The Happiest Song Plays Last* in 2015, *The River Bride* in 2016, *Destiny of Desire* in 2018). Latinx directors directed non-Latinx-themed Shakespeare plays, *Henry IV, Part I, Romeo and Juliet*, and *Macbeth*, from 2017 to 2019 respectively. Along with OSF's programming strategy, in 2013, a Mellon award allowed OSF to name MacArthur Genius Luis Alfaro as the theater's first playwright-in-residence. It was during Alfaro's tenure through 2019 that OSF hosted the first and then subsequent Latinx Playwrights' Projects.

60. Papp had tried to integrate movements of equality—the Civil Rights

movements, LGBTQ rights, the feminist movement—into the organization of the Public through casting choices, the Black/Hispanic Theatre Company, low-priced and free theater, the Festival Latino, and a catalog of other initiatives, some of which were successful and others not.

61. Hildy Gottlieb, "Building Movements, Not Organizations," *Stanford Social Innovation Review*, July 28, 2015, https://ssir.org/articles/entry/building_movements_not_organizations

62. Manuel Morán, telephone interview, November 13, 2021.

63. See Adam Dean, "Racist Incidents Spark Action at Ashland Shakespeare Festival," *Best of SNO*, October 28, 2016, https://bestofsno.com/16708/news/racist-incidents-spark-action-at-ashland-shakespeare-festival/

64. In 2019, Rauch spoke of how saddened he was that "some local community members have gleefully claimed that OSF's current financial challenges are due to audience pushback to our commitment to equity, diversity, and inclusion and not to the $5.2 million in lost ticket revenue from wildfire smoke in the last two seasons." Bill Rauch, "Keynote Address to the 2019 ATHE Conference," *Theatre Topics*, 30, no. 1 (2020): 1–9, 7.

65. "ACLU of Oregon Sues City of Ashland for Illegally Arresting Tony Sancho," *ACLU*, April 16, 2021, https://www.aclu-or.org/en/press-releases/aclu-oregon-sues-city-ashland-illegally-arresting-tony-sancho

66. Eide, "Story of Teatro SEA," 4.

67. Morán, telephone interview.

68. Morán, telephone interview.

69. Kondo, *Worldmaking*, 51.

70. Jose Solís, "How R.Evolución Latina Is Reinventing the Bard," *HowlRound*, May 21, 2018, https://howlround.com/how-revolucion-latina-reinventing-bard

CHAPTER 6

1. Herbert Siguenza, "El Henry," unpublished script, EH Draft 11, 2020, 89.

2. Siguenza, "El Henry," 90.

3. Siguenza, who is of Salvadoran heritage, is one of the original members of Culture Clash, a performance troupe that made its name in the 1990s and still performs to packed audiences today. Culture Clash is one of the few Latinx theater acts/playwrights that are regularly produced at major regional theaters, and it is part of the American theater mainstream.

4. In 2021, they also staged the *Richard III* reinterpretation, *Seize the King*, by Will Power.

5. Miranda based his representation of Hamilton as an abolitionist on Ron Chernow's biography, *Hamilton* (2004). For information on the historical Alex-

ander Hamilton as a slave owner and trader, see Jessie Serfilippi, "'As Odious and Immoral a Thing': Alexander Hamilton's Hidden History as an Enslaver," Schuyler Mansion State Historic Site, 2020, accessed June 6, 2021, https://parks .ny.gov/documents/historic-sites/SchuylerMansionAlexanderHamiltonsHidde nHistoryasanEnslaver.pdf

6. Siguenza, "El Henry," 1.

7. Siguenza, "El Henry," 8.

8. There are several Welsh characters too, and the Welsh are considered a nation of people within the national boundaries of England.

9. There is a larger body of speculative narratives by people of color that *El Henry* is in conversation with, such as N. K. Jemisin's *How Long 'til Black Future Month?*, Colson Whitehead's *The Underground Railroad*, and Octavia Butler's novels such as *Kindred* and *Parable of the Sower*, to name a few.

10. Hall's articulation theory moves away from the potential reductionism of Marxism. Ernesto Laclau and Gramsci also engage articulation, focusing more on class and discourse, respectively. I use Hall's definition and that of those who expanded it from there. See Stuart Hall, "Race, Articulation, and Societies Structured in Dominance," *Essential Essays*, vol. 1: *Foundations of Cultural Studies*, ed. David Morley, Durham, NC: Duke University Press, 2019, 172–221.

11. Catherine S. Ramírez, "Deus ex Machina: Tradition, Technology, and the Chicanafuturist Art of Marion C. Martinez," *Aztlán*, 29, no. 2 (Fall 2004): 55–92, 76–78.

12. Catherine S. Ramírez, "Afrofuturism/Chicanafuturism: Fictive Kin," *Aztlán*, 33, no. 1 (Spring 2008): 185–94, 187.

13. Some examples include Valdez's *Los Vendidos*, Fornés's early play *The Successful Life of Three: A Skit for Vaudeville*, Svich's *Tropic of X*, Rivera's *Marisol*, and Escobar's *Then They Forgot about the Rest*. For a thorough list of Latinx speculative plays, see Teresa Marrero, "Latinxfuturism: Speculating Possible Futures through Sci-Fi Theater," "Forum: What's Next for Latinx?," ed. Chantal Rodriguez and Tom Sellar, *Theater*, 49, no. 1 (2019): 48–51.

14. Cathryn Josefina Merla-Watson and B. V. Olguín, "Introduction: Altermundos: Reassessing the Past, Present, and Future of the Chican@ and Latin@ Speculative Arts," *Altermundos: Latin@ Speculative Literature, Film, and Popular Culture*, ed. Cathryn Josefina Merla-Watson and B. V. Olguín, Los Angeles: UCLA Chicano Studies Research Center Press, 2017, 1–38, 4.

15. Ramírez, "Deus ex Machina," 77–78.

16. Micah Donohue, "Sci-Fi Ain't Nothing but Mojo Misspelled: Latinx Futurism in *Smoking Mirror Blues*," *Chiricú Journal*, 5, no. 1 (2020): 5–23, 6.

17. Moraga's *The Hungry Woman* takes place after "An ethnic civil war," and José Rivera's *Marisol* takes place after "premillennium jitters" cause the moon to disappear.

18. Siguenza, "El Henry," 22.

19. The original music was composed by Bruno Louchoarn. It was influenced by Nortec, a collective of musicians from Tijuana popular in the first decade of the twenty-first century for their electronica/dance music. The sound shares similarities with the grittiness of Nine Inch Nails, with a majestic and classical texture. Herbert Siguenza, Zoom interview, August 15, 2020.

20. Siguenza, "El Henry," 1–2.

21. Siguenza, "El Henry," 1–2.

22. Tomás Ybarra-Frausto, "Rasquachismo: A Chicano Sensibility," *Chicano Aesthetics: Rasquachismo*, Phoenix: Movimiento Artiscico del Rio Salado, 1989, 5–8, 5.

23. See introduction. As Valdez's El Teatro Campesino depicted the struggles in the fields in the 1960s and 1970s, Culture Clash took on the bilingual, bicultural Chicanx in the cities, living, moving, and speaking within white spaces, and made the action comical and satirical.

24. Siguenza, Zoom interview. For an analysis of *El Henry* in the larger body of Siguenza's work with Culture Clash and as a solo artist, see Matthieu Chapman, "Chicano Signifyin': Appropriating Space and Culture in *El Henry*," *Theatre Topics*, 27, no. 1 (March 2017): 61–69, 66–67.

25. Siguenza, "El Henry," 68.

26. Ybarra-Frausto, "Rasquachismo," 6.

27. Cathryn Josefina Merla-Watson, "(Trans)Mission Possible: The Coloniality of Gender, Speculative Rasquachismo, and Altermundos in Luis Valderas's Chican@futurist Visual Art," *Altermundos: Latin@ Speculative Literature, Film, and Popular Culture*, eds. Cathryn Josefina Merla-Watson and B. V. Olguín, Los Angeles: UCLA Chicano Studies Research Center Press, 2017, 352–70, 355.

28. Merla-Watson and Olguín, "Introduction," 25.

29. A production was scheduled for spring 2021 at the University of California, Irvine. It was postponed due to the Covid-19 pandemic.

30. Seating, water, and the position of the stage all had to be conceived and built for the show. Beth Accomando, Hilary Andrews, and Nicholas McVicker, "*El Henry* Gives Shakespeare a *Mad Max* Spin," *KPBS*, June 20, 2014, https://www.kpbs.org/news/2014/jun/20/el-henry-gives-shakespeare-mad-max-update/

31. Siguenza, Zoom interview.

32. This also posed potential issues for the rules established by the Actors Equity Association (AEA) that mandate these technologies for the safety of the actors. All AEA requirements were adhered to for the production. See Laura Zingle, "*El Henry*: Herbert Siguenza's Epic Chicano Version of Shakespeare's *1 Henry IV*," *Theatre Forum*, 46 (2014): 56–61, 60.

33. Zingle, "*El Henry*," 61.

34. Laura Zingle notes that the production also ran during the Theatre Communications Group (TCG) annual conference and was "kind of the highlight" of the conference ("*El Henry*," 61).

35. Siguenza, quoted in Zingle, "*El Henry*," 58.

36. A lowrider is a customized car with a lowered body, a style prominent within southern US Latinx communities since the 1950s. Lowrider communities traditionally value respect for property, family, and community. Several lowrider cars were used in the production. See Zingle, "*El Henry*," 58. Also, in 2016 and again in 2020, Siguenza received the Andrew W. Mellon Foundation National Playwright Residency Program grant, "which fosters the creation and production of theatrically ambitious plays that lend themselves to more effective engagement with audiences and communities"; the grant helps to support his role as San Diego Rep's playwright-in-residence. "Beyond the Boards: Herbert Siguenza," *The Stage*, accessed January 18, 2021, https://www.thestage.org/media/beyond-the-boards/herbert-siguenza

37. Zingle, "*El Henry*," 61.

38. William A. Calvo-Quirós, "The Emancipatory Power of the Imaginary: Defining Chican@ Speculative Productions," *Altermundos: Latin@ Speculative Literature, Film, and Popular Culture*, eds. Cathryn Josefina Merla-Watson and B. V. Olguín, Los Angeles: UCLA Chicano Studies Research Center Press, 2017, 39–54, 51.

39. "SILO in Makers Quarter," *KPBS*, accessed June 5, 2021, https://www.kpbs.org/places/silo-makers-quarter/

40. Chapman, "Chicano Signifyin'," 66–67.

41. Frederick Luis Aldama, *Latinx Ciné in the Twenty-First Century*, Tucson, University of Arizona Press, 2019, 267.

42. See Cherríe Moraga's 1993 foundational essay, "Queer Aztlán: The Reformation of Chicano Tribe," *Latino/a Thought: Culture, Politics, and Society*, eds. Francisco H. Váquez and Rodolfo D. Torres, Lanham, MD: Rowman & Littlefield, 2003, 258–74, 230. Since that time, numerous other scholars have contributed to this discussion.

43. Siguenza, "El Henry," 15, 16, 38.

44. Siguenza, "El Henry," 85.

45. Siguenza, "El Henry," 63.

46. They dance to the music of Big Jay McNeely, the 1950s Black R&B Los Angeles saxophonist whose antics onstage made his famous.

47. Siguenza, "El Henry," 17.

48. Siguenza, "El Henry," 17.

49. Siguenza, "El Henry," 37.

50. LGBTQ characters and story lines were largely absent in the first decades of Latinx theater due to the Latinx community's historical ties with Catholicism.

51. Chapman, "Chicano Signifyin'," 64.

52. Phyllis Rackin, "Women's Roles in the Elizabethan History Plays," *The Cambridge Companion to Shakespeare's History Plays*, ed. Michael Hattaway, Cambridge: Cambridge University Press, 2002, 71–85, 79. Rackin uses *Edward III* to illustrate an exception to this "double-bind" (79).

53. Siguenza, "El Henry," 91A.

54. Georgina Escobar, "Interview: Latinx Futurity with Georgina Escobar," *Sol Talk*, May 10, 2019, https://www.podbean.com/media/share/pb-iusf7-b0bd b7?utm_campaign=w_share_ep&utm_medium=dlink&utm_source=w_share

55. Siguenza, "El Henry," 74.

56. Siguenza, "El Henry," 102.

57. Shakespeare's King Henry orders the death of Worcester and Vernon at the end, but "Other offenders we will pause upon." *The First Part of Henry the Fourth, The Norton Shakespeare: Based on the Oxford Edition*, eds. Stephen Greenblatt, Walter Cohen, Jean E. Howard, and Katharine Eisaman Maus, 3rd ed., New York: Norton, 2016, 1165–244, V.v.15.

58. Herbert Siguenza, "Latinx Superfriends Playwriting Hour," *HowlRound*, June 1, 2020, https://www.youtube.com/watch?v=BkO4G93pRHo&feature=e mb_logo

59. Merla-Watson and Olguín, "Introduction," 4.

60. Siguenza, "El Henry," 16.

61. Siguenza, "El Henry," 17.

62. Cheech and Chong are a comedy pair who were immensely popular in the 1970s and 1980s. They starred in numerous films, television shows, and records.

63. Fernando Martí, "Futuros Fugaces: Latinx Futurism & Ancestral Knowledge," JustSeeds.org, June 29, 2020, https://justseeds.org/futuros-fugaces-latinx -futurism-ancestral-knowledge/

64. Siguenza, "El Henry," 13.

65. Siguenza, "El Henry," 36.

66. This eco-consciousness reflects the current state of California's decades-long drought crisis, as well as the Flint water crisis that began in 2014 when the city of Flint switched the source for its water from Lake Huron to the Flint River.

67. Adjacent to such comedic strands, there is no consistent ethical factor to who is celebrated or commemorated; Cesar Chavez is celebrated on the banknote, but the New Aztlan includes streets named for serial killer "The Night Stalker" Richard Ramirez and for the parricidal Menendez brothers.

68. Siguenza, "El Henry," 10.

69. To note, in the production, these actors were triple cast, so the masks aided in distinguishing characters played by the same actor. The Hispanic characters were in cool-toned makeup and clothing, and the Chicanx characters were in earth tones. Siguenza, Zoom interview.

70. Siguenza, "El Henry," 10. Although *El Henry* director Woodhouse has been a long-standing supporter of Siguenza's work, San Diego Rep is a predominantly white institution (PWI) that has increasingly diversified its programming over the last decade. This imagery serves a double purpose: most of the white audiences would not be expected to recognize the UFW symbol, but

NOTES TO PAGES 167-71 225

Chicanx audiences would likely understand the irony of its presence on the Hispanic city seal.

71. Siguenza, "El Henry," 11.

72. Siguenza, "El Henry," 10.

73. Siguenza, "El Henry," 34, 11, 100.

74. Siguenza, "El Henry," 35.

75. Siguenza, "El Henry," 75.

76. Siguenza, "El Henry," 76.

77. *Cholo* has a variety of meanings, including an aesthetic style of Mexican or Chicanx subculture, a derogatory term for one who is of mixed Indigenous and Chicanx heritage, and a Mexican or Chicanx gangster.

78. Siguenza, Zoom interview. Zingle claims the opposite (*"El Henry,"* 57).

79. Siguenza, "El Henry," 83.

80. Siguenza, "El Henry," 85.

81. Siguenza, "El Henry," 86.

82. In Shakespeare's play, Worcester is uncle to Hotspur (El Bravo) and purposely does not tell Hotspur of King Henry's option to surrender for fear that Hotspur would accept and look weak. After the battle that includes Hotspur's death and Henry's victory, Henry orders Worcester's execution.

83. Siguenza, "El Henry," 95. Created one hundred years before Shakespeare wrote *Henry IV, Part I*, the *Pietà* is considered a masterpiece of the Italian Renaissance.

84. Arthur Laurents, "West Side Story," *Romeo and Juliet and West Side Story*, New York: Laurel-Leaf, 1965, 131–224, 222.

85. This blocking is written in Laurents' 1957 script for the stage musical and remains in the 1961 film and in subsequent stagings until the 2021 film. In the 2021 film, Tony is given a criminal past and is therefore less innocent, and Maria merely leans over him briefly after he is shot. It is Chino who holds Bernardo in the *Pietà* formation upon his death, signaling Chino's loss of innocence and his affection for Nardo. See chapter 2.

86. Siguenza, "El Henry," 95.

87. Marissa López suggests that "a debate thus comes into view about what exactly 'chicanafuturism' makes possible: representing or deconstructing time and technologies of the Latinx self." *El Henry* achieved both. Marissa López, "The Xicano Future Is Now: Poetry, Performance, and Prolepsis," *ASAP/Journal*, 4, no. 2 (2019): 403–28, 411.

88. "Timeline of San Diego History: 20,000 BCE–1798," *San Diego History*, accessed December 1, 2021, https://sandiegohistory.org/archives/biographysubject/timeline/bc-1798/. Juan Rodríguez Cabrillo, who arrived in what is today San Diego in 1542, sailed on behalf of the Spanish Empire, though it is debated if he were Portuguese or Spanish.

89. "History of Old Town San Diego," *Old Town San Diego*, accessed September 6, 2021, https://www.oldtownsandiego.org/historyofoldtown/

90. Martí, "Futuros Fugaces."

91. Jorge Huerta, "Interview with Luis Valdez," Necessary Theatre: Conversations with Leading Chicano & Chicana Theatre Artists, San Diego, University of California Television, May 10, 1998, YouTube video, 57:35, https://www.youtube.com/watch?v=3-DaYL8cx9o

92. Siguenza, "El Henry," 65.

EPÍLOGO

1. Georgina Escobar, "Curating Courage and the Future of Latinx Theatre/Valentía Curatorial y el Futuro del Teatro Latinx," *HowlRound*, August 1, 2018, https://howlround.com/curating-courage-and-future-latinx-theatre-valentia-curatorial-y-el-futuro-del-teatro-latinx

2. Herbert Siguenza, Zoom interview.

3. "NALAC Fund for the Arts (NFA)," National Association for Latino Arts and Cultures, Nalac.org, accessed October 5, 2014.

4. Coco Fusco, "Introduction: Latin American Performance and the Reconquista of Civil Space," *Corpus Delecti: Performance Art of the Americas*, ed. Coco Fusco, New York: Routledge, 2000, 1–22, 4.

5. "BIPOC Theatres: Inherently Political," ArtEquity, "Talking Back," Episode 1, video clip, 2019, artequity.org, https://www.artequity.org/talking-back-bipoc-theatres

6. Jorge Ignacio Cortiñas, "'Fefu' and Her Pleasures," *American Theatre*, January 8, 2021, https://www.americantheatre.org/2021/01/08/fefu-and-her-pleasures/

7. Gloria E. Anzaldúa, *Light in the Dark / Luz En Lo Oscuro: Rewriting Identity, Spirituality, Reality*, ed. Analouise Keating, Durham, NC: Duke University Press, 2015, 78.

8. "Shakespeare in Latinx Communities: José Cruz González and David Lozano," *Shakespeare Unlimited*, Folger Shakespeare Library, 2021, https://www.folger.edu/shakespeare-unlimited/latinx-communities-gonzalez-lozano

9. Frankie J. Alvarez, Skype interview, July 20, 2017.

10. *Love's Labour's Lost* is set in Navarre, which is Basque country, and the traditional language is Euskera (Basque). In Shakespeare's play, Don Armado is Spanish, and culturally distinct from the King of Navarre, the Princess of France, and their attendants.

11. Ben Bartolone, Zoom interview, September 30, 2021.

Bibliography

Abelmann, Nancy, and John Lie. *Blue Dreams: Korean Americans and the Los Angeles Riots*. Cambridge: Harvard University Press, 1995.

"About." Asolo Rep. Accessed June 10, 2015. https://www.asolorep.org/about

"About." Couerage Ensemble. Accessed October 12, 2020. https://www.coeura ge.org/about

Accomando, Beth, Hilary Andrews, and Nicholas McVicker. "*El Henry* Gives Shakespeare a *Mad Max* Spin." *KPBS*, June 20, 2014. https://www.kpbs.org /news/2014/jun/20/el-henry-gives-shakespeare-mad-max-update/

Acevedo-Muñoz, Ernesto R. *West Side Story as Cinema: The Making and Impact of an American Masterpiece*. Lawrence: University Press of Kansas, 2013.

"ACLU of Oregon Sues City of Ashland for Illegally Arresting Tony Sancho." ACLU, April 16, 2021. https://www.aclu-or.org/en/press-releases/aclu-oreg on-sues-city-ashland-illegally-arresting-tony-sancho

"Affluent Barred from Youth Club; Lower East Side Project Gives Poor a Theater." *New York Times*, April 6, 1964.

Aguilar Montes de Oca, Rosa Isela. "The Day of the Dead: One Ritual, New Folk Costumes, and Old Identities." *Folklore*, 66 (2016): 95–114.

Aldama, Arturo J., Chela Sandoval, and Peter J. García, eds. *Performing the US Latina and Latino Borderlands*. Bloomington: Indiana University Press, 2012.

Aldama, Frederick Luis. *Latinx Ciné in the Twenty-First Century*. Tucson: University of Arizona Press, 2019.

Aldama, Frederick Luis, and Christopher González. *Latinx Studies: The Key Concepts*. New York: Routledge, 2019.

Alpharaoh, Alex. "O-Dogg." Unpublished script.

Alpharaoh, Alex. *O-Dogg*. Video performance. Dir. Brisa Areli Muñoz. RED-CAT. October 9, 2020.

Alvarez, Frankie J. "Passion's Slave: Reminiscences on Latinx Shakespeares in Performance." *Shakespeare and Latinidad*, edited by Trevor Boffone and Carla Della Gatta, 45–56. Edinburgh: Edinburgh University Press, 2021.

American Psychological Association Office on AIDS. *Resource Guide for Adapting SISTA for Latinas*. https://hiv.rutgers.edu/wp-content/uploads/2016/05 /SISTA_Latina_Resource_Guide.pdf

Añez, Luis M., Manuel Paris Jr., Luis E. Bedregal, Larry Davidson, and Carlos

M. Grilo. "Application of Cultural Constructs in the Care of First Generation Latino Clients in a Community Mental Health Setting." *Journal of Psychiatric Practice*, 2, no. 4 (2005): 221–30.

Antena Books. "How to Build Language Justice." Antena Are. 2020. Accessed August 17, 2020. antenaantena.org

Anzaldúa, Gloria. *Borderlands / La Frontera: The New Mestiza.* 3rd edition. San Francisco: Aunt Lute, 1999.

Anzaldúa, Gloria. *Light in the Dark / Luz en lo Oscuro: Rewriting Identity, Spirituality, Reality.* Edited by Analouise Keating. Durham, NC: Duke University Press, 2015.

Aparicio, Frances R. "Jennifer as Selena: Rethinking Latinidad in Media and Popular Culture." *Latino Studies*, 1, no. 1 (2003): 90–105.

Aparicio, Frances R. "On Sub-versive Signifiers: Tropicalizing Language in the United States." *Tropicalizations: Transcultural Representations of Latinidad*, edited by Susana Chávez-Silverman and Frances R. Aparicio, 194–212. Hanover, NH: University Press of New England, 1997.

Arellano, Gustavo. ¡*Ask a Mexican!* New York: Scribner, 2007.

Arellano, Gustavo. "Ask a Mexican: Why Do Mexicans Call People with Curly Hair Chinos?" *Houston Press*, October 26, 2006. https://www.houstonpress .com/news/why-do-mexicans-call-people-with-curly-hair-chinos-6544916

Arrizón, Alicia. *Latina Performance: Traversing the Stage.* Bloomington: Indiana University Press, 1999.

Arteaga, Alfred. *Chicano Poetics: Heterotexts and Hybridities.* Cambridge: Cambridge University Press, 1997.

"Ashland City, Oregon; Jackson County, Oregon." Census.gov. 2019. Accessed November 21, 2019. https://www.census.gov/quickfacts/fact/table/ashlandc ityoregon,jacksoncountyoregon/PST045219#qf-headnote-b

Bain, Margaret S. "'White Men Are Liars'—Another Look at Aboriginal-Western Interactions." Booklet. Alice Springs, Australia: SIL Darwin, 2005.

Barnes, Clive. "Theater: Slings and Arrows of Outrageous Papp." *New York Times*, December 27, 1967.

Bates, Karen Grigsby. "25 Years Later, the Enduring Relevance of the Los Angeles Riots." *NPR*, May 2, 2017. https://www.npr.org/2017/05/02/526607419/25 -years-later-the-enduring-relevance-of-the-los-angeles-riots

Battistella, Maureen Flanagan. "'La Comedia' Is a Play with Many Layers." *Mail Tribune*, July 8, 2019. https://www.mailtribune.com/tempo/theater/la -comedia-is-a-play-with-many-layers/

Bebout, Lee. *Whiteness on the Border: Mapping the U.S. Racial Imagination in Brown and White.* New York: New York University Press, 2016.

Beliso-De Jesús, Aisha. "Santería Copresence and the Making of African Diaspora Bodies." *Cultural Anthropology*, 29, no. 3 (2014): 503–26.

Beltrán, Cristina. *The Trouble with Unity: Latino Politics and the Creation of Identity.* Oxford: Oxford University Press, 2010.

Bermudez, Esmerelda. "Column One: 'Vivaporu': For Many Latinos, Memories of Vicks VapoRub Are as Strong as the Scent of Eucalyptus." *Los Angeles Times*, March 26, 2019. www.latimes.com/local/california/la-me-col1-vicks -vaporub-20190326-htmlstory.html

Berson, Misha. *Something's Coming, Something Good: West Side Story and the American Imagination*. Milwaukee, WI: Applause Theatre & Cinema Books, 2011.

"Beyond the Boards: Herbert Siguenza." *The Stage*. Accessed January 18, 2021. https://www.thestage.org/media/beyond-the-boards/herbert-siguenza

Bharucha, Rustom. *Globalization*. New York: Oxford University Press, 2001.

Biggers, Jeff. "Who's Afraid of *The Tempest*?" *Salon*, January 13, 2012. https:// www.salon.com/2012/01/13/whos_afraid_of_the_tempest/

"BIPOC Demands for White American Theatre." We See You, White American Theater. June 8, 2020. https://www.weseeyouwat.com/demands

Blake, Art M. *Radio, Race, and Audible Difference in Post-1945 America: The Citizens Band*. New York: Palgrave Macmillan, 2019.

Boffone, Trevor. "Creating a Canon of Latinx Shakespeares: The Oregon Shakespeare Festival's *Play on!*" *Shakespeare and Latinidad*, edited by Trevor Boffone and Carla Della Gatta, 181–95. Edinburgh: Edinburgh University Press, 2021.

Boffone, Trevor, and Carla Della Gatta. "Introduction: Shakespeare and Latinidad." *Shakespeare and Latinidad*, edited by Trevor Boffone and Carla Della Gatta, 1–20. Edinburgh: Edinburgh University Press, 2021.

Boffone, Trevor, Teresa Marrero, and Chantal Rodriguez. "Introduction, Encuentro 2014: Encountering Latinx Theater and Performance." *Encuentro: Latinx Performance for the New American Theater*, edited by Trevor Boffone, María Teresa Marrero, and Chantal Rodriguez, vi–xxxvi. Evanston, IL: Northwestern University Press, 2013.

Bosman, Julie. "Jets? Yes! Sharks? ¡Sí! in Bilingual *West Side*." *New York Times*, July 17, 2008. https://www.nytimes.com/2008/07/17/theater/17bway.html

Bourus, Terri, and Gary Taylor, eds. *The Creation & Re-creation of Cardenio: Performing Shakespeare, Transforming Cervantes*. New York: Palgrave Macmillan, 2013.

Brandes, Stanley. "Iconography in Mexico's Day of the Dead: Origins and Meaning." *Ethnohistory*, 45, no. 2 (Spring 1998): 181–218.

Brantley, Ben. "Such Sweet Sorrow: Orlando Bloom and Condola Rashad in *Romeo and Juliet*." *New York Times*, September 19, 2013. https://www.nytimes .com/2013/09/20/theater/reviews/orlando-bloom-and-condola-rashad-in-ro meo-and-juliet.html

Breaux, Richard M. "After 75 Years of Magic: Disney Answers Its Critics, Rewrites African American History, and Cashes In on Its Racist Past." *Journal of African American Studies*, 14 (2010): 398–416.

Brown, Ross. *Sound: A Reader in Theatre Practice*. New York: Palgrave Macmillan, 2010.

Brown, Ross. "Towards Theatre Noise." *Theatre Noise: The Sound of Performance,* edited by Lynne Kendrick and David Roesner, 1–13. Newcastle upon Tyne: Cambridge Scholars Publishing, 2011.

Broyles-González, Yolanda. "Rancher Music(s) and the Legendary Lydia Mendoza: Performing Social Location and Relations." *The Chicana/o Cultural Studies Reader,* edited by Angie Chabram-Dernersesian, 352–60. New York: Routledge, 2006.

Bulman, James C. "Introduction: Shakespeare and Performance Theory." *Shakespeare, Theory, and Performance,* edited by James C. Bulman, 1–11. New York: Routledge, 1996.

Burton, Jonathan. "Shakespeare in Liberal Arts Education." *Rock Magazine,* Whittier College, Fall 2013. https://issuu.com/whittiercollege/docs/13-116_wc_f13_mag_final_printer_fil

Butler, Octavia E. *Kindred.* Boston: Beacon Press, 2003.

Butler, Octavia E. *Parable of the Sower.* New York: Grand Central Publishing, 2019.

Cabranes-Grant, Leo. *From Scenarios to Networks: Performing the Intercultural in Colonial Mexico.* Evanston, IL: Northwestern University Press, 2016.

Calvo-Quirós, William A. "The Emancipatory Power of the Imaginary: Defining Chican@ Speculative Productions." *Altermundos: Latin@ Speculative Literature, Film, and Popular Culture,* edited by Cathryn Josefina Merla-Watson and B. V. Olguín, 39–54. Los Angeles: UCLA Chicano Studies Research Center Press, 2017.

Carlson, Marvin. *Speaking in Tongues: Languages at Play in the Theatre.* Ann Arbor: University of Michigan Press, 2009.

Carnegie, David, and Gary Taylor, eds. *The Quest for Cardenio.* Oxford: Oxford University Press, 2012.

Cartelli, Thomas. *Repositioning Shakespeare: National Formations, Postcolonial Appropriations.* New York: Routledge, 1999.

Catanese, Brandi Wilkins. *The Problem of the Color[blind]: Racial Transgression and the Politics of Black Performance.* Ann Arbor: University of Michigan Press, 2011.

Chapman, Matthieu. "Chicano Signifyin': Appropriating Space and Culture in *El Henry.*" *Theatre Topics,* 27, no. 1 (March 2017): 61–69.

Chartier, Roger. *Cardenio between Cervantes and Shakespeare: The Story of a Lost Play.* Cambridge: Polity, 2013.

Choo, Kristin. "Indentured Servants." *Chicago Tribune,* June 23, 1996. www.chicagotribune.com/news/ct-xpm-1996-06-23-9606230346-story.html

Cisneros, Alejandra. "The Community of La Comedia." Oregon Shakespeare Festival. YouTube video, 6:42. December 30, 2019. https://www.youtube.com/watch?v=M-D8bdYTBuE

Cohen, Patricia. "Same City, New Story." *New York Times,* March 11, 2009. https://www.nytimes.com/2009/03/15/theater/15cohe.html

Cohn, Ruby. *Modern Shakespeare Offshoots*. Princeton: Princeton University Press, 1976.

Committee of the Jubilee. "Welcome to the Jubilee." *HowlRound*, October 17, 2015. https://howlround.com/welcome-jubilee

Constante, Agnes. "Years after LA Riots, Koreatown Finds Strength in 'Saigu' Legacy." NBC News, April 25, 2017. https://www.nbcnews.com/news/asian -america/25-years-after-la-riots-koreatown-finds-strength-saigu-legacy-n74 9081

Cortez, Julie. "Oregon Shakespeare Festival Reaches Out." *El Hispanic News*, August 11, 2011. http://www.elhispanicnews.com/2011/08/11/oregon-shake speare-festival-reaches-out/

Cortiñas, Jorge Ignacio. "'Fefu' and Her Pleasures." *American Theatre*, January 8, 2021. https://www.americantheatre.org/2021/01/08/fefu-and-her-pleasu res/

Cross, Lezlie. "Speaking in the Silence: Deaf Performance at the Oregon Shake-speare Festival." *Shakespeare Expressed: Page, Stage, and Classroom in Shake-speare and His Contemporaries*, edited by Kathryn M. Moncreif, Kathryn R. McPherson, and Sarah Enloe, 7–18. Madison, NJ: Farleigh Dickinson University Press, 2013.

Crystal, David. "Early Interest in Shakespearean Original Pronunciation." *Language and History*, 56, no. 1 (May 2013): 5–17.

Crystal, David. *Pronouncing Shakespeare: The Globe Experiment*. Cambridge: Cambridge University Press, 2005.

Cutter, Martha J. *Lost and Found in Translation: Contemporary Ethnic American Writing and the Politics of Language Diversity*. Chapel Hill: University of North Carolina Press, 2005.

Darío, Rubén. "El Triunfo de Caliban." 1898. Accessed November 30, 2020. www.ensayistas.org/antologia/XIXA/dario/

Dávila, Arlene. "Culture." *Keywords for Latina/o Studies*, edited by Deborah R. Vargas, Nancy Raquel Mirabal, and Lawrence La Fountain-Stokes,. 40–42. New York: New York University Press, 2017.

Davine, Lauren. "'Could We Not Dye It Red at Least?': Color and Race in *West Side Story*." *Journal of Popular Film and Television*, 44, no. 3 (2016): 139–49.

Dean, Adam. "Racist Incidents Spark Action at Ashland Shakespeare Festival." *Best of SNO*, October 28, 2016. https://bestofsno.com/16708/news/racist-inci dents-spark-action-at-ashland-shakespeare-festival/

DeKeseredy, Walter S., and Martin D. Schwartz. "Masculinities and Interper-sonal Violence." *Handbook of Studies on Men & Masculinities*, edited by Michael S. Kimmel, Jeff Hearn, and R. W. Connell, 353–66. London: Sage Publications, 2005.

Della Gatta, Carla. "Afterword." *Shakespeare and "Accentism"*, edited by Adele Lee, 198–208. New York: Routledge, 2021.

Della Gatta, Carla. "*Hamlet*: Oregon Shakespeare Festival 2010." *Shakespeare Bulletin*, 30, no. 1 (2012): 72–73.

Della Gatta, Carla. "The Island Belongs to Sycorax: Decolonial Feminist Story-telling and *The Tempest*." Women and Power Symposium, Shakespeare's Globe, December 2021.

Della Gatta, Carla. "Shakespeare and American Bilingualism: Borderland The-atricality in *Romeo y Julieta*." *Renaissance Shakespeare / Shakespeare Renais-sances: Proceedings of the Ninth World Shakespeare Congress*, edited by Martin Procházka, Michael Dobson, Andreas Höfele, and Hanna Scolnicov, 286–95. Newark: University of Delaware Press, 2014.

Della Gatta, Carla. "Shakespeare, Race, and 'Other' Englishes: The Q Brothers' *Othello: The Remix*." *Shakespeare Survey*, 71 (2018): 74–87.

Della Gatta, Carla. "Staging Bilingual Classical Theatre." *HowlRound*, Septem-ber 15, 2020. https://howlround.com/staging-bilingual-classical-theatre

Della Gatta, Carla. "*West Side Story*: A New Take on *Romeo and Juliet*, 60 Years Later." *Shakespeare & Beyond*, January 4, 2022. https://shakespeareandbeyond.folger.edu/2022/01/04/west-side-story-2021-film-romeo-and-juliet/

Desmet, Christy, and Robert Sawyer, eds. *Shakespeare and Appropriation*. New York: Routledge, 1999.

"Despite Father's Claim, Leguizamo Asserts Puerto Rico Ties." *CNN*, June 13, 2011. http://edition.cnn.com/2011/SHOWBIZ/celebrity.news.gossip/06/13/leguizamo.puerto.rico/

Donohue, Micah. "Sci-Fi Ain't Nothing but Mojo Misspelled: Latinx Futurism in *Smoking Mirror Blues*." *Chiricú Journal*, 5, no. 1 (2020): 5–23.

Dramatists Guild Landmark Symposium. "*West Side Story* (1985)." *Shakespeare in America: An Anthology from the Revolution to Now*, edited by James Shapiro, 597–619. New York: Library of America, 2014.

Dyer, Richard. *White*. New York: Routledge, 1997.

Edwards, Michael Donald. "Hamlet, Prince of Cuba." Unpublished script, March 16, 2012.

Edwards, Michael Donald. "La Tragedia de Hamlet, Príncipe de Cuba." Trans-lated by Nilo Cruz. Unpublished script, January 3, 2012.

Eide, Paul. "The Story of Teatro SEA." *Puppetry Journal*, 65, no. 4 (2014): 2–6.

Elam, J. Daniel. "Anticolonialism." *Global South Studies: A Collective Publication with The Global South*. December 27, 2017. https://globalsouthstudies.as.virginia.edu/key-concepts/anticolonialism

Epstein, Helen. *Joe Papp: An American Life*. Boston: Little, Brown, 1994.

Escalante, Alejandra, and Daniel Molina. "Diálogo: On Performing Shakespear-ean Characters as Latinx." *Shakespeare and Latinidad*, edited by Trevor Boffone and Carla Della Gatta, 217–23. Edinburgh: Edinburgh University Press, 2021.

Escobar, Georgina. "The Composition of Latinx Aesthetics." *HowlRound*, August 23, 2017. https://howlround.com/composition-latinx-aesthetics

Escobar, Georgina. "Curating Courage and the Future of Latinx Theatre / Valentía Curatorial y el Futuro del Teatro Latinx." *HowlRound*, August 1,

2018. https://howlround.com/curating-courage-and-future-latinx-theatre
-valentia-curatorial-y-el-futuro-del-teatro-latinx

Escobar, Georgina. "Interview: Latinx Futurity with Georgina Escobar." *Sol Talk*, May 10, 2019. https://www.podbean.com/media/share/pb-iusf7-b0bd
b7?utm_campaign=w_share_ep&utm_medium=dlink&utm_source=w
_share

Espinosa, Micha. "What's with the Spanish, Dude? Identity Development, Language Acquisition and Shame while Coaching *La Comedia of Errors*." *Shakespeare and Latinidad*, edited by Trevor Boffone and Carla Della Gatta, 224–33. Edinburgh: Edinburgh University Press, 2021.

Espinosa, Norge. "Sueño." La Sociedad Educativa de las Artes (Teatro SEA). Unpublished script, 2015.

Espinosa, Ruben. "Chicano Shakespeare: The Bard, the Border, and the Peripheries of Performance." *Teaching Social Justice through Shakespeare: Why Renaissance Literature Matters Now*, edited by Hillary Eklund and Wendy Beth Hyman, 76–84. Edinburgh: Edinburgh University Press, 2019.

Espinosa, Ruben. "'Don't It Make My Brown Eyes Blue': Uneasy Assimilation and the Shakespeare-Latinx Divide." *The Routledge Handbook to Shakespeare and Global Appropriation*, edited by Christy Desmet, Sujata Iyengar, and Miriam Jacobson, 48–58. New York: Routledge, 2019.

Falocco, Joe. "Tommaso Salvini's Othello and Racial Identity in Late Nineteenth-Century America." *New England Theatre Journal*, 23 (2012): 15–35.

Fazel, Valerie M., and Louise Geddes. "Introduction: Bound in a Nutshell—Shakespeare's Vibrant Matter." *Variable Objects: Shakespeare and Speculative Appropriation*, 1–18. Edinburgh: Edinburgh University Press, 2021.

Fazel, Valerie M., and Louise Geddes. *The Shakespeare User: Critical and Creative Appropriations in a Networked Culture*. New York: Palgrave Macmillan, 2017.

Folkerth, Wes. *The Sound of Shakespeare*. New York: Routledge, 2002.

Francis, Penny. *Puppetry: A Reader in Theatre Practice*. New York: Palgrave Macmillan, 2012.

Fuchs, Barbara. *The Poetics of Piracy*. Philadelphia: University of Pennsylvania Press, 2013.

Fusco, Coco. "Introduction: Latin American Performance and the Reconquista of Civil Space." *Corpus Delecti: Performance Art of the Americas*, edited by Coco Fusco, 1–22. New York: Routledge, 2000.

García, Armando. "Freedom as Praxis: Migdalia Cruz's Fur and the Emancipation of Caliban's Woman." *Modern Drama*, 59, no. 3 (Fall 2016): 343–62.

Garcia, Lydia G., and Bill Rauch. "La Comedia of Errors." From the *Play on!* translation by Christina Anderson. Unpublished script, July 2, 2019.

García-Peña, Lorgia. "Dismantling Anti-Blackness Together." *North American Congress on Latin America*. June 8, 2020. Accessed November 7, 2021. https://
nacla.org/news/2020/06/09/dismantling-anti-blackness-together

García-Romero, Anne. "Latino/a Theater Commons: Updating the U.S. Narra-

tive." *HowlRound*, August 8, 2012. https://howlround.com/latinx-theatre-co
mmons-0

Garebian, Keith. *The Making of West Side Story*. Buffalo, NY: Mosaic Press, 1998.

Garner, Steve. *Whiteness: An Introduction*. London: Routledge, 2007.

General Research Division, New York Public Library. "Cream of Wheat." New York Public Library Digital Collections. Accessed September 11, 2021. https://digitalcollections.nypl.org/items/88c29255-0ab0-a090-e040-e00a1806 5550

The Geneva Bible: A Facsimile of the 1599 Edition with Undated Sternhold & Hopkins Psalms. 1990. Buena Park, CA: Geneva Pub. Co.

Gillen, Katherine, and Adrianna M. Santos, "Borderlands Shakespeare: The Decolonial Visions of James Lujan's *Kino and Teresa* and Seres Jaime Maga-ña's *The Tragic Corrido of Romeo and Lupe*." *Shakespeare Bulletin*, 38, no. 4 (Winter 2020): 549–71.

Gonsalez, Marcos. "Caliban Never Belonged to Shakespeare." *Literary Hub*, July 26, 2019. https://lithub.com/caliban-never-belonged-to-shakespeare/

González, José Cruz. "Invierno." Unpublished script, Draft 7, May 21, 2017.

González, José Cruz, and David Lozano. "Diálogo: On Making Shakespeare Relevant to Latinx Communities." *Shakespeare and Latinidad*, edited by Trevor Boffone and Carla Della Gatta, 154–59. Edinburgh: Edinburgh University Press, 2021.

Gooding-Williams, Robert, ed. *Reading Rodney King / Reading Urban Uprising*. New York: Routledge, 1993.

Gottlieb, Hildy. "Building Movements, Not Organizations." *Stanford Social Innovation Review*, July 28, 2015. https://ssir.org/articles/entry/building_mov ements_not_organizations

"The Great *West Side Story* Debate." *New York Times*, December 1, 2021. https://www.nytimes.com/2021/12/01/theater/west-side-story-steven-spielberg -movie.html

Hall, Stuart. *Essential Essays*. Vol. 1: *Foundations of Cultural Studies*. Edited by David Morley. Durham, NC: Duke University Press, 2019.

Hall, Stuart. "Race, Articulation, and Societies Structured in Dominance." *Essential Essays*, vol. 1: *Foundations of Cultural Studies*, edited by David Morley, 172–221. Durham, NC: Duke University Press, 2019.

Hall, Stuart. "The Spectacle of the Other." *Representation: Cultural Representations and Signifying Practices*, edited by Stuart Hall, 223–90. London: Sage Publications, 1997.

Hamilton, Charles. *William Shakespeare and John Fletcher: "Cardenio" or "The Second Maiden's Tragedy"*. Lakewood, CO: Glenbridge, 1994.

Hatzipanagos, Rachel. "'Latinx': An Offense to the Spanish Language or a Nod to Inclusion?" *Washington Post*, September 14, 2018. https://www.washingto npost.com/news/post-nation/wp/2018/09/14/latinx-an-offense-to-the-spani sh-language-or-a-nod-to-inclusion/

Hecht, Stuart J. *Transposing Broadway: Jews, Assimilation, and the American Musical*. New York: Palgrave Macmillan, 2011.

Hendricks, Margo. "Gestures of Performance: Rethinking Race in Contemporary Shakespeare." *Colorblind Shakespeare: New Perspectives on Race and Performance*, edited by Ayanna Thompson, 187–204. New York: Routledge, 2006.

Hensley, Dennis. "Claire Danes: Teen Angst." *Movieline*, December 1, 1995.

Herrera, Brian Eugenio. "Compiling *West Side Story*'s Parahistories, 1949–2009." *Theatre Journal*, 64, no. 2 (2012): 231–47.

Herrera, Brian Eugenio. *Latin Numbers: Playing Latino in Twentieth-Century U.S. Popular Performance*. Ann Arbor: University of Michigan Press, 2015.

Herrera, Brian Eugenio. "Panel Discussion." Latinx Playwrights Project, Oregon Shakespeare Festival, September 26, 2015.

Herrera, Patricia. *Nuyorican Feminist Performance: From the Café to Hip Hop Theater*. Ann Arbor: University of Michigan Press, 2020.

Herreras, Mari. "TUSD Banning Books? Well Yes, and No, and Yes." *Tucson Weekly*, January 17, 2012. https://www.tucsonweekly.com/TheRange/archives/2012/01/17/tusd-banning-book-well-yes-and-no-and-yes

"Hispanic or Latino Origin by Race." Data.census.gov. 2019. Accessed October 7, 2020. https://data.census.gov/cedsci/table?q=HISPANIC%20OR%20LATINO%20ORIGIN%20BY%20RACE&t=Hispanic%20or%20Latino&tid=ACSDT1Y2019.B03002&hidePreview=false

"History of Old Town San Diego." Old Town San Diego. Accessed September 6, 2021. https://www.oldtownsandiego.org/historyofoldtown/

Hodgdon, Barbara. *The Shakespeare Trade: Performances and Appropriations*. Philadelphia: University of Pennsylvania Press, 1998.

Hodgdon, Barbara. "*William Shakespeare's Romeo + Juliet*: Everything's Nice in America?" *Shakespeare Survey*, vol. 52: *Shakespeare and The Globe*, edited by Stanley Wells, 88–98. Cambridge: Cambridge University Press, 1999.

Holderness, Graham. *Tales from Shakespeare: Creative Collisions*. Cambridge: Cambridge University Press, 2014.

"Home." Lean & Hungry Theater. Accessed May 23, 2020. http://www.leanandhungrytheater.org/

Home-Cook, George. *Theatre and Aural Attention: Stretching Ourselves*. New York: Palgrave Macmillan, 2015.

Huang, Alexa. "What Country, Friends, Is This? Touring Shakespeares, Agency, and Efficacy in Theatre Historiography." *Theatre Survey*, 54 (2013): 51–85.

Huerta, Jorge. "From the Margins to the Mainstream: Latino/a Theater in the U.S." *Studies in Twentieth and Twenty-First Century Literature*, 32 (2008): 463–52.

Huerta, Jorge. "Interview with Luis Valdez." Necessary Theatre: Conversations with Leading Chicano & Chicana Theatre Artists. San Diego, University of California Television, May 10, 1998. YouTube video, 57:35. https://www.youtube.com/watch?v=3-DaYL8cx9o

Huerta, Jorge. "Introduction." *Necessary Theater: Six Plays about the Chicano Experience.* Edited by Jorge Huerta, 5–17. Houston: Arte Publico Press, 1989.

Huerta, Jorge. "Looking for Magic: Chicanos in the Mainstream." *Negotiating Performance: Gender, Sexuality, and Theatricality in Latin/o America,* edited by Diana Taylor and Juan Villegas, 37–48. Durham, NC: Duke University Press, 1994.

Inside Asolo Rep. "Hamlet, Prince of Cuba." March 21, 2012. Asolo Repertory Theatre. YouTube. https://www.youtube.com/watch?v=L4vN8kLgeFI

Itzkoff, Dave. "Bilingual 'West Side Story' Edits Out Some Spanish." *New York Times,* August 25, 2009. https://artsbeat.blogs.nytimes.com/2009/08/25/bilin gual-west-side-story-edits-out-some-spanish/

Jackson-Schebetta, Lisa. "'Spain . . . Brought Me Back to America': Ghostings of Other Races in Paul Robeson's Othello and José Ferrer's Iago (1943)." *Experiments in Democracy: Interracial and Cross-Cultural Exchange in American Theatre, 1912–1945,* edited by Cheryl Black and Jonathan Shandell, 213–34. Carbondale: Southern Illinois University Press, 2016.

Jaime, Karen. *The Queer Nuyorican: Racialized Sexualities and Aesthetics in Loisaida.* New York: New York University Press, 2021.

Jemisin, N. K. *How Long 'til Black Future Month?* New York: Orbit, 2018.

Johnson, Hans, Cesar Alesi Perez, and Marisol Cuellar Mejia. "Immigrants in California." Public Policy Institute of California. Accessed November 6, 2021. https://www.ppic.org/publication/immigrants-in-california/

Jopson, Kate. "Theatre: Twelfth Night." Accessed May 20, 2020. https://www.ka tejopson.com/12th-night

Jopson, Kate. "Twelfth Night." Unpublished script, 2016.

Kendrick, Lynne, and David Roesner. "Introduction." *Theatre Noise: The Sound of Performance,* edited by Lynne Kendrick and David Roesner, xiv–xxxv. Newcastle upon Tyne: Cambridge Scholars Publishing, 2011.

"The Kennedy Center Next 50," https://www.kennedy-center.org/our-story/soc ial-impact/next-50

Kern-Foxworth, Marilyn. *Aunt Jemima, Uncle Ben, and Rastus: Blacks in Advertising, Yesterday, Today, and Tomorrow.* Westport, CT: Greenwood Press, 1994.

Knowles, Ric. *Reading the Material Theatre.* Cambridge: Cambridge University Press, 2004.

Knowles, Ric. *Theatre & Interculturalism.* New York: Palgrave Macmillan, 2010.

Kondo, Dorinne. *Worldmaking: Race, Performance, and the Work of Creativity.* Durham, NC: Duke University Press, 2018.

Kozusko, Matthew. "Beyond Appropriation: Teaching Shakespeare with Accidental Echoes in Film." *The Routledge Handbook or Shakespeare and Global Appropriation,* edited by Christy Desmet, Sujata Iyengar, and Miriam Jacobson, 217–26. New York: Routledge, 2020.

Krogstad, Jens Manuel, and D'Vera Cohn. "U.S. Census Looking at Big Changes in How It Asks about Race and Ethnicity." Pew Research. March 14, 2014.

https://www.pewresearch.org/fact-tank/2014/03/14/u-s-census-looking-at
-big-changes-in-how-it-asks-about-race-and-ethnicity/

Kun, Josh. *Audiotopia: Music, Race, and America*. Berkeley: University of California Press, 2005.

Kun, Josh. "Sound." *Keywords for American Cultural Studies*, edited by Bruce Burgett and Glenn Hendler, 2nd edition. New York: New York University Press, 2014. https://keywords.nyupress.org/american-cultural-studies/essay/sound/

Kuner, Mildred C. "The New York Shakespeare Festival, 1966." *Shakespeare Quarterly*, 17, no. 4 (Autumn 1966): 419–21.

"L.A. Speaks: Language Diversity and English Proficiency by Los Angeles County Service Planning Area." Asian Americans Advancing Justice Los Angeles. 2009. Accessed October 28, 2020. https://www.advancingjustice-la
.org/media-and-publications/publications/la-speaks-language-diversity
-and-english-proficiency-los-angeles-county

Lah, Kyung. "The LA Riots Were a Rude Awakening for Korean-Americans." *CNN*, April 29, 2017. https://www.cnn.com/2017/04/28/us/la-riots-korean
-americans/index.html

Lanier, Douglas. "Recent Shakespeare Adaptation and the Mutations of Cultural Capital." *Shakespeare Studies*, 38 (2010): 104–13.

Lanier, Douglas. *Shakespeare and Popular Culture*. Oxford: Oxford University Press, 2002.

Lanier, Douglas. "Shakespearean Rhizomatics: Adaptation, Ethics, Value." *Shakespeare and the Ethics of Appropriation*, edited by Alexa Huang and Elizabeth Rivlin, 21–40. New York: Palgrave Macmillan, 2014.

Lara, Irene. "Beyond Caliban's Curses: The Decolonial Feminist Literacy of Sycorax." *Journal of International Women's Studies*, 9, no. 1 (September 2007): 80–98.

Laurents, Arthur. "Letter to Jerome Robbins." Billy Rose Division, MGZMD 182 — Box 101, Folders 1–3, Series IV: Personalities — Arthur Laurents. Folder 1 (1952–55). New York Public Library.

Laurents, Arthur. *Mainly on Directing: "Gypsy", "West Side Story", and Other Musicals*. New York: Alfred A. Knopf, 2009.

Laurents, Arthur. *Original Story By: A Memoir of Broadway and Hollywood*. New York: Alfred A. Knopf, 2000.

Laurents, Arthur. *West Side Story*. Bilingual version; unpublished script. 2009. New York Public Library Billy Rose Theatre Division.

Laurents, Arthur. "West Side Story." *Romeo and Juliet and West Side Story*, 131–224. New York: Laurel-Leaf, 1965.

"Lean & Hungry Theater: Taming of the Shrew (Audio)." WAMU 88.5, American University Radio. Accessed May 23, 2020. https://wamu.org/story/13/02
/07/lean_hungry_theater_taming_of_the_shrew_audio/

"Lean & Hungry Theater Presents: The Taming of the Shrew." Promotional

video. YouTube. January 27, 2013. https://www.youtube.com/watch?v=K
_npo25_glQ

Lee, Adele, ed. *Shakespeare and "Accentism"*. New York: Routledge, 2021.

Lee, Ashley. "Commentary: Spielberg Tried to Save *West Side Story*. But Its History Makes It Unsalvageable." *Los Angeles Times*, December 12, 2021. https://www.latimes.com/entertainment-arts/movies/story/2021-12-12/west-side-story-puerto-rico-cultural-authenticity

Lind, Paula Baldwin. "Chilean Translations of Shakespeare: Do They Constitute a National Shakespeare Canon?" *Tradução em Revista*, 12, no. 1 (2012): 61–80.

Lipsitz, George. *The Possessive Investment in Whiteness: How White People Profit from Identity Politics*. Philadelphia: Temple University Press, 1998.

Lipski, John M. "Spanish, English, or Spanglish? Truth and Consequences of U.S. Latino Bilingualism." *Spanish and Empire*, edited by Nelsy Echávez-Solano and Kenya C. Dworkin y Méndez, 197–218. Nashville: Vanderbilt University Press, 2007.

"Local Data Search." North Sarasota, FL: Population and Races. USA.com. Accessed February 1, 2014. http://www.usa.com/north-sarasota-fl-population-and-races.htm

Look Up and Live: West Side Story. Hosted by Sidney Lanier. Jerome Robbins Collection. CBS, 1958. VHS.

López, Marissa. "The Xicano Future Is Now: Poetry, Performance, and Prolepsis." *ASAP/Journal*, 4, no. 2 (2019): 403–28.

Lopez, Mark Hugo, Jens Manuel Krogstad, and Antonio Flores. "Most Hispanic Parents Speak Spanish to Their Children, but This Is Less the Case in Later Immigrant Generations." Pew Research. April 2, 2018. https://www.pewresearch.org/fact-tank/2018/04/02/most-hispanic-parents-speak-spanish-to-their-children-but-this-is-less-the-case-in-later-immigrant-generations/

Lopez-Rios, Michelle. "Shakespeare through the Latinx Voice." *Shakespeare and Latinidad*, edited by Trevor Boffone and Carla Della Gatta, 117–22. Edinburgh: Edinburgh University Press, 2021.

Lorde, Audre. "The Master's Tools Will Never Dismantle the Master's House." *Sister Outsider: Essays and Speeches*, 110–14. Berkeley, CA: Crossing Press, 2007.

Ludden, Jennifer. "1965 Immigration Law Changed Face of America." National Public Radio. May 9, 2006. https://www.npr.org/templates/story/story.php?storyId=5391395

Lugones, María. "Decolonial." *Keywords for Latina/o Studies*, edited by Deborah R. Vargas, Nancy Raquel Mirabal, and Lawrence La Fountain-Stokes, 43–47. New York: New York University Press, 2017.

Luhrmann, Baz, dir. *William Shakespeare's Romeo + Juliet: The Music Edition*. 20th Century Fox, 2006. DVD, 120 minutes.

Machado Sáez, Elena. "Reconquista: Ilan Stavans Multiculturalist Latino/a Discourse." *Latino Studies*, 7, no. 4 (2009): 410–34.

Mannoni, Octave. *Prospero & Caliban: The Psychology of Colonization*. Ann Arbor: University of Michigan Press, 1990.

Marrero, Teresa. "Latinxfuturism: Speculating Possible Futures through Sci-Fi Theater." "Forum: What's Next for Latinx?" Edited by Chantal Rodriguez and Tom Sellar. *Theater*, 49, no. 1 (2019): 48–51.

Martí, Fernando. "Futuros Fugaces: Latinx Futurism & Ancestral Knowledge." JustSeeds. June 29, 2020. https://justseeds.org/futuros-fugaces-latinx-futuri sm-ancestral-knowledge/

Martínez, Glenn A. "Mexican-American Code Switching." *Mexican Americans and Language*, 94–108. Tucson: University of Arizona Press, 2006.

Maslon, Laurence. "The Divided States of 'America'—Why Rita Moreno Objected to *West Side Story*'s Original Lyrics." *PBS*, October 8, 2021. https:// www.pbs.org/wnet/americanmasters/the-divided-states-of-america-why-ri ta-moreno-objected-to-west-side-storys-original-lyrics/18671/

Massai, Sonia. *Shakespeare's Accents: Voicing Identity in Performance*. Cambridge: Cambridge University Press, 2020.

Mazer, Cary M. *Double Shakespeares: Emotional-Realist Acting and Contemporary Performance*. Madison, NJ: Farleigh Dickinson University Press, 2015.

Mendoza, Vicente T. *El Romance Español y el Corrido Mexicano, Estudio Comparativo*. Mexico City: Imprenta Universitaria, 1939.

Merla-Watson, Cathryn Josefina. "(Trans)Mission Possible: The Coloniality of Gender, Speculative Rasquachismo, and Altermundos in Luis Valderas's Chican@futurist Visual Art." *Altermundos: Latin@ Speculative Literature, Film, and Popular Culture*, edited by Cathryn Josefina Merla-Watson and B. V. Olguín, 352–70. Los Angeles: UCLA Chicano Studies Research Center Press, 2017.

Merla-Watson, Cathryn Josefina, and B. V. Olguín. "Introduction: Altermundos: Reassessing the Past, Present, and Future of the Chican@ and Latin@ Speculative Arts." *Altermundos: Latin@ Speculative Literature, Film, and Popular Culture*, edited by Cathryn Josefina Merla-Watson and B. V. Olguín, 1–38. Los Angeles: UCLA Chicano Studies Research Center Press, 2017.

"Michael Edwards Talking about *Hamlet, Prince of Cuba*." Video interview. YouTube. May 6, 2012. https://www.youtube.com/watch?v=jUgtTm52guk

Mignolo, Walter. *The Idea of Latin America*, Malden: Blackwell, 2005.

Mignolo, Walter. *Local Histories / Global Designs: Coloniality, Subaltern Knowledges, and Border Thinking*. Princeton: Princeton University Press, 2000.

Miller, Derek. Review of *West Side Story* at the National Theatre, directed by Arthur Laurents. *Theatre Journal*, 61, no. 3 (2009): 480.

Minton, Eric. "Ranking the Bard's Plays by Stage Popularity." Shakespeareances.com. October 13, 2017. http://www.shakespeareances.com/dialogues /commentary/Bard_Board_Popularity-171012.html

Modenessi, Alfredo Michel. "Of Shadows and Stones: Revering and Translating 'the Word' Shakespeare in Mexico." *Shakespeare Survey*, 54 (2001): 152–64.

Modenessi, Alfredo Michel. "(Un)doing the Book 'without Verona Walls': A View from the Receiving End of Baz Luhrmann's *William Shakespeare's Romeo + Juliet*." *Spectacular Shakespeare: Critical Theory and Popular Cinema*, edited by Courtney Lehmann and Lisa S. Starks, 62–85. Madison, NJ: Fairleigh Dickinson University Press, 2002.

Mohler, Courtney Elkin. Review of *Romeo and Juliet*, directed by Laird Williamson at Oregon Shakespeare. *Latin American Theatre Review*, 46, no. 1 (2012): 207–10.

Moraga, Cherríe L. "Queer Aztlán: The Re-formation of Chicano Tribe." *Latino/a Thought: Culture, Politics, and Society*, edited by Francisco H. Vázquez, 258–74. Lanham, MD: Rowman & Littlefield, 2003.

Moraga, Cherríe L. *A Xicana Codex of Changing Consciousness: Writings, 2000–2010*. Durham, NC: Duke University Press, 2011.

Morán, Manuel Antonio. "'Latinizing' Shakespeare." *Puppetry International*, 47 (Spring–Summer 2020): 18–21.

Moreno, Iani del Rosario. *Theatre of the Borderlands: Conflict, Violence, and Healing*. Lanham, MD: Lexington Books, 2015.

Moreno, Rita. *Rita Moreno: A Memoir*. New York: Penguin, 2014.

Morgan, David. "Class and Masculinity." *Handbook of Studies on Men & Masculinities*, edited by Michael S. Kimmel, Jeff Hearn, and R. W. Connell, 165–77. London: Sage Publications, 2005.

Moses, Tara. "Hamlet: El Príncipe de Denmark." With translations by Editorial Porrúa. Unpublished script, 2018.

Muñoz, José Esteban. *The Sense of Brown*. Durham, NC: Duke University Press, 2020.

"NALAC Fund for the Arts (NFA)." National Association for Latino Arts and Cultures. Accessed October 5, 2014. Nalac.org

Negrón-Muntaner, Frances. "Feeling Pretty: *West Side Story* and Puerto Rican Identity Discourses." *Social Text*, 18, no. 2 (2000): 83–106.

Ngũgĩ wa Thiongo. "Decolonizing the Mind." *Decolonising the Mind: The Politics of Language in African Literature*, 4–33. London: J. Currey, 1986.

Nicholson, Amy. "Interview: Olivia Hussey, Star of Zeffirelli's *Romeo and Juliet*: 'I Was Wild.'" *The Guardian*, August 1, 2018. https://www.theguardian.com /film/2018/aug/01/olivia-hussey-romeo-and-juliet-film-franco-zeffirelli

Noe-Bustamante, Luis, Antonio Flores, and Sono Shah. "Facts on Hispanics of Cuban Origin in the United States, 2017." Pew Research. September 16, 2019. https://www.pewresearch.org/hispanic/fact-sheet/u-s-hispanics-facts -on-cuban-origin-latinos/

Ocampo, Anthony Christian. *The Latinos of Asia: How Filipino Americans Break the Rules of Race*. Stanford: Stanford University Press, 2016.

Ocampo-Guzman, Antonio. "My Own Private Shakespeare; or, Am I Deluding Myself?" *Colorblind Shakespeare: New Perspectives on Race and Performance*, edited by Ayanna Thompson, 125–36. New York: Routledge, 2006.

"The Old Globe Presents Finale of *Romeo y Julieta* Bi-national Education Project with Free Performances in San Diego, Chula Vista, and Tijuana." Press release. San Diego: Old Globe, July 6, 2005.

Oregon Shakespeare Festival. *Illuminations, 2012–2013*. Ashland: Oregon Shakespeare Festival, 2013.

Orozco, Gisela. "John Leguizamo: Boricua o No, Presente en Desfile Nacional Puertorriqueño." *Chicago Tribune*, June 12, 2011. https://www.chicagotribu ne.com/hoy/ct-hoy-8007123-john-leguizamo-boricua-o-no-presente-en-desf ile-nacional-puertorriqueno-story.html

Ortega, Carlos F. "Romance." *Celebrating Latino Folklore: An Encyclopedia of Cultural Traditions*, edited by María Herrera-Sobek, 3:998–1000. Santa Barbara: ABC-CLIO, 2012.

Pao, Angela C. *No Safe Spaces: Re-casting Race, Ethnicity, and Nationality in American Theater*. Ann Arbor: University of Michigan Press, 2010.

Papp, Joseph. "Art, the State and Illusion." Address, n.d. New York Public Library Billy Rose Theatre Division.

Papp, Joseph. "For Program." Typewritten notes, n.d. New York Public Library Billy Rose Theatre Division.

Papp, Joseph. *William Shakespeare's "Naked" Hamlet: A Production Handbook*. London: Macmillan, 1969.

Paredez, Deborah. "'Queer For Uncle Sam': Anita's Latina Diva citizenship in *West Side Story*." *Latino Studies*, 12, no. 3 (2014): 332–52.

"Part II: *Hamlet, Prince of Cuba*." Conversation at Asolo Rep. May 6, 2012. YouTube. March 7, 2014. https://www.youtube.com/watch?v=9tD_Jgqo3fQ

Passel, Jeffrey S., and D'Vera Cohn. "20 Metro Areas Are Home to Six-in-Ten Unauthorized Immigrants in U.S." Pew Research. March 11, 2019. https:// www.pewresearch.org/fact-tank/2019/03/11/us-metro-areas-unauthorized -immigrants/

"Paula Vogel on *The Baltimore Waltz*." Comparative Drama Conference. YouTube. September 26, 2012. https://www.youtube.com/watch?v=Mkj7NC9 AU4w

Paz, Octavio. *The Labyrinth of Solitude*. *The Labyrinth of Solitude and Other Writings*, translated by Lysander Kemp, Yara Milos, and Rachel Phillips Belash, 7–212. New York: Grove Weidenfeld, 1985.

Pelaez Lopez, Alan. "The X in Latinx Is a Wound, Not a Trend." ColorBloq. September 2018. https://www.colorbloq.org/article/the-x-in-latinx-is-a-wou nd-not-a-trend

Pérez, Emma. *The Decolonial Imaginary: Writing Chicanas Into History*. Bloomington: Indiana University Press, 1999.

Pilkington, Ed. "Latino Liberation: Sharks Sing in the Language of Their Streets as *West Side Story* Goes Bilingual on Broadway." *The Guardian*, March 19, 2009. https://www.theguardian.com/stage/2009/mar/20/west-side-story-on -broadway

Pollack-Pelzner, Daniel. "Why *West Side Story* Abandoned Its Queer Narrative." *The Atlantic*. March 1, 2020. https://www.theatlantic.com/culture/arch ive/2020/03/ivo-van-hoves-west-side-story-steeped-stereotypes/607210/

Pousada, Alicia. "Being Bilingual in Puerto Rico." 2011. http://aliciapousada.we ebly.com/uploads/1/0/0/2/10020146/being_bilingual_in_puerto_rico2.pdf

"Proclamation of the State of New York Executive Chamber." July 13, 1989. New York Public Library, Billy Rose Theatre Division.

"Prompt Book: *Romeo and Juliet* (2012)." Prompt Book, Folder 1. Oregon Shakespeare Festival Archives, Ashland.

"QuickFacts: California." Census.gov. Accessed November 10, 2020. https://www.census.gov/quickfacts/CA

"QuickFacts: Los Angeles." Census.gov. Accessed November 10, 2020. https://www.census.gov/quickfacts/losangelescitycalifornia

Rackin, Phyllis. "Women's Roles in the Elizabethan History Plays." *The Cambridge Companion to Shakespeare's History Plays*, edited by Michael Hattaway, 71–85. Cambridge: Cambridge University Press, 2002.

Ramírez, Catherine S. "Afrofuturism/Chicanafuturism: Fictive Kin." *Aztlán*, 33, no. 1 (Spring 2008): 185–94.

Ramírez, Catherine S. "Deus ex Machina: Tradition, Technology, and the Chicanafuturist Art of Marion C. Martinez." *Aztlán*, 29, no. 2 (Spring 2002): 55–92.

Rashad, Phylicia, and Debbie Allen. Instagram comments. December 26, 2020. https://www.instagram.com/tv/CJRYxmlgPyR/?utm_source=ig_web_copy _link

Rasmussen, Birgit Brander, Eric Klinenberg, Irene J. Nexica, and Matt Wray. "Introduction." *The Making and Unmaking of Whiteness*, edited by Birgit Bander Rasmussen, Eric Klinenberg, Irene J. Nexica, and Matt Wray, 1–24. Durham, NC: Duke University Press, 2001.

Rauch, Bill. "Keynote Address to the 2019 ATHE Conference." *Theatre Topics*, 30, no. 1 (2020): 1–9.

Rauch, Bill, and William Shakespeare. "Measure for Measure." Unpublished script including prologue, 2011. Oregon Shakespeare Festival Archives, Ashland.

Rauch, Bill, and William Shakespeare. "Measure for Measure." DVD recording, 2011. Oregon Shakespeare Festival Archives, Ashland.

Reid, John T. "The Rise and Decline of the Ariel-Caliban Antithesis in Spanish America." *The Americas*, 34, no. 3 (January 1978): 345–55.

Retamar, Roberto Fernández. "Caliban: Notes toward a Discussion of Culture in Our America." *Caliban and Other Essays*, translated by Edward Baker. Minneapolis: University of Minnesota Press, 1989.

Revill, George. "Music and the Politics Of Sound: Nationalism, Citizenship, and Auditory Space." *Environment and Planning D: Society and Space*, 18 (2000): 597–613.

Rifkin, Mark. *Beyond Settler Time: Temporal Sovereignty and Indigenous Self-Determination*. Durham, NC: Duke University Press, 2017.

Rivas, Tlaloc. "Directors' Panel." Latina Theater Today: New Voices, University of Notre Dame. November 17, 2011.

Roach, Joseph. *Cities of the Dead: Circum-Atlantic Performance*. New York: Columbia University Press, 1996.

Robbins, Jerome, and Robert Wise, dirs. *West Side Story*. 1961. 50th Anniversary Edition, 20th Century Fox, 2011. DVD, 153 minutes.

"Rodney King's LA Riots Speech, May 1st 1992." Press conference. YouTube. Accessed January 8, 2022. https://www.youtube.com/watch?v=tVidK2k agPA

Rodó, José Enrique. "Ariel." StreetLibWrite.

Román, David. *Performance in America: Contemporary U.S. Culture and the Performing Arts*. Durham, NC: Duke University Press, 2005.

"Rooftop Koreans." *Urban Dictionary*. Accessed November 6, 2021. https://www.urbandictionary.com/define.php?term=Rooftop%20Koreans

Rosenfeld, Colleen Ruth. *Indecorous Thinking: Figures of Speech in Early Modern Poetics*. New York: Fordham University Press, 2018.

Rossini, Jon D. *Contemporary Latina/o Theater: Wrighting Ethnicity*. Carbondale: Southern Illinois University Press, 2008.

Rossini, Jon D. "Thinking the Space(s) of Historiography: Latina/o Ethnicity Theatre." *Theatre/Performance Historiography: Time, Space, Matter*, edited by Rosemarie K. Bank and Michal Kobialka, 237–52. New York: Palgrave Macmillan, 2015.

Rubin, Gayle. "The Traffic in Women: Notes on the 'Political Economy' of Sex." *Toward an Anthropology of Women*, edited by Rayna R. Reiter, 157–210. New York: Monthly Review Press, 1975.

Saborío, Linda. *Embodying Difference: Scripting Social Images of the Female Body in Latina Theatre*. Madison, NJ: Farleigh Dickinson University Press, 2012.

Saldívar, José David. "The School of Caliban." *The Dialectics of Our America: Genealogy, Cultural Critique, and Literary History*, 123–48. Durham, NC: Duke University Press, 1991.

Sandoval, Chela, Arturo J. Aldama, and Peter J. García. "Introduction: Toward a De-colonial Performatics of the US Latina and Latino Borderlands." *Performing the US Latina and Latino Borderlands*, edited by Arturo J. Aldama, Chela Sandoval, and Peter J. García, 1–30. Bloomington: Indiana University Press, 2012.

Sandoval-Sánchez, Alberto. *José, Can You See? Latinos On and Off Broadway*. Madison: University of Wisconsin Press, 1999.

Sawyer, Robert. "Country Matters: Shakespeare and Music in the American South." *Borrowers & Lenders*, 1, no. 1 (2005). https://openjournals.libs.uga.edu/borrowers/article/view/2124/2006

Schidlowsky, David. *Neruda y Su Tiempo: Las Furias y Las Pena*. Vol. 2: *1950–1973*. Santiago de Chile: RIL, 2008.

Serfilippi, Jessie. "'As Odious and Immoral a Thing': Alexander Hamilton's Hidden History as an Enslaver." Schuyler Mansion State Historic Site. 2020. Accessed June 6, 2021. https://parks.ny.gov/documents/historic-sites/Schuy lerMansionAlexanderHamiltonsHiddenHistoryasanEnslaver.pdf

Seyffert, Estefania. "*Romeo and Julieta* Opens Door to Future Bilingual Productions in the Borderlands." *Borderzine*. December 10, 2015. https://bor derzine.com/2015/12/romeo-and-julieta-opens-door-to-future-bilingual -productions-in-the-borderlands/

Shakespeare, William. *The Comedy of Errors. The Norton Shakespeare: Based on the Oxford Edition*, edited by Stephen Greenblatt, Walter Cohen, Jean E. Howard, and Katharine Eisaman Maus, 745–98. 3rd edition. New York: Norton, 2016.

Shakespeare, William. *Double Falsehood or The Distressed Lovers*. Edited by Brean Hammond. London: Arden Shakespeare, 2010.

Shakespeare, William. *The First Part of Henry the Fourth. The Norton Shakespeare: Based on the Oxford Edition*, edited by Stephen Greenblatt, Walter Cohen, Jean E. Howard, and Katharine Eisaman Maus, 1165–244. 3rd edition. New York: Norton, 2016.

Shakespeare, William. *Hamlet. The Norton Shakespeare: Based on the Oxford Edition*, edited by Stephen Greenblatt, Walter Cohen, Jean E. Howard, and Katharine Eisaman Maus, 1751–906. 3rd edition. New York: Norton, 2016.

Shakespeare, William. *A Midsummer Night's Dream. The Norton Shakespeare: Based on the Oxford Edition*, edited by Stephen Greenblatt, Walter Cohen, Jean E. Howard, and Katharine Eisaman Maus, 1037–96. 3rd edition. New York: Norton, 2016.

Shakespeare, William. *Othello. The Norton Shakespeare: Based on the Oxford Edition*, edited by Stephen Greenblatt, Walter Cohen, Jean E. Howard, and Katharine Eisaman Maus, 2073–158. 3rd edition. New York: Norton, 2016.

Shakespeare, William. *Romeo and Juliet. The Norton Shakespeare: Based on the Oxford Edition*, edited by Stephen Greenblatt, Walter Cohen, Jean E. Howard, and Katharine Eisaman Maus, 957–1036. 3rd edition. New York: Norton, 2016.

Shakespeare, William. *Romeo y Julieta*. Translated by Pablo Neruda. Buenos Aires: Editorial Losada, 1964.

Shakespeare, William. *The Winter's Tale. The Norton Shakespeare: Based on the Oxford Edition*, edited by Stephen Greenblatt, Walter Cohen, Jean E. Howard, and Katharine Eisaman Maus, 3121–204. 3rd edition. New York: Norton, 2016.

"Shakespeare in Latinx Communities: José Cruz González and David Lozano." *Shakespeare Unlimited*, Episode 176. Folger Shakespeare Library. Accessed November 12, 2021. https://www.folger.edu/shakespeare-unlimited/latinx -communities-gonzalez-lozano

Shapiro, James. *Shakespeare in a Divided America: What His Plays Tell Us about Our Past and Future*. New York: Penguin Random House, 2020.

Shaughnessy, Robert. "*Romeo and Juliet*: The Rock and Roll Years." *Remaking Shakespeare: Performances across Media, Genres and Cultures*, edited by Pascale Aebischer, Edward J. Esche, and Nigel Wheale, 172–89. New York: Palgrave Macmillan, 2003.

Sheen, Martin. "Martin Sheen 1972 Interview about Joe Papp's 1967 *Hamlet*." WV State Archives. YouTube. Accessed November 20, 2020.

Sheppard, Philippa. "Latino Elements in Baz Luhrmann's *Romeo + Juliet*." *Latin American Shakespeares*, edited by Bernice W. Kliman and Rick J. Santos, 242–61. Madison, NJ: Fairleigh Dickinson University Press, 2005.

"Show Introduction January 4, 2012." "Members Lounge Handbook, Oregon Shakespeare Festival." MS. Oregon Shakespeare Festival Archives, Ashland.

Shurgot, Michael W. "Breaking the Sound Barrier: Howie Seago and American Sign Language at Oregon Shakespeare Festival." *Shakespeare Bulletin*, 30, no. 1 (Spring 2012): 21–36.

Siguenza, Herbert. "El Henry." Unpublished script, EH Draft 11, 2020.

Siguenza, Herbert. "Latinx Superfriends Playwriting Hour." *HowlRound*, June 1, 2020. YouTube video, 1:10: 36. https://www.youtube.com/watch?v=BkO4 G93pRHo&feature=emb_logo

Sillen, Samuel. "Paul Robeson's *Othello* (1943)." *Shakespeare in America: An Anthology from the Revolution to Now*, edited by James Shapiro, 451–58. New York: Library of America, 2014.

"SILO in Makers Quarter." *KPBS*. Accessed June 5, 2021. https://www.kpbs.org /places/silo-makers-quarter/

Simeone, Nigel. *Leonard Bernstein: "West Side Story"*. Farnham, Surrey: Ashgate, 2009.

Smith, Amanda M. and Alfredo Franco. "The Politics of Latinx Literature Today." *Chiricú Journal: Latina/o Literatures, Arts, and Cultures*, 2, no. 2 (Spring 2018): 5–19.

Smith, Bruce R. *The Acoustic World of Early Modern England: Attending to the O-Factor*. Chicago: University of Chicago Press, 1999.

Smith, Emma. *This Is Shakespeare: How to Read the World's Greatest Playwright*. New York: Pelican Books, 2020.

Solís, Jose. "How R.Evolución Latina Is Reinventing the Bard." *HowlRound*, May 21, 2018. https://howlround.com/how-revolucion-latina-reinventing -bard

Spielberg, Steven, dir. *West Side Story*. 2021. 20th Century Studios, 2022. DVD, 156 minutes.

Stamberg, Susan. "A *West Side Story* with a Different Accent." *NPR*, December 15, 2008. https://www.npr.org/templates/story/story.php?storyId=98207909

Steffen, Suzi. "A Fingernail Moon Honors a New Oregon Shakespeare Festival Season." Oregon ArtsWatch. March 10, 2012. https://archive.orartswatch .org/a-fingernail-moon-honors-a-new-oregon-shakespeare-festival-season/

Stephens, Thomas M. "Chino." *Dictionary of Latin American Racial and Ethnic Terminology*, 66–69. Gainesville: University of Florida Press, 1989.

Stern, Tiffany. *Making Shakespeare: From Stage to Page*. London: Routledge, 2004.

Stoever, Jennifer Lynn. *The Sonic Color Line: Race & the Cultural Politics of Listening*. New York: New York University Press, 2016.

"Support Us: Corporate Sponsorships, 2011–2012 Season." Asolo Repertory Theatre. Accessed June 28, 2015. https://www.asolorep.org/support-us/corp orate-foundation-sponsors/corporate-sponsors

Tan, Marcus Cheng Chye. *Acoustic Interculturalism: Listening to Performance*. New York: Palgrave Macmillan, 2012.

Taylor, Diana. *The Archive and the Repertoire: Performing Cultural Memory in the Americas*. Durham, NC: Duke University Press, 2003.

Taylor, Kate. "Multicultural Stages in a Small Oregon Town." *New York Times*, August 14, 2009. https://www.nytimes.com/2009/08/15/theater/15oregon.html

"Telling the Story behind the Story behind *West Side Story*." *LA Times Blogs*, February 27, 2012. https://latimesblogs.latimes.com/culturemonster/2012 /02/west-side-story-inspiration.html

Thompson, Ayanna. *Passing Strange: Shakespeare, Race, and Contemporary America*. Oxford: Oxford University Press, 2011.

Thompson, Robert Farris. *Flash of the Spirit: African and Afro-American Art and Philosophy*. New York: Vintage Books, 1984.

"Timeline of San Diego History: 20,000 BCE—1798." San Diego History. Accessed December 1, 2021. https://sandiegohistory.org/archives/biograph ysubject/timeline/bc-1798/

Tizon, Alex. "My Family's Slave." *The Atlantic*, June 2017. https://www.theatlan tic.com/magazine/archive/2017/06/lolas-story/524490/

Torres, Julie. "Black Latinx Activists on Anti-Blackness." *Anthropology News*, September 3, 2020. https://www.anthropology-news.org/articles/black-lati nx-activists-on-anti-blackness/

Traci, Philip. "Joseph Papp's Happening and the Teaching of *Hamlet*." *English Journal*, 58, no. 1 (January 1969): 75–77.

Tuck, Eve, and K. Wayne Yang. "Decolonization Is Not a Metaphor." *Decolonization: Indigeneity, Education & Society*, 1, no. 1 (2012): 1–40.

Tudeau-Clayton, Margaret. *Shakespeare's Englishes: Against Englishness*. Cambridge: Cambridge University Press, 2019.

"Unauthorized Immigrants* California and Los Angeles County." Los Angeles Almanac. http://www.laalmanac.com/immigration/im04a.php

US Census Bureau. *Annual Estimates of the Resident Population by Sex, Race, and Hispanic Origin for California: April 1, 2010 to July 1, 2019 (SC-EST2019-SR11H-06)*. Accessed November 10, 2020. https://www.census.gov/data/tab les/time-series/demo/popest/2010s-state-detail.html

Van Gelder, Lawrence. "Theater Review; Zany Doings on a Ranch, All in

Verse." *New York Times*, January 3, 2003. https://www.nytimes.com/2003/01
/03/movies/theater-review-zany-doings-on-a-ranch-all-in-verse.html

Valdez, Luis. *Theatre of the Sphere: The Vibrant Being*. New York: Routledge, 2022.

Villanueva, Victor. "Foreword." *Decolonizing Rhetoric and Composition Studies:
New Keywords for Theory and Pedagogy*, edited by Iris D. Ruiz and Raúl Sánchez, v–viii. New York: Palgrave Macmillan, 2016.

Villarreal, Edit. "The Language of Flowers." Music by Germaine Franco. Draft
6. Unpublished script, 1991.

"Vilma Silva on Shakespeare's Work." Oregon Public Broadcast, season 10, episode 1001, video clip, October 18, 2015. Opb.org

Vogel, Mike. "Snapshots of Florida's Hispanic Community." *Florida Trend*,
April 30, 2013. https://www.floridatrend.com/article/15521/snapshots-of-flo
ridas-hispanic-community

Watson, Robert N. "Lord Capulet's Lost Compromise: A Tragic Emendation
and the Binary Dynamics of *Romeo and Juliet*." *Renaissance Drama*, 43, no. 1
(Spring 2015): 53–83.

Weber, Bruce. "Stratford-upon-Main Street: Shakespeare to Tour, Thanks to
N.E.A." *New York Times*, April 23, 2003.

Welsh, Anne Marie. "This *Romeo* Will Cross Both the Borders of Love and of
Life." *San Diego Union-Tribune*, July 10, 2005. http://www.utsandiego.com/un
iontrib/20050710/news_1a10romeo.html

Whitehead, Colson. *The Underground Railroad*. New York: Doubleday, 2016.

Williamson, Laird. "Director's Notes." Program for *Romeo and Juliet*. Ashland:
Oregon Shakespeare Festival, 2012.

Williamson, Laird. "Romeo and Juliet." Unpublished script, 2012. Oregon
Shakespeare Festival Archives, Ashland.

Ybarra-Frausto, Tomás. "Rasquachismo: A Chicano Sensibility." *Chicano Aesthetics: Rasquachismo*, 5–8. Exhibition catalog. Phoenix: Movimiento Artiscico
del Rio Salado, 1989.

Yong Li Lan. "Shakespeare and the Fiction of the Intercultural." *A Companion to
Shakespeare and Performance*, edited by Barbara Hodgdon and W. B. Worthen,
527–49. Malden, MA: Blackwell, 2005.

"Young Lords." *Encyclopedia Britannica*. Accessed December 8, 2021. https://
www.britannica.com/topic/Young-Lords

Yu, Henry. "Ethnicity." *Keywords for American Cultural Studies*, edited by Bruce
Burgett and Glenn Hendler, 2nd edition, 100–104. New York: New York
University Press, 2014.

Yúdice, George. "Culture." *Keywords for American Cultural Studies*, edited by
Bruce Burgett and Glenn Hendler, 2nd edition, 68–72. New York: New York
University Press, 2014.

Zentella, Ana Celia. "'José, Can You See?': Latin@ Responses to Racist Discourse." *Bilingual Games: Some Literary Investigations*, edited by Doris Sommer, 51–68. New York: Palgrave Macmillan, 2003.

Zingle, Laura. "*El Henry*: Herbert Siguenza's Epic Chicano Version of Shakespeare's 1 *Henry IV.*" *Theatre Forum*, 46 (2014): 56–61.

Zotolow, Sam. "School Aides Object to Papp's Modern Hamlet." *New York Times*, January 22, 1968.

OTHER CITATIONS

Alpharaoh, Alex. Zoom interview. August 18, 2020.

Alvarez, Frankie J. Skype interview July 20, 2017.

Bartolone, Ben. Zoom interview. September 30, 2021.

Bonilla, Alberto. Personal interview. March 25, 2014.

Briggs, John. Telephone interview. February 8, 2013.

Broznan, Chloe. Telephone interview. August. 25, 2020.

Garcia, Lydia. Telephone interview. February 4, 2012.

Jopson, Kate. Zoom interview. September 8, 2020.

Kanelos, Peter. Personal Interview. September 16, 2021.

Marcus Center. Message to the author. December 20, 2011. Email.

Morán, Manuel. Telephone interview. November 13, 2021.

Moses, Tara. Zoom Interview. August 26, 2020.

Ocampo-Guzman, Antonio. Telephone interview. November 21, 2011.

Ojeda, Julianna Stephanie. Zoom interview. August 17, 2020.

Rivera, Javier. Zoom interview. August 27, 2020.

Siguenza, Herbert. Zoom interview, August 15, 2020.

Index

Page numbers in *italics* indicate figures.

188n24; legacy in musical theater, 31, 33, 36, 42, 176, 186n7, 194n100; and linguistic division, 43–47; masculinity in, 26, 34–37, 39, 48, 50; original film, 31–32, 35, 40, *40*, 43–44, 48–50, 52, 56, 187n16, 189n34, 193n93, 225n85; other productions of, 43, 179n16, 191n62; *Pietà* image in, 169–70; and racialized Other in, 39–41, *40*, 43–44, 105; and re-ethnicization of *Romeo and Juliet*, 8, 15–16, 25–26, 41–42, 51–52; vs. *Romeo and Juliet* plot, 33–35, 37, 39–41, 49–50; songs in, 32, 36–37, 48–50, 192n76; Spanish title of, 194n99; Spielberg film, 31, 44, 47–50, 225n85; trajectory across versions, 29–31, 42–50; whiteness in, 26, 33–41, 48, 52, 57, 101. See also *Romeo and Juliet*

West Side Story effect: argued for, 41–43; and aurality of Latinx Shakespeares, 57–58; conceptualized, 23–26, 29–30; evidenced in Latinx Shakespeare films, 51–57; and performance of difference, 50–51, 65, 71, 134, 141, 203n22; vs. speculative critical history, 28, 152–55, 168; as step toward decoloniality and reparative work, 110, 131, 151, 170
Wetback (Romero), 183n53
White, Frank L., 115
Whitehead, Colson, 221n9
whiteness: and acting/vocal methods, 24; and Arielismo, 9–10; and Brownness as relationship to, 83, 90, 92, 101–3; and characters' accents/heritage, 47, 114; decentering of, 15, 134; defined, 5; in early Latinx-themed Shakespeares, 2, 114; language of, 10–11; as power structure, 5, 38, 40, 44, 48, 50, 92, 103, 203n8; unstable, 36–40, 48, 50, 57; *West Side Story* and, 26, 33–41, 48, 52, 57, 101
Whiting, Leonard, 52

Will & Co., 212n64
William Shakespeare's "Naked" Hamlet. See *Naked Hamlet*
William Shakespeare's Romeo + Juliet (Luhrmann), 26, 29, 52–55, *54*, 204n29
Williamson, Laird, 64, 71, 74, 77. See also *Romeo and Juliet* (Williamson/OSF production)
Winnicott, Donald, 216n9
Winters, David, 52
Winter's Tale, The, 96, 98–101, 140, 178n10. See also *Invierno*
"Without Walls" (WOW) festival, 160
Wiz, The, 149
Women's National Democratic Club, 108–9
Wood, Natalie, 31, 44, 188n28
Woodhouse, Sam, 160, 224n70
Wooster Group, 179n16
worldmaking, 19, 23, 28, 134–36, 147–49, 151. *See also* healing; spectatorship
World Shakespeare Festival, 6
Wynter, Sylvia, 10

Ybarra-Frausto, Tómas, 158
Yong Li Lan, 21–22
York, Y, 10
Young Lords, 209n26, 209n31
Yu, Henry, 107
Yúdice, George, 203n7

Zacarías, Karen, 216n5, 219n59
Zavalla, Nakia, 96–97
Zebrahead, 52–53
Zeffirelli, Franco, 15–16, 52
Zegler, Rachel, 47
Zeller, Caro, *139*
Zellerbach Family Foundation, 216n6
Zentella, Ana Celia, 64
Zingle, Laura, 160
Zinn, Howard, 9
Zoot Suit (Valdez), 168, 190n47
Zoot Suit Riots, 88